Physicians of the Heart:
A Sufi View of the
Ninety-Nine Names of Allah

Physicians of the Heart:
A Sufi View of the Ninety-Nine Names of Allah

❖ ❖ ❖

Wali Ali Meyer
Bilal Hyde
Faisal Muqaddam
Shabda Kahn

Sufi Ruhaniat International
San Francisco, California

Sufi Ruhaniat International
410 Precita Avenue
San Francisco, CA 94110
www.ruhaniat.org

Hardcover ISBN 978-0-983051-76-3
Softcover ISBN 978-1-936940-00-4
Library of Congress Control Number: 2010942872

Book Cover Design: Nuria Stephanie Sabato
Interior Book Design: Joe Tantillo

calligraphy by
murafabba/mike
sufiscribe
all artwork ©2010 murafabba/mike monahan

Contents

Acknowledgments

We wish to acknowledge and express our deep gratitude to an extended family of friends and colleagues who shared the vision behind this work and who supported this decade-long project through all the stages of its evolution. It was truly a group effort—and a remarkably harmonious one.

Samia Bloch was the assistant editor, and the tasks she performed are too numerous to recount. If this had been written at a university, a slew of graduate students would have been employed to do what she did. She has held this book in her heart for a long time. Vakil Polevoy diligently transcribed every group discussion. As a volunteer, he generated thousands of pages of complex transcription, with lots of Arabic transliteration thrown in for good measure, and never complained.

Halim Dunsky also logged hundreds of volunteer hours as our professional copy editor. His skill and intelligence in approaching this material were invaluable. Suria Rebecca McBride became our chief proofreader and brought great clarity and expertise to her work.

Dr. 'Abd al-Haqq Alan Godlas graciously consulted with us in authenticating and researching several hadith. Rabbi Zalman Schachter-Shalomi helped us with some questions related to Judaism and Hebrew. A number of respected colleagues and friends read chapters at different stages and offered suggestions and critical feedback from which we gained a great deal. Our thanks go out to Suhrawardi Gebel, Pamela Frydman Baugh, Paula Saffire, Sabura Meyer, Ruhama Veltfort, and Mary Flowers. Subhana Ansari and Hilal Sala helped facilitate necessary communication, and Tamam Kahn participated in several group discussions.

Nuria Stephanie Sabato contributed her artistic vision and created our beautiful cover design. Muraq'abba Mike Monahan did the calligraphy and design for the collages of the Names of Allah that adorn many of the chapters in the book. Their beautiful design adds an important element to this work.

We are very grateful to Shafee Howard Ballinger, who worked diligently and creatively to develop the website for the book, and Shivadam Adam Burke for editing the sound files.

We especially appreciate the cooperation of Pir Zia Inayat Khan, who made a recording of the 99 Names for our website. His recitation reflects Urdu and Farsi influences on the Arabic pronunciation. We are very grateful to Seemi Ghazi, who recited the Names for us in the classical Arabic of the Qur'an. Our coauthor Imam Bilal Hyde provided a recording in classical Arabic as well, and thus the Names can be heard in both female and male voices. We would also like to thank Sidi Ali Sbai for his beautiful chanted recording of the Names. These recordings can be accessed at www.PhysiciansOfTheHeart.com.

We are grateful to the many people who have supported this project financially. Without their help it could never have happened. This list includes: Fazl Terry Peay, Barakat Carolynn Bryan, Munir Reynolds, Samira Johnson, Paula Saffire, Jane Delozier, Nancy Bancroft, Vadan Nisenboim, Louise Jacobus, Raja Pritchard, Insu Hyams, Malika Merrill Endres, Yaqin Sandleben, Sherdyl Len Wolff, Hayat Rubardt, Peter Lipa, Ayesha Goodrich, Ali Charles, Walia DeMille, Mudita Sabato, Laura Meltsner, Fadhilla Bradley, Raphael Birney, Michael and Joanna Gest, Jelehla Ziemba, Saladin Pelfrey, Zardusht Chet Van Wert, Jilani Esterly, Raqiba Rose, Madri Irani Wagner, Johara Reynolds, Ramdas Ashton, Wali Perry Pike, Diana Scammel, Azima Forest, Marty Kraft, Basira Beardsworth, Farrunnissa Rosa, and Amina Rae Horton.

With thankfulness to all those who have helped us and with gratitude to the Source of all blessings,
Wali Ali Meyer
Bilal Hyde
Faisal Muqaddam
Shabda Kahn

How the Wazifah Project Began

In 1969, I received my first *wazifah* recitation practice from my Sufi teacher, Murshid Samuel Lewis. Since then, daily *wazifah* recitation and contemplation have been part of the rhythm of my life. For years, I searched for texts to illuminate these millennium-old ways of opening the heart but never felt satisfied with available texts on *wazifah* in the English language.

In February 2001, I was appointed spiritual lineage holder (*pir*) of our Sufi family, the Sufi Ruhaniat International, in the stream of the great mystic Hazrat Inayat Khan and his disciple, Murshid Samuel Lewis.

Following inner guidance, in late 2001, I approached my friend and colleague, Faisal Muqaddam, asking if he would join me in bringing through a contemporary, sophisticated guidebook on the 99 Beautiful Names of God, the *sifaat-u-llah*. Faisal is one of the founders of the Diamond Approach to awakening, a native-born Arabic speaker, and a mystic deeply versed in uncovering and healing the wounds of the human condition. He agreed!

Very shortly after that, I was invited to teach and perform at the Sound and Spirit music festival in Bay St. Louis, Mississippi, with another friend and colleague, Imam Bilal Hyde. Imam Bilal is a unique blend of Arabic and Qur'anic scholar, Muslim, and Sufi seeker. As we walked on the beach during a break, I shared with him my enthusiasm for the Wazifah Project. He immediately was inspired to join our concentration.

The three of us met for three-hour sessions year after year. Each session was recorded and faithfully transcribed by our Sufi friend Vakil Cary Polevoy. I had hoped to make time to turn the transcriptions into a readable manuscript, but my responsibilities as *pir*, as well as my inexperience as a writer, kept me from the opportunity.

In 2005, one of my oldest friends and mentors, Murshid Wali Ali Meyer, shared an office with me. In 1969, he was Murshid Sam's esoteric secretary and lived with him at the Mentorgarden. Wali Ali was one of the people who led me to my teacher. During our time in the shared office, Wali Ali—who had become the head of the esoteric school of the Ruhaniat—listened with great interest as I shared the discoveries of our *wazifah* sessions.

Familiar with his writing skills and mystic heart, in 2005 I was moved to invite Wali Ali to join our ongoing conversation and to write our text. He joyfully entered our group, five more years of discussion ensued, and this guidebook is the glowing result. We are indebted to him for so masterfully giving written voice to 10 years of meetings and research.

May the feelings, ideas, and words on the following pages find their way into your hearts and minds. May the practices suggested help you unfold your life's purpose and become streams of blessing, happiness, and generosity.

With all gratitude,
Pir Shabda Kahn

Editor's Preface

This book is the product of a continuing spiritual conversation about the Names of Allah, a conversation that was recorded and transcribed over a period of more than nine years. Almost four years into the conversation, Pir Shabda Kahn, Imam Bilal Hyde, and Faisal Muqaddam invited me to join the project. They also gave me the task of constructing a book.

We decided that the book would communicate best if it were written in a straightforward way. The alternative we considered was to present it as an edited transcript, with the different voices identified. We decided that would not be an effective form for integrating and presenting material from thousands of pages of transcripts.

Writing this book required my blending our four distinct voices into a single voice. This was not as hard a job as might be imagined because there is an essential agreement of heart and inner knowledge among the four of us. Of course, that does not mean that each of us is an expert in every field that is mentioned in the text or that any one of us would have chosen to express what has been said in the particular form that was chosen.

Imam Bilal Hyde, among other accomplishments, is an outstanding Arabic scholar and grammarian. His understanding of the Qur'an is extraordinarily deep on many levels. His knowledge of Qur'an, hadith, and the classical works of Sufism is a constant presence throughout this narrative. Faisal Muqaddam is a master psychologist and a mystic with a highly developed intuition. He has the gift of being able to expose the intimate connection that the divine Names have with the human psyche in its struggles and in its quest to reconnect with its innate wholeness.

In every realm, Faisal was able to show how disconnection from the divine source is caused by various kinds of traumatic wounding experiences, particularly in early childhood, and to connect these experiences with different Names and families of Names. In addition, Faisal often offered a visionary component to our conversation, which on a number of occasions has been incorporated into the text.

Shabda and I bring some practical knowledge as Sufi teachers who have worked with students for more than 35 years. We are also able to draw on a wide range of experience of spiritual practice and study in religious traditions other than Islam to show how the states, stations, practices, and spiritual realities that are discussed from a classical Sufi perspective can in many cases be directly correlated to the Dharma traditions of Hinduism and Buddhism.

Moreover, Shabda brings mastery in the Indian tradition of spiritual music, and I have a classical background in philosophy and theology. So even though we all didn't, couldn't, or wouldn't have said every word that is in the book, we affirm it to be our united voice. The mistakes and inconsistencies that no doubt appear throughout this effort should be attributed to my shortcomings as an editor.

Let me now summarize a few of the ways we have chosen to handle the material.

Aspects of the Arabic Language

We provide a pronunciation guide to the Arabic language. This is a guide to classical Arabic pronunciation as the language was spoken in the time of the Prophet Muhammad. The website www.PhysiciansOfTheHeart.com offers several recordings through which you can hear the Names recited in classical Arabic, in male and female voices, and also in a version showing the Urdu/Farsi influence. Modern Arabic is quite different from classical Arabic, and various countries and regions have adapted the language differently.

We emphasize classical Arabic because we are relying on the roots of the words, and their usage in the Qur'an, as basic sources for probing into their meanings. We have no intention of saying this is the only way to recite these sacred Names, or even the best way.

When a Name of Allah that may be used in prayerful recitation appears in the text, we have transliterated it in the conventional manner, giving the phonetic spelling in parentheses according to the pronunciation guide. When Arabic words and phrases are included in the body of the text, as in a quotation from the Qur'an, we have generally chosen to spell them phonetically, as we think this more appropriate for our readers, most of whom will not know how to sound out the words.

The exceptions to this rule are philosophical terms and words that are already reasonably well known in a conventional transliteration, as well as the Names of Allah. Sometimes we put the alternative spelling in parentheses. On occasion we also include parenthetically the spelling of the word in the phonetic form it took when it traveled to India—for example, *zikr* as a more widely known spelling of the Arabic *dhikr.*

We do not distinguish between the *'ayn* and the *hamza* (glottal stop) but indicate both with a straight apostrophe. For readers with some knowledge of Arabic it may appear that we are placing *'ayn*s where they don't belong, as often the *hamza* is omitted in transliteration. We took the liberty of omitting the *'ayn* mark for definite articles (for example, "al" in al-'Azim) as we thought its presence would be distracting to our readers.

Sometimes we refer to the divine Names with different prefixes. When we write Ya Karim, for example, "Ya" is a vocative form used to indicate that we are calling out, invoking the divine quality. As the Names are traditionally repeated over and over as part of Sufi practice, we use the "Ya" form when the Names are first introduced and whenever the context suggests this usage.

When we write al-Karim we are using the definite article "al" to refer to the divine Name in a respectful way, a way that recognizes its uniqueness. Referring to "the" divine generosity as al-Karim distinguishes it from the ordinary usage of *karim* in the language.

In fact, some of the divine Names have become used in ordinary language in ways that have changed radically from their original meanings. For example, *wakil* in modern Arabic means "lawyer." However, using the definite article and making it al-Wakil clearly refers to the divine quality of a being who manifests complete trustworthiness.

The particular form that the definite article takes depends on the word it precedes. Consequently, you will see ar-Rahim, as-Sabur, at-Tawwab, an-Nur, and so on, as well as the more frequently used al-Quddus, al-Fattah, and so on.

Classical References

Recitation of the 99 Names of Allah is a practice that arose among Sufis in response to a historical tradition of the Prophet Muhammad where he spoke of the Names of Allah and the great benefit to be received by enumerating them. In Appendix A, Hadith Regarding the Recitation of the Names, we have printed a widely accepted hadith from the Tirmidhi collection detailing what the Prophet said.

Virtually all scholars agree that the number 99 is merely a symbol for an unlimited quantity. In fact, there are more than 99 Names by which Allah is addressed in the Qur'an. We offer an expanded, but still incomplete, list of such Names at the end of Chapter 5.

Based on different traditions, the Names that have been included on such lists vary slightly, and the list of 99 that we have used differs slightly from other lists. Our variations reflect the Names of God we have chosen to concentrate on in this book; we do not think scholars should be too doctrinaire as to what specifically can be included on such a list.

The Qur'an is a primary source for the meanings of the Names. In one sense, the Qur'an is an encoded version of the Names. As part of the exploration of each divine Name's meaning we looked at the different root forms that each Name takes in the Qur'an, the context in the Qur'an of the stories and teachings where these qualities are evoked, and the context in which divine Names appear together.

Through these and other factors we sought to elicit the meanings in the Names. Each time we refer to the Qur'an we have cited chapter and verse. We have not footnoted every reference to hadith—the historical traditions of what the Prophet Muhammad said and did. However, in the References chapter we have listed several excellent compilations of hadith, which include all of the ones we have cited.

A number of classical Sufi teachers such as 'ibn 'Arabi, al-Qushayri, and Junayd are referred to throughout the text. Rather than giving page citations, we refer the reader to the primary texts themselves, which are listed in the References chapter, and we invite readers to confirm the accuracy of our memories by investigating these texts.

Exploration of the forms that the Arabic roots of the Names take is an important part of our process, as well as the lexicographical meanings. Several Arabic/English dictionaries and lexicons were used; the principal ones are listed in References.

Primary Organization of the Book

Our investigation of these sacred Names led us to see them as relational families or clusters. We believe this way of grouping them is essential to deepening the understanding of each Name individually as well as to uncovering the skillful application of the Names to the human condition. The organization of the book strongly reflects this insight that the Names can be best understood in relational clusters.

The Names exist as potentialities in the oneness of God. As hidden relationships within the divine field of being, they can best be understood in relationship with one another. The relational groupings we have emphasized are opposites, cognates (those that have the same root), those that are similar in meaning, and those that are similar in grammatical form.

We have included one large chapter (Chapter 5) that offers a brief summary for each Name, and even here we found it important to cross-reference other divine Names. We have also included an alphabetical listing of the 99 Names for convenient reference (Appendix B).

We refer to the 10 grammatical forms in the Arabic language as part of a "sound code" that gives a general meaning to every word. This is based on the word's particular structure of stressed and unstressed vowels, doubled consonants, and the like. It is a fundamental element of Arabic grammar, and every Arabic dictionary is organized in this way.

We have applied these general grammatical meanings to the divine Names in particular as a way of gaining more insight into each Name. This approach is something that has never been done for English readers. Chapter 4 has been devoted to the sound code, and we constantly make reference to it in our analyses of the meaning of the Names throughout the book.

Our discussion of capitalization led us to no conclusions. Some of us felt that it was proper to capitalize many words that refer to God, such as Divine, Essence, Love, Will, and all pronouns. Others felt modern usage would be simplest. We made what is probably a very inconsistent compromise in this regard.

We use the words God and Allah interchangeably throughout the text, and except where the sound quality of "Allah" is specifically the point, we have been deliberately indifferent as to which word we use. Also, in the effort to stay with informal language, we have been flexible in our use of pronouns in general.

Our group process has been a mutual venture of delight. Many friends have supported this vision with their time and skills in transcribing, editing, graphic design, researching, and in many other generous ways. Elsewhere, we specifically try to acknowledge everyone who has helped, and to single out a few whose efforts were central to our success.

Everything has been done in, by, and through the Name of Allah. And that is how we begin: *Bismillah ar-rahman, ar-rahim*. Our prayer, to the one who hears all prayer, is that this labor of love be of real benefit to all beings and that all joyfully awaken to the God reality.

Wali Ali Meyer
San Francisco, California
August 2010

allah

99

chapter 1

Beginning in
the Name of Allah

The words "Allah" and "God" refer to the ineffable reality, the essence of all things. Allah includes everything and depends upon nothing for existence. That absolute state is called *dhat* (often transliterated *zat*). That is the essence of all the Names.

What we are looking into is a relationship between divine essence and divine attributes. The *sifat*, or attributes of Allah, the divine Names, have no independent existence of their own. They only exist as differentiated aspects of Allah. They are neither identical to nor distinct from the essence.

All the divine Names that we will consider in this book are contained in that one Name, Allah. The 99 Names are manifestations of the qualities of Allah, and as you go deeply into the attributes you are led to the essence, because the attributes are manifestations of the essence. Through this means, you can fully awaken to the essential Name, which is unique.

A similar process occurs when a student studies the musical scale. All the notes of the scale are manifestations of the main note, the tonic note. In singing the attribute note, the singer learns about the tonic because the attribute note is fully present in the tonic.

The word "Allah," according to some scholars, comes from the root *waliha,* and this root combines the vast concepts of total love and being passionately beyond all the constraints of mind. Combining these, we get the meaning "to fall madly in love, to utterly dissolve in an insane yearning."

Another jewel of meaning is disclosed by looking into the phrase *la 'ilaha 'illa allah.* At the highest level, *la 'ilaha 'illa allah* means "There is no existence except Allah." The root meaning of the Arabic word for existence, *wujud,* is "a voyage to ecstasy." The Arabic words for "ecstasy" and "to find" both come from the same root as *wujud,* the sound W-J-D.

All this leads us to the affirmation, "Nothing exists except Allah, whose existence is pure ecstasy, and there is no ecstasy to be found except the unrestrained ecstasy of total yearning and love." These thoughts are suggested by that one root, *waliha,* and this derivation may well be something that most readers have not heard about the word "Allah." The derivation of this root for the word "Allah" is not fanciful; it can be found in many dictionaries. (See References for recommended Arabic/English dictionaries.)

The Name Allah is also a sound, and as a sound its real meaning is to directly evoke and point toward the unpronounceable essence, behind all the Names. The sound that you make when you say Allah represents the greatest Name, or the 100th Name, which itself has no sound. The quest to find the one sound that is the greatest Name does not turn out to be very important. What may be of utmost importance is to repetitively chant the sound "Allah" and the sounds of all the wonderful Names of Allah to evoke a direct experience of the essence that is the greatest Name.

Another fascinating subject is the combination of sounds that is used in the word "Allah." There are the two syllables: "Al" + "lah." *Al* is affirmation. It is the definite article in Arabic. If we are referring to a person as "the spiritual pole," for example, we say *al-qutb,* the *qutb.*

La is negation, the word for "no." When you are making the sounds of affirmation and negation together, it points to something that is beyond reason. "Allah" both affirms and negates. It is like a Zen koan. Consider, the 6th Patriarch Hui Neng's koan: "Think neither of the good nor the bad, but tell me what is your original face before your parents conceived you."

Affirmation and negation can be seen to cancel each other out. Taking affirmation and negation together, you can reach a still point that includes and transcends both components. This still point is an entry into the divine, into Allah.

Allah (God) is presence, beyond all affirmation and negation. It includes the negative and the positive, the absence and the presence, the emptiness and the fullness. Allah is an infinite Name that both transcends and includes all positive and negative aspects.

The direct coupling of opposite qualities within the Name Allah inspires further inquiry. Following the example of this construction, we find it illuminating in our discussions to couple apparently opposite divine Names, and we often use these pairs of opposites in the practices we recommend for students. Pairing opposites, called *tazweej* by Shaykh 'ibn 'Arabi, is a process that leads to integration and transcendence.

Such a method of pairing is effective for all of the *'ism-ul-jalal* and *'ism-ul-jamal*, the Names of power and the Names of beauty. Proceeding in this way, we are often led directly to the transcendental reality, and we may discover an *'ism-ul-kamal*, or Name of perfection, which transcends and includes a particular pair of opposites.

The breathy sound of the final "h" of Allah is the beginning of the sacred syllable *hu*. *Hu* transcends both the positive and negative elements: the *al* and the *la*. The word "Allahu" sets up a model with which to look at every single Name of the divine. The opposites included in the Name Allah produce a certain effect on the mind, leading to the still point, which is the *hu*. *Hu* is called the secret of the secret, or the essence of the essence, because it is included unpronounced in an abbreviated form within the Name Allah.

The letter "h" is the first letter of the word *hu* and is called the secret of the secret of the secret, or, the essence of the essence of the essence. The Name Allah, in this way, sets up what is called an infinite progression. It is like a repetitive series ending in three dots, which suggests it should go on forever, essence of essence of essence of essence. . . Mystics often try to describe the indescribable by using finite expressions to suggest the infinite.

Sufis call this "H" sound the breath of infinite compassion, with which God created the universe. God's love is the secret of *hu*. A sacred tradition (*hadith qudsi*) of the Prophet Muhammad, one where he speaks in the voice of Allah, says, "I longed to know myself so I created the heavens and earth with the breath of infinite compassion."[1]

There is yet another surprising and unusual dimension to this Name Allah, one that could resolve an immense difficulty, especially in the Western community. So often the meaning of this Name, like the concept of Buddha-nature or enlightenment, is conceptually framed only in terms of the absolute. It is described as the boundless infinite. But, if only this aspect is stressed, the approach is often unbalancing in a student's development.

We want to emphasize that the Name Allah also suggests the principle of individuation. The word "Allah" has another form: It is not incorrect to express the sound as *al-'ilah*, which means the individuated God. Yes, it can be pronounced *al-lah*, as we have been doing, but in the alternative form of *al-'ilah* it means "the God."

The word becomes individuated. The *ilah* reveals individuation, and individuation is an important aspect of divinity. The meaning of *al-'ilah* can be realized when you become integrated in your own sense of self and know it as a divine manifestation not separate from the real self. It is important to see that the word "Allah" contains both the cosmic and the individual. Both are a part of the inner dynamic of the word. The specific application depends on what is emphasized.

The Name itself, as we have seen, also contains negation and affirmation, and much else besides. So when we explore this Name, we are playing with all of these things. We are playing with the individuated God, the cosmic presence, negation and affirmation, and what is beyond that. It is all streaming through this vibration.

The word "Allah" is also a form; it is a visual design. The letters have a shape. If you write it, it makes an amazing design. There is a practice called *irfan* or *ma'rifah*, which means understanding at the deepest level of the soul. It is a meditation practice with the shape of this Name. One writes the Name Allah in letters of light. It makes an imprint of light in the center of the heart so that wherever the spiritual student looks and whatever sounds they hear, or whatever thoughts arise, all are perceived as coming from and going to Allah. In both the Arabic and Hebrew languages, the mystical shape chosen for each letter of the alphabet is considered to have inner meaning.

There is a classical Sufi teaching of the five Presences that can be described by using the Name Allah as a basis. This teaching is based upon the letters in the word: *aliph, lam, lam, aliph, ha. Aliph* is said to refer to *nasut*. This is the realm of the material universe where humanity finds itself. The first *lam* refers to *malakut*. Literally this means angels, but heaven and hell and all the unseen spiritual worlds are contained in this realm. The second *lam* represents *jabarut*, which is the realm of divine power. This is actually the place where we find the manifestation of these 99 Names as Names.

The second *aliph* represents *lahut*. This is the world of Allah, insofar as we are able to know Allah. There's a hadith that says, "I am as my servant imagines me to be." So, whether we imagine God to be Jesus, Krishna, the wind, or the universe, that particular formulation is just how we are imagining or idealizing God to be. The realm of *lahut* is the reality of God, as we know God. It is how we individuate it, and according to this sacred tradition God affirms being in that form. *Hahut*, the last of the five Presences, is described by the letter *ha*, which stands for the God that we can never know definitively. It is beyond mind. It is how God is to God: God's self-knowing.

Humanity has been using variations of the word "Allah" as a Name of God since Proto-Semitic times, long before the Muhammadan Era. Both Jews and Christians in the Middle East use Allah as a Name for the One God, and have done so for thousands of years. Its usage is not unique to Islam. Other names from the same root were used, such as *Allat* and *Allaha*. Even *El* in Hebrew is historically the same word as Allah. It is no more a stretch to make this statement than it is to say the French *magnifique* and the English "magnificent" are the same word.

Simply considering the sound of the word "Allah," we notice that the initial "A" sound is a natural heart sound. It is opening out into the universe, into the infinite. The "L" sound in Allah is a shimmering or a tingling in the heart, called *wujilat*. The "LLLLL" sound in the practice of *dhikr* (remembering Allah through reciting the Name) has this effect on the heart. This thrilling sound is sometimes referred to as the "shimmering being." Then you say "A" again, bringing the release of the heart, the relaxation of the heart.

Thus the shimmering is brought to the heart and then emanates back out. And finally you pronounce the "H" sound, the aspirant, the breath sound. It is the breath of infinite compassion and the initial of *hu*, which transcends all qualities. The letter "h" (*ha*) is represented as a circle in Arabic, and this form also is a symbol for the infinite.

Sound is a universal language, no matter how it may be transliterated into any given alphabet, and the mysticism of sound will be given an important place in our investigations. What we are striving to emphasize is that the divine Names create, and they go on creating. And this is beyond the linguistic meanings we give them. In this sense, sacred language is that language which is developed according to the sound's effect. We could easily say that definitions came after the effects of the sounds were discovered.

The form of the Qur'an as an encoded book that contains the 99 beautiful Names of God in Arabic is only part of the story that needs to be told. The universal essence of each divine attribute may be shown through the various levels of sound found within each word. A demonstration of this is in the hadith that says sometimes the revelation of the Qur'an was heard by the Prophet Muhammad as the ringing of bells, at other times as the buzzing of bees, or the chanting of the human voice.

The Sufis say that if we had the ears to hear and listened with an open heart, we could actually hear, interpret, and understand the deeper sounds and the universal message contained within each Arabic word in the Qur'an. This goes far beyond any specific meanings contained at the ordinary denotative and connotative levels of the language. This is an indication of why the Qur'an is called "the ocean of meanings," in which each verse contains hundreds of thousands of levels of interpretation.

Only the outward levels of meanings are called the Qur'an, or the recitation, but when the heart is opened to the inner levels of meaning, it is called *al-furqaan*, discriminating wisdom. The deepest meanings are called *al-nujmaan*, which means the light of a shower of shooting stars. These mystical meanings are experienced as a shower of lights falling from heaven directly into the human heart. Such a mystical light of direct experience is what each beautiful Name communicates at the deepest level.

All the Names of the absolute, whether in Sanskrit, Pali, Hebrew, Greek, Aramaic, Arabic, or other sacred languages, contain this essential light. The proof of this is contained in the Qur'anic verse, "We make no distinction between any one of the Books or the Messengers who bring them."[2] The reason no distinction is made between the sacred books is because they all point to the same essential reality. And this is true because they all come from the same source, called the Preserved Tablet ('al-lawh 'al-mahfoodh).

This symbol, also called the Mother of the Book, 'umm-ul-kitab, represents the universal message of unity that each sacred book contains at its deepest level, and true source. Just as, from one point of view, each of a mother's children is different, from another point of view each child "contains" the same mother in his or her own way.

That the preserved tablet has been read as Sanskrit, Hebrew, Greek, Arabic, and so on, is an accident of history. Such readings occurred solely for the practical purpose of communicating with people belonging to a particular place and a particular time. Although sacred texts do differ from one another in some ways, like daughters of one mother, from a deeper perspective each book reveals the universal message in its own particular way.

In the same way that the New Testament accepts the Old Testament, the Qur'an accepts the books that preceded it. The root for Qur'an, Q-R-A, means "to gather together" as well as "to recite." The main function of the Qur'an was to gather together and affirm what had come before. Fully seen, the Qur'an gathers together all the divine signs in the heavens and earth. The word for a chapter of the Qur'an, *ayat*, also means "sign." In the book of nature itself we also have a collection of signs. Each sign is a Name of God.

It is interesting to note that each Arabic consonant has seven different possible pronunciations depending upon the vowel mark that is put on it. The original transcribed Qur'an, like the Hebrew Torah, was written without any vowel marks at all. The vowel sounds themselves were considered sacred. Later it was decided that to avoid confusion the vowels would be written out fully in Arabic. But we can look at all the infinite possibilities present in the book without the vowel marks, as another indication of its universal message.

The Prophet Muhammad said, "All of the creation, all that there is, is included in the Qur'an. And all the Qur'an is summarized in the opening chapter, *al-Fatiha*. All of *al-Fatiha* is summarized in *Bismillah ar-Rahman ar-Rahim*." Sufis later said that this could all be condensed into the dot under the "B" in *bismillah*. All spiritual traditions have one thing in common: the universal unity of existence, and that is expressed by the dot. There is an infinite circle, but within the circle is the dot of absolute oneness. It contains everything. If you string out these dots you get everything that can be written in all scriptures and beyond.

Bismillah can literally mean "I yearn for the protection in the Name Allah." But its deeper meaning could better be expressed, "In saying *bismillah*, I invoke the actualization, the presence, of Allah." Seen in this way, the 99 Names of Allah come as an invocation. They are an invocation of the presence of Allah, through different Names, different qualities, and different emanations.

Sound is what pulls together this whole discourse. Even the root of *'ism* means sound. We begin in the sound. We find the same thing in Hebrew, with the word *shem*. In Hebrew, the word for "heaven" is *shemayim*. *Shem* is "sound" or "name." What is called heaven is the place where the Name is flowing.

As travelers on the spiritual path, we are aiming to experience both the manifestation of God and the transcendence of God as a unity. Most of us are caught in the stage where we experience the manifestation of the universe and all its forms as something separate. However, manifestation is not really separate. It is individualized, but not separate. All manifestation is pervaded by the same reality. There is an inseparability of the limited and the absolute.

At the level of the absolute you experience total unity. It might actually be more philosophically complete to simultaneously affirm that both manifestation and transcendence are the true reality, that neither manifestation nor transcendence is the true reality, and that total unity is the true reality. Thankfully, there is a realization beyond these intellectual formulations. The nature of the heart is central to achieving a unified view.

Shaykh Junayd teaches that the wonderful thing about the heart is that it is able to "turn." The heart can turn toward the *nafs* and see a separation, and it can turn toward the *ruh* and see a total union. Both *nafs* and *ruh* have the meaning of "soul." Sometimes they are called lower self (ego) and higher self, or lower soul and higher soul, but both words mean soul.

The beautiful quality of the heart is it can simultaneously look at the separation and union of the soul. It can see both working at the same time. The heart has the capacity to accept simultaneously both your experience of separation from God and your feeling of union with the source. That is why the heart is so important in Sufism—because it has an almost infinite capacity.

A sacred tradition has Allah affirming, "The heavens and the earth cannot contain me, but the heart of my loving servant can." Everything is taking place within the globe of the heart. It is in the infinite space of the heart that the possibility exists for the integration of the limited and the absolute.

There is a much-quoted sacred hadith in which the voice of Allah is heard to say, "I was a hidden treasure and wished to be known." What could it mean to say that all-pervading reality is hidden?

One answer is to say the hidden treasure is the unmanifest potential. Take the white light of the sun. When you put its clear light through a prism, it begins to differentiate. In this way you come to see the ultimate beauty and majesty of differentiation. Before that, all there was to know was the pure essence that held all potentialities. But, viewed only as essence, the potential remains potential. It has not yet differentiated in all its capacities and come to know itself in a more complete way.

We could say it is all a divine love play. Allah fell in love in order to be known. Falling in love with the imagined potentialities means Allah starts to differentiate. The different qualities have not yet manifested, but the seeds of manifestation have already become the object of Allah's love.

Sacred sounds can affect the universe by activating the whole universal field. The absolute is like clear space, clear luminosity. Consider a glass of clear water. . .If you put a drop of cherry essence in it, it becomes red. If you put a drop of mint in it, it becomes green. When you put a given sound in it, the whole field of the absolute resonates, and in so doing reveals the gradations of what each divine Name truly means.

The *sifat*, or divine qualities, are sound formulas, and they have a historical context. They were organized, we understand through several hadiths, into the 99 Names in the time of the Prophet Muhammad. What do we know about their history before that time? Simplistically put, all the particular powers, such as the kinds of powers represented by ar-Rahman and ar-Rahim and the other Names, were looked upon as independent deities that stood on their own. This is polytheism. Polytheism can be viewed as pure multiplicity. It is the conception of a multiplicity with no all-pervading unity.

The change that the Prophet Muhammad brought, which is viewed as a revival of the ancient Abrahamic tradition, the tradition of the *haneefah*, was to revive the idea of a pristine, unified consciousness. Understanding this means to see that the divine Names are not independent existences. They are interrelationships, or *nisab*, as 'ibn 'Arabi says. They describe interrelationships within the unity of existence. Consequently, the divine Names are all doors to a single essence, to Allah.

The Names evoke relationships that reveal God's presence. They describe, for instance, the lover's relationship with the beloved. It is a relationship between two individuated aspects of a single whole, not a connection between two fundamentally or intrinsically separate things. Thus, the great change brought by Muhammad was a return to essential unity.

Vajrayana Buddhism does a similar thing. In Tibetan Buddhism, there are multiple deities (*yidam*). But when Tibetan Buddhists do the practice of any deity, at the very end is a necessary stage of recognizing the representations of deity as insubstantial. They dissolve and resolve the deities into what is called the *dharmakaya*, or what Sufis would call Allah. It all dissolves in the formless, just as the divine Names all dissolve in Allah. Tibetan deities are ultimately insubstantial, from the point of view of the all-pervading reality. It appears to us as simply a different way of getting at the same truth.

Let's put it in personal terms. You are known as so-and-so, which name we could say stands for your essence. But then we go on to describe you as mother, wife, mathematician, and so on. These names are not different things that are attached to you. They are your attributes. They describe different relationships of your existence. In the same way, the sacred Names bring out endless, multifaceted relationships that Allah has in the universe.

We say there are 99 Names, which as 100 less one, is actually a code for endlessness. One hundred is a number that expresses completion. Ninety-nine is a finite way of suggesting an infinite stream, and so it should not be surprising that there are more than 99 Names that are acknowledged as Names of God. And most mystics and Sufis say that all names are the Names of Allah. It is just that these particular divine Names, all of which are encoded in the Qur'an, were brought out in the tradition for an enumerative purpose that suggests the infinite.

Historically, the Names of Allah have also been applied as remedies for diseased, disconnected, habitual, and confused existence. And they have historically been invoked as aids for awakening consciousness of the divine. Over the centuries, the Names have been a spiritual pharmacopoeia used by true physicians of the heart. Many great Sufis have said they are the cure for every ill.

There are several beautiful traditions of the Prophet Muhammad that recommend reciting the whole list as a practice. It says whoever enumerates them all by singing the full set will receive great benefit. There are a few variants of the Names, even on these lists. We have printed the most widely accepted account of the Prophet speaking of reciting all these Names in Appendix A.

What is wonderful about the whole list of 99 Names is that, while we can of course invoke any single Name, we can never isolate it from Allah. We need to continually remember that the divine Names, as described by Shaykh 'ibn 'Arabi, are a network of intertwined relationships with the divine, and can never be isolated entities.

In this divine pharmacopoeia of the Names, any one of them might be applied as a remedy for a condition or as a cure for a set of ailments. However, we generally prescribe the invocation of pairs of divine Names that bear an intimate relationship with each other. It is important for a physician of the heart to know, for example, that to amplify the effect of a Name, it should be chanted along with a Name that expresses its opposite, when possible. And, it is also important to learn that Names that share a similar divine quality often cooperate together in a systematic process of growth.

A *wazifah* is the name for the spiritual practice of invoking the divine Names as a prayer. Our whole conversation of many years, which we called the Wazifah Project, started when we agreed that the material that was available in English was insufficient. One of the limitations of what was available on this subject was that it rarely showed any relationships between the Names.

In our view, it is rather silly, and in some instances even somewhat irresponsible, to only do 99 Names one page at time. They invite being grouped together. In fact, it may be spiritually dangerous in some cases to only recite one Name of an opposite pair, because at the level of human psychology, the objective of working with the divine Names is to grow into an integrated wholeness.

For simplicity's sake we have included a chapter (Chapter 5) where we offer brief summaries of each Name, along with cross-references. In the main body of this work, we treat the divine Names as parts of families or clusters. It is very helpful when inquiring into the depths of meanings in these divine qualities, to have relational groups to consider. In fact, all of the divine Names occur in different clusters of meaning.

Consider what is called *omnipresence* in theology. Briefly summarized, it means God is everywhere: an infinite presence. This is a challenging subject to communicate. But by grouping together in a cluster all the divine Names that have the quality of omnipresence, we have a fresh way of coming to understand that divine quality. Not only can we gain insight into the nature of this whole cluster of Names and insight into a more complete meaning of omnipresence, but by considering each Name in relation to a family cluster, the particular meanings also are more clearly differentiated. Throughout this book, in general, we take a relational approach.

There are several important ways that the 99 Names can naturally be viewed in relation to each other. We group the divine Names according to: 1) meanings (similar and opposite); 2) roots (cognates); 3) the context and frequency of their appearance together in the Qur'an; and 4) the general meaning of each one's form as determined by the sound code that is embedded in the grammatical structure of the Arabic language.

These relational families of divine Names impel us toward a more complete understanding. They make for a beautiful journey of discovery, which we sincerely invite you to join. *Bismillah ar-rahman ar-rahim.*

bismillah
ar-rahman
ar-rahim

chapter 2

Our Psychological Perspective

When their inherent potential is realized, the sacred Names of Allah offer a remedy for each and every human disability. Indeed, they offer the key to resolving our whole existential dilemma. Throughout this book, we focus on bringing out specific applications of the Names as divine medicines. They provide a full array of skillful means for psychological healing when wisely applied by those whom we call "physicians of the heart." When students seek guidance, the Names become a vehicle of healing wisdom.

Any complete psychological view should delineate a clear path for human beings to achieve successful integration, and it should also be capable of explaining and addressing the typically wounded and alienated state of our ego-structures. In each layer of the psyche, human beings identify with an idea of self that they have constructed themselves. This false idea of the self configures and coalesces around an intense sense of being wounded, an impression that is stored in the ego.

Each Name of God and each relational cluster or family of divine Names provides a unique opportunity for psychological and spiritual growth. Because our psychological perspective is integral to the discussions of specific Names and clusters of Names throughout this book, we want to briefly summarize it at the outset. We will cover it here in general terms, but the most complete way to observe it will be in seeing how this view plays into discussions of particular human conditions in the chapters that follow.

The need of a human being to achieve individuation should not be ignored in the delineation of the process of spiritual awakening. Too often, spiritual teachers only emphasize the goal of merging with the absolute or the cosmic reality. Such an approach is incomplete and confusing for the student. As was emphasized in Chapter 1, the Name Allah ought to be seen as both a cosmic and an individuated reality.

Several of the hadiths of the Prophet Muhammad relate his experience of observing God take particularly beautiful physical forms on the cosmic throne—the *'arsh*, or Heart Throne. God as an individuated entity takes a limited form, which nevertheless embodies perfection. It is not the cosmic self but the individuated self.

Al-lah is the cosmic self. *Al-'ilah* is the individuated self. The individuated self is embodied in the heart. It is a ray of the infinite sun, so to speak. Philosophically, these two types of self can be characterized as the impersonal God and the personal God. In conveying spiritual teachings to the West, the aspect of divine individuation has often been bypassed.

We would even go as far as to say that this important aspect of God's nature has been trespassed. God, as an individuated being, is the theme that can crack the ego's shell. If students can find the way to connect with that individuated value, then cosmic value can enter from just that point of light.

It is quite ironic that Westerners often suffer from a lack of individuality, even though many think they are trying very hard to individuate. What happens is that people tend to be isolated, and they think that being isolated is being individuated. This mistaken notion is idealized in the hero in the western movie, who walks into the sunset alone. Individuality is essential, but when you isolate yourself in your constructed sense of self, the result is to become disconnected and alienated. Such disconnection in your relationships leads to suffering, in the East or the West.

When teachers ask their students to bypass the dimension of individuation and go directly to the absolute, what happens is often a big mess. The students try to jump at the teacher's direction, and many even have an experience of the absolute, but they are left even more puzzled, because *Al-'ilah* is not seen.

Hazrat Inayat Khan emphasized individuation when he said in his widely known Sufi invocation that we should orient ourselves to be "United with all the illuminated souls, who form the embodiment of the Master, the Spirit of Guidance." This recognizes an important principle. By orienting in this way, the traveler on the spiritual path affirms there is only one Spirit of Guidance and that there are many individual points—the illuminated souls—that are available to merge into.

We are therefore encouraged to come to know the God reality as Abraham, Christ, the Buddha, Muhammad, and so on. Such a teaching honors and evokes divine individuation. When someone says, "Jesus is God," or "Buddha is the ultimate reality," they are calling out to that divine individuation. We should not skip over that point. There is a progression. You should move through the process of individuation, and this ultimately will allow for a full merging with the universal cosmic absolute.

Having emphasized the principle of individuation as it relates to our quest for wholeness as human beings, we now need to direct our attention to the structure of the human ego. The overall ego structure is made of many layers. In each layer, the ego appears as a separated and isolated reality with which each of us have self-identified because of what has been missing in our earthly experience and because of being wounded in our relationships.

We will explore some aspects of the ego structure by examining the wounds that the ego bears, and by considering some very central issues of self-value. As we see it, the ego bears two major wounds. Because of the excruciating sensitivity of these deep wounds, the ego sets out with great determination to defend them from being touched and thereby activated. The way you defend your wounds from being touched by the experiences of your life creates and reflects your specific personality structures.

There is a major wound of humiliation, of shame. It is caused by your overall relationship with humanity, and by your relationship with your own family in particular. Children often feel like failures because there was something the parents needed them to fulfill, and it was something that the child could not do.

Confronting this failure, the child feels very unworthy and very shamed. Your act of self-identifying with this shameful and isolated condition is because of the intensity of your wound. It is a defensive act. However, self-identification with your own perceived deficiency isolates you. Configuring your sense of self in this way disconnects you from the joy of an ongoing relationship with the divine source, a relationship that is the birthright of every soul.

The second wound, the deepest layer of wounding, is experienced as being caused by your relationship with God. There is a profound feeling that even God has abandoned you. In this place, you feel you have been abandoned because you have failed to fulfill your divine destiny. You ask the question, "Why have you forsaken me?" And the ego gives its answer: "There must be something wrong with me for me to feel so abandoned."

Human beings thus feel put to shame by both the worldly and the heavenly. At the level of worldly relations, we call it the "family hole." There is something missing in the household and you should have fixed it but you didn't. Mom's still unhappy. Dad's still unhappy. Children believe they are supposed to manifest what the family really needs: to be the most loving, the strongest, or the most intelligent person. They were supposed to be whatever was required to fill the family hole. Since that is an impossible task, they feel shame.

Not having healed the deficiency felt in the family, they do not feel worthy of happiness. The ego, or basic sense of self, narcissistically identifies with a powerful sense of deficiency, and in so doing it disconnects from the greater reality. It disconnects from source. We call this secondary narcissism.

Primary narcissism carries a much deeper wound. "I failed the divine." There is a sense of not fulfilling the soul's destiny, not fulfilling what God wants you to do. Each soul comes into existence with a purpose connected to the cosmos and the great being. Often children feel they have not been allowed to fulfill the purpose with which their soul entered. Their environment demanded that they give up their own purpose in order to make Mom or Dad happy.

As a result, children feel they were never allowed to fulfill God's purpose, and now, because of that, they are incapable of fulfilling it. They feel both wronged and deficient. They feel that they are not being helped to fulfill what their soul came to do. Perhaps their soul came to learn about compassion, for example, but they are put into an environment that entices them to cruelty. Consequently human beings constantly carry around this wound, and feel like they have failed God.

The ego is caught between two major obstacles. One obstacle is trying to fill the family hole, and this leads to a sense of failure. And the other obstacle is trying to fulfill the divine purpose, but because the ego is trying to accomplish this goal from the place of fundamental isolation, this quest also leads to a sense of failure. Since you cannot fulfill God's wish, and you cannot fulfill the family's wish, you always feel like you are a failure, you always feel deficient, and you narcissistically maintain yourself in self-identification as "the lowest of the low."

Once you get stuck in this identification, it is very painful. But to let go of the identification, to break its grip, may open up a nightmare for you. As long as you identify with your perceived deficiency, you don't fully feel the pain. It is muted. When you disengage from the identification, the pain hits you in a massive way because now the protective layer of your defenses has been broken. Then you feel the shame, the humiliation. You feel that everybody is better than you, that you are lesser than all.

The deepest narcissistic wound in the ego structure is this sense of failure and worthlessness and shame. Such a deep wound can ultimately only be healed by the God reality. Only through the gracious touch of the all-compassionate and loving being of God can there be a healing for your alienation from the divine source and for your shame at having gotten stuck in the lesser identity at this deepest layer of narcissism.

A wonderful thing occurs when you reach your deepest wound and, at the same time, find the courage not to defend against the intense feelings that are aroused by reaching it. Then grace comes with a healing touch of love and divine generosity. Then the layer of ego containing the inner child feels that he or she is being loved all the time. You experience constantly being created by God. You are valued.

Now there is a profound sense of the preciousness of your soul, right in this very embodiment. It is an individual light of empowerment. It is the light of self-value or inner worth. The divine Name al-'Aziz expresses such true worth. It comes up as a theme of healing in Chapter 8 (Divine Forgiveness) and elsewhere. Al-'Aziz is the true value and strength that comes directly from God and needs no intermediary. Real strength comes from your sense of inner worth. If you have no sense of self-value, you can't feel strong.

When you feel full of worth and value, because you have identified your self with the eternal reality of the soul, strength arises spontaneously from within. It is something to be cherished, and it gives you the courage to be, the strength and dignity to protect the divine quality within, and to honor it throughout your life. When you let down your ego defenses, you are able to see that you don't personally have the power to do what needs to be done in order to heal the wound of being disconnected from God. The dawning of this light of self-value comes when you truly surrender the healing into God's hands.

Psychologists observe that there is a primary narcissism, but they don't know exactly how it is generated. That is because psychology doesn't know what happens in the womb, which is where the answer lies. We should not forget that all souls are emerging from their origin in the divine womb of love, the *rahm*. When a soul enters incarnation, this earthly realm is experienced as a kind of disconnection from the divine source. The Buddhist teacher Chogyam Trungpa described birth as a kind of reverse *samadhi*, just the opposite of the experience of merging with the one.

Because the soul now experiences interference with its connection to the divine, entering the earthly realm is like entering disconnectedness. The disconnection may be in a very minute way, a very subtle way, but it is present. We can easily say that all sin, or error, arises from our disconnectedness with the divine. So in this one sense, sin does come with our birth.

Human beings generate primary narcissism through the experience of disconnectedness from God. When the ego is engaged in a narcissistic identification with limitation, based on disconnection from the source, you doggedly hold onto this limited identity in your heart. And it remains constant no matter what realm you may enter. If this ego enters the dimension of the all-seeing one, the identity that is revealed there is "I am blind," and if it enters the domain of power, the identity that comes up in the ego is "I am weak."

Because of this narcissistic identity, the negative aspect that is aroused when divine qualities are introduced is very important for physicians of the heart to understand when making use of the divine Names as tools for psychological healing. The divine Name needs to be consciously drawn into the specific wounded places in the layers of ego, so that each human being can ultimately overcome their stubborn sense of separation and disconnection.

Each of us may have a thousand blind spots, but there is one that is primary. It has to do with a visceral feeling that something fundamental is missing in you. When your soul comes into this incarnated realm, it is full of divine qualities. Due to what is missing in the family, one or more aspects are blocked. These could be intelligence, creativity, compassion, peace, or something else. These blockages occur before the development of the ego—connection with these qualities is lost in the womb and in the first stages of incarnation.

There is no recognition in the ego about what the particular missing qualities may be. All the ego knows is that there is something fundamentally missing. It doesn't know what is missing, and it doesn't know how to get it. In time, with the aid of divine compassion, you may come to see that you have this blind spot, and by accepting the need and making the journey even through pain and anguish, you can return. The sincere desire is developed to seek back to the source of all. The pain of separation creates the longing. And since it requires you to acknowledge that you don't really know what you need, it may lead to real humility.

Self-surrender is important. Inner wholeness requires each of us to make space for the generous manifestation of loving compassion. Human suffering serves the purpose of wholeness as well. It is a way of return and a means to see that there is something beyond your immediate scope. Knowing there is something beyond your ability to know enables you to bring in the divine. Otherwise, you may remain stuck in a grandiose view of your ego-self, and quite forget about the God reality.

Truly speaking, recollection of self would be *dhikr* (*zikr*) or remembrance of God. Because in its essence the soul is an activity of God, the soul would then have the remembrance of God activated within it. But the grosser ego level doesn't have access to this kind of remembrance because at that level of isolation in which you have self-identified, you have lost your connection with the source.

There is a mystery about remembrance, about that *dhikr* which is the recollection of self. You are reconnecting with a whole process of continuously becoming. There is a famous tradition where Allah says, "I was a hidden treasure; I wished to be known." Allah's great loving wish to be known brings forth something new. It is the manifest reality. The perfection that manifests in the individual soul was always there. It was pure potential energy, so to speak. What incarnation brings is the possibility of a new form that can continuously flow from the source.

Such recollection of self is more than just remembering. "Remembering" suggests getting back to where you were. But this kind of remembering is not a static thing. It is not like two pieces of a train connecting. *Dhikr* is a generative process. The one who remembers Allah is constantly in a connected flow of the divine power. Our aspiration is to work with the sacred Names of Allah in just this kind of connected way.

Recitation of the sacred Names can be a great vehicle for healing wisdom to manifest in your life. The Names are best recited aloud for a certain period of time each day and with a devotional feeling of calling out to the source of all perfection. While doing this, you also know that God is in the very vibration of the sound. The quality of God that is evoked moves in and through you.

By listening to the sound you make when you recite the Names, you begin to gradually bring the tone of your voice into harmony with their essence. Often you will be asked to let down your defenses around a wounded place so that a particular quality of God can reach you. It is important to feel the sound in your body. That will give you a vehicle to sense your own resistance to a particular quality and your own profound resonance with it.

Recollecting self, through reconnecting with your ultimate source in the God reality, is the culmination of the individuation process. You realize how you have been stuck in a fixedness of ego, but now you see that your real self is in constant motion, and the fixedness breaks. The ego surrenders its stubborn clinging to an idea of itself that is isolated and deficient, and comes into a continual influx with being.

In this way, the ego transforms into an image of God. It is no longer an image of the parents. The soul realizes that it is the inner reality at the core of the ego-self, and that it is made in the divine image and likeness. It is immortal and filled with divine qualities. Such union, or continual remembrance, produces a wholesome fluidity of being that is the desired goal of the psychological process.

chapter 3

Pronunciation Guide

Each Arabic vowel and consonant has a unique sound. This is not the case for every English letter. Where there is no English equivalent for a consonant, we have indicated this with a dot below the letter that gives the closest approximate sound in English. Example: Rahim is shown as ra-ḤEEM. Where two consonants together make one sound we have put a line underneath. Example: Mudhill is shown as mu-DHILL.

The glottal stop (*hamza*) and the *'ayn* (which is a different letter in Arabic than the English "a") are vowel sounds for which there is no direct English equivalent. We have indicated both of these with a straight apostrophe. When the mark appears at the end of one of the 99 Names, except in the case of al-Bari', it is an *'ayn*, and it should be sounded like an "a" that is swallowed or muffled.

As these specific Arabic sounds can only be learned directly by listening and practice, we offer this website as a way to hear the pronunciation of these Names: www.PhysiciansOfTheHeart.com. The Names are recited in classical Arabic by a male and a female voice, and another version of the Names is recited reflecting Urdu and Farsi influences.

The syllables in each word have been separated with a hyphen.

The capitalized syllables are stressed.

The sounds of all the Arabic vowels we can approximate in English letters are listed below:

Long "a"	aa	as in "last"
Short "a"	a	as in "father"
Long "e"	ee	as in "feel"
Short "i"	i	as in "fit"
Long "u"	oo	as in "cool"
Short "u"	u	as in "lute"

Two diphthongs are rendered as follows:

ow	as in "how"
ai	as in "lanai"

The sound of the following combined consonants is rendered in this way:

<u>sh</u>	as in "should"
<u>th</u>	as in "think"
<u>dh</u>	as in "this"

Throughout the book we have transliterated passages from the Qur'an and other Arabic phrases using a phonetic notation based on this pronunciation guide. We made a few exceptions to this rule. The Names themselves and certain well-known philosophical terms are transliterated here in the conventional manner.

When doubled consonants are used in Arabic they are strongly doubled! There is a pause between syllables, and each consonant is given a definite emphasis. For example, the "b"s in al-Jabbar would sound as in "lab book"; the "y"s in al-Qayyum or al-Hayy would sound as in "funny yellow"; the double "f" of al-Ghaffar would sound as in "laugh fest."

With regard to pronunciation, as a general rule long vowels become stressed syllables and short vowels become unstressed syllables. For example, yaa BAA-siṭ and yaa ba-ṢEER.

Following is a list of the 99 divine Names with the phonetic spellings expressed as we have described above:

Ya Allah (yaa 'al-LAAH)

1. **Ya Rahman** (yaa raḥ-MAAN)

2. **Ya Rahim** (ra-ḤEEM)

3. **Ya Malik** (yaa MA-lik)

4. **Ya Quddus** (yaa ḳud-DOOS)

5. **Ya Salam** (yaa sa-LAAM)

6. **Ya Mu'min** (yaa MU'-min)

7. **Ya Muhaimin** (yaa mu-HAI-min)

8. **Ya 'Aziz** (yaa 'a-ZEEZ)

9. **Ya Jabbar** (yaa jab-BAAR)

10. **Ya Mutakabbir** (yaa mu-ta-KAB-bir)

11. **Ya Khaliq** (yaa ḴHAA-liḳ)

12. **Ya Bari'** (yaa BAA-ri')

13. **Ya Musawwir** (yaa mu-ṢOW-wir)

14. **Ya Ghaffar** (yaa g͟haf-FAAR)

15. **Ya Qahhar** (yaa ḳah-HAAR)

16. **Ya Wahhab** (yaa wah-HAAB)

17. **Ya Razzaq** (yaa raz-ZAAḲ)

18. **Ya Fattah** (yaa fat-TAAḤ)

19. **Ya 'Alim** (yaa 'a-LEEM)

20. **Ya Qabid** (yaa ḲAA-biḍ)

21. **Ya Basit** (yaa BAA-siṭ)

22. **Ya Khafid** (yaa ḴHAA-fiḍ)

23. **Ya Rafi'** (yaa RAA-fi')

24. **Ya Mu'izz** (yaa mu-'IZZ)

25. **Ya Mudhill** (yaa mu-D͟HILL)

26. **Ya Sami'** (yaa sa-MEE')

27. **Ya Basir** (yaa ba-ṢEER)

28. **Ya Hakam** (yaa ḤA-kam)

29. **Ya 'Adl** (yaa 'ADL)

30. **Ya Latif** (yaa la-ṬEEF)

31. **Ya Khabir** (yaa k͟ha-BEER)

32. **Ya Halim** (yaa ḥa-LEEM)

33. **Ya 'Azim** (yaa 'a-D͟HEEM)

34. **Ya Ghafur** (yaa g͟ha-FOOR)

35. **Ya Shakur** (yaa s͟ha-KOOR)

36. **Ya 'Aliyy** (yaa 'A-leeyy)

37. **Ya Kabir** (yaa ka-BEER)

38. **Ya Hafiz** (yaa ḥa-FEED͟H)

39. **Ya Muqit** (yaa mu-ḲEET)

40. **Ya Hasib** (yaa ḥa-SEEB)

41. **Ya Jalil** (yaa ja-LEEL)

42. **Ya Karim** (yaa ka-REEM)

43. **Ya Raqib** (yaa ra-ḲEEB)

44. **Ya Mujib** (yaa mu-JEEB)

45. **Ya Wasi'** (yaa WAA-si')

46. **Ya Hakim** (yaa ḥa-KEEM)

47. **Ya Wadud** (yaa wa-DOOD)

48. **Ya Majid** (yaa ma-JEED)

49. **Ya Ba'ith** (yaa BAA-'i̱th)

50. **Ya Shahid** (yaa s̱ha-HEED)

51. **Ya Haqq** (yaa ḤAḲḲ)

52. **Ya Wakil** (yaa wa-KEEL)

53. **Ya Qawiyy** (yaa Ḳ O-weeyy)

54. **Ya Matin** (yaa ma-TEEN)

55. **Ya Waliyy** (yaa WA-leeyy)

56. **Ya Hamid** (yaa ḥa-MEED)

57. **Ya Muhsi** (yaa MUḤ-ṣee)

58. **Ya Mubdi'** (yaa mub-dee')

59. **Ya Mu'id** (yaa mu-'EED)

60. **Ya Muhyi** (yaa MUḤ-yee)

61. **Ya Mumit** (yaa mu-MEET)

62. **Ya Hayy** (yaa ḤAIYY)

63. **Ya Qayyum** (yaa ḳaiy-YOOM)

64. **Ya Wajid** (yaa WAA-jid)

65. **Ya Wahid** (yaa WAA-ḥid)

66. **Ya Ahad** (yaa A-ḥad)

67. **Ya Samad** (yaa ṢA-mad)

68. **Ya Qadir** (yaa ḲAA-dir)

69. **Ya Muqtadir** (yaa muk-TA-dir)

70. **Ya Muqaddim** (yaa mu-ḲAD-dim)

71. **Ya Mu'akhkhir** (yaa mu-'AKH-k̲hir)

72. **Ya 'Awwal** (yaa OW-wal)

73. **Ya Akhir** (yaa AA-k̲hir)

74. **Ya Zahir** (yaa ḌHAA-hir)

75. **Ya Batin** (yaa BAA-ṭin)

76. **Ya Wali** (yaa WAA-lee)

77. **Ya Muta'ali** (yaa mu-ta-'AA-lee)

78. **Ya Barr** (yaa BARR)

79. **Ya Tawwab** (yaa tow-WAAB)

80. **Ya Muntaqim** (yaa mun-TA-ḳim)

81. **Ya 'Afuw** (yaa 'A-fooww)

82. **Ya Ra'uf** (yaa ra-'OOF)

83. **Ya Malikal-Mulk** (yaa MAA-li-kal-MULK)

84. **Ya Dhal Jalali wal 'Ikram** (yaa DHAL ja-LAA-li WAL 'ik-RAAM)

85. **Ya Muqsit** (yaa MUK-sit)

86. **Ya Jami'** (yaa JAA-mi')

87. **Ya Ghaniyy** (yaa GHA-neeyy)

88. **Ya Mughni** (yaa mugh-NEE)

89. **Ya Mani'** (yaa MAA-ni')

90. **Ya Mu'ti** (yaa mu'-TEE)

91. **Ya Darr** (yaa DAARR)

92. **Ya Nafi'** (yaa NAA-fi')

93. **Ya Nur** (yaa NOOR)

94. **Ya Hadi** (yaa haa-DEE)

95. **Ya Badi'** (yaa ba-DEE')

96. **Ya Baqi** (yaa baa-KEE)

97. **Ya Warith** (yaa WAA-rith)

98. **Ya Rashid** (yaa ra-SHEED)

99. **Ya Sabur** (yaa sa-BOOR)

ishq
allah
ma'boud
lillah

chapter 4

The Sound Code at the Heart of the Arabic Language

A significant part of the meaning of the 99 Beautiful Names of God is conveyed by a sound code that is embedded in the grammatical structure of the Arabic language. In this chapter we will examine what the sound code looks like, how it occurs, and why it is so important. From the grammatical point of view we should also note at the outset that almost all of the 99 Names of Allah in the form they are given on the list express activity. They are active participles. In other words, God is a verb.

There are ten grammatical forms that an Arabic word can take. All words of a given form have a specific, overarching meaning that must be included as part of the basic meaning of the word. This meaning necessarily must be understood no matter how the rest of the meaning of the word is elaborated.

We have found this principle of Arabic grammar to be especially useful in our attempt to get closer to the meanings of the Beautiful Names in a book intended primarily for English-speaking readers. Our wish is to introduce an important teaching in a simple way. In this chapter, we will not try to cover every divine Name or every variation but will concentrate on some of the main groupings and also provide a summary in list form.

This sound code is a significant key for a deepening understanding of the 99 Names. To our knowledge, the kind of analysis we are presenting here has not been done before in English. To familiarize the reader with this approach, we will begin with some concrete examples of how the sound code works. Then we will systematically present most of the divine Names grouped into formal categories.

The ten grammatical forms in the Arabic language are distinguished by the vowels or vowel combinations that the words employ and by whether the vowel sounds are long or short. Whether the middle consonants are doubled is also significant, as that changes the meaning of a word.

You can find nothing like this in the structure of the English language. Just imagine a rule in English that said every time you double the second consonant in a word it intensifies the meaning of the word in a very specific way. So if you occasionally drove to work you would be a "comuter," but if you did so continuously you would be a "commuter." That is exactly the kind of orthographic/semantic rule we are looking at in the sound code.

Please see the full Pronunciation Guide for help with the Arabic pronunciation of the divine Names. For further help, access the recordings of the 99 Names that we have made available online at www. PhysiciansOfTheHeart.com.

A Fresh Start at Explaining the Sound Code

Let's make a fresh start at explaining how the sound code works in Arabic and how we will apply it to our explorations of the divine Names. Words in Arabic, including the divine Names, grow from a root formed by three seed letters that together have a basic meaning. These seeds grow in each word into a more fully shaped reality, and the way they do that reveals forms that are much more specific in meaning. To see how this works, we will look at some examples.

The divine Name al-Basir has three seed letters: B-S-R. This root has the basic meaning: seeing inside or having insight into. The three seed letters can grow in several ways. If we put a long "aa" sound after the first letter and a short "i" after the second letter, we get *baasir*, with a specific meaning of the one and only source of deep insight. But if we add a short "a" after the first letter, double the middle letter, and add a long "aa" after the middle letter we get *bassaar*, which would mean something like "the divine one who perceives everything all the time without interruption."

And finally, if we add a short "a" sound after the first seed letter and a long "ee" sound after the second, we get *baseer*, which means "the one who perceives each and every thing everywhere without exception." This last form is the form of the actual divine Name for seeing, al-Basir, that appears on the list of the 99 Names of Allah. Incorporating our understanding of what it means that al-Basir and other divine Names make up a particular class allows us to better uncover their full meaning.

Theoretically, any three seed letters can grow into any of the three forms we have just given and into more forms as well. Let's take some further examples to see how this principle works for the 99 Names. Remember the form *baasir*. It emphasizes the first syllable of the word; it has a long "aa" sound after the first seed letter, and a short "i" sound after the second seed letter. It would mean "the one and only one who perceives." This general meaning of "the one and only one who. . ." holds true for every Name that is formed around any root of three seed letters using this same pattern. For example, the root B-S-T means expansion. The divine Name al-Basit, which has a long "aa" sound in the first syllable, will then mean "the one and only one who expands."

Let's take another example. As we have seen, when we took the three seed letters of the root B-S-R and constructed the form *bassaar*, it meant "the one who perceives all things everywhere, all at the same time." Every divine Name that takes this particular form will have the general meaning "the one who continually. . ." The root W-H-B has a basic meaning of providing. The divine Name al-Wahhab will then mean "the one who continually provides without interruption."

Returning to the seed letters B-S-R, we will take a final example. We saw that it can take the form *baseer*, with a short "a" after the first consonant, a long "ee" after the second consonant, and the emphasis on the second syllable. It means "to perceive all things without exception all the time, everywhere." All the divine Names that are formed in this pattern have the meaning "the one who does something all the time everywhere, without exception." The root K-R-M means generosity. The divine Name al-Kareem thus means "the one who is generous all the time everywhere without exception."

The reader should be aware that we always take the sound code into our consideration when defining divine Names whether we specifically mention it analytically or not. Often in our discussion of a Name we will refer to an "earthy" meaning of the Name. Semitic languages have a very physical base. We found these meanings that we call earthy by surveying all the words of different forms the root of a given Name can take and finding the most physical images among them.

One final point, which we cannot emphasize too much, is the importance of the sound quality, the vibration of the Name when it is recited. While it is true that conceptually understanding a Name is important, it should always be understood that the inner quality of the divine Name can be perfectly received by a practitioner who is sincerely chanting and meditating on it without the benefit of complex linguistic explanations. Sound has effect apart from meaning.

What follows is a more formal presentation of the sound code. We will limit our discussion to only the forms that include divine Names. So as to not overburden our readers with too many very finely defined meanings, we will not try to cover all of the many subcategories of Form I. We are also omitting some of the groups with very few members. We will omit listing some of the Names that grammarians disagree about where to place and whose placement in a group is not obvious.

We are taking this simplified approach because we want every reader, not just those who love the structure of language, to be encouraged to understand and use the sound code. When each list below is read aloud, the similarity of sounds and stresses will help demonstrate its members' shared quality. To help with the process, we have included a phonetic spelling beside each Name listed to facilitate pronunciation. We have used the vocative form "Ya" in this list, which is the way you call out to God in prayerful invocation. For an explanation of how to use the phonetic system, please see the Pronunciation Guide.

Form I

In all the members of the first form, the meaning of a Name can be described by the key phrase(s): "The only one who," "the only source of all," "the unique," "the only actor who acts in the universe." Form I has many subcategories, but all the Names in Form I are constructed particularly to emphasize the quality of uniqueness.

Each subcategory of the first form shows a way that the special meaning of uniqueness is particularly intensified. These nuances of meaning will become quite important later in this book when the divine Names are applied as curatives for human problems and needs.

Form I-1: *Faa'il*

The first form (*faa'il*) emphasizes uniqueness. The first syllable is a long "aa" sound, and the last syllable is a short "i" sound.

Faa'il: aa/i. The syllable stresses are long/short. Descriptive phrases for this category: "The only source of all," "The only one who," The only actor of all actions," "The unique or exclusive."

Ya Khaliq	(KHAA-lik)	Ya Wahid	(WAA-hid)
Ya Bari'	(BAA-ri')	Ya Qadir	(KAA-dir)
Ya Qabid	(KAA-bid)	Ya Akhir	(AA-khir)
Ya Basit	(BAA-sit)	Ya Zahir	(DHAA-hir)
Ya Khafid	(KHAA-fid)	Ya Batin	(BAA-tin)
Ya Rafi'	(RAA-fi')	Ya Jami'	(JAA-mi')
Ya Wasi'	(WAA-si')	Ya Mani'	(MAA-ni')
Ya Ba'ith	(BAA-'ith)	Ya Nafi'	(NAA-fi')
Ya Wajid	(WAA-jid)	Ya Warith	(WAA-rith)

Form I-2: *Fa'eel*

Musically, this variant (*fa'eel*) is just the opposite of its predecessor. It uses the same vowels, so the sound is "a"/"ee," but the stress of the syllables is now short/long instead of long/short. This variant begins to emphasize another aspect in addition to uniqueness. The Names in this subcategory still carry the basic meaning of uniqueness, but over and above that, the sound code emphasizes another divine aspect.

These Names have a quality that pervades into everything and all things, individually and generally. It is "the All." In theology this quality is called omnipresence. It infinitely pervades everywhere. Consequently, if we take the root R-H-M as divine Mercy, then, ar-Rahim is not merely the only One who possesses this Mercy, or the One who is the source of all Mercy, but ar-Rahim also overflows this Mercy into every single being. It is all-pervading. It reaches the good, the bad, and the ugly without distinction. This is very important theologically. It is an infinite presence manifesting into each and every thing *ad infinitum*. This first variant of the first form expresses actualization and not just transcendence. Its transcendental reality is brought right into the relative.

Fa'eel: a/ee. The syllable stresses are short/long. It traces the manifestation from transcendence into infinite particularization. All-pervading, it flows into each and every thing. "The All. . ."

Ya Rahim	(ra-ḤEEM)	Ya Hasib	(ḥa-SEEB)
Ya 'Alim	('a-LEEM)	Ya Karim	(ka-REEM)
Ya Sami'	(sa-MEE')	Ya Raqib	(ra-ḲEEB)
Ya Basir	(ba-ṢEER)	Ya Hakim	(ḥa-KEEM)
Ya Latif	(la-ṬEEF)	Ya Majid	(ma-JEED)
Ya Khabir	(kha-BEER)	Ya Shahid	(sha-HEED)
Ya 'Azim	('a-ḎHEEM)	Ya Wakil	(wa-KEEL)
Ya Halim	(ḥa-LEEM)	Ya Matin	(ma-TEEN)
Ya 'Aziz	('a-ZEEZ)	Ya Hamid	(ḥa-MEED)
Ya Kabir	(ka-BEER)	Ya Badi'	(ba-DEE')
Ya Hafiz	(ḥa-FEEḎH)	Ya Rashid	(ra-SHEED)

Form I-3: Fa'ool

We now come to the second intensive variant (*fa'ool*). This variant emphasizes the "heart" or the "essence of." Its form is determined by its having a short "a" sound followed by a long "oo" sound. The quality is to penetrate to the deepest place, the most subterranean reaches of the heart. It permeates even to the deepest so-called "unholy" place. The Sufi poet Hafiz said, "If you want to see the face of God, sift the dust in a bar-room floor." There's no place you can't find the quality. Note the stress in the pronunciation—for example, Ya Ghafur (Ghafooooor), Ya Shakur (Shakooooor), Ya Wadud (Wadoooood).

Fa'ool: a/oo. The syllable stresses are short/long. "The Heart or Essence of. . ." It permeates the deepest places.

Ya Ghafur	(gha-FOOR)	Ya Ra'uf	(ra-'OOF)
Ya Shakur	(sha-KOOR)	Ya Sabur	(ṣa-BOOR)
Ya Wadud	(wa-DOOD)		

Form I-4: Fa'aal

In the next variation of the first form, the first syllable has a short "a" sound, the middle consonant is doubled, and then a long "aa" is added after it. It is called a frequentative. The emphasis here is "always" or "ever." The key descriptive phase is, "the one who always. . ." These Names reveal the always-continuing heart. It is divine eternity, with no beginning, no end, and no breaks in between. Frequentative doesn't mean frequent. It means a steady flow, like water.

Fa'aal: a/aa. The syllable stresses are short/long, with a double consonant in the middle. It connotes perpetual, repetitive, and continuous action. "The One who always. . .," "the ever-becoming."

Ya Jabbar	(jab-BAAR)	Ya Razzaq	(raz-ZAAK̲)
Ya Ghaffar	(g̲h̲af-FAAR)	Ya Fattah	(fat-TAAḤ)
Ya Qahhar	(k̲ah-HAAR)	Ya Tawwab	(tow-WAAB)
Ya Wahhab	(wah-HAAB)		

Form I-4A

Though it only has two members among the divine Names, there is an important subcategory of the variant just discussed above. There are three levels of meaning in the structure of the Names in this group. It would be no stretch to call them triple intensives. Like the category above, the middle consonant is doubled. In this subgroup the final vowel sound is a long "oo." The initial vowel is a short "u" or short "a." It means, "always happening without a beginning or an end," but because it belongs to three categories at the same time its meaning combines the aspects of "the unique," "the eternal," and "the heart/essence."

Form I-4A: u/oo or a/oo. Syllable stresses are short/long, with a double consonant in the middle, and oo at the end. This subcategory is a combination of I-3 and I-4, the two variants that precede it. Descriptive phrase: "The unique, the eternal, and the heart/essence."

| Ya Quddus | (k̲ud-DOOS) |
| Ya Qayyum | (k̲aiy-YOOM) |

Form I-5: Fa'l

The next intensive variant (*fa'l*) describes a quality of the divine that is not always manifesting but it is always an inherent quality. Whatever meaning we put on al-Barr, as say "the perfect" or "the complete," we must include the key thought of it being an essential characteristic, not one that depends on a transient container for its meaning. In no sense does it rely on secondary causes or accidental characteristics.

Fa'l: a. Short vowel. It indicates a permanent state, but it is a naturally inherent quality, an essential characteristic. The sound code doesn't emphasize the continual manifestation of it.

Ya 'Adl	('ADL)	Ya Barr	(BARR)
Ya Haqq	(ḤAKK)	Ya Hayy	(ḤAIYY)

Form I-6: Fa'al

The next variant of the first form (*fa'al*) has two syllables, both with a short "a" sound. With the other categories of forms, there is always activation of the absolute. This "naturally inherent" category refers more to the nature of the absolute itself, the original nature of things. Like all the Names in Form I, Names in I-6 carry the overall meaning of uniqueness, but these specifically connote uniqueness as potential, even unmanifest.

Fa'al: a/a. While neither syllable is particularly stressed, the first syllable receives slightly more emphasis. The focus here is on inherent qualities that haven't been expanded. This may indicate a permanent state like the previous category, but it also means a continual becoming or process itself. For example, part of the meaning of al-Hakam is "to become wise."

Ya Hakam	(ḤA-kam)	Ya Samad	(ṢA-mad)
Ya Ahad	(A-ḥad)	Ya 'Awwal	(OW-wal)

Form I-7: Fa'laan

There is another most important variant (*fa'laan*) of Form I, and it has one Name and one Name only, ar-Rahman. We always begin with *Bismillah ar-Rahman ar-Rahim*. There is a beautiful Qur'anic verse, *Kataba 'alaa nafsi-hi-r-rahmah*.[3] "Allah has written on the heart, the divine heart, this word *rahma*." That's why God is ar-Rahman. It is a permanent or inherent characteristic. We can translate this quality as "endless," or something poetic like that, but it means that the thing named wouldn't be itself without this characteristic.

Fa'laan: aa-aa. The syllable stresses are long/long. "Endlessly. . ." The thing wouldn't be itself without this attribute. It is the most inherent or most essential permanent quality. Called the gate or the mother of all the divine Names.

Ya Rahman   (raḥ-MAAN)

Others

There are some divine Names that are members of subcategories of Form I that we have not included in the summary above for the sake of simplicity. They include Ya 'Aliyy ('A-leeyy), Ya Qawiyy (ḲO-weeyy), Ya Ghaniyy (GHA-neeyy), Ya 'Afuw ('A-fooww), Ya Baqi (baa-ḲEE), Ya Hadi (haa-DEE), Ya Muhaimin (mu-HAI-min), Ya Salam (sa-LAAM), Ya Malik (MA-lik), Ya Malikal-Mulk (MAA-li-kal-MULK), Ya Wali (WAA-lee), Ya Waliyy (WA-leeyy) and Ya Dhal Jalali wal 'Ikram (DHAL ja-LAA-li WAL 'ik-RAAM).

Form II: *Mufa'ail*

Form II is a frequentative, which means that its members embody continuous action without beginning or end and with no break. They do not rest or sleep. Allah is manifesting every moment, as explained in the Qur'an. But unlike the previous frequentative, it does not also emphasize the uniqueness of the divine Being. It simply emphasizes continuous, endless, and beginningless activity. This concept is very important for Creationists to try to understand. Take al-Musawwir, for example. Do not think of God making something and leaving it for even a breath. Al-Musawwir is continuously shaping forms, shaping the heart and the soul, and everything else. There is no beginning and no end to its activity.

Members of this form have "mu," plus consonant, plus "a," plus double consonant, plus "i," plus consonant. There is a frequentative continuous action without beginning, end, or break.

Ya Musawwir   (mu-ṢOW-wir)
Ya Muqaddim   (mu-ḲAD-dim)
Ya Mu'akhkhir   (mu-'AK͟H-k͟hir)

None of the 99 Names are found in Form III.

Form IV: *Muf'eel*

The fourth form (*muf'eel*) is causative. The key phrase is "the cause of all causes." There are no secondary causes, such as "my mom made me unhappy and that's why I'm unhappy." There is one single cause. Allah works through the agency of the Names, and reveals itself as the only being, the cause of all causes and of all effects. The veil of secondary causes is completely resolved, and the ultimate cause becomes evident. The stresses in this group are mostly short/short, but one finds some longs included because they are weak longs.

In this form we have "mu," plus consonant, plus usually short "i," plus consonant. This form emphasizes the sacred source before actual manifestation comes to fruition. The veil of secondary causes vanishes.

Ya Mu'min	(MU'-min)	Ya Mu'id	(mu-'EED)
Ya Mu'izz	(mu-'IZZ)	Ya Muhyi	(MUḤ-yee)
Ya Mudhill	(mu-D͟HILL)	Ya Mumit	(mu-MEET)
Ya Muqit	(mu-ḲEET)	Ya Muqsit	(MUḲ-siṭ)
Ya Mujib	(mu-JEEB)	Ya Mughni	(mug͟h-NEE)
Ya Muhsi	(MUḤ-ṣee)	Ya Mu'ti	(mu'-ṬEE)

Form V: *Ta'fa'al*

Form V is both intensive and continuous. There are two concepts going on here: the eternal, timeless element, which comes from the double consonant, and the reflexive aspect, which comes from the "t." There is also a third element between the two that is called the affective. It affects or produces a state, and we must use our will power for it to become activated. So *mutakabbir* would mean "to become *kabir*." It is to possess or produce a state within. Allah is using the divine power within itself to produce this state, and this reality is continuous and eternal.

Members of this form are intensive, continuous, reflexive, and affective. Form V is Form II with a "ta" inserted after the "mu," that is: "mu," plus "ta," plus consonant, plus "a," plus double consonant, plus "i." If Form II is continuous or frequent action, Form V is the result of the state of this continuous action. God is ever becoming great but the state of always becoming great refers only to the divine self, so it is reflexive.

There is one divine Name in this group. Ya Mutakabbir, "to become Kabir," does not make reference to anything else and is without comparison.

Ya Mutakabbir   (mu-ta-KAB-bir)

None of the 99 Names are found in Forms VI and VII.

Form VIII: Mufta'il

Form VIII (*mufta'il*) is reciprocal. This is expressed by the "t" in the middle after an initial "mu." There are two divine Names that are in the eighth form, al-Muqtadir and al-Muntaqim. This infix, the "t" sound in the middle, makes members of this group have a reciprocal quality, as is expressed in the phrase, "they met each other." Since it is reciprocal, al-Muqtadir means that the lovers make use of whatever power, *qadir*, that the beloved has granted them and wisely direct it toward creation. The beloved of God uses the power that the divine beloved has given.

That's one side of the reciprocal formula. The other side is that Allah will manifest the divine in limitless power with wisdom and beauty and just measure toward the lover. This combination makes it reciprocal. A person takes responsibility and, at the same time, feels Allah is the only one.

Remember, al-Qadir is Form I, which emphasizes the uniqueness of the source. The source of all *qadir* is Allah, and Allah alone manifests it. Notice the difference? There is no real reciprocity emphasized in al-Qadir. In al-Muqtadir, it is reciprocal. It becomes more interactive. The reciprocal aspect of this form throws a great deal of light on our whole discussion of a widely misunderstood Name al-Muntaqim, which is discussed in Chapter 7, Allah's Opposite Qualities.

This form is "mu," plus "ta," plus "i." It is fully reciprocal in the realm of action and reaction. It makes a full circle. It has a reciprocal quality that indicates mutual love between lover and beloved. It is a merging of will. The lover says, "Let Thy wish become my desire." This means taking full responsibility for one's action while knowing Allah is the only one who acts.

Ya Muqtadir   (muk-TA-dir)
Ya Muntaqim   (mun-TA-ḳim)

None of the 99 Names are in Form IX.

Form X: 'Istaf'la

While none of the 99 Names are in Form X, we have included it because one divine Name loved by Sufis is in this category.

Words that are members of Form X express the lover's deepest and most fervent yearnings and desires. An intimate relationship of trust allows you to ask for what you really want. While none of the 99 Names of God appear in this group, the example below is an oft-repeated phrase that Sufis use to express their yearning for the forgiveness of Allah for their failure to constantly remember divine presence.

'Astaghfiru-llaah   ('as-TAGH-fir-ul-laah)

"I long for the sweet forgiveness of God." The verbal root is *'astaghfiru-llaah*, one longed for forgiveness.

ar-rahman ar-rahim al-malik al-quddus as-salam al-mu'min al-muhaimin al-'aziz al-jabbar al-muta-kabbir al-khaliq al-bari' al-musawwir al-ghaffar al-qahhar al-wahhab al-razzaq al-fattah al-'alim al-qabid al-basit al-khafid ar-rafi' al-mu'izz al-mudhill as-sami' al-basir al-hakam al-'adl al-latif al-khabir al-halim al-'azim al-ghafur ash-shakur al-'aliyy al-kabir al-hafiz al-muqit al-hasib al-jalil al-karim ar-raqib al-mujib al-wasi' al-hakim al-wadud al-ma-jid al-ba'ith ash-shahid al-haqq al-wakil al-qawiyy al-matin al-waliyy al-hamid al-muhsi al-mubdi' al-mu'id al-muhyi al-mumit al-hayy al-qayyum al-wajid al-majid al-wahid al-ahad as-samad al-qadir al-muq-tadir al-muqaddim al-mu'akhkhir al-awwal al-akhir az-zahir al-batin al-wali al-muta'ali al-barr at-tawwab al-muntaqim al-'afuw ar-ra'uf malik al-mulk dhal-jalali wal-ikram al-muqsit al-jami' al-ghaniyy al-mughni al-mani' ad-darr an-nafi' an-nur al-hadi al-badi' al-baqi al-warith ar-rashid as-sabur

chapter 5

99 Names of Allah Discussed in Brief Summaries

There are more than 99 Names of Allah that are encoded as such in the Qur'an and in various hadith. We offer an expanded list at the end of these summaries. This expanded list, while quite incomplete, does include the additional Names of Allah that are mentioned in various chapters of our text.

The summary paragraphs below offer one version of the 99 Names. The selection of 99 Names given here is slightly different from other lists. This mainly reflects what we have chosen to concentrate on in the book. It is also a statement that we think one should not be too fixated on one idea of what ought to be included in, or excluded from, a list of the 99 Names of Allah, since it is generally agreed that the number 99 is symbolic of an unlimited quantity.

The practice of reciting 99 Names of Allah is based on historical traditions preserved about the life of the Prophet Muhammad. We have printed the most widely accepted hadith on this subject in Appendix A.

Ya Allah (yaa 'al-LAAH)

Allah is the Name of the essence. All the Names of Allah, or divine manifestations, are nothing but Allah. Nonmanifestation itself is Allah. For a full treatment of this centrally important Name, see Chapter 1.

1. Ya Rahman (yaa raḥ-MAAN)

Ar-Rahman is endless love. It is the infinite, unconditional reality of love. This is the Name said in the Qur'an to be inscribed on the heart of Allah.[4] In other words, God's essence necessarily includes this quality of love. Ar-Rahman might be imagined as the inner self of God, an infinite container that is incredibly compassionate, kind, and tender. It is the sun of loving compassion that is endlessly shining. Ar-Rahman includes all the other divine Names. It is the source of all; it is the gate that opens onto all God's qualities, and an inner secret of each one.

The root meaning comes from the word *rahm*, "womb." In human beings, this quality is naturally felt in relation to pregnancy. Allah provides human beings a womb to be born into and through which to have the realization of the love that is at the very foundation of all that exists. Invocation of Ya Rahman is a healing remedy for all who feel disconnected from God and for those marked by a wound of self-loathing. See Ya Rahim (2), with which it is paired in repetition.

2. Ya Rahim (yaa ra-ḤEEM)

Ar-Rahim is the embodiment of loving mercy, and it brings the gentle touch of divine mercy. Nothing other than ar-Rahim possesses the mercy that pours forth freely and fully reaches all beings and all things, without exception. It is an all-pervading infinite presence that is manifesting into a boundless number of finite things.

Its root meaning, like that of Ya Rahman (1), comes from the Arabic word for womb, *rahm*. It carries an inner feeling that is naturally connected with childhood. Ar-Rahim actively brings divine love into human relationships. It enables each and every being to more fully manifest loving mercy. Recitation of Ya Rahim is an antidote for all who feel abandoned by God and who need to experience the healing activity of divine love reaching deeply within them. See Ya Rahman (1), with which it is paired in repetition.

3. **Ya Malik** (yaa MA-lik)

The quality of al-Malik is to hold everything in the universe in the hands of the one and only being. It is an all-inclusive and majestic embrace. The word for angel, *malak*, is closely related to this name. Angels are made of light and are held in the hands of Allah. The light of al-Malik holds the inner essence of each and every thing. Each thing's essence never leaves this majestic embrace and never returns to it because it is permanently rooted in it. Ya Malik, thus experienced as holding everything's essence in the inner world, is naturally paired in repetition with Ya Malikal-Mulk (83), the majestic force that holds all outer forms.

By combining the two Names in repetition, you are brought to a balanced confidence in heaven and earth. Invocation of Ya Malik, Ya Malikal-Mulk is an antidote for all who feel abandoned and don't believe they belong anywhere. A person in this condition is constantly negating the reality of inner majesty or denying the reality of outer majesty. The recitation of these two related Names as a pair is also useful for those who do not feel entitled to possess things and who are afraid of the grossness of the material realm. See Ya Malikal-Mulk (83). See also Chapter 7, Allah's Opposite Qualities.

4. **Ya Quddus** (yaa ḳud-DOOS)

Al-Quddus is the ever-purifying one. It requires us to take leave of what we cling to in order to experience intimate union. Al-Quddus allows the spiritual traveler to transcend the lower self and keep going toward the one. Al-Quddus is a force that constantly cleanses us from the conceptual mind and its differentiations. It is continuously purifying our experience of the world through inward intimacy and union with the absolute.

A variation of the root of this Name means to return home to one's village. Al-Quddus is always purifying and always distancing, in the sense of leaving behind the ephemeral to go fully into the eternal. What is constantly moving toward Allah is al-Quddus. The union given by al-Quddus is one of continually becoming the eternal reality. See Ya Jami' (86), which is its opposite Name, especially when viewed in the context of divine ecstasy. See also Chapter 12, The Secret Of Ecstasy, and Chapter 13, The Arc of Ascent and Descent.

5. **Ya Salam** (yaa sa-LAAM)

As-Salam is peace itself. Such peace is not the result of anything and is nothing that can be said to manifest. There is no peace except the peace found in as-Salam. In another sense, as-Salam is the one who is peaceful. It is the *maqaam*, or spiritual station, of complete peace, where this perfect peace is embodied in every peaceful act. This divine quality is recommended as a greeting when meeting others, and its recitation is an antidote for disharmony in our relationships. One form of the root of Ya Salam means "to be safe."

The peace of as-Salam is not a dead place, nor should it be seen as simply the end of hostilities, or any kind of mere cessation. It is the divine energy that bestows peace itself on us, and it is the miraculous word, or *qawl,* that Allah speaks to our souls. Ya Salam may be repeated as a prayer of blessing for those who have departed. It brings the knowledge of not being abandoned at death to those who may be grieving, and to the departed souls as well. See Chapters 16, 18, and 19 on the emanations of divine abundance.

6.   **Ya Mu'min** (yaa MU'-min)

Al-Mu'min is the one who offers to us a real faith and a trust that is free of all fear, craft, and deceit. From its root we learn that al-Mu'min is a divine gift that allows us to feel safety, confidence, and security in our hearts. It allows human beings to have trust in God alone and not to be taken in by secondary causes, or what appear on the surface to be the causes of conditions.

Invocation of Ya Mu'min is an antidote for hypocrisy. It is a remedy for those who only give lip service to their faith or who trust in Allah but lack fullness of heart. And it is also an antidote for fanaticism or what is sometimes called blind faith. It shares the same root as al-Muhaimin (7) and may be combined with it in recitation.

7.   **Ya Muhaimin** (yaa mu-HAI-min)

Al-Muhaimin is the divine quality that preserves the essence of a thing from corruption through all the vicissitudes of time. The eternal in the thing, the purity of what it is in reality, is protected from being harmed by any temporal cause. It is an attribute used to describe the Qur'an.[5] Al-Muhaimin affirms that translation and addendum will not diminish the Qur'an's essence. In a more general sense, what is transient passes away and therefore never truly had existence. *Baqa,* the eternal, is, always was, and always will be.

Thus al-Muhaimin is linked with al-Baqi (96), the eternal essence that remains. The essence of each thing, the *malakut,* is held in the hands of God. Al-Muhaimin describes the immutable quality by which all the 99 Names of God work in the world. A full way to invoke the protection of this sacred quality would be to recite Ya Baqi, Ya Malik, Ya Muhaimin. See Ya Baqi (96) and Ya Malik (3). See also Ya Hafiz (38), Ya Muqit (39), Ya Wakil (52), Ya Wali (76), and Ya Mani' (89), and Chapter 11, Divine Protection.

8.　**Ya 'Aziz** (yaa 'a-ZEEZ)

Al-'Aziz is a kind of divine strength or power that is beyond the dualism of praise and blame. It is the strength that naturally flows from intrinsic, essential worth. The power of al-'Aziz is sweet, and it actually carries an inner meaning of sweetness. It also means precious and rare, like a baby eagle among birds.

The strength of al-'Aziz is the power of God itself. It is the true worth, utmost dignity, and strength that manifests directly from God, without an intermediary. It can be contemplated in the incredible precious value of the human soul. Invocation of Ya 'Aziz brings freedom without limitations and is a remedy for our experience of being powerless and under great restraint due to restrictions that may be real or imagined.

Repetition of Ya 'Aziz is also an important remedy for the common human experience of feeling undervalued and worthless. Al-'Aziz is the marriage of strength and self-worth. See Ya Mu'izz (24), with which it is often paired in repetition. See also Ya Jabbar (9), Ya Qawiyy (53) Ya Matin (54), Ya Qadir (68), Ya Muqtadir (69), and Ya Dhal Jalali wal 'Ikram (84). See Chapter 7, Allah's Opposite Qualities, and Chapter 9, Omnipotence.

9.　**Ya Jabbar** (yaa jab-BAAR)

Al-Jabbar is an expression of divine power that allows you to accomplish things or to act in the world. It is a healing strength. It carries the root meaning of setting a broken bone to heal it. Al-Jabbar means the strength to continuously heal all things all the time, the strength to heal brokenness. It is compelling, but only in the sense of stabilizing you in a consistent direction of movement.

When recited, Ya Jabbar empowers the sincere practitioner with an enduring strength so that nothing can shake you. Through embodying this quality your existence becomes unified. It is the mender of our fractured existence. See Ya 'Aziz (8), Ya Qawiyy (53), Ya Matin (54), Ya Qadir (68), Ya Muqtadir (69), and Ya Dhal Jalali wal 'Ikram (84). See also Chapter 9, Omnipotence.

10.　**Ya Mutakabbir** (yaa mu-ta-KAB-bir)

Al-Mutakabbir is the path to vastness, an ever-expanding cosmic wave removing all boundaries. Its grammatical form in the Arabic language means always moving. It is continually moving beyond the present understanding or experience. Al-Mutakabbir is about as transcendental as one can imagine.

No matter what your relationship to Allah is, al-Mutakabbir goes beyond that. It is going beyond, constantly going beyond limitation. It corresponds to the mantra for the Heart of Perfect Wisdom sutra in Sanskrit, *gate gate paragate parasamgate bodhi svaha*. There is the continual action of going beyond.

Al-Mutakabbir is the means of producing a state within that will enable one to become al-Kabir, incomparably vast like God. Its root includes the meanings of dignity, honor, and goodness of action. Al-Mutakabbir means becoming incomparably bigger, but this sense of "bigger" makes no reference to anything else by way of comparison. It is a steady state of becoming infinitely great. See Ya Kabir (37), with which Ya Mutakabbir may effectively be paired in repetition.

11. **Ya Khaliq** (yaa ḴHAA-liḵ)

Al-Khaliq is the only one who creates. It is the active, dynamic source of creation, and the continuous activity of creation. There is no beginning to it and no end, nor any rest in the middle. Every moment reveals al-Khaliq in action, as well as the fruits of the action. A variation of al-Khaliq's root means to measure a piece of leather or any material and see that it is beautifully proportioned in design before cutting it and sewing the pieces together.

Prior to anything being made, al-Khaliq is the one who imagines all the possibilities. It is the innate disposition of God to imagine the universe. Metaphorically, it is like imagining all the possible letters that might be written with the ink in a bottle. Al-Khaliq is reflected in human beings, and as a consequence we have the innate ability to imagine the beloved. See Ya Bari' (12) and Ya Musawwir (13), which further express divine creation, as well as Ya Mubdi' (58) and Ya Mu'id (59). See also Chapter 14, God the Creator.

12. **Ya Bari'** (yaa BAA-ri')

Al-Bari' is the originator of individuation. Continuing with the metaphor of leatherworking mentioned above, al-Bari' would be the act of cutting out the individual pieces of the design that has been measured on the leather. While it is the beginning of individuation, nevertheless it still remains in the condition of creation before physical manifestation. Al-Bari' defines the realm called *jabarut*, where we find the origination of the divine Names. It is how they exist. They are still not manifested in physical form, but they are individuated as potentialities.

What God creates is well proportioned and in a manner free from inconsistencies, faults, blemishes, defects, and imperfection. The nature of al-Bari' is to make the universe like that. On a personal level, it can mean to free yourself from any unclean thing, to become free from guilt, and to become pure of soul. The healing aspect of al-Bari'—to remove or free oneself from disease—is also an important part of the meaning of this divine Name. See Ya Khaliq (11) and Ya Musawwir (13). See also Chapter 14, God the Creator.

13. **Ya Musawwir** (yaa mu-ṢOW-wir)

Al-Musawwir is the one who continuously shapes the heart and continuously shapes all things. What it creates is not left for even a breath. This Name completes the creative activity described above with Ya Khaliq (11) and Ya Bari' (12). The individually cut-out pieces of leather are now sewn together and made into a three-dimensional form.

Of these three Names of creation, al-Musawwir is the one that moves closest to material objects in the universe. But it doesn't yet fully manifest into the visible, sensible world, the world described by az-Zahir (74). Al-Musawwir continuously and increasingly goes toward that final manifestation. Nevertheless, the individuation process has been completed and the infinite is given a finite shape—in just the way, as it is said in the scriptures, that Adam is created in God's own image and likeness. See also Chapter 14, God the Creator.

14. **Ya Ghaffar** (yaa g̱haf-FAAR)

Al-Ghaffar is inexhaustible forgiveness. It is repetitive. Even though you may repeat the same error over and over again, you never come to the end of God's forgiveness, which is inexhaustible. A form of the root of al-Ghaffar means a substance bees make that the Arabs used to fill in the cracks of a dried-out, old leather water skin, so that it no longer leaks. Divine forgiveness repairs human dryness and brittleness in a similar way.

Invocation of Ya Ghaffar offers a healing salve that is an antidote for self-loathing, guilt, and blame. It is especially useful to bring this emanation of divine forgiveness into the places where you have been marked by impressions of self-deficiency that have been reinforced time and again. Al-Ghaffar brings moisture back into the system. An even more complete realization of the nature of divine forgiveness may occur when this Name is paired in repetition with Ya Ghafur (34), which shares the same root. We recommend prayerful recitation of Ya Ghaffar, Ya Ghafur. See also Ya Tawwab (79), Ya 'Afuw (81), and Chapter 8, Divine Forgiveness.

15. **Ya Qahhar** (yaa ḳah-HAAR)

Al-Qahhar is a strength that overwhelms all else. A physical-plane meaning from the same root is the searing effect that fire has on a piece of meat, which gets the juices flowing. The fire is the love ('ishq), and the meat is the heart. Al-Qahhar is continuous and repetitive. It brings the passionate fire of longing. Its presence means that regardless of outward circumstances you still long for God in your heart, and nothing will put out this flame.

Al-Qahhar's reality causes the personality shell to dissolve. The process may feel like hell on earth, but al-Qahhar overwhelms all attachment. It consumes otherness, leaving only Allah. It defeats your lower self but doesn't break you in doing so. It shows you that, in truth, you are un-defeatable. It transforms what you are from raw meat to cooked meat. Because of its intensity, it is best recited in combination with other divine Names that would tend to balance its manifestation. See Chapter 9, Omnipotence.

16. Ya Wahhab (yaa wah-HAAB)

Al-Wahhab gives divine blessings continually and universally. It is a flow that is without disruption and which is freely given without any expectation of return. It is the one who constantly refreshes. There is no restraint based on scarcity, as its source is super-abundant. A form from the same root, *mawhibah*, is a cloud that rains freely on everything. Another form, *mawhoob*, is a child or any blessing given to you by God.

By invoking Ya Wahhab you become identified with a stream flowing continuously from the divine source, and everything you need in life is already fully present and flowing in that stream. It is closely related to Ya Razzaq (17) and Ya Fattah (18). In the sound code of the Arabic language, all three share a form that conveys continuous activity.

There is a developmental aspect in considering these three Names together. Al-Wahhab is the free rain that is given to all. Ar-Razzaq is the water that flows into irrigation ditches. Al-Fattah is all the fruit you harvest from all the trees you've irrigated. In other words, Al-Wahhab is a free gift; ar-Razzaq offers the means for achieving abundance; al-Fattah is the continuing action of all that will be accomplished. See Chapters 16, 18, and 19 on the emanations of divine abundance and Chapter 4, The Sound Code.

17. Ya Razzaq (yaa raz-ZAAḲ)

Ar-Razzaq is the one who continuously provides the means for each of us to get what we need for our daily sustenance, our bread and butter. The noun *rizq*, formed from its root, means a gift of blessing from which all can benefit. The adage "The bounty of the dates can be seen at the bottom of the well" illustrates the meaning of ar-Razzaq. If you make use of the water of the well and draw it up and irrigate your palm trees every day, you will get the dates.

There are endless opportunities to benefit from the divine gifts that are offered by ar-Razzaq, and endless ways to make them available to others. Ar-Razzaq is also seen in a person's openness to receive divine provenance. The word *al-arzaaq* means "endless gifts." The truly endless gifts are the gifts of *rahma*: compassion, mercy, and love. The one who always gives these gifts has an infinite supply in treasure houses of infinite love. See Ya Wahhab (16) and Ya Fattah (18). See also Chapters 16, 18, and 19 on the emanations of divine abundance.

18. **Ya Fattah** (yaa fat-TAAḤ)

Al-Fattah means both to begin and to open. Through it you begin to open your heart to the infinite possibilities of the divine presence. With al-Fattah, the opening is continuous. It is an enlightenment that keeps happening. Al-Fattah brings great power to clear the way of obstacles and open the path of your life for success. It is the one who opens the heart to love and ecstasy.

Al-Fattah means to open something with something else, a key. It is the key to opening the heart to Allah, the key to finding the God within. Reciting Ya Fattah is a very powerful practice because, even in the midst of despair, it brings the possibility of awakening to love and ecstasy. Its activity in us is opening up the veils of darkness over the heart to uncover the light within. Al-Fattah is the continuous action of all that will be accomplished. Invocation of Ya Fattah sets up the dynamic of going deeper and deeper in the process of opening. See Ya Wahhab (16) and Ya Razzaq (17). See also Chapters 16, 18, and 19 on divine abundance.

19. **Ya 'Alim** (yaa 'a-LEEM)

Al-'Alim is the omniscient knowledge of God. Its ultimate meaning is all-inclusive. It includes inner knowledge, al-Khabir (31), and outer knowledge, ash-Shahid (50), the unseen and the seen. Al-'Alim means the emanation of knowledge that reaches everything without exception. Considering all of its various forms, al-'Alim is mentioned in the Qur'an more than any other single attribute of Allah.

The variations and different syllable stresses of the forms taken by the root of al-'Alim produce divine Names that express God's omniscience in a variety of ways. *'AA-lim* is the only source of knowledge; *'al-'AAM* is ever-continuing knowledge; *'a'lam* is ever-widening knowledge. *'Aalameen* is an animate plural of *'aleem*. It is the word for universe in the sense of a collection of all possible worlds, and it occurs in the first surah of the Qur'an, which says that Allah is the lord of all possible universes.[6] At the physical level, *'alaamah* means a water source that is under a mountain.

Al-'Alim is often paired in the Qur'an with al-Wasi' (45), which emphasizes that it is both all-knowing and infinitely present. It is also frequently paired with *kullu shayin*, which affirms knowing every possible thing in an absolute way. God is described as the knower of the essence, or inward secret of hearts. God-consciousness, *taqwaa*, is this ultimate secret of the heart. True knowledge leads to a continuing relationship with wisdom that heals and discerns. See Ya Hakim (46) and Ya Hakam (28). See Chapter 20, In Quest of Wisdom; Chapter 22, God's Omniscience; and Chapter 23, The Ground of All Knowing.

20. **Ya Qabid** (yaa ḲAA-biḍ)

Al-Qabid is the only source of all contraction and the only one who actually contracts. At the physical level, continual contraction and expansion are seen throughout nature. It is in the natural physical rhythm of the heart and lungs. Contraction and expansion are also aspects of the greater sphere of heart. Transient states, called *ahwal*, constantly are experienced in the wider sphere of heart, which could be called the depth of feeling.

Al-Qabid has a sober quality; its opposite, al-Basit (21), expansion, has the quality of ecstasy. Ya Qabid, Ya Basit, when recited as a pair, provide a necessary balance for those who stubbornly cling to the pleasurable spiritual states that they have become attached to by their desire. Repetition of this pair is also useful for those who have a strong aversion to contraction and who are desperately trying to escape from lower states. Equanimity comes from realizing that God is operating through both these poles of experience.

The four divine Names beginning here with al-Qabid are the regulators of spiritual states. They describe the action of God in contracting, expanding, lowering, and raising beings. They should all be considered together. See Ya Basit (21), Ya Khafid (22), and Ya Rafi' (23). See also Chapter 7, Allah's Opposite Qualities.

21. **Ya Basit** (yaa BAA-siṭ)

Al-Basit is the only one who expands, the only source of expansion. Often there is great joy in the expansion of al-Basit, and its meaning is connected with ecstasy. There are many stages of its expansiveness. Al-Basit brings a kind of ecstasy in eating, drinking, and smelling, in music, in great natural beauty, and in grander and grander ways until your joy uplifts all beings. You become absent to yourself and find God's presence completely within.

Even though the states that may be reached are impressive, they are transient, and the movement between al-Qabid and al-Basit consequently should be seen as horizontal. One's actual *maqaam*, or established station of realization, may be unaffected by temporary states of ecstasy; after they pass, there is a tendency to return to the habit of grieving over the past and fearing the future. The more mature a spiritual traveler becomes on the path, the more fully they understand how sobriety and ecstasy naturally go together. See Ya Qabid (20), Ya Khafid (22), and Ya Rafi' (23). See also Chapter 7, Allah's Opposite Qualities.

22. **Ya Khafid** (yaa ḴḤAA-fiḍ)

Al-Khafid is the only one who lowers beings down through the spiritual stations. It facilitates real descent. The movement described by the pair al-Khafid and ar-Rafi' is vertical. These two Names of God relate to *maqaam*, or spiritual station, a nontransient stage of spiritual realization, rather than to *ahwal*, which are temporary states described by al-Qabid and al-Basit. Al-Khafid's lowering of your spiritual station is out of loving protective concern for the soul of the wayfarer. It is a kind of constriction, but the job of the heart is to make the infinite finite.

With the realization of al-Khafid, there is a grasping of the secret deep within the contraction of the heart. One meaning of the root of al-Khafid is to lower the wing, like a mother chicken lowers her wing over her chicks to protect them. Ya Khafid should be recited paired with its opposite Ya Rafi'. When you understand that God alone is the facilitator of your grade of realization, you become content with the raising or lowering of the spirit as God wills.

The combination of these Names in repetition helps to protect you from your own spiritual greed or desire, and to protect you from going too high too fast when you are not prepared. Repetition of Ya Khafid may also be an antidote for spiritual burnout, especially when a person feels that spiritual practices are not working to change their condition. See Ya Qabid (20), Ya Basit (21), and Ya Rafi' (23).

23. **Ya Rafi'** (yaa RAA-fi')

Ar-Rafi' is the only one who raises beings through the spiritual stations, by which they draw near to Allah. It is the only cause of such exaltation. Ar-Rafi' is the exalter; it facilitates movement to the higher planes. It allows you to transcend lower states, opinions, prejudices, and even to overcome obsession. Through its activity, a traveler on the spiritual path goes through every single healing process until they are truly free.

The action of al-Khafid and ar-Rafi' is not an action in time. It is not evident even in the movement of the heart's expansion and contraction. It occurs in God's time, which is eternal. When invoking this Name you are attending to God's causality, and thus it is not a technique for getting high. To truly benefit from it, you cannot be attached to being high or low. When Ya Rafi' is paired in recitation with Ya Khafid, the sincere practitioner may be allowed to unveil and observe the inner workings of the soul. See Ya Qabid (20), Ya Basit (21), Ya Khafid (22), and Ya Wajid (64).

24. **Ya Mu'izz** (yaa mu-'IZZ)

Al-Mu'izz is the one who gives the gift of self-esteem. It brings true dignity. Al-Mu'izz has the same root as al-'Aziz (8), the strength that flows from a knowledge of essential worth or inner value. Its root means "sweetness," as well as "special" and "rare," like an eagle among birds. Al-Mu'izz is the one who can take us to the state of al-'Aziz. Repetition of Ya Mu'izz is an antidote for attachment to reputation and a remedy for the habit of self-aggrandizement. We recommend that it be paired with its opposite Name, al-Mudhill (25).

In reciting Ya Mu'izz, Ya Mudhill, you are invoking the one who is both the ultimate cause of your being honored and of your being brought to shame. The Names balance each other. There is an inner dynamic. When you truly reach a depth of anguish of the soul, then the truth that your soul is created in the divine image is of necessity remembered and honored, and the quality of al-Mu'izz naturally arises. There is a similar dynamic that occurs when egotistical pride evokes the need to be dishonored. See Ya 'Aziz (8) and Ya Mudhill (25). See also Chapter 7, Allah's Opposite Qualities, where these pairings are more fully discussed.

25. **Ya Mudhill** (yaa mu-<u>DH</u>ILL)

Al-Mudhill is the one who leads you to the domain where you see yourself as the lowest of the low. This domain is where the original disconnected and isolated ego identity has been constructed. Al-Mudhill's root means to seek or yearn for the object of a long cherished wish. This divine quality empowers you to face your lower self, to bow low before God and to engage the lowest regions of the self. Until you reach this place, you cannot begin to dissolve the false self.

Al-Mudhill brings us, willingly or not, to our knees with our head on the ground. For someone who is stuck in a place of shame, humiliation, or shadow, this sacred Name can actually be a powerful antidote. However, we recommend that it should rarely be recited alone. It is best repeated in combination with Ya Mu'izz (24). See Chapter 7, Allah's Opposite Qualities.

26. **Ya Sami'** (yaa sa-MEE')

As-Sami' means divine hearing. This is hearing in the sense of hearing everything without limitation, both in detail and as a totality. It includes possible and impossible sounds, manifest and unmanifest sounds. As-Sami' endows you with true hearing so that you might hear the sound of God's signs and hear all sounds as sacred. The essence of sound itself is discovered in the heart. The heart becomes an ear.[7]

With as-Sami' the true ears may be opened, the mystical ears, and we can hear the sound beyond all sounds, the sound that is not an effect of a secondary cause. From a personal perspective, repetition of Ya Sami' is an antidote for those who, on an emotional and spiritual level, cannot hear what others are saying because they only hear the words but are unaware of the underlying meaning. See Ya Basir (27), with which it is paired in repetition.

27. **Ya Basir** (yaa ba-ṢEER)

Al-Basir is seeing in its totality, which means seeing everything all at once as well as every single individual thing in detail—visible, invisible, possible, impossible, manifest, and unmanifest. Al-Basir is the eye of the heart, *'ain-'al-qalb*.[8] It is a divine seeing that is complete in understanding and realization.

Such is the organ of inner perception through which human beings may perceive the greatest sign of the divine presence.

It is seeing from the inside out and the outside in. This absolute seeing overcomes your sense of separation, loneliness, and alienation, and you are allowed to live in the vision of God. See Ya Sami' (26), with which it is naturally paired in repetition. See Chapter 20, In Quest of Wisdom; and Chapter 23, The Ground of All Knowing.

28. Ya Hakam (yaa ḤA-kam)   يَا حَكَمٌ

Al-Hakam is discerning wisdom, a wisdom that is utterly pervasive and very precise. Al-Hakam is the one who discerns and who makes wise decisions. This divine quality is described by such words as sagacious, judicious, clear-headed, intelligent, subtle, and discreet. In its deepest sense, it is a seeing from the eye of the heart, by means of the light of God. A hadith says, "Be aware of the penetrating insight (*firaasah*) of the believer, because such a one sees by the light of God."

The nominative form of H-K-M is *al-hikmah*, which means both wisely reflecting on the secrets of divine essence (the silent or still wisdom), and living actively in harmony with that reflection. Through this kind of wisdom, you become able to discern between what is real and what is transient. It erases all doubt so that you can focus on the truth amidst the most confusing of conditions.

Invocation of Ya Hakam offers a way out of the feeling of powerlessness in the face of all the raging desires. It is a means of objectifying situations to gain clarity of insight. We recommend it be paired in recitation with its cognate Ya Hakim (46), healing wisdom, which is a more inclusive Name of wisdom. See Chapter 23, The Ground of All Knowing.

29. Ya 'Adl (yaa 'ADL)   يَا عَدْلُ

The essence of al-'Adl is a fluid, merciful quality that mediates and brings all that exists into true balance and harmony. It is the balanced and the balancer, as well as the harmonious balance of all things. Al-'Adl balances all the Names of beauty and the Names of power. It is particularly important in balancing the opposite Names. Al-'Adl even balances the balance. It is the harmonizing of the total system so that everything is moving toward the one. Invocation of Ya 'Adl is a remedy for all those who are out of balance with themselves and with the world. It brings reintegration. See Chapter 7, Allah's Opposite Qualities.

30. Ya Latif (yaa la-ṬEEF)   يَا لَطِيفٌ

Al-Latif is a subtle love that reveals the finest of mysteries. To know this quality is to know the subtlest of things that are unknown, and thus not to be limited by finite conditioning. The subtle mystery of al-Latif is within all things. This divine Name is strongly related to the kind of knowledge brought by Ya Khabir (31). The magnetic centers in the body used in spiritual practices of the Sufis are called *lata'if*. Al-Latif is a gentle and refined love. It is the secret of kindness, tenderness, and love.

Al-Latif offers a subtle strength in the taming of the *nafs*. It is the most essential quality for human beings in developing a refined character and a harmonious manner in all relationships. Invocation of Ya Latif is an antidote for coarseness of ego. It brings gracefulness, resiliency, and a softening of our defensive behaviors and rigidities. It is often paired in repetition with Ya Khabir (31) to express very refined and subtle knowledge. See Chapter 6, Love's Mysteries.

31. **Ya Khabir** (yaa k͟ha-BEER)

Al-Khabir includes the whole realm of inner knowledge. It is depth of insight that penetrates into the most secret and buried places of the earth. Root forms of the word mean "to till the soil" (*khabara*) and "a field where a tree is growing" (*khabr*). Part of its inner meaning involves being tested to get to the depth of the secret.

Al-Khabir is very closely related in meaning to al-Latif (30), and they frequently are paired in the Qur'an. We need to combine the skillful knowing of al-Khabir with the refinement of al-Latif to uncover the subtle mysteries of knowledge. Reciting Ya Latif, Ya Khabir is helpful to this end. Al-Khabir's natural complement is its opposite, ash-Shahid (50), which means the witnessing of God in the outer world through all the senses.

We recommend pairing them in recitation: Ya Shahid, Ya Khabir. The interplay of these two Names leads us to al-'Alim (19), a name for transcendental knowledge that contains them both, as omniscience must embrace both the inside and the outside. See Chapter 20, In Quest of Wisdom; and Chapter 22, God's Omniscience.

32. **Ya Halim** (yaa ḥa-LEEM)

Al-Halim is tender love, gentle and kind love. The tenderness of al-Halim is physical, emotional, and nurturing. God manifests this quality anywhere and everywhere, without exception. One physical root meaning is the shyness and gentleness that is found in an early pubescent girl. There is a kind of retiring or monastic quality to al-Halim. It offers a softness and kindness that makes for perseverance. Al-Halim is the place where the dreams can arise, which are really visions. Forms of the word, *hulm* and *'ahlam*, are categories in dream interpretation.

Al-Halim offers an avenue for creative imagination, even as God is said to lovingly dream the universe. Repetition of Ya Halim brings a mildness of manner that is an antidote for anger and impatience. It expands with immense openness. Al-Halim's harmonious qualities allow it to be beneficially paired with many other divine Names to enhance their effects. See Ya Rahman (1),

Ya Rahim (2), Ya Latif (30), Ya Wadud (47), and Ya Ra'uf (82), with all of which al-Halim is grouped in Chapter 6, Love's Mysteries.

33. **Ya 'Azim** (yaa 'a-DHEEM)

Al-'Azim actualizes the divine presence. It involves feeling this presence in the depth of your soul, literally in your very bones. Al-'Azim comes from *al-'adaam*, which means to grow strong in the bones. It is the experience of the infinite in your deepest, essential self, as well as in the world outside. Al-'Azim means to embody the divine presence in a complete way, a physical way. A most difficult part of human actualization is reaching the stage of being able to bring the structure of your inner realization into balance with the structure of your outward manifestation in the world.

The invocation of Ya 'Azim is a very helpful practice for all who pay attention to realization in an abstract sort of way, but who cannot bring their realization out and function with it in daily life. It is a divine quality that is called on for the accomplishment of extraordinary aims. There is an awesome or overwhelming feeling connected with this Name. The root of 'Azim alludes to the hundredth or greatest Name of God, the unknown Name. See Chapter 10, Infinite Presence.

34. **Ya Ghafur** (yaa gha-FOOR)

Al-Ghafur is the essence of forgiveness, because it reveals the depth of the divine heart. Al-Ghafur means to forgive all the way into the deepest possible place, all the way to the ground floor. It is the divine forgiveness that penetrates into the most repressed secrets in our hearts. Its presence allows us to accept that there is forgiveness even for the worst crime we have ever committed in our life, or the worst crime ever done to us.

Al-Ghafur is a healing salve for human beings' deep sense of being wounded that is due to self-identifying with shame and unworthiness. It shares the same root as al-Ghaffar (14). A physical-plane meaning from the same root tells us it is like the substance bees make to repair their hives, which then is rubbed into the dried-out, cracked leather water skin so that it no longer leaks. See Ya Ghaffar (14), with which it is paired in repetition. See also Ya Tawwab (79) and Ya 'Afuw (81), as well as Chapter 8, Divine Forgiveness.

35. **Ya Shakur** (yaa sha-KOOR)

Ash-Shakur is the One who sends gratitude into the depth of the lover's heart. Several of the root forms of ash-Shakur have physical meanings that refer to udders or breasts filling up, and to the sensation of the letting down of a mother's milk. As reflected in human beings, it means to turn your attention with thankfulness toward inward perfection. Repetition of Ya Shakur is an antidote for dissatisfaction with the falseness or incompleteness of the world. When you feel gratitude in your heart, your gaze can then be directed outward to the signs of Allah in the world.

Ultimately, the heart overflows like a fountain with gratitude onto the tongue, the limbs, and all the actions of the thankful servant. That is how the Prophet Muhammad described himself to his wife Khadija: Am I not *'abdun shakurun*, a grateful slave? Another root meaning of ash-Shakur is to forgive and to bless. Invocation of Ya Shakur is a remedy for the perpetual dissatisfaction of the complaining *nafs*, or lower self. See Ya Hamid (56), and Chapter 16, Names of Gratitude.

36. **Ya 'Aliyy** (yaa 'A-leeyy)

Al-'Aliyy is the exalted, beyond form. It is purely transcendent. Al-'Aliyy means absolutely above, totally beyond. Beyond it there is nothing. It is a vision of the highest, like the vision of the Heart Throne of God suspended above oceans of infinite mercy.

Al-'Aliyy is emanating transcendence just as the sun must reach its zenith in the sky to shine its light and fully illuminate each and every thing. Al-'Aliyy is fully exalted, and it manifests that transcendence in its immanence. Repetition of Ya 'Aliyy is an antidote for the ego's attachment to reputation, rank, and hierarchy. See Ya Muta'ali (77), which is closely related in meaning. See also Chapter 10, Infinite Presence.

37. **Ya Kabir** (yaa ka-BEER)

Al-Kabir is incomparable greatness or vastness, an unrestricted expansiveness. It is not a comparison. It is a state beyond the boundaries of time and space. Al-Kabir is the infinite presence of Allah, which includes what we call presence and absence simultaneously. It is beyond expansion and contraction.

It is not enough to say al-Kabir is the biggest, the greatest, and the beyond. Language is inadequate for such realities, so poets endeavor to use finite images to describe the indescribable. Al-Kabir is like an ocean without a shore. Al-Akbar, as in the often-repeated phrase Allahu Akbar, shares the same root as al-Kabir and essentially has the same meaning.

Al-Kabir refers to the infinite nature of God and is so vast it is beyond the rational mind's ability to comprehend. Invocation of Ya Kabir is a remedy for being imprisoned by limited mental constructs. See Ya Mutakabbir (10), with which it is often paired in repetition. See also Chapter 10, Infinite Presence.

38. **Ya Hafiz** (yaa ḥa-FEEDH)

Al-Hafiz means that everything in the heavens and earth, down to the smallest particle, is within the protection of Allah. For human beings, it involves becoming mindful, considerate, respectful, and cherishing deeply in your heart. This makes it exactly parallel with *dhikr* (*zikr*), which means "to re-member." It is in this sense that God says in the Qur'an, "Remember me, and I will remember you."[9] Al-Hafiz is protecting and remembering everyone. To realize al-Hafiz is to be conscious of the greatest of secrets, to know the secret, and to keep it. The order, sequence, and timing of the universe are pre-served through this quality.

Invocation of Ya Hafiz is useful for all who need protection from fear, despair, and hopelessness. Al-Hafiz is a matrix for the whole family of the divine Names of protection because it contains within itself all the specific qualities they each evoke. See Ya Muhaimin (7), Ya Muqit (39), Ya Wakil (52), Ya Wali (76), and Ya Mani' (89). See Chapter 11, Divine Protection.

39. **Ya Muqit** (yaa mu-ḴEET)

Al-Muqit is the unlimited ability to provide for each and every thing. It is the trusted, reliable source of sustenance. With al-Muqit, the divine protection arrives to feed and to nourish, to allow for survival. A physical meaning that its root takes is to provide a measure of grain in a reliable way to guard against starvation.

There is also a variation of the root that means the fat of a camel's hump. *Qut al-quloob*, a classical Sufi work,[10] presents al-Muqit (*qut*) as the quality that nourishes our spirit, breath after breath. Breath itself is a kind of nourishment from God that protects us from the death of the heart.

Ya Muqit may be paired in invocation with Ya Shahid (50) to evoke the one who has the power of watching over everything and protects everything from want. See also Ya Muhaimin (7), Ya Hafiz (38), Ya Wakil (52), Ya Wali (76), and Ya Mani' (89). See Chapter 11, Divine Protection.

40. **Ya Hasib** (yaa ḥa-SEEB)

Al-Hasib is the action of accounting for the full meaning of everything. Nothing goes unrecorded and nothing is ever lost. It means taking full responsibility for one's actions, words, and even one's thoughts. To become completely accountable allows for a new beginning of what is possible. It brings realization. A root meaning of al-Hasib is to record a business transaction in an account book with ex-actitude and honesty.

An advanced Sufi technique called *muhaasibah* is an honest taking account of oneself while never forgetting that you are within the ocean of divine mercy. Repetition of Ya Hasib can be an antidote for those of us who get lost in minutiae. It is also recommended for those who are fearful or who get caught up in the habit of scheming. See Ya Raqib (43) and Ya Muhsi (57). Together with Ya Hasib, these Names are considered in relation to divine knowledge and the psychological challenges of the superego in Chapter 22, God's Omniscience.

41. **Ya Jalil** (ja-LEEL)

Al-Jalil is the omnipotent divine power and strength that manifests into each thing and everything without exception. Its opposite is al-Jamil, the divine beauty that likewise penetrates all. Al-Jamil is often, but not always, found on traditional lists of the 99 Names. In considering the relational families of the Names as we have done in this book, the largest clusters of Names within the 99 Names of Allah are the *jalali* and *jamali* Names, the Names of Power and the Names of Beauty. There is a small group of perfectly transcendent and eternal Names that can be called *kamali*. Because we felt it was more useful to focus in detail on family clusters of smaller size, our discussion of al-Jalil and al-Jamil mostly occurs in the sections devoted to the Name that combines power, beauty, and absolute perfection, Ya Dhal Jalali wal 'Ikram (84).

42. **Ya Karim** (yaa ka-REEM)

Al-Karim is fully manifested generosity that reaches everything without exception. It can be found in every particular thing and in everything altogether. Al-Karim bestows endless gifts with full integrity. It is an inexhaustible, bountiful energy that keeps on giving, like a flowing stream of water from a fathomless well. Those who embody al-Karim are generous with whatever they have, whether it actually reaches people or not, or whether others respond or not. Another form of the word is *'ikram*, which means incomparably generous. It is found in one of the divine Names: Ya Dhal Jalali wal 'Ikram (84). The common root K-R-M means unconditional giving from the inner intention of love.

A physical form of the root has the meaning of fertile ground. Al-Karim also expresses dignity and integrity. When the angels perceived the quality of God's fully manifested generosity in Adam, they fully prostrated in *sajdah* before the mystery of divine manifestation in the human being. Repetition of Ya Karim is a remedy for miserliness in all realms and directly addresses the densest core of the ego. See Chapter 18, Divine Generosity, and Chapter 17, The Seven Levels of the *Nafs*.

43. **Ya Raqib** (yaa ra-ḴEEB)

Ar-Raqib combines the qualities of protection and watchfulness. Its meaning of "watching over" integrates two concepts: to watch the stars until the dawn comes, and to watch a baby while it is sleeping. Ar-Raqib means to fully give loving attention, and at the same time to possess the inner quietude that makes real concentration possible. The best technique for learning to concentrate is to awaken loving interest for the object of concentration and to use this love as a focus for one-pointed attention. Concentration can best be held and grow within the context of caring for what we love.

From Ar-Raqib comes *muraaqabah*, an advanced Sufi technique of concentration that begins with *hush dar dam*, watching the breath. Ar-Raqib brings expanded awareness of the inner world, taking one beyond the physical into the metaphysical. Repetition of Ya Raqib is helpful in attaining focus in your concentrations. See Ya Hasib (40) and Ya Muhsi (57). These three Names are considered in relation to divine knowledge and the psychological challenges of the superego in Chapter 22, God's Omniscience.

44. **Ya Mujib** (yaa mu-JEEB)

Al-Mujib is the one who answers all prayers. This response to prayer matches the genuineness of the asking. The Qur'an says, "Call to me and I will answer you."[11] The imperative here is to act. Not knowing the time, manner, and place in which al-Mujib answers is actually a protection from getting trapped by our limited expectations.

A physical form of its root means to dig into a rock to reach water. Another form means to penetrate the blackness of the night like the light of the moon that, when it rises, renders clear what has been obscured. These physical meanings of the root of al-Mujib suggest that the act of asking in prayer is a light that penetrates your inner darkness of confusion and shines upon your own self, and in this way reveals what you are really asking for. This addresses the often-repeated question of why we should pray when God already knows what we need.

Invoking Ya Mujib is not simply seeking an answer; it means to pay attention and listen. If we are not listening, or are distant in our feeling, we may not be near enough to al-Mujib to receive the answer that is always there. Its repetition allows us to listen with our heart and hear God's answers. See Chapter 18, Divine Generosity, and Chapter 17, The Seven Levels of the *Nafs*.

45. **Ya Wasi'** (yaa WAA-si')

Al-Wasi' is the infinite, all-surrounding, embracing presence of God. "Wheresoever you turn, there is the Face of God."[12] "Face" here means essence. Al-Wasi' is the infinite omnipresence of the essence. In another Qur'anic passage we have, "The compassionate presence of God (*rahma*) surrounds all things." From the root meaning of *rahm* an image of the womb of love is implied: encompassing, comprehending, and surrounding all things.

Al-Wasi' is an embracing expansion. It embraces without containing, narrowing, or limiting. It is infinite vastness that can be said to curve back into itself. Al-Wasi' transcends all opposites and reveals the full potential of the one and only being. The heart has this capacity to unite and harmonize the higher and lower realms. A sacred hadith of the Prophet Muhammad says in the voice of Allah, "The heavens and earth cannot contain me, but the heart of my faithful servant contains me."

Al-Wasi' allows old boundaries to be melted down so that we can relax and merge into an inclusive state. Repetition of Al-Wasi' is an antidote for all who are locked into rigid habitual boundaries. It is a door for the opening of the heart. See Chapter 10, Infinite Presence, and Chapter 7, Allah's Opposite Qualities.

46. **Ya Hakim** (yaa ḥa-KEEM)

Al-Hakim is the universal manifestation of healing wisdom. It is the essential wisdom that brings all experience into balance and harmony, and it is the one whose wisdom is manifested everywhere. It is the heart of diamond-like clarity that gives you access to an active spirit of guidance.

Al-Hakim is born of inner certainty and it is manifested as outward calm and determination. The word for bridle is *hakama*, meaning to rein in. The ability to control unbridled passions, such as anger, requires a wisdom that expresses itself in skillful action, and through the actual practice of all that you know. Realization of this divine quality gives you the ability to determine exactly how wisdom can promote healing in each and every instance.

A most concrete meaning of al-Hakim is a physician, a physician of hearts. Invocation of Ya Hakim provides help for those of us who easily get lost in generalities, and have difficulty translating knowledge into practical wisdom. Al-Hakim is the Name of wisdom that is most inclusive; its universal meaning includes the meaning of its cognate, Ya Hakam (28), discerning wisdom, with which it is paired in repetition. See Chapter 20, In Quest of Wisdom; and Chapter 23, The Ground of All Knowing.

47. **Ya Wadud** (yaa wa-DOOD)

Al-Wadud is divine love's most intimate manifestation. It is the constant embrace of the affectionate, loving universe. The way we learn to love Allah is by learning how to love, and human beings especially learn how to love by learning how to be intimate. Repetition of Ya Wadud is an antidote for all who have difficulty achieving intimacy with others. Al-Wadud includes sexual intimacy. A physical-plane meaning from the same root is "tent peg." The peg of our deepest desire holds down the tent of our existence.

Al-Wadud offers an avenue for seeing divine love in tumultuous relationships and within strong love/hate relationships. It consciously uses the densest elements of a situation as an inner impetus to turn toward God. This transformative quality is also found in Ya Tawwab (79), and these two Names may be paired in repetition to enhance such a process of turning from the lower self toward the one. See Chapter 6, Love's Mysteries.

48. **Ya Majid** (yaa ma-JEED)

Al-Majid is sublime and infinite super-abundance that radiates into the whole of manifestation. Al-Majid, in all its root forms, emphasizes abundance, along with the conscious realization of being satiated. When you receive al-Majid's gift you know you have been filled.

It has a quality of an unexpected gift that is wonderful, astonishing, and surprising. A good example is the bounty of numberless heirs given to Abraham and to his wife Sarah, who had already reached the age of menopause. She laughed at the outlandish news brought by the angel, and this laughter is the meaning of the name "Isaac" given to her son.

Another reference to this quality of al-Majid is in the Qur'an where it is reported that people are amazed that one of their own, an illiterate man, has been given such a revelation as the Qur'an.[13] Al-Majid is like the light of the rising sun. When it arises, the more you are lost in admiration, the more it illuminates your mental horizons. Its meanings become inexhaustible. See Chapter 18, Divine Generosity.

49. **Ya Ba'ith** (yaa BAA-'i<u>th</u>)

Al-Ba'ith is the one who fully sends forth the message of God and the messengers of God. It removes all blockages to the divine flow. It is the quickener. It means to throw off death-like sleep or inertia to fully wake up. Al-Ba'ith is the power that resurrects all souls, and it is the power that revives dead hearts so that they can be open. *Ba'atha*, a form of the same root, means to remove that which restrains you from free action. Another form means to remove the barrier from a stream of water so that the water can flow forth.

The story of Jonah and the whale gives a vivid example of a similar physical meaning. "He would certainly have remained inside the stomach of the fish until the day when he was spewed out."[14] Spewed out (sent forth) is *yub'athun*. It means the day or time for being sent forth. Ya Warith (97) and Ya Ba'ith are divine opposites that are most beneficial when recited as a pair. Their realization enables you to become unstuck in the spiritual process of dying before death and awakening into what is more enduring. See Ya Warith (97), Ya Baqi (96), and Chapter 21, Actualizing the Knowledge of Unity.

50. **Ya Shahid** (yaa <u>sh</u>a-HEED)

Ash-Shahid is the quality that expresses God's witnessing all things without limitation. It is the whole realm of outer knowledge that is perceived by the five senses. Human beings who fully reflect this quality are able to witness whatever arises in their perception without prejudice. They know God in nature, through all their senses. *Mushaahidah*, awe-full contemplation, is an advanced Sufi practice that involves fully embodying the flow of actively witnessing God in all possible aspects within the globe of the heart.

In the Qur'an, transformers or angels are described as ash-Shahid, and *al-'insaan kaamil*, or the complete human being, is also called ash-Shahid, as is Allah in the most complete possible sense of witnessing. Allah witnesses Allah's own reality. *Shahaadah*, one of the forms of the root of this Name, has the same root meaning as the word "earth." The sense of this is that the earth is a silent witness. Its natural complement is the divine opposite al-Khabir (31), which means the whole realm of inner knowledge. Pairing Ya Shahid and Ya Khabir in recitation is recommended. It is an antidote for attachment to either the outer or inner world. See Chapter 20, In Quest of Wisdom; and Chapter 22, God's Omniscience.

51. **Ya Haqq** (yaa ḤAḲḲ)

Al-Haqq is the one and only reality. It is truth itself. Al-Haqq is Allah, or God, as Allah actually is, and not in the form the mind tries to conceive or imagine it. It is the very ground of being, a field that is both active and potential, known and unknown, manifest and unmanifest. It is the basic field from which any manifestation or activation can be generated.

As a verb, the root of al-Haqq becomes *haqhaqa. Haqhaqa* means to journey into the heart of the night, and, at the same time, to exert oneself to the utmost degree. A second physical-plane meaning refers to when the sun begins to rise and its light makes everything visible. That is called *haqqat-nee ash-shams.* A third meaning of al-Haqq is to become necessary, incumbent, or obligatory. It is associated with *taqdeer,* which expresses the whole realm of al-Qadir (68), the inexorable power of divine purpose moving through all of manifestation.

One interesting form that the root of al-Haqq takes is *hulkh,* which means the spiderweb. This suggests a lattice-work of veils of light and dark of form and emptiness, of the absolute and the relative. Al-Haqq is the matrix of all. Invocation of Ya Haqq is a remedy for our attachment to the mind's limited concept of the infinite. See Ya Hayy (62), the ever-living, with which Ya Haqq is often paired in repetition. See Chapter 23, The Ground of All Knowing.

52. **Ya Wakil** (yaa wa-KEEL)

Al-Wakil is the only one who is worthy of complete trust in every affair. It is said that the person who trusts completely in Allah is like an infant who knows nothing but to resort to the mother's breast. For Sufis, *tawakkul* means complete trust in Allah. It is a station of realization, not a passing state. There are stages in the development of this kind of trust that correspond to abandoning the qualities of the lower self and at the same time embracing and embodying divine qualities.

Recitation of Ya Wakil calls forth a protection that is full of reliability. It is steadfastness along with resilience and lack of defensiveness. It has cohesiveness. It brings solidity without rigidity. Invocation of Ya Wakil is a remedy for those of us who have deep issues with being able to trust. See Ya Muhaimin (7), Ya Hafiz (38), Ya Muqit (39), Ya Wali (76), and Ya Mani' (89). See Chapter 11, Divine Protection.

53. **Ya Qawiyy** (yaa ḲO-weeyy)

Al-Qawiyy is overpowering strength. Its omnipotent power persists through all the possible permutations of temporal being. Al-Qawiyy is the strength to overcome the impulse of self-expression. It is the strength to not use the power that we feel is ready to burst forth from within us.

Realizing al-Qawiyy allows us to overcome the feeling of always being the doer, or active controlling agent, in every situation. A physical form of the root means to completely empty out one's house. Al-Qawiyy's power is strong enough to overcome the superego, the lusts, and the desires. Al-Qawiyy is in command of the commanding self, a self that is very primitive and adamant. It disarms the commanding self so that human beings can see that all personal power is the result of the real power that is coming from the divine source.

In addition, recitation of Ya Qawiyy is an antidote for those who feel that they have to be in control. Control issues in the personality often stem from fear of death, and al-Qawiyy can be experienced as a pathway for conquering the fear of death. See Ya Jabbar (9), Ya 'Aziz (8), Ya Matin (54), Ya Mu'id (59), Ya Qadir (68), Ya Muqtadir (69), and Ya Dhal Jalali wal 'Ikram (84), and Chapter 9, Omnipotence.

54. **Ya Matin** (yaa ma-TEEN)

Al-Matin is the kind of strength that makes one consistent and dependable. At the scale of the whole universe, this balanced rhythm is an expression of divine omnipotence. It gives the strength to keep on keeping on. It involves mastery as well as stability. You become like a rock or a mountain. You feel grounded in the world because you are grounded in your own self, and this gives you integrity as a human being.

A quality that indicates al-Matin in your life is the presence of rhythm, daily rhythm. The power that comes from this rhythmic existence is a kind of balance, harmony, and wholeness. Al-Matin gives you the strength to handle both success and failure. It is the strength to balance and harmonize your individual needs with the needs of the group. See Ya Jabbar (9), Ya 'Aziz (8), Ya Qawiyy (53), Ya Qadir (68), Ya Muqtadir (69), and Ya Dhal Jalali wal 'Ikram (84). See also Chapter 9, Omnipotence.

55. **Ya Waliyy** (yaa WA-leeyy)

Al-Waliyy is the nearest friend, the one who realizes a deep, intimate, and loving relationship with everything and everyone without distinction. Knowing God as this kind of intimate friend evokes complete and unreserved love. What is most human about each one of us is our intimate relationship with God, and al-Waliyy is the most intimate expression of divine love that is possible. Its root *waliha* expresses intimacy with an ecstatic passion that is beyond rationality.

Al-Waliyy manifests complete and total unity, a unity that is greater than what can be achieved simply by merging. It is both transcendent and immanent. Invocation of Ya Waliyy is a remedy for all who have been deeply marked by lack of intimacy, especially in their home environment. In general, it is a remedy for loneliness and alienation. See Ya Wali (76), which shares the same root but also involves an aspect of divine protection. See Chapter 10, Infinite Presence.

56. **Ya Hamid** (yaa ḥa-MEED)

Al-Hamid is contained within the often-repeated Name Alhamdulillah, which means that all gratitude and praise return to Allah. Al-Hamid also means, in an eternal way, that all gratitude, all *hamd*, has its source in God, and that the emanation of *hamd* reaches every aspect of existence. Each individual thing, and everything as a whole, returns that *hamd* to the source. The Qur'an says that among rows upon rows of birds, each one knows its own mode of *hamd*.[15] Each bird that sings shows the diversity of gratitude. Every single atom of the universe is saying Alhamdulillah in its own way.

There are physical meanings of the root of al-Hamid that express an intense flaming fire and a day of fierce heat. Drawing from this, we can say that al-Hamid manifests into each and every thing in creation like a burning heat or a burning love. It is very close in meaning to ash-Shakur (35), but it tends to manifest more as gratitude for divine qualities, while ash-Shakur manifests more as thankfulness for specific blessings. See Ya Shakur (35). See also Chapter 16, Names of Gratitude.

57. **Ya Muhsi** (yaa MUḤ-ṣee)

Al-Muhsi is the one who quantifies and enumerates. Al-Muhsi is omniscience, in the sense of the full knowledge of each and every thing. It is the one who knows every hair on the head. Al-Muhsi reveals that Allah is the direct cause of any and all knowledge, intelligence, and mental perception. The root *ahsa'* means to take everything into account without losing track of anything.

Nothing is ever lost in the knowledge of God. A physical form that the root takes means to count sheep with little black stones. By contrast, Ar-Raqib (43) is more like the action of accounting for everything. Ar-Raqib has a definite active element to it, while al-Muhsi emphasizes knowledge. Invocation of Ya Muhsi is an antidote for those who think that what they know really doesn't count and who consequently feel that their lives don't count. Al-Muhsi, ar-Raqib (43), and al-Hasib (40) are considered in relation to divine knowledge and the psychological challenges of the superego in Chapter 22, God's Omniscience.

58. **Ya Mubdi'** (yaa mub-dee')

Al-Mubdi' means to cause to begin. It is to initiate something for the first time, like the first creative thought. It differs from, al-'Awwal (72), the first, in that al-'Awwal is transcendent. Al-'Awwal is the first without a second, but al-Mubdi' means to do something first, and to go on to the second thing. A physical meaning of the root, *'abda'a*, means to grow a second set of teeth. Spiritually, al-Mubdi' means to cause a thing to be found, to cause it to come into existence. Al-Mubdi' offers a childlike sense of wonder and discovery to manifestation.

Recitation of Ya Mubdi' is an antidote for getting bogged down and ceasing to care. The movement from al-'Awwal to al-Mubdi' is from the infinite to the finite. It is from the unseen world to the visible world, from al-Batin (75) to az-Zahir (74). Invocation of Ya Mubdi' and Ya Mu'id (59) together is often recommended. Al-Mu'id completes the full circle, as it returns the visible manifestation to invisible essence. Pairing them is especially useful if you have difficulty starting and ending anything. See Ya Khaliq (11), Ya Bari' (12), and Ya Musawwir (13). See also Chapter 13, The Arc of Ascent and Descent, and Chapter 14, God the Creator.

59. **Ya Mu'id** (yaa mu-'EED)

Al-Mu'id is the one, the only one, who is capable of mercifully giving refuge to every single thing. It returns the visible manifestation to invisible essence. It is the one who brings things to their ultimate end. Al-Mu'id is different from Al-Akhir (73), the Last, which has a transcendent quality. Al-Akhir is the last, without a next-to-last. Al-Mu'id means to return, in stages, until you get to some ultimate place.

This divine quality accepts each one, and everything, without exception, in its return to the source, which is Allah. It is the opposite of Al-Mubdi' (58), with which it may be paired in repetition. Ya Mu'id can also be paired with Ya Hayy (62), Ya Muhyi (60), and Ya Qawiyy (53) to help human beings overcome fear of death and the weakness of feeling overpowered in life. See Chapter 13, The Arc of Ascent and Descent.

60. **Ya Muhyi** (yaa MUH-yee)

Al-Muhyi is the one who gives life, the one who is the only cause of life. It quickens. Nothing that is living is outside of al-Muhyi. It is the opposite of al-Mumit (61), which is the giver of death. Both these divine Names are about causation, and serve the function of taking us beyond secondary causes. Sperm and egg cause life; disease and old age cause death, but God is the ultimate cause of both. Repetition of these two Names together is recommended.

When Ya Muhyi is paired with Ya Mumit, you are inwardly directed toward the realization of the one who bestows reality on what we call life and death. By invocation of these qualities as a pair, you are led to a transcendental Name, al-Hayy (62), the perfection of everlasting life. Al-Hayy includes both these divine opposites in its meaning. Reciting first Ya Mumit, Ya Muhyi and then gradually adding Ya Hayy is also recommended as a way of approaching grief.

Recitation of Ya Muhyi is helpful for those who have lost vitality or who are so depressed they want to die. Al-Muhyi is related through its root to *al-hayawaan*, the gradation of *nafs* called the animal soul. See Ya Mumit (61) and Ya Hayy (62). See Chapter 7, Allah's Opposite Qualities, and Chapter 13, The Arc of Ascent and Descent.

61. **Ya Mumit** (yaa mu-MEET)

Al-Mumit is the only one who causes death. It is the other side of al-Muhyi (60). Ya Mumit should be paired with Ya Muhyi to bring a person to equanimity about the life and death of individual beings, and to rise above secondary causes, as described above. There is a hadith of the Prophet Muhammad where we are invited to "die before death."

Essential to Sufism is the teaching that physical death is a symbol for *fana*, the dissolving of the ego-self. When God sends you a type of death—spiritual, mental, or physical—it is a mechanism for spiritual transformation. The lover realizes with every death of the self that they are being drawn in toward the Beloved. It is a process that leads to *liqaa'*, the union of lovers. A person's death day, or *'urs*, is seen as a wedding day.

In the Qur'an, al-Mumit and al-Muhyi are described as temporary states, when viewed from the infinity of God's being. See Ya Hayy (62), and Ya Muhyi (60). See Chapter 7, Allah's Opposite Qualities, and Chapter 13, The Arc of Ascent and Descent.

62. **Ya Hayy** (yaa ḤAIYY)

Al-Hayy is the perfection of everlasting life, and the only one who truly lives. It is the one source of all life and the very life of everything that lives. It is the life principle that never dies, and it is inside every being. This divine Name is also the living presence of everything, whether it is dead, alive, animate, inanimate, material, spiritual, or anything in-between. No distinction is made among these states because al-Hayy lives in everything. Because of this infinitude, it is truly a transcendent Name, beyond the apparent relativity of al-Mumit (61) and al-Muhyi (60).

Al-Hayy is filled with vitality; it is the inner life of the heart. Repetition of Ya Hayy arouses a kind of life energy and freedom that is an antidote to the deadened condition of the heart that is often the result of grief and sorrow. See Ya Qayyum (63) and Ya Haqq (51), two similarly transcendent Names with which Ya Hayy is often paired in recitation. See Chapter 15, Names of Time and Eternity.

63. **Ya Qayyum** (yaa ḳaiy-YOOM)

Al-Qayyum is the only one who remains through all the permutations of time and space. It is an existence beyond being or appearance, form, or continuance of form. Al-Qayyum manifests in everything, down to the very heart of every being. It is eternal time and omnipresence. Al-Qayyum is a continuous unending activity that bestows existence, or *kun*, to everything else.

The very fact that anything exists, including the very existence of being itself, is because of the nature of al-Qayyum, which transcends the passage of time. A variation of the root, *qaama*, means to stand. Things come and things go. Al-Qayyum stands. Due to the reality of al-Qayyum's nature, all things continually exist, even after death, as living entities in the mind of God. It is recommended to pair Ya Qayyum with Ya Hayy (62), in chanting. Both have the same root H-Y-Y, the life principle inside each one that never dies. See Chapter 15, Names of Time and Eternity.

64. **Ya Wajid** (yaa WAA-jid)

Al-Wajid is the only source of ecstasy. It is perfectly present in the very fabric of existence itself. Existence, *wujud*, shares the same root W-J-D, which at the deepest level means ecstasy. Al-Wajid is the ultimate stage of divine ecstasy and contains all the stages within it, beginning with expansion or *bast*, which shares a root with al-Basit (21). Ecstasy's spontaneous manifestation is incrementally described as gleams, glimmers, and the shining of stars. It is experienced further through the deliberate practices of a Sufi *tareeqah*, used to evoke ecstasy.

There is an inner development of this quality that leads you to opening the eye and ear of the heart, so that God becomes the eye through which you see and the ear through which you hear. Finally, it manifests in the practice of *mushaahidah*, which is rooted in a continuous balanced and awe-filled witnessing of all senses together.

In the progression through these stages, the *wajd*, or ecstasy, becomes increasingly reliable. Al-Wajid is a measure of one's spiritual station. Ultimately, ecstasy becomes fully stabilized in al-Wajid, and one is truly receptive to the action of God. See Ya Basit (21) and Ya Ghaniyy (87). See Chapter 12, The Secret of Ecstasy.

65. **Ya Wahid** (yaa WAA-ḥid)

Al-Wahid is the unique one present in the many, the one that is in everything. Al-Wahid is also the one underlying the many, the uniqueness of God that is reflected in each and every aspect of manifestation. As an abstract noun, it is identified with the state of oneness itself, but it also has the meaning, "the one who is in all." Everything is a mirror for God's face.

Al-Wahid brings the vision of infinity in a grain of sand. Every speck reflects the infinite. The result is that we can see a thing as finite and as infinite at the same time. That is called *waahidiyyah*. The totality—the infinite—can be perceived within each and every finite element. Anything you hear, you hear the one; anything you see, you see the one. See Ya Ahad (66) and Ya Samad (67). See Chapter 15, Names of Time and Eternity.

66. **Ya Ahad** (yaa A-ḥad)

Al-Ahad means total and absolute oneness. It is the one of the one. It should not be confused with the conception of the totality of all things. Oneness is an essential characteristic of Allah. God is absolutely singular and unique. Al-Ahad is the one without a second. It is a unicity. You can't add the one of al-Ahad to itself and get two. In its concreteness, only one is. It has no opposite. Nothing is like this one.

From the view of al-Ahad, of unity, no distinctions are made between the different prophets of God. Each one of them is a complete entity of the whole. Al-Ahad is the center of a circle without a circumference. See Ya Samad (67), with which it is often paired in recitation, and Ya Wahid (65). See Chapter 15, Names of Time and Eternity.

67. **Ya Samad** (yaa ṢA-mad)

As-Samad is the continuity of eternity. It is the circumference of the circle that expands eternally, whose center is everywhere. It is infinite expansive space. The root form *samad(an)* means continuously. As-Samad is the relationship between al-Ahad, the one of the one, and al-Wahid, the one of the many. Although it may be impossible to conceptualize the coexistence of these two kinds of oneness, in as-Samad they are reconciled.

In recitation, you invoke Ya Ahad, the infinite dot or singularity, and pair it with Ya Samad, the infinite circle that expands eternally. Invoking them as a pair will assist in bringing you true balance in life. As-Samad is connected with the word *samdah*, which means castle or citadel. It conveys the sense that the ground on which you stand is infinite. See Ya Wahid (65) and Ya Ahad (66). See Chapter 15, Names of Time and Eternity.

68. **Ya Qadir** (yaa ḰAA-dir)

Al-Qadir is the expression of all the purpose and all the strength and will in the universe as one power. Nothing is unconnected from this divine power. Through awakening to it, the traveler on the spiritual path realizes that there is a path and a specific destination. Al-Qadir gives a definite meaning and a real purpose to everything in life.

Al-Qadir also means unlimited capacity, and that every person has that capacity. Such a realization gives you a sense of value, power, and spaciousness, as well as a confidence that all things are possible. You are inherently able to receive and contain anything that may come, and to regard it as a divine gift. Al-Qadir expresses omnipotence, power, endurance, and proportionality. It is the power to both manifest and contain manifestation.

Invocation of Ya Qadir is an antidote to feeling worthless and powerless and offers relief to those who believe that they are living wasted lives. We recommend that it be combined with Ya Muqtadir (69). See Chapter 9, Omnipotence.

69. **Ya Muqtadir** (yaa muk-TA-dir)

Al-Muqtadir is the one who places you on a particular path to God and enables you to firmly put your feet on that path, and keep going on that path, step by step. It brings the ability to actualize the divine purpose in your life. The power that is guiding you has put you in this very specific situation, here and now. There are no mistakes, and nothing is ever wasted or lost. Each soul is unique, with a unique purpose in life. That is the meaning of al-Muqtadir.

To realize its meaning, each person needs to recognize al-Qadir (68) and lovingly engage his or her will to fulfill it. The lover thus makes use of whatever power the beloved has granted and uses that power in the wise and beautifully proportioned way present in its very nature. To accomplish this, repetition of Ya Qadir, Ya Muqtadir is recommended. One of the root meanings of *qadara* is beautifully proportioned to get the right fit, as in cutting leather. See Ya Qadir (68) and Chapter 9, Omnipotence.

70. **Ya Muqaddim** (yaa mu-ḲAD-dim)

Al-Muqaddim is the one who continually moves things forward in time. A form the root takes, *qaddama*, means to step forward, putting one foot in front of the other. When this quality is reflected in a human being, they realize how it is that everything happens in its own time in perfect sequence. Al-Muqaddim is, step by step, making the pilgrimage to the inner sanctum.

Invocation of Ya Muqaddim is a remedy for impatience, and a remedy for all who have trouble letting go of the feeling that they have to be in control of the timing and sequence of events. It brings inner ease with which to engage the feeling that you must push things forward faster. See Ya Mu'akhkhir (71), with which it can be paired in recitation. See Chapter 13, The Arc of Ascent and Descent.

71. **Ya Mu'akhkhir** (yaa mu-'AḴḤ-ḵhir)

Al-Mu'akhkhir is the one who is continually moving each thing back to its perfect placement in time to fully manifest that which is already complete at its source in Allah. The root *'akhara* means to step back toward the source of all Being. One consequence of this is that al-Mu'akhkhir is also the one who fully engages in the process of manifesting each thing at the perfect time. It is the one who brings a thing to closure in complete perfection and in its own time. It helps you to fulfill what you have already begun.

Invocation of Ya Mu'akhkhir offers help to those who have trouble setting the right pace in life to achieve success and to accomplish goals. It may effectively be paired in recitation with Ya Muqaddim (70). See Chapter 13, The Arc of Ascent and Descent.

72. **Ya 'Awwal** (yaa OW-wal)

Al-'Awwal is the first, without a second. It is the first, without a before. Al-'Awwal never was born and never initiated anything. It is pure potentiality. In meditative practice, it may be discovered in the perfectly still point, the *kamal* point that you briefly experience at the apex of each inhalation of breath.

Al-'Awwal is the primary source from which all things arise. It is different from al-Mubdi' (58), which is the one who begins things in the finite sphere. Al-'Awwal's sacred quality should be considered in conjunction with the three divine Names that follow on the list. See Ya Akhir (73), Ya Zahir (74), and Ya Batin (75). See Chapter 13, The Arc of Ascent and Descent.

73. **Ya Akhir** (yaa AA-k̲h̲ir)

Al-Akhir is the last, without a penultimate. In other words, there is no next-to-last, or anything previous to it. And al-Akhir is the last without an after. Nothing can possibly follow it. Al-Akhir is the one fully manifest in time. In meditative practice, it may be discovered in the perfectly still point that you briefly experience at the end of the exhalation of the breath. Al-Akhir is the final destination of the ultimate return of all things. It is different from Al-Mu'id (59), who is the one who brings all things in the finite realm to closure. See Ya 'Awwal (72), Ya Zahir (74), and Ya Batin (75). See Chapter 13, The Arc of Ascent and Descent.

74. **Ya Zahir** (yaa D̲H̲AA-hir)

Az-Zahir means completely present in space. It is fully materialized, fully visible. Az-Zahir is the most outward and the most manifest. There is no otherness with which it could be in relationship. Like the Sun at its height, it is so evident, so bright, that you may not even notice its existence. Allah's quality of being most manifest is hidden in plain view. Az-Zahir should be considered along with Ya 'Awwal (72), Ya Akhir (73), and Ya Batin (75). See Chapter 13, The Arc of Ascent and Descent.

75. **Ya Batin** (yaa BAA-t̤in)

Al-Batin is the most hidden treasure, the secret of secrets. The essence of God is utterly hidden, but it is not hidden inside of something else. There is nothing for it to be hidden within. The four corners of the transcendental throne of God, as described by 'ibn 'Arabi, are four beautiful Names: al-'Awwal (72), al-Akhir (73), az-Zahir (74), and al-Batin. Sometimes they are described as four angels. In the center is stillness. This is the throne of God, the *'arsh*, or Heart Throne. These four divine qualities seem to revolve about the *'arsh*, like spheres.

In meditative practice, as you consider these four divine attributes together you become aware of the eternal still point in the center that is not first or last, not manifest or unmanifest, and has no beginning or end. Invocation of Ya 'Awwal , Ya Akhir, Ya Zahir, and Ya Batin together is recommended, along with contemplation of the *'arsh*. See Chapter 13, The Arc of Ascent and Descent.

76. **Ya Wali** (yaa WAA-lee)

Al-Wali is the kind of protection or safety that arises from a truly intimate relationship. A form of the root has a physical meaning to turn back toward a loved one with familiarity and closeness. It also means to turn away from anger and alienation. With al-Wali, you feel that you are safe in the arms of the beloved.

A metaphor for al-Wali is to lie down next to someone to offer protection. You feel protected be-cause of the intimacy of your relationship with the power of God's love. The friends of God are pro-tected and provided for by this shared love and friendship. Al-Wali has the same root as al-Waliyy (55) and is closely related to it in meaning, but al-Wali emphasizes the protective aspect of the intimate relationship with the beloved. Invocation of Ya Wali is recommended as a healing *wazifah* for those who have been wounded by powerful people that they lovingly looked to for protection. See Ya Waliyy (55). See Chapter 11, Divine Protection.

77. **Ya Muta'ali** (yaa mu-ta-'AA-lee)   يَا مُتَعَالٌ

Al-Muta'ali is the means by which you connect to Allah through what is called the higher self, the soul, or *ruh*. With al-Muta'ali there is an elevating journey, which is like an ascending flight of the spirit. Al-Muta'ali's divine quality is the invitation to pure transcendence. It offers a path for the wayfarer to travel from immanence to transcendence. In this way, you progress to the center beyond the beyond, higher than the high. You are moving toward pure transcendence.

Al-Muta'ali brings the awareness that every manifested thing is pervaded by pure transcendence. Invocation of Ya Muta'ali offers an antidote for the experience of getting mired down and stuck in your journey on the spiritual path. See Ya 'Aliyy (36), with which it may be beneficially paired in repetition. See Chapter 10, Infinite Presence.

78. **Ya Barr** (yaa BARR)   يَا بَرٌّ

Al-Barr announces the mystery of the perfect state. It manifests the quality of unconditional love. Al-Barr is uniquely perfect and complete. A variation of the root of this Name means to be sweet, through and through. There is not even a subtle distinction in it between inner and outer. It is a per-fection of love both in its potential and its manifestation. Its perfection transcends good and evil, but al-Barr can be seen as all the possible variations of "the Good" in the Platonic sense of that term.

Realization of al-Barr brings a continuum of action that has a seamlessness of thought, word, and deed, of inner and outer, and of lower self and higher self. Al-Barr radiates perfection of the whole, and is seen in a serenity of soul that is maintained in all conditions of life. Invocation of Ya Barr offers a remedy for feeling broken because of having your ideals shattered in life. See Ya Rahman (1), Ya Rahim (2), and Ya Latif (30). See Chapter 6, Love's Mysteries.

79. **Ya Tawwab** (yaa tow-WAAB)   يَا تَوَّابٌ

At-Tawwab is the forgiveness that enables you to turn away from grudges, and perceived indi-vidual defects, toward the perfection of Allah. It comes with the realization that the divine beloved is always turning toward you, continually offering a gaze of deep forgiveness and endless compassion.

At-Tawwab conveys the real meaning of repentance, the turning from the limitations of the false self and toward the perfection of your immortal soul, which is not separate from the divine reality.

Realizing at-Tawwab involves giving up the attachment to being right. It means giving up self-righteousness and letting go of the grudge. It is to turn your face toward someone else with forgiveness and compassion. Like Ya Wadud (47), it consciously uses the densest elements of a situation as an inner impetus for transformation, and to turn toward God. Repetition of Ya Tawwab allows you to turn toward the divine face in every face. It is an antidote for clinging to, and identifying with, a wounded sense of self-deficiency. See Ya Ghaffar (14), Ya Ghafur (34), and Ya 'Afuw (81). See Chapter 8, Divine Forgiveness.

80. **Ya Muntaqim** (mun-TA-ḳim)

Al-Muntaqim is a powerful balancing force that is completely reliable and uncompromising. It is the embodiment of the principle of reciprocity, or the holy wheel of karma as described in the Dharma traditions. Whatever you put into the universe comes back to you. The force of al-Muntaqim equalizes and seeks to create harmony in the universe in ways that may appear tragic and violent from the human perspective.

As a starting point, its repetition is an antidote for those caught in the cycle of revenge. A number of its root meanings have to do with revenge. It should rarely be recited alone, but it can be effectively combined with other divine Names. Ya Muntaqim's true opposite is Ya 'Afuw (81), and they are paired in prayerful recitation as a means for us to come into balance in relation to both impulses and emotions. See Chapter 7, Allah's Opposite Qualities, in which this process of working with al-Muntaqim is highlighted, as well as Chapter 8, Divine Forgiveness.

81. **Ya 'Afuw** (yaa 'A-fooww)

Al-'Afuw is the perfection of divine forgiveness. It does not even notice the fault. Al-'Afuw can be compared to the wind completely erasing the footprints in the desert sand, as if no one had ever walked there. This image is one of the physical-plane meanings that its root takes. Al-'Afuw is to completely forgive without a trace of residue. No resentment, memory, or impression is left to obscure your heart or mind. Such forgiveness requires the erasing of the "I" that is usually clung to in the thought, "I forgive you."

With al-'Afuw there is no false self to grasp at the concepts of who is the forgiver and who and what is forgiven, or to cogitate about the process of forgiveness. Al-'Afuw simply emanates the pure essence of forgiveness itself. As described in Chapter 8, Divine Forgiveness, Ya 'Afuw may be effectively recited with Ya Ghaffar (14), Ya Ghafur (34), and Ya Tawwab (79) as the last in a sequence for inner healing. Also see al-'Afuw's opposite, Ya Muntaqim (80). See Chapter 7, Allah's Opposite Qualities, and Chapter 8, Divine Forgiveness.

82. **Ya Ra'uf** (yaa ra-'OOF)

Ar-Ra'uf is a quiet, gentle, indwelling love that actively penetrates to the deepest and most profound place. This kind of love goes right to the essence of what it truly means to be human. Ar-Ra'uf helps heal the crucial problem of the ego-personality's self-identification with deficiency and inability, which is caused by its wounded condition. It works to heal the effects of not being seen and accepted by humanity. It manifests a peaceful calm, a resting in God that especially arises in the midst of difficulties and trials.

Ar-Ra'uf's inner quality is awakened in a similar manner to the way steel is tempered in the process of making a sword. It is not a passive calm. It faces hostility, slander, and corruption with serenity, while at the same time it has a soothing effect that reaches the very core of the apparent enemy. Ya Ra'uf is close in its meaning to Ya Rahim (2), and they are quite beneficial when chanted together. Realization of these two qualities in your heart and in your life brings what is most necessary to become wholeheartedly human. See Chapter 6. Love's Mysteries.

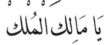

83. **Ya Malikal-Mulk** (yaa MAA-li-kal-MULK)

Malikul-Mulk expresses that each and every manifestation in the universe completely depends on being held by God. Malikul-Mulk describes permanence in the midst of change. Things (*mulk*) are always in flux—coming and going, strong and weak. They are transient. Even though the world has this appearance, invocation of Ya Malikal-Mulk brings the realization that all manifestation never leaves the hands of Allah. In accord with Arabic grammar, when using "Ya" we say Ya Malikal-Mulk; without the "Ya" the name is slightly different: we say Malikul-Mulk.

Both elements of the Name, *malik* and *mulk*, derive from the same root—*malaka*—which means to hold in the hands. Calling on this divine quality is like reaching down into the stream of time and grasping eternal essence in its majesty. It is king and controller. Invocation of Ya Malikal-Mulk helps you overcome the dichotomy that arises from how you may be perceived by others because, from the perspective of this divine Name, whether you are viewed as high or low is irrelevant.

Repetition of Ya Malikal-Mulk is especially recommended for all who, because of lack of intimacy in their family experience, are hesitant to trust relationships with people. It is also a remedy for all who are afraid to fully engage in this world because of its coarseness. See Ya Malik (3), with which we recommend it be paired in recitation.

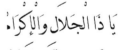

84. **Ya Dhal Jalali wal 'Ikram** (yaa DHAL ja-LAA-li WAL 'ik-RAAM)

All manifestation of power (al-Jalal) as well as all manifestation of beauty (al-Jamal) come from God's absolute essence. The first word, "Dhal" of this Name, is the same as *dhat* (or *zat*), which means the absolute essence. Dhal is the utterly transcendent source of the ceaseless flowing of divine manifestations. It is the source of the flow of divine strength, al-Jalal, into everything everywhere, without distinction. In accord with Arabic grammar, when using "Ya" we say Ya Dhal Jalali wal 'Ikram; without the "Ya" the name is slightly different: we say Dhul Jalali wal 'Ikram.

The 'Ikram in this Name is a most beautiful or *jamali* quality. It means the unconditional and loving generosity of God that fully manifests into everything. It is an intensive form of al-Karim (42). 'Ikram adds emphasis, making it incomparably kind and generous, noble and giving. Paired, as they are in this Name, al-Jalal and al-'Ikram express the omnipotent strength and incomparable divine generosity that are present in the absolute essence of all, and harmonize them. The balanced combination of qualities in this great Name produces balance.

Ya Dhal Jalali wal 'Ikram is recommended as a useful practice for all who are out of balance in relation to strength and its proper use. It is similarly effective when people may not be able to set appropriate personal boundaries, as a result of being out of balance in the sphere of generosity. See Ya Jabbar (9), Ya 'Aziz (8), Ya Qawiyy (53), Ya Matin (54), Ya Qadir (68), and Ya Muqtadir (69), which are also treated in Chapter 9, Omnipotence. See also Chapters 16, 18, and 19 on the emanations of divine abundance and Chapter 7, Allah's Opposite Qualities.

85. **Ya Muqsit** (yaa MUK̄-sit)

Al-Muqsit is the ultimate divine cause that ensures all gifts are apportioned in a just and equitable way. Since the way that gifts are given out often does not appear to be just at all, this just apportionment is the case even though we may not know it. Unlike al-Majid (48), al-Muqsit does not always come to you with the knowledge that your need has been satisfied. Allah makes each person's lot in life a portion of subsistence, and makes it little or much according to the divine purpose, which may be hidden from our view.

Qist, which is the noun form of al-Muqsit, refers to God's action in the lowering and raising of the scales of the balance. Repetition of Ya Muqsit is an antidote to our sense of life's unfairness. This is particularly true in relation to the distribution of shares, as among siblings. Its recitation also helps overcome the mistaken notion that the rich must be better and more favored by God than the poor. See Chapter 19, Completing the Family of Abundance.

86. **Ya Jami'** (yaa JAA-mi')

Al-Jami' is the gatherer. It means to come back together, to bring all the parts into a whole. Al-Jami' is to return home, to return to the real self. It is a constant process of becoming reconnected with wholeness. It is sometimes called the grand synthesis, the joining of all joinings. Al-Quddus (4) is an opposite of al-Jami', especially when viewed in the context of divine ecstasy. Through al-Quddus, you are continuously purifying yourself of remnants of the *nafs*.

The two pathways of realization complement each other. Al-Quddus offers purification of *nafs*, while al-Jami' offers integration of the various aspects of *nafs*. Classically these paths would be called the *via negativa* and the *via positiva*. When all the aspects of the *nafs* begin to gather together, through the action of al-Jami', a quality of ecstasy enters.

As this continues, the *nafs* begins to merge with the *ruh*, or soul. It is an ecstatic union. Then, varying aspects of the higher self or soul manifest into the lower self, or *nafs*, and reintegrate. With al-Quddus, sobriety enters after the ecstasy of union. To receive great benefit from these Names, we recommend invoking Ya Quddus and Ya Jami' together. See Ya Quddus (4). See Chapter 13, The Arc of Ascent and Descent, and Chapter 12, The Secret of Ecstasy.

87. **Ya Ghaniyy** (yaa GHA-neeyy)

Al-Ghaniyy is the source of all being and the source of all ecstasy. It is an indescribably rich container, a treasure house of all existence. Al-Ghaniyy manifests the very essence of existence to every single thing, at all times, and is the one who gives existence to that which has no existence. Al-Ghaniyy is a flowing forth from God's inexhaustible treasure house to all. The Qur'an says, "We found you in want and then gave sufficiency."[16] In the quoted passage, you are *fuqaraa'* (want) and Allah is *ghaniyy* (sufficiency).

Al-Ghaniyy is richness and fullness. It is an infinite source that can never be exhausted. Your existence may seem to be empty of meaning, but al-Ghaniyy transforms it and fills it from within. Sufis who sought to become *faqeers*, giving up everything and especially the clinging of the ego, followed in the footsteps of Jesus, who announced the treasures awaiting the "poor in spirit."

Invocation of Ya Ghaniyy is a remedy for the fixation that there are not enough riches or success in your life. It is a remedy for joylessness, boredom, and meaninglessness. Invoking Ya Ghaniyy calls out for ecstasy and increase of being. This divine Name has an alchemical quality of transforming experience. It answers the existential question, "Why do I exist?" See Ya Mughni (88), with which it is often paired in recitation. See also Ya Wajid (64). See Chapters 16, 18, and 19 on the emanations of divine abundance and Chapter 12, The Secret of Ecstasy.

88. **Ya Mughni** (yaa mugh-NEE)

Al-Mughni has an important and complex relationship with al-Ghaniyy (87). Allah causes al-Ghaniyy's rich state to be bestowed on temporal creatures, who then can temporarily act as the embodiments of infinite and inexhaustible ecstatic reality. The source and primary cause of this divine quality is al-Ghaniyy, and the causal manifestation of it is al-Mughni.

The root of al-Mughni means to dwell in one place and rest firm in that. All multiplicity swims around one still point in the primal waters of blessing. Everything gains its existence and movement from this stillness. The root of "dwelling in a place" also has the meaning of being constant in love and affection.

Repetition of Ya Mughni is a remedy for dependence and neediness on another. It serves to give contentment, protection, and guidance from the essence of reality. We recommend pairing it in recitation: Ya Ghaniyy, Ya Mughni. In this way it can serve to bring fullness to the process of actualizing happiness. See Ya Ghaniyy (87). See Chapters 16, 18, and 19 on the emanations of divine abundance and Chapter 12, The Secret of Ecstasy.

89. **Ya Mani'** (yaa MAA-ni')

Al-Mani' is the divine protection that guards against all attacks. It means to make a fortress inaccessible and impregnable. Al-Mani' defends against encroachment. It is a spiritual guardian, so to speak. At the inner level, al-Mani' guards you from surrendering to inner doubts and weaknesses. It emanates the inner power necessary to abstain from giving in to negative impressions of yourself. The presence of al-Mani' also brings the ability to hold back from engaging in revenge or from acting out of anger. Preventing these reactions broadens al-Mani's scope of protection beyond the purely personal sphere.

Invocation of Al-Mani' along with its opposite Name, Ya Mu'ti (90), brings a kind of stabilization between fortification and openness. Repetition of Ya Mani', Ya Mu'ti is recommended as a remedy for habitual patterns of aggression and weakness, as well as other expressions arising from a particularly deep sense of personal vulnerability. Also see Ya Muhaimin (7), Ya Hafiz (38), Ya Muqit (39), Ya Wakil (52), Ya Wali (76). See Chapter 11, Divine Protection.

90. Ya Mu'ti (yaa mu'-ṬEE)

Al-Mu'ti is the one who is the cause of all causes. It is a form of 'ata'ullah, which means gift of God. This gift is behind the whole chain of events. It is the ultimate cause of all existence. All manifested being, as well as all unmanifested being, is the effect of this single cause. Al-Mu'ti carries the inner meaning of accepting the gift that is being offered and not resisting it.

Invocation of Ya Mu'ti is an antidote for being overly concerned about the effects of your good deeds or the rewards you might get as a result of your good deeds. Its repetition is also helpful for those who are convinced that conditions will not allow them to make progress. See its opposite, Al-Mani' (89), with which it can be effectively paired in recitation. See Chapter 16, Names of Gratitude, and Chapters 18 and 19 on the other Names of divine abundance.

91. **Ya Darr** (yaa DAARR)

Ad-Darr is the only source that produces the failure to make use of something for a higher good or that causes us not to profit or benefit from the gifts, opportunities, and events that come our way. Ad-Darr is the only source of what we perceive to be harm. It is the only source of harmful or profitless behavior. Ad-Darr means to become blind to the divine intent in the unseen worlds.

It puts you in a state of great want or need, and at the same time it makes you unable to use a remedy for a good purpose. Letting the denseness of ego dwell in the heart is what produces real blindness. When God blinds, it is in the heart. Reflection on ad-Darr is helpful for all who need to pray for enough sight to see their own blindness. In invocation, Ya Darr should in almost all cases be paired with its opposite, Ya Nafi' (92). See Chapter 7, Allah's Opposite Qualities.

92. **Ya Nafi'** (yaa NAA-fi')

An-Nafi' is the only source of what is truly profitable and beneficial. It is the only cause that allows us to make use of something for a higher good. A form of the word, *nafa'a*, means both "to use" and also "to benefit from." An-Nafi' brings purification. It also means to wash the eyes clear of impurities by using water.

An-Nafi' allows you to use a remedy for a good purpose. It offers a beneficial inner and outer cleansing. It is a most helpful quality with which to heal your inner eye, the eye of the heart. When that eye is opened, there is no separation from Allah. See the opposite divine Name, Ya Darr (91). See also Chapter 7, Allah's Opposite Qualities.

93. **Ya Nur** (yaa NOOR)

An-Nur is the essence of light, luminosity itself. A Qur'anic verse says, "Allah is the light of the heavens and the earth."[17] An-Nur is the light of every soul and an inherent characteristic in every pore of your body. *Munawwir* is a form of the same root and means the one who illuminates.

It is interesting that the word for "hell" in Arabic is *naar*, which has the same root as Nur. What makes it hell is that the burning heat there is lacking in light. That kind of burning heat is our inner condition if we don't embody God's loving mercy and compassion (*rahma*) and instead become full of rage.

Whatever way we may turn, we see the all-pervading light of an-Nur. Even the darkness shines from within it. All the various forms of wisdom and guidance are expressions of an-Nur. For example, *nur-ul-haqeeqah* is the light of truth and guidance on the path. What continues to live on in God when we die is also a legacy of light. See Chapter 20, In Quest of Wisdom; Chapter 22, God's Omniscience; and Chapter 23, The Ground of All Knowing.

94. **Ya Hadi** (yaa haa-DEE)

Al Hadi is the most general and inclusive Name of divine guidance. It means the source of all guidance, and its guidance is for the whole of humanity, or a whole community of people. In societal terms, al-Hadi manifests in canonical guidance from a holy book and a structured religion. Repetition of

Ya Hadi is especially recommended at the stage when the spiritual wayfarer is ready to actualize insights, to walk their authentic walk in life, to function in an integrated way, and to become a part of a spiritual community.

Al-Hadi is an invitation to remember God (*dhikr*) and to remove the coverings over our heart (*kufraan*) that cause forgetfulness. It offers the light of guidance that illuminates the way for humanity to overcome self-delusion, anger, and panic and to find the broad and balanced road, the straight way that offers patience and hope, and is life-giving water, *hady(un)*. Al-Hadi represents an advanced stage in the process of awakening to guidance. It should be considered as part of a cluster of Names including ar-Rashid (98) and al-Mulhim. See Chapter 24, Names of Guidance.

95. **Ya Badi'** (yaa ba-DEE')

The activity of al-Badi' takes you back to the beginning of the creation process, as far back as can be conceived, to that which is eternal and does not perish. This divine Name manifests the artistry of God in the act of formation, through the process of gathering together and leaving behind elements, as in sculpting. Al-Badi' is the originator that has no preexistence. It is the ultimate cause of being and nonbeing and manifests into each thing and into every thing in an unlimited way.

Through al-Badi's arc of ascent, or return to timelessness, you ultimately come to al-Baqi (96). In going back to the ultimate source, you find the ground of being, the unborn foundation of existence, the continuous divine power in all its infinitudes. In other words, by returning to your original nature, you find the capacity to discover and express what is real. Repetition of Ya Badi' offers a remedy for the ego's need to impose its sense of truth on others and make it an obligatory duty for them.

96. **Ya Baqi** (yaa baa-ḲEE)

Al-Baqi is what eternally remains. It is the everlasting, continuous, abiding duration of the real. It is revealed in the process of *fana* and *baqa*, dissolving the false self and realizing the true self. According to Sufi teachings, *fana* is what never was. What never was can be said to die since its existence is derivative and passes away.

Baqa is what always was, always is, and ever shall be. Thus, al-Baqi includes pre-eternity and post-eternity. There is a physical-plane root meaning of al-Baqi, "to stay in a place." It is firmly established without change in space and time. Its nature returns you to the eternal and to love. As seen with al-Azaliyy and al-Abadiyy, time is continuous, without beginning or end, and cannot be divided into specific segments.

We recommend the invocation Ya Azaliyy, Ya Abadiyy as an antidote for those who are stuck in their lives by the pressures of time and space. Ya Baqi can then be added to this pair, for completion, as the integrative, transcendental Name. See Chapter 13, The Arc of Ascent and Descent, and Chapter 15, Names of Time and Eternity. For further summary information on Ya Azaliyy and Ya Abadiyy, see the section at the end of this chapter, "More than 99 Names of Allah."

97. **Ya Warith** (yaa WAA-ri<u>th</u>)

Al-Warith expresses the aspect of God that is the inheritor of all. Everything will return to Allah. The Qur'an says, "We (Allah) give life and we give death, but We are the inheritors (*warithun*)."[18] Al-Warith manifests the divine activity of leaving your limited self behind. From the human standpoint, it means to "die before death." It is a process of letting go of the transient (*fana*) and identifying with what does not die (*baqa*).

The physical meaning of the verb *warratha* is to put out a fire, to stir around the ashes to kill it. Even from the physical point of view, the heat of the fire disappears but the light continues, just as the light of an extinct star continues. Al-Warith shows that Allah is the ultimate inheritor of whatever of value is left behind at death, a legacy of light. It puts a different emphasis on the process of annihilation, for death is not simply a disappearance. That which has been awakened returns to Allah in the end.

We recommend that Ya Warith be paired together with its divine opposite, Ya Ba'ith (49). Together, these Names point to a cosmic process that manifests the great return to unity of all separated entities. See also Ya Baqi (96). See Chapter 21, Actualizing the Knowledge of Unity.

98. **Ya Rashid** (yaa ra-<u>SHEED</u>)

Ar-Rashid is the state of unerring guidance that is infinitely, and in an unlimited way, manifesting into each and every thing. The word for the one who is constantly evolving so that they can manifest this state is Murshid (*mu-ra-sha-da*). Ar-Rashid brings an established and clear consciousness that balances inner experience and worldly life.

To discern and communicate a wisdom that addresses the specific needs of individual souls, the quality of divine guidance must be brought into a particular focus. Ar-Rashid is the emanation of guidance that has the clarity and capacity to discern and communicate healing wisdom to all types of human beings. It brings hope to humanity, while its opposite, *ghayy*, leads to despair.

Ar-Rashid offers the nexus of balance between the unstructured nature of inner inspiration or guidance (*ilham*) and the structure of formal guidance (*hudaa*). Because of its quality of clarity, Ya Rashid can effectively be paired in repetition with several Names, including Ya Matin (54), Ya Hadi (94), and Ya Mulhim. See Chapter 24, Names of Guidance, and the teachings on the diamond body of awareness in Chapter 20, In Quest of Wisdom; Chapter 22, God's Omniscience; and Chapter 23, The Ground of All Knowing.

99. **Ya Sabur** (yaa ṣa-BOOR)

As-Sabur is the divine power that will always see things through to the end. At the human level, it means to maintain inner equanimity through all trials and circumstances and to persevere to the end of the test. A physical-plane variation of its root means to endure and to stop complaining.

As-Sabur embodies development of complete inner capacity. It is a great container that enables a spiritual student to endure the long journey of the path and actualize every detail and technique of the teachings. It is a powerful solidarity that allows you to stand firm. The divine manifestation of as-Sabur as a quality of God emphasizes that God doesn't act hastily but forgives or defers judgment.

Invocation of Ya Sabur is a remedy for all who lack patience, especially on the spiritual path, and it is recommended for those who find it difficult to defer judgment or forgive. It may be effectively paired in recitation with Ya Halim (32). According to the story in the Qur'an of Khidr and Moses, *sabr* is the one essential element for following the path of mystical union.[19]

❖ ❖ ❖

More Than 99 Names of Allah

Below is an alphabetized list of some of the other Names of Allah that appear in our text and that can be identified as Names of Allah in the Qur'an. We provide them here with phonetic pronunciation and a very brief definition.

Ya Abadiyy (yaa AB-a-deeyy) and **Ya Azaliyy** (yaa AZ-a-leeyy)

Al-Azaliyy is the continuation of time without respect to a beginning. It is not preceded by non-existence. In most spiritual traditions we find descriptions of events happening in pre-eternity, but pre-eternity has layers or levels within it. For example, at the level of ideas in the mind of God, there are descriptions in the Qur'an of God's interactions with the angels. Just as al-Azaliyy is freed from the limit of a beginning, al-Abadiyy is freed from the limit of an end and has been called post-eternity. See Ya Baqi (96), which is what remains, both in pre-eternity and post-eternity. See Chapter 15, Names of Time and Eternity.

Ya 'Alim (yaa 'AA-lim) — The only source of all knowledge

Ya 'Allam (yaa 'al-LAAM) — The one who is ever-continuous knowledge

Ya 'A'lam (yaa 'A'-lam) — The infinitude of knowledge that is always more

Ya Bayaan (yaa bay-YAAN) — The one who guides by making clear distinctions

Ya Dafi' (yaa DAA-fi') — Protector from attack

Ya Da'im (yaa DAA-im) — The circular form of eternity

Ya Dahr (yaa DAHR) — Time itself

Ya Hakim (yaa HAA-kim) — The source of all healing wisdom

Ya Jamal (yaa ja-MAAL) — Beauty itself, God is beautiful, and loves beauty

Ya Jamil (yaa ja-MEEL) — Divine beauty that reaches everything without exception

Ya Jalal (yaa ja-LAAL) — Power itself, vast and timeless

Ya Kafi (yaa kaa-FEE) — Sufficient remedy for healing

Ya Mannaan (yaa man-NAAN) — The one who gives a true gift with no restrictions

Ya Majid (yaa MAA-jid) — The source of sublime and infinite super-abundance. This form of al-Majid also appears on most lists of the 99 Names.

Ya Mu'allif (yaa mu'-AL-lif) — The one who gives intimate connection and heart attunement

Ya Mubin (yaa mu-BEEN) — The one who makes clear

Ya Mulhim (yaa MOOL-him) — The inner guidance that comes to one directly from the source without intermediation

Ya Muqallib (yaa mu-ḲAL-lib) — The quickener of the heart

Ya Qa'im (yaa ḲAA-'im) — The eternal

Ya Qarib (yaa ḳa-REEB) — The intimate

Ya Sahib (yaa SAA-hib) — Intimate friend

Ya Salim (yaa sa-LEEM) — The emanation of peace that reaches everything without exception

Ya Shafi (yaa s̲h̲aa-FEE) — The healer

Ya Yaqin (yaa-ḲEEN) — Certainty

rahman·rahim
allah
wadud halim
barr latif
rauf

chapter 6

Love's Mysteries

Because all the divine qualities emerged out of the infinite heart of Allah as an act of love, it would be no exaggeration to say that the entire collection of divine Names are members of the love family.

The Names featured in this chapter have been singled out because they particularly emphasize divine love, and because they reveal the variety of its manifestation. Grouping them together as a cluster will expose layers of meaning that deepen our spiritual search.

Ya Allah

(yaa 'al-LAAH)

In modern Arabic, some of the original meanings of love contained within the divine Names have faded from usage and thus became lost or hidden from view. The word "Allah" is an example of how meanings have been lost. It is based on the verb *waliha*, meaning to love passionately, to love madly. As Allah is the Name of the Essence, all the other Names are contained in this one word.

This idea of "crazy love," which is based on a linguistic derivation, is a good starting place for our discussion. To go out of our mind with passion, to go insane with love, to long for it, to pine away, to fall helplessly in love with, to lose our self-control, is a key to opening our understanding of the kind of love suggested by the invocation of Allah.

There are many hadith where we are told to repeat "Allah" until people will say we are *majnun*, or totally possessed with love. Because the root meaning of the Name Allah is passionate love, it is centrally important to recognize that all the divine Names are aspects of this love.

We have seen how the word "Allah" combines yes and no, *al* and *lah*. There is a secret in the final "H" sound of *lah*—that is, *hu*. And *hu* is both inclusive and transcendental. *Allahu* points to the essence and brings out the inner secret of love and ecstasy. (This secret ecstasy is discussed more fully in Chapter 12, The Secret of Ecstasy.) For our purposes here, we want to focus on Allah simply as the foremost member of the love family. Allah is the first Name of love.

La 'ilaha 'illa allah appears in the Qur'an three times, and *la 'ilaha 'illalla hu* 30 times. It is almost as if there is an intention of giving away the secret of *hu*. *La 'ilaha 'illalla hu* can be seen as the ultimate stage of all the possible formulations of this phrase. It conveys ultimate freedom. The word *hu* doesn't say "you" or "me." It doesn't say "I." It doesn't have a gender. It says, "huuuuuuuuuuuu."

The sound *hu* breaks all the categories of separation and union. It is just *hu*. And don't forget, it is present as an unspoken secret in the Name Allah, as the essence of the essence. When you say Allah you are saying *hu* without verbally saying it. That's why it is one of the secret Names—and the secret is love! This is of paramount importance. All of the Sufi tradition is contained in this one word.

In the Qur'an we have *Shahi da-llahu 'anna-hu laa 'ilaaha 'illaa hoo*.[20] The passage defies conventional translation. Here, Allah witnesses *'anna-hu*: there is no Allah but *hu*. Essentially, this is the teaching that Moses received at the Burning Bush. In the quote above it seems that there is a subject and an object, but actually the meaning goes full circle. Technically, *hu* is a pronoun, but it is neither male nor female. *Hu* includes everything.

This secret of the all-inclusive divine reality is metaphorically expressed in the love story of Layla and Majnun. Majnun follows his mad, passionate love (*waliha*) of Layla for his entire life, in the process becoming more and more absorbed in the beloved. His state makes the rational progression of courtship impossible, and they both endure difficulty after difficulty.

Layla literally means night. It can be interpreted as the beauty of being empty of the thought of self. In one part of the story, Layla's parents agree to marriage on the condition that Majnun act normally. He is sitting up on the dais waiting for the wedding party to come, and he hasn't seen Layla for years. Her dog happens to precede the wedding procession. He is so enraptured to see this dog—Layla's dog—that he jumps down from the dais to the floor and starts kissing the feet of the animal. Naturally, they call off the wedding.

After many years of travail Layla and Majnun meet one more time in the Sahara. She says, "I'll come back. I have to go back to my parents just now." And he has practically wasted away; he's nothing. He leans up against a tree and he kind of melts into the tree. After many months Layla finally returns, and she sees a woodcutter there. She says, "Have you seen my Majnun?"

The woodcutter replies, "No, but I wouldn't go near that tree. It's haunted. When I struck it, it cried out, 'Layla!'" So she goes to the tree and she sees Majnun merged into the tree. She says, "Majnun, Majnun, I've come. It's Layla. I'm here." He replies, "No, I'm Layla." "Come to your senses. I am Layla." "If you are Layla, I am not." And he dies. Giving up his separated sense of self in this way, his act of dying represents the complete merging of lover and beloved.

In earlier times everyone knew the meaning of *waliha* behind the word Allah, but it was lost through continual usage. Over time, most people have come to see "Allah" as a sort of father figure or lawgiver, often projecting what their fathers were like to them onto their idea of Godhead.

To keep the core meaning of love alive, the Sufis began to use the word *hu*. By medieval times they said *'ishq*, which also conveys the quality of non-rational, all-inclusive, overwhelming love. The important point is that this particular meaning of love, this *waliha*, is present in the original word "Allah" even if people lost view of it.

Ya Rahman, Ya Rahim

(yaa raḥ-MAAN, yaa ra-ḤEEM)

The first two Names of Allah on the list of 99 are ar-Rahman and ar-Rahim. They also mean love, the divine love that is the essential quality within compassion and mercy, which is how these attributes are conventionally translated. Thus the phrase *Bismillah ar-Rahman ar-Rahim* invokes love three times.

We suggest as a simple translation of ar-Rahman and ar-Rahim, "compassionate love" and "merciful love." Such compassion involves the sense of beneficially connecting with all beings in the radiant manner of the sun. Mercy makes its loving connection with all beings in the reflective manner of the moon. The way we ordinarily understand compassion and mercy in English can lack depth of feeling, the depth of love that accompanies the beneficence expressed by these qualities.

Ar-Rahman and ar-Rahim both come from the same root, *rahm* (R-H-M), which means the womb of love. Variations of this root include *rahim*, which means womb, and *rahma*, which means love. *Rahim* is sounded differently from the divine Name ar-Rahim (ra-HEEM). This metaphor of the womb of love allows us to sense both ar-Rahman and ar-Rahim. Reflect on how the mother's love for the fetus in the womb is compassionate and merciful. It is embracing, nourishing, and unconditional.

Birth and death are both related to the central concept of *rahm* The word *marhoom* means "whom God has had mercy upon," which is said for the dead. *Rahmatu-llah 'alayh* means "May God have mercy upon him or her," another prayer for the dead.

Remember that before birth we are all in this *rahma*. The *rahma* reaches from womb to womb. In the manner of a Sufi meditation, lie down and imagine yourself in the grave while feeling this earthly cycle of traveling from a womb of love to a womb of love. Murshid Samuel Lewis of San Francisco often shouted at his students, "Allah is your *lover*, not your *jailer*!" We can now see he was just saying, "Allah is Allah."

Allah is this mercy and compassion embodying the endless love of the *rahma*. Ar-Rahman is called the gateway to all the other Names and also is called the inner self of God. It expresses the inherent love within the heart of Allah that must be there for Allah to be Allah.

Ar-Rahim expresses how intensely this infinite merciful love is poured into every being and thing, without exception. The chapter of the Qur'an devoted to Mary (Mariam) demonstrates these qualities to perfection. The context is pregnancy, and the soul of Jesus is the divine spirit.

Ar-Rahman has a masculine, sun-like quality and ar-Rahim has a feminine, moon-like quality. Together they indicate the union, or holy communion, of the male and the female. When they are truly brought together in your practice, you are led to the transcendental yet all-inclusive divine love or *rahma*. This brings *rahma* into the organs that can perpetuate creation. Creation is intrinsically holy. Recitation of Ya Rahman, Ya Rahim generates healing energy, not only for the heart but also for the organs of reproduction.

The qualities of ar-Rahman and ar-Rahim address the deepest wound in the human psyche, a wound formed as far back as your own experience in the womb, well before the ego developed. The wound is engendered by an experience of disconnection with God. In this wounded consciousness, you identify with a deficiency that you feel makes you unlovable. Such narcissistic self-identification leads to defensiveness, self-loathing, shame, hate, rejection, and a deep sense of being abandoned by God.

When you finally navigate your way to the bottom of this inner hole, or perceived deficiency, there is nothing that you can actually do. Every action you take generates a sense of alienation, of wound-edness, and defiance. Only the grace that comes from the intervention of the deep loving mercy and loving compassion of the rahma can heal this primary wound and allow you to become fully connected with the source. This process is discussed in more detail in the section on Ya Ra'uf later in this chapter.

The quality of rahma is most tender and gentle and therefore does not arouse the defenses that the ego musters up to guard this most sensitive wounded place. Consequently, truly calling on Ya Rahman, Ya Rahim is everyone's remedy. It will prepare the ground to allow for healing of our fundamental impression of deficiency of self, and we can then feel abundant and flowing with endless love.

Realizing and accepting the essence of ar-Rahman and ar-Rahim brings self-healing, as well as a healing of our relationships with others and the world. Invoking Ya Rahman allows us to become individuated entities and to embody divine love, and invoking Ya Rahim enables us to bring this divine love into all our human relationships.

Ya Barr

(yaa BARR)

Al-Barr is perfect unconditional love. It is like the pure love that a mother has for her baby. Al-Barr can be described with synonyms such as merciful, compassionate, very benign, or good. But if we take it as being "good" we should understand it more in the Platonic sense of the Good, like a sun that is all-encompassing and complete in its essence.

Such goodness contains what are conventionally viewed as the opposites of good and bad. The Greek equivalent is *agape*. The all-merciful and womb-like love of God that is the meaning of ar-Rahman, is also the meaning of al-Barr. Associated meanings in the Name al-Barr are: gentleness toward parents and loved ones, kindness to strangers, and consideration of the circumstances that have shaped people as they are. Al-Barr is both inward and outward in its meaning. There is no distinction of sun and moon.

The root of the word al-Barr appears in the word *birrah*, which means a first fruit from a plant that bears sweet berries. *Burrah* means sweet through and through—inwardly and outwardly. This is a perfect love. A variation of the root of al-Barr, *barra fi qawlihi*, means to be true to your word, veracious, prudent, sound, and honest: if you say you will do something, you will do it. Your inner condition and your outward appearance never contradict each other. 'Ibn 'Arabi calls this one of the highest stations of the Saints. Perfect love is a seamless whole.

When applied to life in the world, those who live in this way are called *muhsin*, people of a perfected station of realization. They are also called *siddiq* or *'abrar*, people of perfect love, true Sufis. A famous oral tradition about the Prophet Muhammad is his saying that what would be a good deed for a pious believer would be a defect in the *'abrar*. Another way to look at the perfection embodied in this sacred Name is faultless action, *burra al-'amal*. It is to be free from errors and faultless, and we are especially enjoined to be sure to give others food and to be sweet in speech.

The last associated meaning of al-Barr has to do with location. It manifests in the *birr*, which means in the mind, heart, and soul. One is serene in all these aspects of one's being. With this serenity or equanimity one is able to accept without reaction what is perceived as a blessing or a nonblessing. If we call *birr* "good," then we are saying it is every variety of goodness. In the dictionary we find a synonym for al-Barr, *'altaf*, subtle love, as in al-Latif.

There is a hadith that deliberately plays with the ambiguities in the word, because *birr* (mind, heart, and soul) also means goodness, and *barr* also means the dryness of the earth. The tradition says that when you can't find water to do your ablutions in, wash yourselves with the dust of the earth, for she (the earth) is a *barr* to you.

Al-Barr, through all these variations, can be seen to be an example of a perfect quality, one that is *kamal*. What is usually translated in the opening chapter of the Qur'an as "the straight path," *siraat-ul mustaqeem*,[21] could just as easily be translated "the pathway of balance." It brings harmony. The secret (*sirr*) is perfection or completeness (*birr*). This *kamal* quality balances the extremes of power (*jalal*) and beauty (*jamal*).

The heart is the treasure house of all the divine Names. It is the perfect container created in the essence of all human beings in God's creation of the prototype of humanity, Adam. This has to do with al-Barr. One Name does not dominate or predominate over the others at any given moment. There is perfect balance.

What allows for the completeness of the Names in manifestation is al-Barr, or perfection. The perfected human being, *al-'insaan kaamil*, is thus seen as the complete mirror of all the Names. In fact, the very word for human being, *al-'insaan*, comes from *'uns*, which means intimacy. So the very essence of the human being is intimacy or nearness with Allah. Invocation of Ya Barr is a general tonic that helps humanity awaken to this intimacy.

Ya Halim

(yaa ḥa-LEEM)

Al-Halim is tender love. The sound code in the Arabic language informs us al-Halim means God is manifesting tender love everywhere without exception. There is no place we cannot find it. This quality of al-Halim is manifest in the totality of existence.

We like to begin our inquiry with some of the physical meanings of a word. We do this by examining various forms the root of the word takes that are quite concrete. One such physical meaning is found in the word *halama*, which means to attain puberty. *Halama* means to fill something like an animal water skin with water. The connection between puberty and filling a skin is to grow big breasts with tender nipples. The tenderness is physical, and we could say a maturing of this kind of nurturing love brings tenderness.

Tenderness is a physical feeling, but it is also an emotional feeling. Al-Halim is so tender. It is mild, meek, and gentle. The connection between a young girl and this tenderness would be shyness, withdrawal, and dreaminess. What a way to talk! We are offering a metaphor of God as a young girl, withdrawn, shy, and dreamy.

Forms of the root of al-Halim (H-L-M), *hulm* and *'ahlam*, are categories in dream interpretation. These terms refer to a sexual fantasy dream, and, in the case of men, actually refer to a wet dream. So the Name al-Halim suggests a quality that, in a sense, may be shy and withdrawn, but that also includes active imagination in the manner of dreams. Dream interpretation is an important subject in the inner life.

It is God who dreams us and we who dream God. Round things like soap bubbles are created and burst. 'Ibn 'Arabi calls this *khalq jadeed* and says that in every moment there is a new creation. Between the breaths, everything is wiped out and then recreated. *Khalq jadeed* matches up nicely with ancient Hindu teachings. It is moment-to-moment, each breath a creation and dissolution. Allah is the bubble blower creating these *'aalameen*, as in the phrase from the first surah of the Qur'an, *Al-hamdu li-llahi rabb-il-'aalameen*.[22] *'Aalameen* means God is dreaming all the possible Universes.

One of the sacred Hadith has Allah saying, "I am as my servant imagines me to be." Such imagining is creative imagination. And what allows us to dream Allah is the manifestation of al-Halim. This divine quality is erotic and creative. Al-Halim gives this *'ahlam*. And God is experiencing an *'ahlam*, an inner ecstasy, about all these possible universes or worlds that God is masterfully dreaming.

There is another set of meanings. *Hulm*, which is the tender quality, also means the ability to maintain calm or reason when we are overcome by anger or extreme emotion. It is the ability to remain calm especially in the midst of boiling anger. It is to be deliberate and measured, to calm one's soul and restrain one's temperament on the occasion of such excitement.

This allows for introducing a delay into our instinct of payback or revenge toward the perceived evildoer. Al-Halim is the opposite of hastiness or quick temper. Consequently, by offering such restraint, it is an antidote for *an-nafs ul-'ammaarah*, the ego state of just blowing up and flying off the handle. Mastery of al-Halim means gaining the ability to maintain a calm over the condition of the soul.

There is a related word *halamah*, which is a small tick that digs into the skin and torments an animal. The negative earthy meanings associated in some way with words formed from the roots of the divine Names give us clues to areas of application of the Names for healing human conditions of disease. So if we experience something like being tormented by that tick, we bring in al-Halim.

Invocation of Ya Halim allows us to maintain calmness. Al-Halim should not be thought of as simply calmness itself; it is more like calming down. It is the ability to maintain calm in the midst of emotional upheaval.

Hulm is connected in its meaning with the word *sakeenah* (*shekinah* in Hebrew). *Sakeenah* is called an indwelling emptiness. It appears in the Qur'an: "Inner peace descends like rain upon the hearts of those who are agitated."[23] This phrase is often recited in the *bayat* or initiation pledge that is made in joining a Sufi order. The word *bayat*, or initiation, comes from an incident under a tree when the companions of the Prophet thought they were going to die. The *sakeenah* came down at the moment of *bayat*.

One of the most famous hadith is about when there is a ring or a circle, a *halak*—for example, a circle of people who are doing *dhikr*. It is said that there is a ring of angels, wing to wing. Some people can see this. From on high, the *sakeenah* flows down upon them and into the hearts of the people in the circle.

One of the companions asked if even somebody who comes to do something like borrow a cup of milk gets the *sakeenah* from God. Prophet Muhammad said even those persons who had no idea what they were doing in the circle receive the *sakeenah*. Al-Halim sends the *hulm* down, or you might say al-Halim allows us to let this quality in.

There is another way to look at al-Halim that is found in the Qur'an. Halim is the tender love that can forgive. It is the love that always forgives, or can forgive anything. In this way it is like al-Ghafur and al-Ghaffar. Forgiveness cannot be fully experienced until we feel sympathy and tenderness.

We must empty out all the revenge, all the anger, and allow love to come in, which is perfect peace. It is a kind of flowing out. What flows out is very forgiving and loving. But it must be very strong too. It must be a strong power of love because it can forgive anything, and it can forgive everything all the time.

Abraham (Ibrahim) manifested this kind of forgiveness, and he did it time and again in his life. He is called *Khaleel-ul-allah*. It means a friend that you hug, a bosom buddy. Abraham had this kind of relationship with Allah. It was intimate in an almost physical way. Abraham is also called Halim.

In the Qur'an we have, *'inna 'Ibraaheema la-'awwaahun haleem* [*Halim*] *'awwaahun muneeb*.[24] In this context, it would mean turning away from anger and toward al-Halim, turning away from thoughts of revenge and toward al-Halim. Where does he get his forgiveness? He gets it from al-Halim, the One he is turning toward. This word *'awwaa* in the passage reveals a secret of tender-heartedness.

The secret is in constantly saying "Ah." The sound "Ah" is actually one of the secret Names of Allah. It is the first letter and the last letter of Allah. Ibrahim said "Ah" all the time as a way of continuously letting go and forgiving after, for example, an argument with his polytheistic father.[25]

This "Ah" is the closest to expressing what al-Halim is giving him. He prays for his father, who is rejecting him and kicking him out of the family. He could have instead had a big argument and a battle of wills. The verse ends with the phrase, *'inna 'Ibraaheema la-haleemun 'awwaahun muneeb*. In his worst moments, he could still say Ah. That's what al-Halim did for him. It expresses forgiveness that is specific, but he didn't say, "I forgive you, Father." He said, "Ah." It is tender and loving. Instead of beating the polytheists over the head with invective, he just said, "Ah."

It is always a challenge for us to be *halim* because, in the midst of frustration and anger, the last thing that generally comes to us is al-Halim. However, we might find that in the midst of such upheaval there is a dark place we may go that is like dark matter in physics. Dark matter is the basic ingredient from which creation can take place. In this place, we can create.

But most often we create our own nightmare. We recreate our continual dream, and it perpetuates our false self and our alienation. We can either create this dream, which is the mess we usually make, or we can release our attachments and wait for divine guidance. It is possible for us to find the way to wait in this dark place and receive grace and guidance.

Then creation can happen in the direction of evolution rather than in the direction of self-serving. Al-Halim is the place where true dreams can arise, and the dreams here really are visions. They are full of inspiration and guidance. Then the creation that flows from them will be meaningful. It will be evolutionary, and it will have a feeling of salvation.

Seen in this psychological context, al-Halim has to do with salvation rather than what we might call enlightenment or revelation. Salvation comes through grace, not through work. And for grace to happen, you have to reach that place that feels like the greatest sigh of relief, like Abraham's "Ah." Even though in one sense you may be broken, you know yourself as unbreakable even in the midst of suffering.

You release and wait on the divine to come and touch you. In this place one might say, "Humanity could not break me, even though my relationship with the world disconnected me from the divine. Yet

I am broken because I am disconnected from the divine." When you reach that state of deep surrender, a certain yearning and longing happens such that you feel "Now I turn to You. Where are You? I cannot cross this ocean of darkness to reach You. Only through Your grace can I be transformed, can I be touched."

When you reach that state there is nowhere to go. There is nothing but patience, calmness, *sakeenah*, and the potential of the dream. The potential for *hulm*, the potential for the activation of al-Halim is in that state. The dream in that domain is not like the dream we have in our conceptual mind. The dream that arises from that potent and calm state becomes reality. There the dream is the creative imagination or the pure creative aspect. The descent of the *hulm* so that we may receive it is the result of surrender.

As you approach such a condition of soul, a huge amount of terror begins to be released from the system. It is a congestion that has to do with anger and revenge. Upheavals of anger are maneuvers to avoid the deep dark place of abandonment. Anger gives us continuity. Revenge gives us something too. But this place takes away everything. It is a place of woundedness in your relationship with the divine. It brings up the ultimate revenge of the ego toward God. "You forsake me? Then I forsake you."

And even when that woundedness is released, what may be waiting is a ring, a vicious circle of terror. It is called "fear and trembling." This is no ordinary fear. There is fear of annihilation, but there is also fear of losing reality. It all goes to the survival instinct, which is located in the perineum, the lower center. "I've got to survive, I've got find my way, I've got to know what is my destiny. I've got to go home." All of those survival issues start to come up. And the terror is that a tidal wave is going to erase everything so that you will never know your direction or your soul's purpose.

It is a deep seemingly irrational terror. "I am all alone. Where have you taken me? Why have you forsaken me? Why have you thrown me into this?" We often avoid this dark place by daydreaming, by going to sleep, or by hypnotizing ourselves with our stories. We repeat our stories continuously. Or we engage in watching a lot of television, narcotization, and concern about conventional standards of what life is and what we should do, or about what offers apparent safety in existence.

Ultimately, the ring of terror is released, and the abyss, the deep, is waiting. In this deep place you find infinite patience and an infinite sigh of relief. Whenever the relative world comes to get you, you sigh, and the sighing releases the relative world from catching you. It releases the mind from gripping you, and you dip again into the abyss.

Each sigh takes you to the abyss, to the deep, to the dark, to the gentle. And there the Beloved is waiting. The tender love of al-Halim arises. "I am beyond my anger, I am beyond my hurt. I am beyond my pride; I am beyond my brokenness. I am waiting in this eternal peacefulness, and I know that in this infinite patience is the womb of creation. In this place, I can create or I can be created." This is *hulm*. And it is a feminine quality in the love of God.

Each time you excavate the inner terrain, there is constant ebb and flow in both directions: the terror arises, but also the source flows forth with a sense of great tenderness and support. Back and forth you go. One day you discover your fear, another day you discover your attachment, and so on. You undo each one and rest deeper in the grace. Ultimately you may have a station you can go into again and again, and rest in, but that often takes years of work.

Ya Halim is a wonderful practice for a person to start with when there is a great amount of anger at the surface. Repeating Ya Halim will start the process of calming down. You can follow the thread of it all the way to the abyss. Just the sound quality of this Name brings so much calmness, so much comfort.

The physician of the heart may therefore prescribe Ya Halim to those who are out of control and full of temper. However, repetition of Ya Halim is also called for when students are on the verge of a major breakthrough or when they face the biggest disappointment of their life. Both of these occasions are often experienced as a kind of ultimate bankruptcy. If a person has not done a great deal of spiritual work, they will struggle and panic at these times, and they will not be able to release the extreme impressions.

Ya Halim is also appropriate to prescribe to those who are in their final stages of surrender. They are reaching the stage where they need to sigh. It will help them understand that here is the last place to rest. It is the fertile ground of infinite creativity. Now it is only up to the divine to touch and transform. Two pairs of divine Names repeated together at this point may be quite effective: Ya Ghafur, Ya Halim, Ya Sabur, Ya Halim.

"The Supreme Terror will cause them no grief and the angels will receive them with the greeting, 'This is your promised day.'"[26] For the Saints of Allah, the worst nightmare that comes true doesn't affect them. Their inner calm is so empty, so strong, that the greatest fear doesn't color that emptiness, doesn't disturb it. It just passes through.

They are in the *halim*. In the beginning was the deep and the spirit of God pervaded the deep in pre-eternity. It is unfathomable, but it is the great potential. From it, all creation can be manifested. With the realization of this grand station comes an amazing ecstatic love. The uncovering of this ecstatic love, as we have seen, is nothing but Allah. In that place, nothing is left but Allah.

In the Hindu myth of creation the primordial state is "the waters." Vishnu is the God asleep in the primordial waters of infinity beyond time and space. Then Vishnu awakens, and the next cycle of the manifest universe comes out of his awakening from his dream in that primordial, undifferentiated space of pure potentiality.

Ya Wadud

(yaa wa-DOOD)

Al-Wadud is the most overtly erotic word that is used as a Name for Allah. It is intimate love, a secret love that may be hidden in the heart even from the lover. A general meaning of al-Wadud is heart love. It is the way Allah is loved in the hearts of the divine friends. One form of the root has the physical-plane meaning of a wooden peg that holds the tent down.

An erotic connection can be seen in al-Wadud's purposeful meaning of "attached to." We are attached to al-Wadud in the same way we would be attached to a lover. It is the most deeply penetrating connection we have. That is why al-Wadud is love in the heart. It is in our heart of hearts, our secret heart, our *sirr*. We are physically pegged to Allah in our depths.

We may think that what is the moving force in our desires is finances, or physical attraction, or the will to power, but if we could get deep enough we would see it is really the love of al-Wadud. Our most intimate connection is what stirs us. This quality is mysterious because our conscious mind may make an idol or false god of it and try to say it is one particular thing while in reality it is this deeper pull.

Historically there has often been a misreading of Sufi poetry because Westerners thought the poets were writing about their earthly lovers, or wine, or something literal like that. Well, they may have been, but such a reading is woefully incomplete.

The sound code embedded in Arabic grammar intensifies the meaning of al-Wadud. It emphasizes deep penetration, going right into the heart of things, into the essence. It is as if we are saying, "All appearances notwithstanding, what do you really love in your heart, and in your heart of hearts, and then in your secret heart?" Such love, al-Wadud, attaches each one of us to the universe. It is the peg that holds down the tent of existence.

Let's look at some of the contextual ways al-Wadud is used in the Qur'an, where it appears 29 times. *Amilus-saalihaati sayaj-'alu lahumur-Rahmaanu[Rahman] wuddaa [Wadud].*[27] "On those who believe and work deeds of righteousness will (Allah) Most Gracious bestow love." Al-Wadud always appears along with loving compassion, which in this verse is expressed by ar-Rahman. Ar-Rahman gives a kind of certainty, an inner certainty. It is an action that promotes peaceful, harmonious coexistence with the rest of the universe. In the context of this Qur'anic verse, we have both inner certainty and outer action. The kind of action that ensues is in line with the natural flow of the universe.

Such action involves loving surrender rather than self-will. It can truly and literally, therefore, be called *islam*, and it naturally gives rise to peace and harmony. The verse is saying that the manifestation of the divine is ar-Rahman, and brings al-Wadud. This is another excellent example of how ar-Rahman is the gate for all the other *sifat*, or divine Names.

Another reference in the Qur'an is *Wa-stagh firoo [Ghafur] rabba-kum thumma too-boo [Tawwab] 'ilayh 'inna rabbee raheemun [Rahim] wadood [Wadud].*[28] *Wa-stagh firoo* is like super forgiveness, loving forgiveness. It involves *tawbah* (turning), which is reflected in the divine Name at-Tawwab. It constantly turns away from hate, specifically, toward loving forgiveness. In romance and marriage it is often said that hate is the other side of love.

The sense of this passage is of literally facing away from hate toward love. In this context, al-Wadud is moving from nonforgiveness to forgiveness. Its relationship with the negative aspect gives it its dynamic thrust. Because both at-Tawwab and al-Wadud have the quality of using the appearance of a negative as a springboard to realization of the positive quality—hate to love, for example—they are good to recite together: Ya Tawwab, Ya Wadud.

Let's take one more Qur'anic reference: *Wa huwa-l-ghafoor(un)-wadood dhoo-'arsh-il-majeed* (Allah alone is truly forgiving, all-embracing in divine love).[29] On the soul's return journey to Allah there are certain attributes that it might reflect because of its self-effacement, or *fana*. Two most essential ones, according to this verse, are al-Ghafur and al-Wadud. They share the form in the sound code of penetrating deeply into the heart of hearts.

Al-Wadud is erotic love, attached love, but you can't get to the depth of such love if you have the kind of blockage that comes from coagulating your identity around some wound deep down in your heart that you haven't forgiven. With the forgiveness of al-Ghafur, the depth of al-Wadud will arise as a loving intimate connection with the manifest universe. Consequently, pairing these two in prayerful recitation is recommended: Ya Ghafur, Ya Wadud.

What al-Wadud offers is what has been called the spiritual erotic. Erotic poetry is used in many Arabic, Persian, and Turkish expressions of Sufism because it is easily connected with our common experiences. Metaphysical love is a rare experience. To explain such a rare experience, the poet takes a common experience to indicate how the rare experience might feel to those who haven't had it. Being in love with God is something like being in love with a beloved in the flesh.

There is a celebrated hadith in which the Prophet Muhammad says the three things he likes most are women, perfume, and prayer. And 'ibn 'Arabi takes a whole chapter to interpret this statement, showing that all these words carry an erotic connotation. The long and the short of it is, if we look around for the door to the presence of the beloved, we find the erotic, we find sexual intercourse. Of course this may be playing with fire, but playing with fire is a necessity with al-Wadud.

Erotic love is another opportunity to know God. It is essentially Love, the same as every other love—both mystical and material. It is a part of the path, and its deepest manifestation is called al-Wadud. Sexual intercourse is one of the pathways to God and has been recognized as such by many of the Prophets and Saints. There is also a strong core of this path in some forms of Hinduism.

Certainly we can make erotic love an idol and remain trapped in the material aspect of it. In fact, it was embodied as an idol in Mecca in the pre-Islamic era. Freely acknowledging all the inherent complications, our point is simply that from the divine perspective, intimate, passionate love is a doorway to union.

Al-Wadud also materializes or manifests on the prophetic level. We see this in the Qur'an: *'Asa-llaahu b'an yaj'ala bayna-lladheena 'aaday-tum min-hum mawaddah. Wallaahu qadeer; wa allahu ghafoorun raheem.*[30] The context is that it was a time of great adversity for people. We are advised that even though people may be our enemies and hate us, through al-Wadud we transform hatred into love. Hatred transforms in the heart into forgiving love, compassionate love. Right at the end of the passage it emphasizes the way Allah does this transformation: Ghafur-Rahim—deep forgiveness and infinite compassion.

The Buddhist practice of Taking and Sending (*tonglen*), which is a practice of embodying the compassionate Buddha, is essentially the same as this transformation of hatred into love. Negativity is transformed into the blessing of loving-kindness. Compassion spontaneously arises because it is inherent in the essence of all.

We are asked to take the essence of al-Ghafur and ar-Rahim that Allah has established in our heart and transmute the dense emotion that arises in our desire nature. Hate turns into love. Whatever feeling is arising is intended to be a vehicle for our transformation. *Wad* means intimate. We find al-Wadud at the very depth of what we most desire. It is the most intimate love possible.

Ya Ra'uf

(yaa ra-'OOF)

Ya Ra'uf is an invocation of quiet, gentle, profound love. One of the ways to understand ar-Ra'uf is to compare it to ar-Rahim, with which it is close in meaning. Nine of the 11 times that ar-Ra'uf occurs in the Qur'an, it is paired with ar-Rahim to describe Allah.[31]

These divine names are close in meaning, but the sound code embedded in the Arabic language helps to distinguish them. It makes ar-Rahim omnipresent; thus it spreads into every particular thing without exception. Ar-Rahim has a very immanent quality.

The sound code for ar-Ra'uf reveals it to be a kind of love that emphasizes a deep, deep penetration into the core of being, into essence. *Wa kaana dhoo-l-'arshi binaa 'araafiy. Rafi* here is a variant of Ra'uf. *Dhoo-l-'arshi* means the essence, thatness. Such love moves right into the essence of what could be called divine placelessness.

Ar-Ra'uf has a reputation for being virtually untranslatable. The variation of the root *a'rafu* has a physical meaning of wine. But it would have to be a very gentle and mellow wine. Another level of meaning is peaceful, calm. It is the peacefulness of resting in God in the midst of suffering, difficulties, and trials. One of the words for difficulty and trial is *fitnah*. In sword making, you find this way of perfecting through difficulties. To make the steel strong and flexible, it is tempered, heated, and then plunged into water.

There are many words for peacefulness, such as the Name as-Salaam. Ar-Ra'uf is the quiet, loving peacefulness that appears within the context of difficulties. It is internal but not passive. It is maintaining peace, preserving peace, and not just calming down. You center on this peaceful calm to lovingly relieve the suffering of others. That's why it is so close to ar-Rahim. In both cases the Names compassionately reach out to other people who are suffering.

With ar-Ra'uf, human beings use a calm inner strength to help others when conditions are at their worst, and everyone is panicking. There is a manner of serenity that allows you to overcome hostility, anger, and hate. That calm has a way of going deeply into the essence, and it has a soothing or pacifying effect on others.

Another meaning of ar-Ra'uf is to be able to extract or bring forth. The Qur'an says, "Allah brings

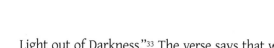

Light out of Darkness."[33] The verse says that we are able to bring forth a "pure light of peace." With this inner peace, this *ra'afah*, we turn toward compassion. Here it is aligned in meaning with the divine Name, at-Tawwab. Like at-Tawwab, ar-Ra'uf is always turning toward those people who are the most hostile, the most hateful, and the most negative. It is not passive. It is outwardly compassionate, and it empowers us to turn repeatedly toward hostile people.

Occasionally some of the 99 Names are used at the end of a chapter of the Qur'an to give a key to the whole meaning of the chapter. At the end of many chapters there are two Names. In technical language this is called *daleel*. In the Qur'an there is a statement about the Prophet: *La-qad taab-allaahu 'al-an-nabiyyi wa-l-muhaajireena wa-l-'ansaar.*[34] It says the Prophet is always turning toward these groups of people who are suffering from inner corruption. *Tawwab* and *rahim* appear as the tag at the end of the verse. And as we have seen, *rahim* and *ra'uf* are extremely close in meaning.

The essential thing that should be emphasized is the quality of deeply rooting ourselves in inward compassion while turning outward toward the people who are really suffering. It also involves turning toward those who have gone from bad to worse. You face the people who are giving you the most trouble. That means active turning out and not just a maintaining one's own state. The best way to establish the calm of ar-Ra'uf is in the midst of hostility, or in the midst of the worst of difficulties and suffering, because it goes to the very heart of our deepest fears.

Another Qur'anic reference is *Wa-llahu ra'oof(un) bi-l'ibaad.*[35] The passage is describing the Last Day: "You'll be faced with the very best of what you've done and the very worst of what you've done." A form of *ra'uf* is used here. It means that we can face the very worst that we have done with loving compassion, with this gentle, gentle indwelling love.

We need to learn to face the gnawing fears that waste us away by realizing and embodying ar-Ra'uf. Specifically mentioned in relation to ar-Ra'uf's manifestation is our difficult struggle to survive, to make ends meet, to wrest a livelihood from the earth in time of drought.

Embodiment of ar-Ra'uf is particularly recommended when hostility is focused directly at you—aggressive hostility that causes you mental anguish. We are talking about backbiting, innuendo, carrying tales, and lying about you. Ar-Ra'uf is even subtler and quieter than saying, "I forgive so-and-so for causing me harm." It is similar to the divine Name al-'Afuw, perfect forgiveness.

In both cases there is no trace of any kind of fault that is held. With ar-Ra'uf you are quietly expressing love from your deepest place. You express this quiet, gentle love to very hateful people right into the depth of their being. And of equal importance, at the same time you have no aversion or reaction to the extremity of their condition. You are acting from a calm, quiet, internal love rather than from a wounded place. Most of us are wounded, yet we try to overcome our wounds and be compassionate. Ar-Ra'uf is beyond that; it is compassion taken to the utmost degree.

You should invoke Ya Ra'uf to overcome the deep place that an accuser is coming from, and not as an effort to overcome their accusations against you. It allows you to become capable of getting into the heart of the one who is directing the hostility toward you. You recognize the negative environment but get past that by penetrating deeply inside. Jesus said, "Resist not evil." There is no resistance, no conquering, no giving life to the impressions by reacting to them.

This is illustrated in a Zen story about a monk who was accused of getting a young girl pregnant. The family attacked him. He didn't deny it even though it was a total fiction. He said, "Is that so?" They then forced him to take the child and raise it, which he did. Years later they found out the truth and tried to apologize to him. He didn't react to that either but again responded, "Is that so?" He wouldn't ever give life to the charge.

With ar-Rauf, you don't deal with the outward stuff but simply go to the inner heart of the person who is directing all of that hostility. The Prophet Muhammad profoundly demonstrated ar-Ra'uf when he returned to Mecca after the ruling tribe had carried out a reign of terror against him and his followers.

He took every possible means to be compassionate toward people who had been hostile to him, to take pity upon them, to take extraordinary pains to show utmost respect in order to benefit them. He didn't punish anyone. There was no revenge. He used every way possible to show compassion and esteem for the people in Mecca. It is a shining example of quiet love in the midst of difficulty.

Just the sound of the word *ra'uf* has a frequency in the heart that is gentler than the wings of a butterfly. It is a kind of love that has conquered any defenses the ego might put up. There is no longer anything to defend against for this love to flow within you. You have surrendered your defenses and worked to overthrow whatever nightmares and pains these defenses have been protecting.

So ar-Rauf touches the deepest wounds there are. It goes to the place within you where there are sensitive hurts and wounds that you have lived your whole life defending from being touched. But this simple love can reach it. It is so quiet that it can penetrate the armor. It is even subtler than what we generally understand by compassion. It is a gentle perfume.

The Secondary Narcissistic Wound

There are two major wounds in the human psyche. We discuss them in different contexts throughout this book and in Chapter 2, Our Psychological Perspective. What we call the secondary narcissistic wound arises because we feel shamed. We feel somehow we have failed to fulfill what our family or society has required of us.

What makes it narcissistic is our self-identification with the deficiency of this wounded condition. The result of this identification is that we feel deficient in our sense of self, in the sense of our very soul. Because this wound is so tender, it usually is defended by our whole personality structure.

We develop strategies so that the wound won't be touched, because it is very delicate and vulnerable. It is not like a wound that happened through gross encounters or hurts. It is a wound in the delicateness of the soul. As a child, in our soul, we felt that nobody could see what we were trying to do. We felt like a failure because we were not able to heal mother or to heal father.

So children ultimately become wounded in the *ra'afah* itself, wounded in the inner peace that is at the core of ar-Ra'uf. Then when somebody attacks them, they may collapse and become aggressive toward their own selves. Or they may become aggressive toward others and start attacking them.

Both kinds of activity mean that the delicate wound is activated. We could say that all aggression is coming as a defense against deep shame, deep vulnerability, and deep woundedness. And we would further say that everybody is trying to cover up this shame, because the pain is so devastating that when they reach it they don't know how to handle it. It can even lead to suicidal impulses.

When we approach the core, the wound is so raw, so delicate, that some forms of love and compassion may be too thick to use. The wound requires a more delicate frequency of compassion because it is really such a tender wound in the sacred heart. It is feeling wounded by the human condition, by the parent, by the community, by humanity.

So now we call on Ya Ra'uf, and that is when *ra'afah* comes. It can touch this delicate wound because it is of a delicate frequency. This is a wound that needs a feather rather than an ointment. Even an ointment may be too powerful.

When the quiet love of ar-Ra'uf is present, there is nothing to defend. You are in a space of utmost light and gentleness, and you are not reacting to all the defenses of the other person. You gently touch their wound. You gently calm the anguish in the soul—the anguish and the vulnerability and the fear and the extreme terror.

The *ra'afah* goes through all those layers, calming them down with gentleness. It soothes the nervous system, the glandular system, and the heart. The whole system becomes calm. Because the tenderness of ar-Ra'uf is open to the hurt of being wounded by humanity, reciting Ya Ra'uf can begin to mediate the extremity of the anguish that the soul may feel in life.

The Primary Narcissistic Wound

What we call the primary narcissistic wound is even deeper, more sensitive, and more full of despair than the secondary wound we have just described. It is our feeling of being wounded by the divine. "Why have You forsaken me?" When this deep crisis occurs, another kind of love needs to come. The Qur'an says, "God has written on His own heart *Rahma*" (*Kataba'alaa nafsi-hi rahmah*).[36] This is the kind of love needed to heal this primary wound.

The primary narcissism comes from feeling wounded by the divine, that, as a soul, as a being, you feel, "I am not loved by God. That must be why God put me in all these difficulties. There must be something wrong with me. I have failed and I feel hurt about it."

The wound from humanity is a secondary hurt. Even though it is very devastating for a child, it is a secondary hurt. The primary hurt comes when a person turns to God and says, "Okay, I understand how my family and society have made me suffer, but why are you persecuting me? You are supposed to be the all-compassionate. There must be something about me that is so bad that it makes you reject me, makes you not protect me or not give me divine mercy."

This deep human condition is asking for something that only the manifestation of the essential love, the *rahma*, can offer. We recommend invoking Ya Rahim. Its quality has the total substantiality of the inherent love in the heart of Allah, and at the same time no quality could be gentler. The *rahma* touches a wound that no human can touch. Only the divine can touch it.

It is interesting to observe that ar-Ra'uf and ar-Rahim appear together everywhere as a pair. This is true both in the Qur'an and in the dictionary. We have come to see that ar-Ra'uf is the antidote for the secondary narcissistic wound, and ar-Rahim is the antidote for the primary narcissistic wound.

When both of these qualities of divine love are present, you become able to reach the unbearable tenderness in the human soul. Filled with this *ra'afah*, you are so delicate, so gentle that you can go through all the armaments and all the defenses. You can be the delicate feather that touches the most unbearable wound inside, the wound in the soul that has human beings screaming day and night.

There are two divine Names that Allah specifically bestows upon the human being, and they are ar-Ra'uf and ar-Rahim. We see this quite specifically in the Qur'an: "A Messenger has come to you for your *nafs* and has been *harees*,"[37] which means he has the quality of embodying this kind of extraordinary extreme of respecting people. And it then says, "Ra'uf, Rahim," describing the Messenger with these two divine Names.

These are the divine Names that Allah applies to the Messenger, the Prophet Muhammad, peace be upon him. They definitely go together: Ya Ra'uf, Ya Rahim. Fully realizing them is what it means to be human. They are the most human attributes, if you will, of the divine Names. Without their essence, humanity is lost. They are both Names for love, different qualities of love, and they are very powerful when used in combination.

We cannot reach such profound states simply by our own efforts. Such states are bestowed by grace. Spiritual work ultimately has to be crowned by grace. Something in the soul finds itself on the cross and must wait for that which is beyond all achievement. It is a waiting for the appearance of divine love.

Ar-Ra'uf is active in one sense, yet it is always there on the inside. That's why we can't exactly work toward it. It is to be discovered. It comes from an essential place of the heart. Otherwise, it could not reach the hearts of others, as it does, without a trace of attachment, resentment, or defensiveness. All of us need this ar-Ra'uf. If we resonate with this quality, it will respond to all our defensive layers of ego because its frequency is so gentle. Just like water can melt rocks, if this stream is actively flowing, it will melt all our defensiveness.

If students have not done enough inner work, it may not be wise to administer this *wazifah* right away, as they may not be able to handle all the dismantling of the personality structure. It might take them years to dismantle one piece after another. However, when they get very deep, when they are in touch with the deep longing in their soul for the divine, and when something is really anguishing them deeply and the wound is very close and tender, that is the best time to prescribe Ya Ra'uf.

Prayerful repetition of Ya Ra'uf addresses the wound that we have received from humanity. Our instinctive response to this wound may be to reproach ourselves for being blameworthy, or it may be to fill ourselves with spiritual pride. So repetition of Ya Ra'uf can be a great antidote for spiritual pride as well. And repetition of this sacred Name is especially recommended for those who are going through the passage of deeply wondering what is their purpose in life.

When you have been wounded by what was missing in your family, part of your self-identity has to do with wanting to heal this family hole. In life, you often try to fix things in a particular way, a way that is based on this narcissistic identification, and you are often quite adamant about fulfilling that purpose. You have to fulfill the family mission. Consciously or unconsciously, the family asked you to do something, and now you are going around trying to fulfill that mission.

There comes a time when you realize that this is not what you really feel like doing in life. But still you see yourself compulsively doing it. You cannot let go of it because you feel overwhelmed. You feel you are going to fail. It is as if something is required of you to do, and you are conflicted between what your mind is telling you to do and something inside saying, "I need to do something different."

Now you are not so much driven by the ego. The ego is beginning to slow down, beginning to relax, beginning to see that its pattern in life might be out of harmony. In that state of navigating between what the family or society requires and birthing what the soul truly desires—in that transitional state— calling on Ya Ra'uf is most useful. It touches the tenderness in you, the vulnerability in you. It touches your identification with the wound that makes you feel you will fail as a person.

And a physician of the heart may only need to genuinely say, "I can be with you in the unbearable-ness that you feel." Gentle love. This is the manifestation of ar-Ra'uf, to dare be with somebody in the most unbearable vulnerability that they go through. It is simply to be present in the divine quality, and gently touch that very tender place.

To succeed then, both the physician of the heart and the student must drop all their defenses. The presence of ar-Ra'uf is very dismantling of all the defenses and all the structures. When the defenses go the divine mercy comes, the divine guidance comes, and the soul shows itself. That is when under-standing kicks in, and that is how the picture opens up.

Forgiveness spontaneously happens. The soul shows you where it wants to journey. Ar-Ra'uf en-ables you to pass through the extreme vulnerability of the feeling that you have failed the family mis-sion. And the *rahma* enables you to heal your innermost wound. Ar-Rahim communicates that the di-vine has never forsaken you.

We recommend prayerful repetition of this pair of divine Names—Ya Ra'uf, Ya Rahim—for those who are caught up in the stream of extreme vulnerability that comes from the wound felt from humanity. By such invocation, the proper space within is activated to receive *ra'afah*. Rep-etition of Ya 'Afuw, and the other Names in the forgiveness family, also prepares the way for this inner healing.

For the primary narcissistic wound, the divine woundedness, it may eventually be more suitable to wait in the silence with willing surrender for the response of divine love. It is relatively easy to write about these stages, but the concept is not the reality. To actually go through these advanced stages requires much dedicated work as well as divine grace.

Ya Latif

(yaa la-ṬEEF)

Al-Latif has also been considered virtually untranslatable. We are translating it as subtle love, and that is as close to the meaning as we can get in a simple gloss. One physical meaning of al-Latif is the sheerness of a piece of cloth such as a fine silk. In another dimension, this fineness of manifestation is a quality of the subtle centers of spiritual magnetism in the body, which are called *lata'if*.

Let's systematically go through various levels of meanings of al-Latif. *Latoofa* is a form of the root. It means to be kind or loving, but it has a passive feeling. The dictionary tells us: "loving, affectionate, affable, lovely, charming, courteous, civil, agreeable, friendly, polite, and then mild." "Mild and soothing" is important.

It is also noteworthy that al-Latif means polished in manners. It is the original, non-corny version of gentleman—someone who has a kind of power yet whose actions are gentle, kind, and loving, rather than just the opposite, which all too often is a consequence of power and money. Al-Latif therefore came to be considered the essence of *adab*, the highest standard in human relationships of refined behavior and refined intellect.

One important root meaning for al-Latif is found in the process of tanning. To tan hide is to make it more soft, more natural and delicate through soaking the hide in some liquid, classically urine. It softens the hide. A further meaning is to be thin and refined in stature, to be graceful in the limbs. The form of the word *latifah* means to caress, to pet, to rock, or to shake gently as one might fondle a child's head.

Still another form of the word has a healing aspect: to treat with an emollient, which softens the skin or soothes an irritation. With this in mind, al-Latif might easily be called a medicinal, healing kind of love. One other group of meanings is to jest, to tickle someone under the ribs gently. It is wit and witticism. Funny love. Subtle humor. It is a gentle touch in a gentle place to bring out laughter.

The other aspect in al-Latif is knowing the subtle, mysterious, or hidden knowledge. That is why it is most often paired with al-Khabir, the depth of mystical insight. Six out of seven times al-Latif is mentioned in the Qur'an, it is paired with al-Khabir in the context of this subtle depth of knowing. Al-Latif works together with al-Khabir to uncover and reveal the subtleties, the mysteries, the hidden mysteries, the obscure, abstruse mysteries.

This quality brings extraordinary intellectual skillfulness, an adeptness in the sense of knowing what is hidden. An example is Solomon knowing the speech of the birds. The Seven Sleepers of the Cave in Ephesus, according to the Qur'an, were also endowed with deep insight, so they would know the subtle mysteries, such as how long they had been asleep in the cave.[38] They knew the mystery of what occurs in the bowels of the earth in a hidden place. That is what is meant by al-Khabir. It is subtle knowledge, and mystical insight as well.

Al-Latif and Al-Khabir are attributes of the legendary teacher Khidr. At the end of *Kahf*, the Surah of the Cave, in the Qur'an, there is the story of Khidr and Moses. At first glance, Khidr may appear to be just the opposite of al-Latif because of the roughness of his manner in his role as spiritual guide to Moses. But he was actually manifesting hidden knowledge, and the lessons he gave were so subtle that Moses at first did not get the point. The story of Khidr and Moses is related in Chapter 17, The Seven Levels of the *Nafs*.

Al-Latif is everything that is the opposite of being violent or violating others, or violating their feelings. It is the opposite of tearing things apart. It is the opposite of clumsy, stupid, awkward, overbearing, and loud. The tension between inner and outer appearances makes the story of Khidr and Moses full of dramatic tension.

The story in the Qur'an also reveals the *ta'wil*, the subtlest, most hidden interpretation that requires the most penetrating kind of knowledge to be understood. That level of explanation is most important. To be *latif* is to know the most subtle things that are not yet known, realities that are not limited by finite knowledge but are knowledge from the depth of the heart.

The Qur'an speaks of the feminine nature of this depth of wisdom, *hikmah*, saying *'Inna allaha kaana lateefan khabeeraa.*[39] It refers to a specific group of women and the way they understood the outward message as well as the inner wisdom. Their accomplishment should be seen in the context of Allah manifesting as al-Latif, demonstrating subtle love, and then manifesting skillful or penetrating wisdom. The continual pairing of al-Latif and al-Khabir demonstrates just how intimately related are the meanings of these two divine Names.

As part of the divine pharmacopoeia, we can easily say that invocation of Ya Latif brings refinement of character. It moisturizes and softens grossness of ego. So it is very useful in dealing with a personality that is gross and heavily defended. Here the meaning of softening and moisturizing the hide in tanning can be seen.

Dry and brittle personalities need this moisturizing action. There is a layer in the human being that is like jerky. It is a layer that has dried out and become calloused inside. It is not the most defended layer, but it is very calloused. And the subtle dimension of the *lata'if*, the whole subtle body, can moisturize and soften this layer and make it alive—make the fleshly jerky more juicy and permeable.

We'll offer a metaphor here in reference to the subtle body. An oil lamp has a wick that holds the moisture of the oil. You light up the wick, and there is a flame. The flame comes down through the *lata'if* or chakras. The moisture is like the perfume. It is not the oil, itself, but the scent of the perfume. That is the dimension of the *lata'if*, the subtle body. When we can condense the moisture and go deeper, it may lead to essential states.

A physician of the heart needs to look at moisturizing and softening different kinds of grossness by bringing in this subtle power. Is there grossness in a person's mind, in their emotions, or in their behavior? Do they realize they are gross or not? Some people don't know that they are not refined. Al-Latif can be focused in all these areas and more.

Invocation of Ya Latif activates the whole subtle body of refinement, exquisiteness, and gentleness. It can be called a kind of love, and it surely has love in it, but it is more than just love. We learn to know people skillfully by developing a refined quality of empathy that comes in part from not projecting our own ego condition on them.

There's a kind of skillfulness that penetrates, a sensitivity that takes knowledge to a very deep and subtle place that isn't obvious to everyone. Even sincere love doesn't always involve this kind of skillful insight. So the quality of al-Latif is also the kind of skill we get in knowing a person very well at a very deep level.

We see that this subtle love goes together with a kind of skill and knowledge and refinement. Al-Latif is heartful, but from heartfulness it can travel to any domain. Its subtle power can also go to the mind. It can come from the heart and affect the mind. This allows the mind to become refined in its depth of understanding and gentleness. Our actions then reflect that.

The reason we group al-Latif in this cluster of Names of divine love is its heartful quality. In a love relationship we want the intimacy of being able to get into the *latif* of another person, to truly get under the skin to that soft, delicate place.

The explanation of *fana*, or self-effacement, is not the destruction of the *nafs*, or lower self. What happens is the *nafs* becomes ever more refined. And there are many grades of *nafs*. At the highest level, the ego covering becomes so sheer, so thin, so *latif* that it is the thinnest sheer membrane. It becomes so transparent you may not even know it is there. That is what *fana* feels like. And a real physician of the heart can tell what is inside the mysterious realm of the heart by looking into how your *nafs* is covering your heart.

Originally the ego is a delicate, transparent membrane. It gets thickened and calcified by beliefs, ideas, and images and becomes a thick membrane. Much of the actual work of dismantling the ego is in dismantling gross beliefs and ideas, including your idea of self. The use of the English word "annihilation" to describe the process of self-effacement or *fana* falls short in conveying these associations.

Our aim is not to kill the ego but rather to allow for its transformation. In giving birth, the cervix of the mother is effaced, not annihilated. It softens and becomes transparent. The absolute has no membrane, but we must respect the relative condition of human beings in our work. Trying to take people to the absolute too fast is inappropriate. To work with them properly, their membrane needs to be intact.

If the ego-covering over the heart is thick, rigid, and stiff, it is lacking the quality of al-Latif. If the membrane is more transparent, it allows the *ruh*, the pure light of the soul, to penetrate and shine through it. *An-nafs ul-saafiyah* is this high stage of purity. The word Sufi also means pure. The covering over the heart has become so subtle and transparent that it lets the light of the *ruh* shine right through it.

There is a story told in the Hebrew Kabbalah that when Moses experienced the Burning Bush he was glowing with unbelievable intensity. There was no veil over him, and the divine light was shining so much that people couldn't endure his presence. They couldn't stand the intensity of that light. So what he did was make a mask that was transparent and subtle. When he put it on, the mask veiled the light, and thus the light did not overpower the others. Through such a membrane the soul shapes itself to harmonize with others. The mask, in the Kabbalistic teaching, is called *nefesh*, the Hebrew word for ego that is identical with the Arabic *nafs*.

Invocation of Ya Latif is recommended as a general tonic for the transformation of the *nafs* from a coarse to a refined condition. In terms of health, al-Latif softens up what has become calcified in your body. Recitation of Ya Latif and Ya Khabir together is also highly recommended, especially when the subtle heartful quality of al-Latif needs to become activated in the sphere of mystical knowledge and insight. Such a combination brings the skillful means to gain insight into your own difficulties and self-delusion.

mu'izz ❖ mudhill

❖ malikal-mulk ❖

mumit ❖ muhyi

❖ hayy ❖

muntazim ❖ 'afuw

❖ 'adl ❖ aziz ❖

darr ❖ nafi'

❖ malik ❖ malikal-mulk ❖

chapter 7

Allah's Opposite Qualities
—Journey into Balance and Transcendence—

All the divine Names, in truth, exist as relationships within Allah. They are potentialities within God's infinite nature. It is fundamental to their very nature to exist relationally. It is helpful to delve into their inherent relationships as a way to uncover more of their meanings. Discussions of the depth of meaning within each divine Name and within each family of Names may then lead to a deeper realization of Allah.

Exploring the relationships that exist between the divine Names is a recurring theme in our work. As a general approach, we give particular attention to families or clusters of Names whose meanings overlap or that collectively reveal processes; to cognates, or Names that share the same linguistic root; to groupings based on the formal structure in the sound code; to the context of the Names appearance in the Qur'an, and to the important subject of the pairs of divine Names that reflect opposite meanings.

Mevlana Jalaluddin Rumi says the secret of Allah is found between the opposites. Looking deeply into pairs of opposite divine Names is interesting and significant. In this chapter we will consider some divine opposites. We recommend prayerfully reciting these opposite Names together as pairs.

Sincere devotion to Allah is a great benefit in the process of waking up to the divine qualities in one's own soul. We find that when students explore the divine opposites in such a way, they are brought into a balanced state in which they see God's causality working in both opposite extremes.

At this point in the process, a transcendent divine Name often suggests itself. Such a Name includes in its meanings both the apparent opposites and transcends the opposites. Repetition of such an inclusive and transcendent Name may then lead to completion of the inner process.

Ya Mu'izz, Ya Mudhill, Ya Malikal-Mulk

(yaa mu-'IZZ, yaa mu-<u>DH</u>ILL, yaa MAA-li-kal-MULK)

We begin with al-Mu'izz, the honorer or strengthener, and al-Mudhill, the dishonorer or weakener. God is the only source of being raised up in honor, and the only source of being brought down in shame. These divine qualities appear to be true opposites.

Let's begin at the human level. Right at the core of what most people experience in life is the play of honor and dishonor, of praise and blame. When we look at the honoring and dishonoring, the raising up and tearing down that manifest in human affairs, it seems clear at first glance that al-Mu'izz and al-Mudhill appear to embody not only opposite but also relative qualities. Are you honored or dishonored by others? How is your life colored by constant concern about how other people perceive you?

Al-Mudhill is a divine Name that can be quite problematical. Al-Mudhill is the one who takes you to the domain of the "lowest of the low," the place where your ego has self-identified with being worthless. But why would a divine quality make us feel terrible? The answer can be found in the meaning of the root from which the Name Al-Mudhill derives: to seek or yearn for the object of a long cherished wish.

In other words, al-Mudhill is the divine power that gives you a real desire and yearning to face your lower self, to bow low and to fully engage with the lowest regions of the self. Al-Mudhill brings you to your knees with your head on the ground. This is the outer form of *sajdah*, which means to bow down as in prayer. You go low. You surrender.

Being brought low in your life could mean the opportunity to learn from the presence of al-Mudhill. By going low—which you thought was terrible—you may actually be drawn nearer to Allah. By going through such a process, you come to see that no matter how you are perceived, you are always in the hands of Allah, who cannot be limited by humanity's ideas of high and low. You may be perceived as wonderful or you may be seen as beneath contempt, but in both instances you are completely held by God.

To help realize that how you are perceived is irrelevant, we recommend prayerful recitation of the opposites Ya Mudhill, Ya Mu'izz. In this way, through touching both extremes as divine emanations, you are gradually brought to an equanimity that encompasses the extremes. You come to understand that being perceived as high or low are, in the depth, just different ways of being in the hands of Allah.

At this point, if there is an extreme wound around self-worth it may be beneficial to work with the invocation of Ya 'Aziz. By invoking the omnipotent power behind al-Mu'izz, you are connected with the strength that comes from knowing the intrinsic worth of your immortal soul. You can then move on to the invocation of the transcendent Name Ya Malikul-Mulk. (In accord with Arabic grammar, when using the vocative "Ya" we say Ya Malikal-Mulk; without the "Ya" the name is slightly different: we say Malikul-Mulk.)

The realization of God's presence in both extremes of being honored and being shamed marks the appearance of the transcendent Name for this pair of opposites: Malikul-Mulk. The point of view of Malikul-Mulk is that all manifestation, no matter how transient and changeable, never leaves the hands of Allah. After you come to the realization of Malikul-Mulk, then you can break through the veil of darkness.

This veil of darkness may be experienced as a cover of feeling badly about yourself, of feeling badly about how you are perceived in the world. The ego has identified with this depth of negativity. So when you undertake the process described here of opening to God through the quality, and you go down into it, you see that through every experience of being brought low, al-Mudhill is really bringing you nearer to Allah. When that happens you awaken to a glow in *sajdah*. You truly prostrate yourself. There is a light within the surrender.

We are dealing with opposite qualities, and so it is natural to see a parallel in the other direction. There is also a veil of light. Suppose you were widely perceived as the best, smartest, richest person in the world. You still might be stuck in the limited, or relative, aspect of al-Mu'izz and think that your ego is the cause of such honor. Then you are in a different kind of trap. A cure for pride is needed. In other words, to grow in understanding, there are times when you actually need to be perceived as low. Then the overall dynamic of the situation will arouse al-Mudhill.

Whichever way you may be veiled, you may receive benefit by invoking Ya Mu'izz and Ya Mudhill together. That is a feature of this kind of practice. There is a process here that allows a sincere practitioner to see a truth arising that unites and transcends the apparent opposites of high and low.

Further Psychological Considerations

Al-Mudhill is usually experienced in our psyches as the humiliator. Consequently, it is very much connected with shame in the personality structure. *Dhalil*, a form of the same root, means not only being shamed but also includes in its meaning the feeling that you are the lowest of the low. This is the deepest humiliation. After you have been brought face to face with that stage of self-identity that has to do with being the lowest of the low, then you are able to rise.

You cannot rise until you hit the feeling, "I am worthless. I am the most shamed. I am the most deval-ued." That is the core of alienated identity. It constitutes the deepest level of the paranoia. Having reached the bottom, you are isolated in the lowest domain of existence, where because of a deep woundedness a kind of narcissistic self-identity is generated from the feeling, "I am the least of the least."

There is the pervasive but deeply hidden feeling of "I am unworthy and I don't have what it takes." What happens is your whole personality structure is created as a defense against having to feel this sense of deficiency. So unless you find the key to fully penetrate into this most defended place of self-identification, you cannot rise. Anything that stops short of this deepest place will leave you still need-ing to defend against feeling some hidden deficiency.

We see that al-Mudhill is the Name of the one that takes you to the domain of the lowest of the low, which is the original ego identity. And that's the place of shame. The shame there is two-fold. There is the shame that comes from feeling rejected by humanity. The other shame is an anguish of soul that comes from feeling rejected or abandoned by God. When you personally bottom out in such a place, it is natural for you to feel like doing nothing about all this negativity, because after all, you have identified with being the lowest of the low, so there is no escape. Now al-Mu'izz comes to the rescue.

Before, we saw how al-Mudhill delivers you from debilitating pride when you are caught up in the relative aspect of al-Mu'izz and your ego has identified itself in a grandiose way. Now we see how al-Mu'izz can deliver you from despair when you are identified with the relative aspect of the lowness of al-Mudhill. At this stage, al-Mu'izz, the one who honors, arises as causality from Allah and offers you a real spiritual breakthrough.

Our strong recommendation is to recite these opposite Names together and not separately. You would say, "Ya Mu'izz, Ya Mudhill." That leads to the integrative or transcendent experience. It points to the majesty with which all things are held in the hands of God. Then when that feeling begins to emerge you can invoke the divine Name Ya Malikal-Mulk. The transcendence and inclusiveness of this Name, brought up after ripening with the opposites, allows you to open to the realization of the omni-presence of Allah.

Through invoking the opposite Names, you are led to a transcendent Name and are now able to rise above the limitation of being caught in only seeing what are called secondary causes. Part of our purpose in writing this book is to continually point to the essence of the divine Names as the primary cause, and thus to help spiritual travelers overcome being limited by their concepts of secondary causes.

Ya Mumit, Ya Muhyi, Ya Hayy

(yaa mu-MEET, yaa MUḤ-yee, yaa ḤAIYY)

Al-Mumit is the one who brings death, and al-Muhyi is the one who brings life. These two divine Names manifest as opposites, and we can safely say that most human beings have a more reverential feeling for the one who causes life than they have for the one who causes death.

We need to get deeper than this surface layer of fears and ideas about life and death if we wish to bring clarity of understanding to the discussion of these two Names of Allah. The sound code shows that al-Muhyi and al-Mumit are causatives: the one who causes life and the one who causes death.

To properly understand what it means for a word to have the form of a causative in the sound code, we first need to understand the difference between a primary cause and secondary causes. From the standpoint of secondary causes, sperm and egg cause life; accidents, disease and old age cause death. From the standpoint of primary cause, Allah is the ultimate cause of life and death.

In the Qur'an, death is said to be a temporary state in the same way that we think of life as a temporary state. By refusing to separate the apparently opposite emanations of these two qualities, because they are both divine, you are led through inner contemplation and inquiry to the reality of the ever-living one, who transcends and embraces the phenomenon of what we call life and death.

Let's look further into other aspects of these two Names. Another meaning of al-Muhyi is related to *al-hayawaan*, corresponding to *an-nafs ul-'ammaarah*, which is called the animal soul. In human beings, it is a life force that appears in our egos with tremendous density and heat. Typical of this particular level of ego is quickened anger and, especially, quickened lust. When *an-nafs ul-'ammaarah* dominates, something is out of balance.

It is good to be alive and to have all the feelings that come with being alive, even such feelings as mentioned above. Yet, at the same time, we need to balance this animal tendency with al-Mumit. It softens these feelings and balances these urges, because al-Mumit brings death into them.

Pairing the two Names in repetition can be highly beneficial for those who feel they have lost their vitality, or who are so depressed they want to die. Even in this kind of depressed condition, instead of saying Ya Muhyi alone, we recommend calling out Ya Muhyi, Ya Mumit, as this lends stability and balance. For a very extreme condition it may be appropriate to recite only the single Name that is the antidote. However, when the emergency passes, there should be a second stage of practice where this person is asked to balance their two urges by invoking Ya Mumit, Ya Muhyi.

Pairing these Names in practice is especially useful for someone who has suffered the death of a loved one. At such a time the only practice we might suggest is repetition of the invocation, "Ya Mumit, Ya Muhyi." In Biblical terms this is expressed by the phrase, "The Lord giveth and the Lord taketh away."

The number of days devoted to this practice should not arbitrarily be cut short. Everyone should be allowed ample space to work through the grieving process. Invoking these opposites, and reflecting on them as aspects of God's nature, offers a container for their process to continue and for healing to begin. In the ripeness of time, a counselor can recommend going further.

By invoking the cause of death and the cause of life together as a related pair, your grief is ultimately brought to an inner balance, and you become ready to accept a reality that is transcendent and ever-living: al-Hayy. Now the *kamali* or perfect Name Ya Hayy appears as the meeting place of the *jamali* Name Ya Muhyi and the *jalali* Name Ya Mumit.

Shaykh Junayd said that when we are contracted God sends us joy and ecstasy, and when we are expanded God sends us contraction. We should recognize, in both cases, that God is the source. In the third stage, Junayd says that sometimes God withholds both expansion and contraction to lead us to essence itself, everlasting love.

Sufis understand the physical death referred to by al-Mumit to be a symbol for *fana*, physical transformation and dissolving of egocentricity. The anniversary observance of a teacher's death, the *'urs*, is actually considered to be similar to a marriage celebration. The famous hadith, "Die before you die," is really about spiritual death and rebirth, *fana* and *baqa*.

When Allah sends human beings death of any type, be it spiritual, mental, or physical, that death is a vehicle of spiritual transformation. Al-Mumit is the cause of anything that ends or passes away. A kind of spiritual death, a death of ego, is necessary for you to awaken to the innate divinity of the real self. As Mevlana Rumi says, "When have I ever grown less by dying?" The "passing away" of all temporal phenomena is one half of the proof of the existence of al-Hayy, the ever-living.

Seen in this way, Al-Mumit is drawing the lover toward the beloved, stage by stage. This process ultimately leads to *liqa'*, the union of lovers. The lover realizes with every death of the self that he or she is being drawn in toward the beloved.

Mediating your relationship with death by viewing it in this way reverses your ordinary aversive outlook about it. The very nature of the infinite being demands that al-Mumit and al-Muhyi, *fana* and *baqa*, go together. You can't have one without the other. They are alternating aspects of the same thing.

This leads us to see that desperately clinging to life is as imbalanced as actively seeking death. What we call life and death are both transient states from the divine perspective. There is a continuous cycle of the flow of being that is called the arc of ascent and descent. Our whole discussion here moves us toward understanding this great circle; we devote Chapter 13 to the arc of ascent and descent and the divine Names that serve to illustrate its nature.

In coming into manifestation, creation is going from the invisible to the visible world. That is the activity of al-Muhyi. Al-Mumit returns things from the land of the living back to the invisible world. The whole process goes in an endless circle.

Al-Muhyi begins in al-Hayy, the transcendent all-inclusive ever-livingness. Through the process of birth and life it eventually approaches al-Mumit. Then al-Mumit goes through the process of dying and shedding of ego-self and ultimately returns to al-Hayy. The beginning is the end and the end is the beginning. In Chapter 13, The Arc of Ascent and Descent, al-Mumit and al-Muhyi are treated along with al-Mubdi' and al-Muid, two Names that also deal with beginnings and endings.

The ever-living one is a reality beyond time and space that transcends and embraces the two apparently opposite qualities of birth and death. 'Ibn 'Arabi's view of the invisible hidden reality (al-Batin) and the fully visible one (al-Zahir) takes the same path. This type of circular map may well apply for all of the opposite Names. For a more detailed discussion of opposites viewed in this way, see Chapter 13, where the Names surrounding the *'arsh* (Heart Throne of God) and the arcs of ascent and descent are discussed.

The divine Names al-Ba'ith and al-Warith describe in another way the same process of *fana* and *baqa*. In this context, we might say that all human beings can be described as renters. Through death,

God is the sole possessor, or inheritor, of what we truly have. That is what remains. This is part of the meaning of al-Ba'ith and al-Warith. They are fully discussed in Chapter 21, Dying to the False Idea of Self and Actualizing the Knowledge of Unity.

We suggest that, as a way to fully open to the process of inner transformation expressed by *fana* and *baqa*, it may be fruitful to contemplate these four divine Names together: Ya Mumit, Ya Muhyi, Ya Warith, Ya Ba'ith.

Ya Muntaqim, Ya 'Adl, Ya 'Afuw, Ya 'Aziz

(yaa mun-TA-ḳim, yaa 'ADL, yaa 'A-fooww, yaa 'a-ZEEZ)

How do you like the description of God as the one who takes revenge? We felt uncomfortable with that simple gloss of one of the divine Names. Thus began for us a most interesting exploration. We started to probe the meaning of the problematical divine Name, al-Muntaqim, which is usually translated as something like "The Avenger," and then we looked for its opposite. This proved an unexpectedly fruitful process, and we think it worth describing in some detail.

The root of the word *muntaqim* in Arabic is *maqaam*, which means to take revenge on somebody. The sound code tells us *muntaqim* is both reflexive and reciprocal. This is an important complication that needs to be considered, and we will deal with it in a moment. There's an initial problem that should be faced first. The most puzzling part about a divine Name with this root meaning of revenge is that, even from a strictly legal point of view, taking vengeance or revenge on anyone is prohibited. In virtually all ethical and moral codes, including the Islamic *sharee'ah*, people are taught to avoid revenge.

Even if you see morality as spontaneously arising from your heart in its natural state, when you are feeling unity with all of creation, even from this point of view, it would not be wise to attack your own self. So vengeance still would be ruled out. Vengeance is lack of compassion. Basically, it is justice without compassion. Yet, al-Muntaqim is one of the aspects of Allah. And so to put the problem in crude terms the question is, "Why is it okay for God to do it but not for me to do it?"

In the conventional view, al-Muntaqim has come to mean revenge. Human beings have a tendency to settle scores. Vengeance is an attempt to achieve a kind of balance, but an attempt that is without compassion. However, it is impossible to imagine that there can be a divine quality that is essentially absent of compassion. So, we contend that this interpretation of the meaning of al-Muntaqim as vengeance cannot be correct. It must have another meaning.

Everyone understands vengeance quite well in everyday language. It is hard to avoid vengeful behavior. However, we all need to find a way to leave it up to Allah, because God is the only one who can balance out rights and wrongs. God is the balancer *with* compassion, with fairness. We think we can show that the activity of al-Muntaqim is best understood as the action of the great balancer.

Human beings have fractured personalities. Each person sees primarily from his or her own particular and limited perspective. "I am going to get back at him." But even the thought, "I'm going to get back at him some day," is a poison to your inner spirit, a kind of disease. Awakening to the reality of al-Muntaqim is intended to cure that vengeful tendency in yourself and allow you to surrender the poison. You do this by letting go of your personal grip on it. You truly leave justice to Allah. God is the only one who fully knows justice.

From the vantage point of a fractured personality it is natural to imagine that a balancing action of the divine being is revenge. But we need to learn to take the rancor out of the quality we are attributing to the divine consciousness.

We think it is more accurate to call this balancing action a powerful application of the principle of reciprocity: "As you sow, so shall you reap." Repetition of Ya Muntaqim might then become a remedy for you when you become trapped in a cycle of vengeance in your heart. It presents an avenue of change—a way to recognize that Allah is the only one who understands how to maintain a balance with compassion for all.

To deepen our understanding of al-Muntaqim, a crucial point to understand is that, according to the sound code of the Arabic language, the word *muntaqim* is reciprocal. Its activity is a two-way street. We might have to wrestle with this a bit intellectually to understand what that reciprocal quality means. How could we take vengeance on God?

On deeper reflection, we recognize there is a human feeling in us that wants revenge on God. We are mad at God. We feel wounded and disconnected and abandoned by God. And, in fact, we do take revenge upon God every day. This is a very common, normal state. "I'm smoking a lot because I'm mad at God. I don't meditate because I am mad at God. If the light and the blessings come, I go and spoil it because I'm mad at God." But it is also reciprocated.

Whatever we put into the universe comes back to us, and we get out as much as we put in. But, with God, the justice, or karmic balancing if you like, will be administered with a compassionate understanding.

Objectively speaking, as human beings we grow through pain. Sometimes we grow through joy, but often it is through pain. And then, sometimes, there are really big tragedies to face. And through all this you may come to understand that the whole drama of life can be viewed as a setup for you to become illuminated. It is almost as if your unconscious has hired the universe to provide exactly what it needs to grow. And in some cases, you may become part of enormous tragedies. Through all of this, somehow, you learn to experience the hand of God as an equalizer.

Many people say, "I am benevolent. I am not vengeful." But when a physician of the heart challenges them and says, "Show me all the ways you are vengeful," they will show you how their unconscious is actually vengeful all the time. They are habitually cutting off from the light, from the essence. Once this is seen they can move forward.

It is uncertain how a person's unconscious may respond to repetition of Ya Muntaqim alone, and so we hesitate to prescribe it by itself. We recommend it be done as part of a pairing, such as with Ya 'Afuw or Ya 'Adl. These pairings will be discussed later.

It is wise, especially when dealing with extremes in the human psyche, to always give a balancing pair of divine Names to work with. In this way the Names can become better instruments of transformation. This psychological principle led us to look for something to balance the force of al-Muntaqim.

The worst part of the present misunderstanding of al-Muntaqim, from a religious point of view, is that it seems that some people have used their misinterpretation of this Name to justify their ego's right to be vengeful in the Name of Allah. Instead of turning to Allah and away from the ego's lust for revenge, they have turned the whole process upside down! As a result of this confusion, horrible atrocities have been perpetrated by those who mistakenly believe that they are entitled to act out their rage on behalf of Allah.

There is a better way for us to understand al-Muntaqim than as the avenger. The concept of revenge suggests some personal dissatisfaction that must be assuaged. We should understand al-Muntaqim as the balancer, the one who has to bring things back into balance, even through what may appear from our ordinary human perspective to be a violent act. For example, if there is an earthquake, you don't generally think God is angry; that would be a projection of your ego condition on God.

It is crucial for the spiritual traveler to find a clearer way to look at the so-called unhappy or wrathful face of God. Making God "the avenger" implies that God is getting back at something or someone because of holding a grudge. It creates confusion. Al-Muntaqim needs to be understood as a correcting force, a dramatic correcting force. At this critical juncture, the process of finding a balancing divine Name or balancing Names to al-Muntaqim becomes very important.

Al-Muntaqim always appears next to al-'Afuw, perfect forgiveness, in the lists of the 99 beautiful Names. We see them paired in the Qur'an.[40] As with other opposite pairs, it is significant that al-Muntaqim and al-'Afuw occur together. By looking at both Names in a single verse or a cluster of verses we can usually get a sense of how they interact with each other.

These two Names are also contrasted in the Thesaurus: al-Muntaqim, "unforgiving;" al-'Afuw, "forgiving." When al-'Afuw is fully explored, as it is in Chapter 8, what emerges is a whole cluster of qualities, grades, and processes of divine forgiveness.

In the Qur'anic passage mentioned above where these divine qualities are joined, we are also pointed to a transcendent Name for this pair: al-'Adl. The essence of al-'Adl is a fluid, merciful quality that mediates and brings all into balance and harmony. Al-'Adl is the balanced and the balancer, the harmonious balance of all things.

Actually, al-'Adl balances all the opposite Names, but this role is particularly true for al-Muntaqim and al-'Afuw. Al-'Adl in this case is that which mediates or balances these two attributes, which we are describing as the "lord of reciprocity" and the "complete forgiver."

It will be helpful now to fully bring our attention to other aspects of al-Muntaqim. To begin with, we will look at *muntaqim* simply as a word. We have all these negatives associated with the word's ordinary meaning: hateful, spiteful, angry, merciless, cruel, hardhearted, mean, harsh, severe, and compassionless.

We look upon all the Names of Allah as a great pharmacopoeia. It might just be that a divine Name that brings along with it such negative associations needs to be part of a homeopathic treatment. In that case, it would be prescribed for someone who is feeling mean, harsh, cruel, compassionless, and unforgiving.

The root meaning for *muntaqim* includes to find fault, to dislike, or disapprove, but it also has the more positive meanings of the center of the road, to be strong and steady, and to be a reliable guide. In this positive respect it is rather like al-Matin.

Al-Muntaqim doesn't appear in the Qur'an in the particular grammatical form that it is found in the lists of Names. (This is also true of some other Names, such as al-Basit.) One form of *muntaqim* does, however, appear four times in the Qur'an.[41] Each appearance is identical: the phrase is *Allahu 'azeezun dhu-ntiqaam*.[42] The word *dhu-ntiqaam* combines *dhul*, which means essence or suchness, or simply "that," with *ntiqaam*, which is a form of *muntaqim*.

Now this word "dhul" is used only one other place in the 99 beautiful Names: Dhul Jalali wal 'Ikram. Allah is *jalal*—overwhelmingly brilliant, like looking directly into the Sun. In essence, Allah has this hard *jalal*-like center. It is completely reliable and uncompromising. And it is from the standpoint of divine essence that Allah can be seen to manifest as al-Muntaqim, as that which seeks equity and balance.

To richen the picture, al-'Aziz also comes into these passages paired with al-Muntaqim, and its quality is a kind of riddle or enigma. We can relate to it in two ways because al-'Aziz itself has two meanings. *'Aziz* means powerful, and it also means rare, precious, and highly valued. The divine Name al-'Aziz is both strong and rare. An eagle is *'azizah*. *'Uzayzah* means a young eaglet, which is a rare phenomenon in nature.

Every single time a form of al-Muntaqim appears in the Qur'an, it never appears alone. This tells us about its need to be balanced by other qualities. In all its references to al-Muntaqim, the Qur'an is pointing out a door for our entering into a relationship with this quality, and that opening is through al-'Aziz. Quite a balancing factor is being offered to us by this Qur'anic pairing. It is because of hidden teachings like this that Sufis regard the Qur'an as a text encoded with the inner mysteries of the divine Names.

We are suggesting the proper way to call on Ya Muntaqim is as a vehicle to change your consciousness away from seeing God as a vengeful God. You do this by taking the meanness out of it and recognizing that al-Muntaqim is simply a process of creating equity or balance. Al-Muntaqim is the reliable guide to that balance and equity.

The way we get to this dimension of the divine Name is through invoking Ya 'Aziz. The strength of Al-'Aziz is not in a hardening of ego but in the identification of your true nature with the soul, whose value is boundless. Invoking this quality is the best way to get to the real meaning of al-Muntaqim.

A Homeopathic Approach to Our Impulse for Revenge

We may want to begin with the homeopathic approach, although it seems a bit backwards. Such an approach would require that you tap into that negative stuff, that merciless revengeful urge. Then you can begin to understand that what is manifesting is a form of strength that is getting balanced. It is a strength that allows you to move toward balance.

When this is accomplished, you are more prepared to come out of that state into al-'Aziz, which is a kind of a sweet strength. Such a realization will allow you ultimately to turn to al-'Afuw, the true opposite of al-Muntaqim and more fully complete the process. We are looking at al-Muntaqim as the balancer, or the one that seeks equity or reliable principle in the universe. It is not vindictive. It is simply correcting the imbalances.

One of the severe imbalances in the human system has to do with a certain kind of love. It is called *'ishq*. The wine that runs in the blood is called *'ishq*. It is a pomegranate-like essence. When this *'ishq*, which is the most ecstatic and passionate of all the loves, is frustrated, it creates imbalance in the system. It is as if the blood itself gets poisoned, and then the mind cannot think clearly, the heart cannot feel clearly, and the body gets sick and weak from all of this.

This particular passionate, ecstatic love manifests at the Oedipal stage of the child. When the passion at that stage is allowed, then the pomegranate is integrated. When this passion is not allowed, and, for example the daughter's love is rejected by the father, or the mother feels jealous and in competition with the daughter, then the wine of *'ishq* becomes vinegar. It becomes toxic. It transforms into a deep desire for revenge.

When the jealousy and the desire for revenge arise, a primal passion is moving you. Here you can see the ego reflection of al-Muntaqim coming in, and it reveals the part in you that seeks revenge. This revengeful impulse gets activated the most when you fall in love. When you are in a relationship and are frustrated in love, revenge comes up. You feel passionately.

With any form of rejection by your partner, no matter how small, you tend to go right to revenge. You want to be the Muntaqim. You are seeking al-Muntaqim at the level of your passion where it is felt as revenge and anger and frustration. A deeper psychological level is reached if a physician of the heart allows the revenge to come through fully in the student's mind.

The student will then express revenge on a certain person, or revenge on God, or revenge on the universe. When that energy is given the chance to completely explode and release, what happens is that the pomegranate (*'ishq*) starts to flow in the system, and that naturally recreates a sense of balance. So spiritual students may then open into the depth of al-Muntaqim, as the restorer of the balance.

The way to this realization is through first engaging with primal passion. You need to first embrace that feeling. You embrace the ostensibly negative Name as being not separate from the divine reality, and you take it in like a homeopathic medicine. You are invited to feel revenge, and keep feeling it until revenge is released. You do this instead of always trying first to reduce it. You ask yourself what are all the ways you can have revenge? If you had the chance to revenge, who would you take revenge on? Mother? Father? Lover? Humanity? The universe? God?

When the entire world is completely reduced into your ultimately taking revenge on God for all the suffering in existence, what happens is that the pomegranate opens, and that can create a sense of harmony and balance in the system. You now have a sense that everything is running in perfect rhythm and harmony. You reach inner harmony, al-'Adl, and every part is functioning according to its natural capacity.

Fully calling on the divine *'ishq* enables you to ultimately release your feeling of vindictiveness and instead uncover an inner empowerment. However, the beginning stages of this process feel like revenge and vindictiveness. One thing to remember about the *jalali* Names of God is that focusing on power can be a very seductive activity. You really need to be alert to where you can get stuck in misunderstanding. We saw this quite dramatically in our earlier discussion of al-Muntaqim.

People make the mistake of imagining God as if God's qualities are really the limited human qualities we are so familiar with, and then they may even identify themselves as God's agent for dispensing the quality. Even with al-'Aziz, as with all the *jalali* Names, you can get seduced into taking the power in and identifying it with your ego. The power you experience belongs to Allah and not your ego. The fundamental mistake is to not understand this.

One thing to reemphasize from the sound code is that the eighth grammatical form, of which al-Muntaqim is a member, is reciprocal. That *teh* makes it reciprocal. It makes it interactive. So when you try to just have al-Muntaqim and cut it off from al-'Afuw, you are already out of balance! But because the inner meaning of the Name itself is intrinsically reciprocal, you will be corrected. You will be corrected from above, so to speak, and that will be a kind of reciprocity. It is exactly like a circle. That is the grammatical form of al-Muntaqim.

There is a physical metaphor offered by a form of the verb *'afuw*: the wind completely erases the footprints that have been made in the desert sand, as if no one had ever walked there. This strongly suggests an awareness of not even noticing the fault. At the beginning stage of forgiveness you may notice the fault or choose to overlook it. But al-'Afuw is beyond that. It is the exact opposite of al-Muntaqim, and it is what al-Muntaqim ultimately needs to be paired with.

If the place where you are stuck is your ego identification with power, you won't be able to make the inner journey to al-'Afuw. You will just understand al-Muntaqim as the power to take vengeance on somebody. However, movement can be attained if you begin to contemplate the quality of al-'Aziz as a more refined strength, as rare or graceful. The sense of power that comes will be detached from the ego and you will start to be able to forgive.

Remember, to forgive is a type of *fana*. You give away the power, or the illusion that you possess the power. Then you can stop holding onto the vengeful, spiteful stuff you think you have on somebody. The more you stop identifying the ego with power, or your illusion of power, the more your inner process builds forgiveness.

What contrasts al-Muntaqim with al-'Afuw is the inner relationship of each Name with power. When you are stuck in the ego identification with power, you need to realize al-'Aziz. The power of al-'Aziz is precious and carries with it a sense of utmost dignity, and this is what will allow you to proceed. In truth, it is a dignity that arises from knowing the preciousness of the human soul. The strength that you feel is married with an experience of inner value, of self worth.

The ultimate stand of the ego is that it wants to take itself and replace God. "Since there is no God, I will be God. I'll be the most powerful; I'll be anything; I'll do anything." Actually, that stand is exhausting and it serves to weaken the ego because the ego thinks it must do everything and that there is nobody else who can do anything.

A physician of the heart will always uncover fear when they examine the grandiosity of the ego's stand of "I am the ultimate one." The ego's grandiosity becomes deflated by the invocation of Ya 'Aziz, because al-'Aziz actually *is* the ultimate strength. So it makes sense that the way to *tawbah* (repentance) and to *'afuw* (complete forgiveness) is through relinquishing the ego power. It begins with *'istighfaar*, the healing salve of the essence of forgiveness. That is why Sufis repeat *'astaghfiru-llaah* so much. It expresses a yearning for forgiveness for all the times they have become unaware of the divine presence.

Al-'Afuw is a lofty and sublime station, but how can we really contrast it with al-Muntaqim? What is the most profound thing we can say? In one sense they are one and the same. They bring balance. But al-Muntaqim approaches balance from the lower end of the scale, and al-'Afuw from the higher. Given a band of existence, if we consider the lower aspect and seek balance, we have al-Muntaqim. Al-'Afuw engages the higher aspect, and if balance is attained at that level, the lower aspect is balanced as well. Both Names are balancing in their activity, but the action of each Name occurs in a different domain.

The domain of the 'Afuw is much more refined than the domain of the Muntaqim. Al-'Afuw is dealing with emotional hurt, wounds of the heart, while al-Muntaqim is dealing with primal instincts. Al-Muntaqim's balancing activity works through the primitive energies.

Primitive energy is like the energy of the tiger looking at the deer and jumping. The tiger is not thinking. It is not feeling. There is no emotion here. What we have is a big charge, a big libidinal charge. Such energy is very primitive and very strong. It just jumps for the kill. Al-'Afuw's balancing activity is working through the imbalance that has been engendered by a wounding of the heart. It is a terrain of emotional collapse. But both divine qualities are seeking the same thing: the balancing of the system. They are seeking Al-'Adl.

Al-'Afuw corrects the imbalance with forgiveness, and it helps us grow by coming to understand that in reality the wounding impressions are actually nonexistent. It allows us to see that the universe heals itself. Now we can stop looking at our own wounds as being something personal to identify with.

Al-Muntaqim works in a different way, correcting the imbalance with powerful action to right the scales. It requires us to detach our ego and surrender to that correcting presence. We now see these opposite Names Al-Muntaqim and Al-'Afuw are intimately related. This helps us realize they both are doorways to the divine.

And then al-'Adl comes in to unite the two, to provide a union of the opposites. This is not just the act of balancing some negative qualities and some positive qualities: it is balancing the most negative and the most positive.

Al-'Adl is related to *al-miyzaan*, the scales, the balance. The Qur'an says the whole universe is set up in accordance with the manifestation of al-'Adl, or else it would fall apart immediately.[43] Seeking balance in everything is like a universal constant, a movement toward the One. Specifically, with regard to this pair of Names, it is like two pans of a scale. The opposites move toward the unity of balance. This is the activity of al-'Adl.

We need to avoid the conventional translation of al-'Adl as "justice," because of the way the word justice is used with a connotation of revenge in today's world. Even 60 or 70 years ago justice still meant harmonious balance.

Repetition of Ya 'Adl is useful for those who lack equanimity and are imbalanced in their minds and their behavior. Repetition of Ya 'Adl, which in itself is the essence of balance, can be used as a corrective. It has a constant harmonizing function, which all can recognize.

Al-'Adl comes between every particle of creation and throughout the whole fabric of the *'asma' ul-husnaa*, the 99 Names. It offers a vehicle for balancing all the pairs of Names, but it is also serves as a super balance for all the opposing Names and all the opposing manifestations. Al-'Adl is complete embodiment, and that means integration.

To bring balance between al-Muntaqim and al-'Afuw, it is necessary for al-'Adl to embody the integration of feeling and instinct. The instinctual nature comes from a certain level of *nafs*. *An-nafs ul-'ammaarah* is the instinctual *nafs*, and is the lowest of the seven gradations of *nafs*. (See Chapter 17, The Seven Levels of the *Nafs*.) According to Shaykh Junayd and other Sufis, on the opposite end of the scale of *nafs* is the *ruh*, which could be called higher spirit or higher self, or soul. This is more like al-'Afuw. The needed integration must take place within the heart.

In one of the sacred traditions of the Prophet Muhammad, called sacred because he speaks in the voice of Allah, it is said, "The heavens and the earth do not contain Me, but the heart of my lover contains Me." The heart has the capacity (al-Wasi') to contain heaven and earth, or in other words, the higher and lower realms. A real capacity for integration can come with the embodiment of al-'Adl in the heart center.

An important piece for us in any exploration of the divine Names is to understand each one's practical application to the human condition. An inspiring aspect about this project is that in the course of investigating the meanings of a particular Name, certain indications arise to guide us in using it for specific diseases and human frailties. One approach, which is like allopathic medicine, offers the opposite as a remedy. For instance, roughly speaking, if you have a vengeful type of person, you might give them Ya 'Afuw to repeat.

Naturally, there are many positive meanings in the great variety of words which have the same root as the divine Name, and we like to explore those. However, there sometimes are negative meanings within words sharing the same root as the divine Name, meanings that are descriptive of diseases. Consequently, we feel there is also an important place for homeopathic remedies, where the physician uses a small amount of the very same quality that is similar to the problem.

This may be a good time to relate an old joke, or truism, that every Arabic word has four meanings: the primary meaning, the secondary meaning which means the exact opposite of the primary meaning, something to do with sex, and something to do with camels.

Ya Darr, Ya Nafi'

(yaa DAARR, yaa NAA-fi')

An-Nafi' is the only source whose activity allows human beings to make use of anything for a higher good. Ad-Darr is the only source whose activity produces our failure to do so. Roughly speaking, it appears that we are talking about what appears to be good versus evil.

In the sound code of the Arabic language, these two Names have the same grammatical form, even though it doesn't appear so at first glance. Their form indicates that an-Nafi' and ad-Darr share a defining quality: "the only source of…, the unique, the only one who…" They also share the quality of being inherent and natural. We will examine them together.

An-Nafi' means to profit, to benefit, to take advantage of, to make use of for good purposes. *Nafa'a* is the root. It means both to use and to benefit from. It is always contrasted with ad-Darr, even in the common Arabic dictionary. The earth-plane meaning for Nafi' is more than simply "beneficial." It means to use a remedy for a good purpose, namely to cure a disease.

There is a specific sense in an-Nafi' of purification from a disease using water. We can think of all the ways we use water in purification—on bodies, clothes, food, and so forth. This specific sense of how an-Nafi' embodies purification should be incorporated into our use of it in the pharmacopoeia.

While an-Nafi' gives us a sense of a kind of remedy, its opposite, ad-Darr, gives us more specifics about the disease! Ad-Darr's primary meaning is just the opposite of al-Nafi'. So taken together we have, "the only source of…benefit" and "the only source of…harm," and so on. To fully go through the process of recognizing God in both these aspects is priceless from a theological perspective. God is the only source of both. It forces one into acknowledging *la 'ilaha 'illa allah.* Unity alone exists.

Mevlana Jalaluddin Rumi has said that the secret of discovering the essence of Allah is in the opposite Names. We can actually find a way to essence through the relativity of these opposites. By consciously invoking both opposite Names, we come to see logically that there is no secondary agent for evil. It just wipes out the whole notion of a separate agency, as it is called in theology.

It is a wakeup call for western theological consciousness, a call to get us to the totally unitive state. There is no other agent but Allah. We recommend reciting Ya Darr and Ya Nafi' together for balance and to lead to this unitive realization.

We may come to recognize that our difficulties ultimately enable us to become self-sufficient—not in our small self, but in Allah. In fact, the word for self-sufficient is *daroorah* , which is one of the nouns that comes out of ad-Darr. Great difficulties also make us realize that what we thought we could lean on is illusory, and we have nothing else to lean on but Allah.

An-Nafi' can be a cure for the specific disease of blindness. But *dareer* , a form that comes from ad-Darr, means to become blind, to lose one's sight. An-Nafi' comes to restore the sight, and one's sight becomes purified, literally purified with water. Ad-Darr has two primary earthly meanings: to come near, and to deprive someone or put someone in a state of want or need. First we are led to the meaning "self-sufficient," and then the other shoe drops. The word itself points us to our need for Allah.

The story of Job raises the question of how the good can suffer. God takes children away, property away, health away. But all of that suffering leads to Job becoming self-sufficient, being able to stand self-sufficient before God. That is to say, he becomes self-sufficient in the sense of identifying with the higher self. We now see how Ya Darr could be invoked to refine our *nafs* for a specific purpose—so that we can willingly surrender to the one and only being and become less dependent on secondary causes.

Being patient and long-suffering are tests of the *nafs*. On the last day, or what is called the day of judgment, no one will be blind to the face of God. There will be no disagreements because the eye of the heart will be opened. This "last day" is not a day on the calendar: from God's perspective, the last day is the first day. It's called a "day" because it happens in the light. But we can say that in that moment there will be an end to all confusion and disagreement. Hearts and minds will be truly opened. All will see reality from their own perspective, but there will be nothing to disagree about.

The Qur'an always talks about events that occur in what is called the unseen world. When you recite the divine Names one of the things that happens is that time and space are very, very different. The whole world is a cosmic display of divine Names, manifestations of the Beautiful Names. Everywhere you look is an aspect of Allah. Everywhere you turn is the face of God. Questions about when and where fade in importance.

Reciting this pair of opposites, Ya Darr, Ya Nafi', may provide a deep healing for episodes of victimization. It allows you to come to understand how cause and effect operate in your life. Things don't happen just because God is in a particular mood today. It is your responsibility to see how you differentiate. If you turn in a particular way, a particular kind of influx comes, and if you turn another way, a different kind of influx happens.

If you are stuck in the place where you are playing the victim, saying to yourself that God is doing everything and who are you to do anything, then it is time to open the eye in the heart. The blindness (*darrir*) in the heart is the blindness of holding onto the little self. Most people think the ego is centralized in the head. The belief system about your ego is centralized in the head, but the real sense of the ego is centralized in the middle of the chest, in the heart.

Human blindness happens because of the clinging in our hearts to that identity of being separate. That is causing the blindness. It causes us to experience ourselves as separate from the world and disconnected from God. In that state, stuff always happens *to* us. It is like being a perpetual victim.

Then, with each dimension you enter, the *nafs* takes on an identity that reacts and identifies with the opposite of that dimension. For example, if you enter the dimension of seeing, the identity that the *nafs* will grasp would say, "I am blind." If you enter the dimension of power, the identity that is in the ego would be, "I am weak."

So each attribute of Allah, every divine Name, reveals a layer in the ego that believes it is the opposite. It is natural for us to take this negative view because we habitually and constantly are identifying ourselves as a separate ego. In the domain of ad-Darr the ego says, "I am the victim."

A student needs to come to the recognition that all the layers of a healthy ego are attributes of Allah. In this way you identify with all the Attributes of Allah. There is really no other self, no other being but Allah. All things are aspects of that reality, and the divine attributes are now seen as different identities that you may experience within yourself.

When people are blinded by self-pity, blinded by the feeling of victimization, they believe that the goodness or badness in the universe happens to them. They believe they are not an active participant. Then a physician of the heart needs to show them their own causality in the process. If you keep banging your head against the wall you will have headaches.

By reciting these divine Names Ya Darr, Ya Nafi' as a pair, you may be graced to transcend both of them and relate to *al-jam'ah*, the unity of soul. In Sufism, this is called *ruh*. You identify with *ruh*. The full light of the soul is your real self. You no longer cling to self-pity, or to the idea of self-benefit. You become integrated or unified in *jaami'ah*.

When a physician of the heart begins to focus on the process of victimization with a student, the student responds with statements or feelings like "I must have done something pretty awful to deserve this." From the first encounter, whenever the counselor works with a negative issue that is arising, the student will blame and attack himself or herself.

In every domain the physician of the heart enters, every issue he or she deals with, it is necessary to pay attention to this negative activity of self-blame, which is the activity of the superego. The superego is playing the role the person has imagined for God to play. It admonishes, it punishes, and it condemns. Students are in an imagined day of judgment and they are passing judgment upon themselves.

Over time they awaken to how much judgment there is inside them and how much they empower the superego to judge as if it were God. It is easy enough to say, "Leave that stuff to Allah. Don't play God." But they first need to recognize that they have already blindly enthroned a God inside—but that God is a fake! They have identified out a separate *nafs*, the superego part, and given it the role of playing God. It has no *hikmah*, no wisdom. It has no heart. The superego does not go beyond "You have been wrong, and you are bad." It simply cracks the whip.

When you begin to grasp that you are carrying an idol inside, which is a false God that has nothing to do with God at all, then you can demolish that idol and address all your shortcomings with more openness to change. You can dismantle both the judgment and the judge. The superego is no longer in the way. Then the guidance can come and God can begin to reveal to you whatever you have done, including the distortions and the shortcomings. And when guidance comes, it comes along with understanding and healing.

Whenever guilt appears, or the sense of deficiency arises, it also brings with it the presence of the superego. You need to liberate yourself from this impression. Only then can you go deeper into cause and effect. You awaken to your own causality in the process. "I did this and this is the result."

An-nafs ul-'ammaarah and *daroorah* carry the meaning "to compel." It is the *nafs* that compels. We just saw how it acts in a compelling way in the activity of the superego. This compelling *nafs* is what must be softened and dissolved.

If you call on Ya Darr, along with Ya Nafi', you surrender the *nafs*, piece by piece, and become more able to go with the divine flow. You can go where ad-Darr takes you because you know it is going to take you to a patient, refined place. It is *fana*, the place of self-effacement. It comes with a kind of poverty. It is where the ego dissolves. That is where ad-Darr is taking us.

You have the option of looking at every episode where ad-Darr manifests as an experience of victimization, as a time to hold on tight to a negative identity. But, on the other hand, the appearance of ad-Darr may be taken as an opportunity for graceful surrender into the unknown, the formless. Admittedly, this can be scary. It asks you to trust more, and to love more.

The bottom line is really to love enough. Then when you are calling Ya Darr, Ya Nafi', you are calling "the Beloved, the Beloved!" If you contemplate these divine Names together like this as a pair, it doesn't matter if you are on the up side or the down side, the fat side or the lean side, the rich side or the poor side, the blind side or the seeing side. When you chant them as divine opposites, it takes in all those circumstances and more.

In your psychological processes, you can pull on negative forces or positive forces. If you want trouble you get it, and if you want benefit, you get it. The reality you are invoking by doing the practice is evoked as a pure potential. It mirrors your interaction with it.

When you are caught up in the blindness caused by viewing yourself as a victim, what you may need to see in the mirror is that you are held responsible for what you invoke. You are responsible for what you ask for, so your intention should be to overcome the blindness of the ego in the heart. Ego in the heart is blindness. When God blinds, it is in the heart.

As to which to invoke first in the pair, Ya Nafi' or Ya Darr, it may not really matter. But if a physician of the heart is working with a student who is very strongly invested in a victimized posture, it might be better to start with Ya Nafi', just to accentuate a fresh taste.

In the model we have used before in working with opposites, we can examine Qur'anic passages to try to determine what the transcendental Name might be. A survey of verses where ad-Darr and al-Nafi' appear together gives the following: 5:76, 7:188, 10:49, 13:16, 20:89, 34:42, and 48:11.

In every single one of these instances Al-Malik or Malikul-Mulk also appears. This is a simple textual demonstration that the transcendental Name for Ya Darr and Ya Nafi' is the pair: Ya Malik, Ya Malikal-Mulk. This pair of Names describes the reality that ties the two opposites of benefit and harm together. All things are in the hands of Allah.

All the scriptures talk about God in this way, as a truly transcendental being beyond good and evil. Reciting Ya Malik, Ya Malikal-Mulk offers the nondualistic connection of these two extremes.

Ya Qabid, Ya Basit, Ya Wasi'
(yaa ḲAA-biḍ, yaa BAA-siṭ, yaa WAA-si')

We will briefly take up one more pair of opposites. For a more complete treatment of al-Qabid, al-Basit, and al-Wasi' see Chapter 12, The Secret of Ecstasy. There they are treated along with their companion pair of al-Khafid and ar-Rafi'. Al-Qabid and al-Basit can be described as the divine states of contraction and expansion. Al-Qabid is contraction, the opposite of al-Basit, expansion.

At the physical level everyone can observe the continual contraction and expansion of the heart and the lungs. Human beings have a wider sphere of heart that expands and contracts on a larger scale. You feel high, and then you come down. Such fluctuations of states within the greater sphere of heart are called *ahwal*. This is sometimes expressed by saying one enters into a *hal*, which is a form of *ahwal* that is often used in Sufi circles.

The experience of shrinking after being expanded can be quite disturbing to a spiritual traveler. You may have been taken to a most beautiful and elevated state of vision and feeling, and then you are plunged back into the limitations of your mundane world. In this contracted condition, the pain caused by stubbornly clinging to an expanded but transient state becomes exacerbated, because now you feel the loss much more than before you had the expansive experience.

Repetition of Ya Qabid, Ya Basit as a pair will bring you to equanimity about this transient process and point you to the transcendent reality that includes both expansion and contraction. This allows you to move toward balance and begin to surrender your attachment and aversion to the expanded and contracted states. Al-Wasi' is the Name of that transcendent reality. It is a *maqaam*, an established station of realization that is not subject to the fluctuations of states.

The Qur'anic verse says that the mercy (*rahma*) of Allah is so wide (*wasi'*) it includes everything. It is so wide it includes its opposite. That kind of capacity is not susceptible to contraction and expansion. It is an infinite embrace of all conditions. A full experience of *ahwal* leads you toward that reality. Being infinite, it transcends expansion and contraction, and yet it also embraces those apparent opposites. It is important to contemplate Ya Qabid and Ya Basit as a pair. Then you can invoke the transcendent Name Ya Wasi'.

Each time we have become engaged with a pair of divine opposites we have been led toward transcendence and unity. There appears to be a built-in process that continues to lead us toward a realization of essence. This approach is an important gift and a resource to call on when seeking to understand all the divine Names.

ghaffar · ghafur

tawwab · 'afuw

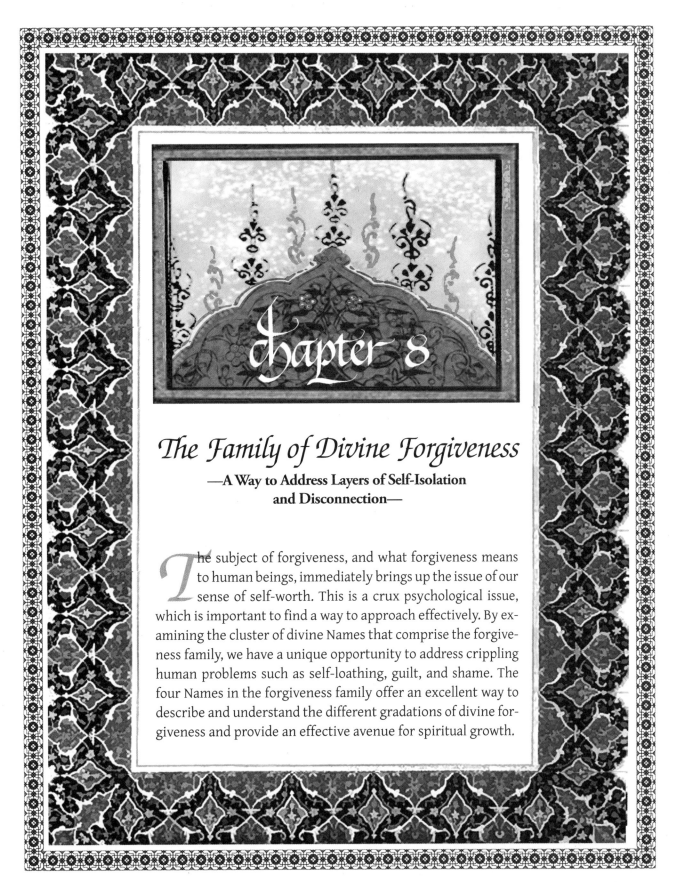

chapter 8

The Family of Divine Forgiveness
—A Way to Address Layers of Self-Isolation and Disconnection—

The subject of forgiveness, and what forgiveness means to human beings, immediately brings up the issue of our sense of self-worth. This is a crux psychological issue, which is important to find a way to approach effectively. By examining the cluster of divine Names that comprise the forgiveness family, we have a unique opportunity to address crippling human problems such as self-loathing, guilt, and shame. The four Names in the forgiveness family offer an excellent way to describe and understand the different gradations of divine forgiveness and provide an effective avenue for spiritual growth.

Ya Ghaffar, Ya Ghafur, Ya Tawwab, Ya 'Afuw

Al-Ghaffar, al-Ghafur, at-Tawwab, and al-'Afuw have a very intimate relationship with one another. By exploring each Name's meaning, as well as the interrelationships of the Names, different layers in the human psyche are exposed. Contemplation of these emanations of divine forgiveness leads directly to a process for remedying deep psychological wounds.

It is interesting how we were first guided to look into the forgiveness family. We were considering the moral and psychological problems connected with revenge that could be seen around al-Muntaqim, a Name often mistranslated as "the avenger." Something in this Name was calling out for balance. We noticed that on the list of 99 Names, al-'Afuw appears right before al-Muntaqim, and it is a true opposite to al-Muntaqim. Al-'Afuw then became very important in our discussion of how the dynamic of divine opposites works. This directed us toward our present focus on the inner relationships in the forgiveness family.

Divine Names can have a meaningful relationship with each other both as opposites and as similars. As opposites they create balance, and this leads to integration and transcendence (see Chapter 7, Allah's Opposite Qualities). In dealing with similars, as we are in this discussion, we often come to see how gradations of essentially the same divine quality may reveal developmental stages of growth.

Ya Ghaffar, Ya Ghafur

(yaa g̱ẖaf FAAR, yaa g̱ẖa-FOOR)

The ground floor in the forgiveness cluster of Names, the starting point, is al-Ghaffar. It is appropriate to begin with this divine quality as it relates to a low point in the human process. People at this stage are usually unable to even consider the possibility of forgiveness. They are caught up in disbelief, grief, and judgment—often self-judgment. There is a progression of forgiveness implied in the Qur'an. Do the big forgiveness, and if you can't do that, do a lesser forgiveness, and if you can't do that, do a still lesser forgiveness. This is similar to the progression we are presenting in this chapter, but we are starting with the most basic level of forgiveness and working up to the most profound.

In the concluding part of this chapter we will focus on applying the healing properties of the forgiveness family to the human condition, and in particular to our emotional and mental health. Before we can properly do this, we will first focus on the layers of meaning in each divine Name in this family. Then we can turn our attention to each Name's application in the various layers of the human psyche and in our psychological states.

The form of al-Ghaffar in the sound code of Arabic grammar gives it a quality that is both continuous and repetitive. You may make the same mistake over and over again, a hundred or a thousand times a day. Every day. But such repeated errors never place you outside the realm of divine forgiveness. Repetitiveness is no problem for al-Ghaffar. Its nature makes it repetitive. Al-Ghaffar's forgiveness is continuous and repetitive.

There is a memorable hadith where a Bedouin says to the Prophet, "What if I do this really bad thing?" And the answer is, "Allah forgives." "But what if I do it again and again and again?" "Allah continues to forgive." Then the Bedouin says, "Doesn't Allah ever get tired of forgiving?" And the Prophet Muhammad says, "No, but you might get tired of doing that same thing over and over again."

It must have been a great moment. At such a time you can see a simple mind becoming enlightened. This tradition of the Prophet beautifully shows the quality of al-Ghaffar. It is not simply an act of forgiveness, but continuous, repetitive acts of forgiveness. It puts in mind the thought inscribed on Mevlana Rumi's tomb—that even if you have broken your vows a thousand times, you should always feel the invitation to return again. God's forgiveness is inexhaustible, and it is continuous.

But we cannot properly introduce al-Ghaffar without introducing its partner, al-Ghafur. They share the same root and are basically emanations of the same divine forgiveness. Not only are they cognates, and thus naturally close in meaning, but they complement each other in another most fulfilling and wholesome way.

Earlier we saw that the sound code of Arabic makes al-Ghaffar repetitive and unending. Now we see that the sound code places al-Ghafur in the group that carries the meaning of "penetrating right into the essence of a thing." It goes right into the deepest place in the heart. Therefore al-Ghafur goes right to the worst crime we have ever committed in our lives. It goes right to the worst thing that has ever been done to us. *Whether it is a grudge of self-loathing or a grudge held against another, the depth of feeling is the same.* Allah's forgiveness reaches that deepest place. From a medical point of view we might say that al-Ghaffar is a remedy for a chronic condition and Al-Ghafur is for an acute condition.

Contemplation on al-Ghafur is a profound and healing practice for anyone. It is even recommended for prisoners on death row. It reaches the deepest wound. It goes right to the heart of the matter. It penetrates to the essence. Divine forgiveness reaches that which we imagined was unforgiveable. That is the quality of al-Ghafur.

The very concept of forgiveness, even in English usage, is to give up the grudge, to let go of that revenge fantasy. Forgiveness comes by giving that away. So at this first stage in the process of learning to forgive, you need to learn to give up the revenging impulse that arises many times a day. And you also need to give up the grudge you hold about the inner wound you believe to be unforgiveable.

At this beginning stage in the process, you notice the fault either in other people or in your own self. Again and again you are asked to give up the grudge you are holding, and to invite in al-Ghaffar and al-Ghafur. You can then awaken to a kind of compassion that actually reaches the wound and covers over the fault in a soothing way.

Both al-Ghaffar and al-Ghafur have this same root meaning of covering over in a healing kind of way. One of the physical-plane variations of the root of these Names refers to covering over the cracks in a leather water skin using the sticky substance that bees use to repair their hives. In a desert culture, a whole tribe could die of thirst from a leaky waterskin. This is a very earthy image that helps us understand the importance of this basic kind of forgiveness.

By calling on these two sacred Names we can actively moisturize and heal the cracks in our being that allow the water of life to dissipate and our hearts to dry up. Repetition of Ya Ghaffar, Ya Ghafur brings a pliability that allows us to overcome brittleness of character. It is a soothing balm to our woundedness. It begins to ease the pain that has caused us to isolate ourselves in our relationships in life.

Ya Tawwab

(yaa tow-WAAB)

Going beyond this, there is an inner stage called *tawbah*. Now you actually become able to turn away from perceived defects and shadows and face directly toward the divine perfection. At-Tawwab is both the divine reality that you turn to in such a way and the activity of turning. The form in Arabic is *wa taaba 'ila-llah*. We literally turn from the defect and toward Allah. "From" and "toward" are expressed simultaneously by the same verb in Arabic.

Tawbah has an Aramaic equivalent *tiyuvtah* and a Hebrew equivalent *teshuvah*, which both have the same meaning. In Judaism, the ten days beginning with Rosh Hashanah (the New Year) and ending with Yom Kippur (the Day of Atonement) are called *Aseret Yemey Teshuvah*, the ten days of repentance. These ten days and the Hebrew month of Elul which precedes them are a time set aside to account for our actions; to ask forgiveness from those we have wronged, from God, and from ourselves; to turn away from what isn't working in our lives; to turn toward God, forgiveness, and healing; and to ask for a good year and for help with the difficulties we face in our lives, our communities, and our world.

What does it mean to say we turn from a defect and turn toward Allah? We are turning toward, or are returning to, at-Tawwab. Because of the sound code embedded in Arabic grammar, we know that at-Tawwab must have a quality that manifests continuously, without beginning, end, or interruption. This allows us to see Allah is always turning toward us, always returning to us. When we give God bad words, God gives us good words. That is God's way of turning.

At-Tawwab is always turning toward you without interruption. This is very important to understand! It allows us to overcome certain theological confusions that can arise in relation to our usual understanding of the English word "repentance." With the invocation of Ya Tawwab, you turn from the defect that you perceive to the face of Allah, who always is facing you. It allows you to let go of the grudge you have been holding onto and to face toward the light.

Taaba'an literally means to forgive someone by facing away from the defect toward Allah who is always forgiving. That is a very high stage of forgiveness. You are not stuck in the rights and wrongs of your personal relationships. What is quite remarkable is that it is by noticing the faults in the first place that you are impelled toward Allah, toward the One. The process of truly invoking Ya Tawwab is deeply healing, because negativity is transformed into its opposite. This is spiritual alchemy.

A hadith says, "If you make a mistake and ask for forgiveness, Allah will immediately turn your grief and sorrow into joy and gladness. God will give you sustenance from an unknown source and will deliver you from all difficulties and hardship into ease." That is at-Tawwab in action.

When, through the realization of at-Tawwab, the student on the path has learned to use every particular event as an opportunity to become aware of the face of Allah, surely it is not out of place to ask what more could there possibly be?

Ya 'Afuw

(yaa 'A-fooww)

The ultimate stage of forgiveness is expressed by al-'Afuw. Let's begin with a physical metaphor that is part of the word's root meaning: *'Afat-ir-reeh ul-'athar*. This is an image of the wind blowing across the desert vastness and completely erasing all the tracks in the sand. It is as if no one had ever walked there. Such a fundamental image in the root of the word shows us that with al-'Afuw you do not even notice the fault.

In the first stages of forgiveness you definitely do notice the fault, but you feel there is a possibility for forgiveness, a chance for some healing salve to reach your wounded places. Then you find the strength to overlook it. Eventually you are moved to turn away from the fault toward Allah whenever awareness of the fault arises, thus transforming negativity into a vision of the divine face.

Finally we come to al-'Afuw, which means to completely forgive, with no trace of the fault even subtly retained. There is not even a trace of resentment or memory. There are no footprints in the sand. There are no impressions. Your awareness is clean and incapable of being stained. Such is the highest stage of divine forgiveness.

We want to strongly emphasize that the state of "not seeing" we are referring to here should not in any way be considered to be unconsciousness or lack of awareness. Rather, it is that your consciousness has been raised to the level of seeing in accordance with the divine reality.

There's a story of a teacher who goes to a town, and when he comes back to his students they ask him what he saw. He says, "It is beautiful, but I don't want any of you going there." Nonetheless, one of them goes to the town; however, he experiences it to be utterly ugly. He comes back and says, "It's a horrible place. What were you talking about?" The teacher replies, "Well, you'd have to be able to see it through my eyes."

With al-Ghaffar and al-Ghafur, you see the shadows. You even see the worst ugliness when you look at the "unforgiveable place" into which al-Ghafur penetrates. In at-Tawwab we notice patches of light and shade, so to speak, because there is still awareness of that fault you are turning from. But with al-'Afuw, there is none of that. You no longer have any negative connotation about whatever events have happened to you. We want to make it emphatically clear to our readers that this is not a stage that you should try and rush into. It is the culmination of a lengthy inner process. If the negative conditions are not respected sufficiently, they become masked and remain active in the unconscious.

Al-'Afuw is the doorway in the heart where all attachment to hurt and pain, and memories regarding hurt and pain, are absolved from within. In that station, such impressions are gone like the footprints in the desert after the wind. It is like they were never there. There is no sense of a mistake that needs to be corrected.

If you are graced to have this realization, you are with humanity, but you are not caught up in it, because you are beyond being touched in a reactive way. You leave the relative perspective, which evaluates people and their limitations. You merge in al-'Afuw in the absolute state of the divine heart. There is forgetfulness of duality and of separation. There is no such thing as poison anymore. Divine forgiveness has come.

The phrase *'astaghfiru-llaah*, often repeated by Sufis, shares the same root as both al-Ghaffar and al-Ghafur. Its meaning is both penetrating and continuous. The "ah" sound at the end of the word adds a sense of yearning or longing. The phrase includes the sense of an "I" that yearns. It is the separated "I" that is the persona of the longing lover. That is why the great Saint Rabi'ah of Basra said, "'*Astaghfiru-llaah* to Allah, for having to say *'astaghfiru-llaah*." She wanted forgiveness for still needing to overcome that "I" of separation.

With al-'Afuw there are no gradations any more. There is the erasing of the "I." No more is there the feeling, "I got hurt yesterday." There simply is a state of Being itself, a being that is continually flowing. No more is there the ego's wound-engendered self-identification that causes people to hold on to their grudges and experience themselves as something separate.

People often repress memories. They say that they don't remember some event, and then they imagine that they have actually forgiven the parties involved because they don't remember an incident any more. But when a counselor shakes them up a little bit, all their memories come out. This is very different from the state we have been discussing.

In the spiritual state, there is no barrier between you and al-'Afuw itself, and it is flowing gently all the time. Nothing is repressed. Every system is released and there is just the continual emanation of that presence. Such a person is very much awake, not asleep and forgetful. They are awake, but they are not carrying the past.

Specific Applications of These Four Emanations of Divine Forgiveness

Ya Ghaffar and Ya Ghafur invoke the capacity within you to feel that you can perform an act of forgiveness, or to feel that it is possible that you could be forgiven. When that arises as a real possibility, you can become unstuck. When you are stuck there is a momentum that carries you on and on in the same groove, and you feel that you personally don't have any other option. We need to see that as human beings, no matter how deeply we are wounded we still have the capacity to remove the grudge where we are stuck. Each occasion is an opportunity to develop understanding and, ultimately, forgiveness.

In early childhood, or even before, people develop the misconception that they are supposed to be perfect. Then when they make a mistake they often feel rage, anger at themselves. By engaging in self-blame, people block themselves from being truly able to make amends. The first step to overcome such confusion may be to recognize that humans are designed to make mistakes in order to learn. This very much applies to our habitual behaviors. So we have to continually allow for forgiveness of the mistake to be able to learn from it.

If you can forgive yourself, you can forgive others. To awaken such forgiveness is part of the healing process. Some people feel, "I don't have that capacity." And, because of this feeling, they say, "I cannot forgive." Forgiveness is not part of their inner constellation of possibilities, especially when they are dealing with hate. Revenge is their specialty. They are focused on having their revenge.

Forgiveness is not in their ego structure. Their ego structure is generated around a kind of notion of justice. By pursuing their revenge, they believe justice will take place. So, for such people, the first principle they need to know is that there is a higher capacity within them. It needs to dawn on them that a human being is capable of forgiving.

Al-Ghaffar is so merciful that it never wavers through failure after failure, and through this process, some healing begins to occur. As they travel along this path, wounded people may begin to feel, "I can open up, through repetition and contemplation of al-Ghaffar, to this work on my ongoing mistakes, to habits like smoking, or overeating, or something similar, but there are some things that I've done or that have happened to me that no power on heaven or earth can make right."

It's so bad they just hopelessly carry it around. They figure their life is ruined, and there is nothing that they can do to change it. It can never be healed. It can never be undone. It can never be forgiven. It is as if they are saying, "I can't let go of that, that's who I am." Without that wound they don't have an identity.

Thus you find that as you work with the recitation of Ya Ghaffar, a second stage is reached. It happens when you find a pain that is so big you feel, "I cannot deal with this one. It's so bad that I can't forgive, and I can't give up this grudge." That is when you really need to draw on al-Ghafur. For example, if somebody harms your son or daughter you feel at that moment that you need a bigger force to meet this than your capacity as a human being. It is just much bigger than what you can do. When it reaches a level that is unbearable, you need to go beyond the known forgiveness capacity that you have as a resonance of God within and call on the greatest divine power of forgiveness to remove the poison of the grudge from your heart.

Consider such an extreme situation. Every time a thought comes such as "What did I do to cause my daughter to commit suicide?" or "I can't bear this and I'd rather be dead," every single time these thoughts of self-blame arise we recommend that you repeat "Ya Ghaffar, Ya Ghafur," over and over and over again. As long as a person is actively engaged in dealing with their wounded condition we recommend staying with this practice. When they are ready to turn from the pain and see the divine purpose through it all, then invocation of Ya Tawwab is appropriate.

Following Shaykh 'ibn 'Arabi, we are viewing these Names as relationships. They are divine relationships. They aren't entities. Every situation in life then is an opportunity to enter into these divine relationships. By continually thinking that you have to be perfect, not only do you beat up on yourself when you fall short, but you are also cutting off a natural divine relationship with Ya Ghaffar and Ya Ghafur. Committing the sin actually allows you, in a backwards kind of way, to tap into the potentialities of your relationship with divine forgiveness by creating a situation that calls for that remedy.

Forgiveness, as we have seen from a study of these Names, is a continuous presence. So it may seem odd to ask for forgiveness when the rain of divine forgiveness is pouring all the time. What we may need to do is ask for the removal of the umbrella that we ourselves have used to block the rain of mercy.

We must respect that the spiritual path requires us to pass through these stages and not to simply understand them intellectually. Repetition of Ya Tawwab reminds us that the all-forgiving one is facing us all the time. We just need to let go of our absorption with the limited self and turn toward the light of the divine source.

To focus more specifically on psychological processes, the period when a student is working with Ya Ghaffar and Ya Ghafur should also entail a process of increasing self-understanding. Some people, for example, are angry at their parents. They need to be allowed to feel their anger. Through such a process they begin to understand that their parents are human. Before expressing their anger, they saw them as something more than human. And perhaps they also saw the parents as making inhuman demands.

When understanding comes, spontaneous forgiveness comes. The dynamic of this stage requires the counselor to have an in-depth understanding of a person's belief system. The physician of the heart needs to see the distortions, feel the feelings that have to be felt, and not jump the gun. With understanding, a person becomes able to clearly look at the anger, the rage, the abandonment, the grief, or whatever is there.

In the next stage, where practitioners are invoking Ya Tawwab, a physician of the heart may have to deal with an attitude of grandiosity. Those who suffer from grandiosity are turning toward themselves, not to God. In the example we were considering, a sense of grandiosity can make the mother think she had that much power over her daughter's soul that the child committed suicide. What about her daughter's own choices, her own destiny?

For the mother to believe she had that much power over her child is a kind of grandiosity, which is actually a defense against an even deeper wound. The mother feels helpless because she believes that she is totally isolated and has to do everything by herself. Consequently, when the student is ready, the counselor should expose the grandiosity and show that it is a defense against vulnerability.

As vulnerability shows up more and more, the desire arises to turn to a greater source, and this is the birth of at-Tawwab. The physician of the heart should expose the defense mechanism, which is the grandiosity that comes from a deep sense of loneliness, a deep sense of being wounded, a deep sense that there is no God to turn to. The person may be asking of God, "Why have you forsaken me?" and that is a very deep wound.

Grandiosity becomes a defense. The ego, experiencing itself as isolated, thinks it is doing everything on its own. So when you turn to at-Tawwab, you begin to see the inflation in your ego as well as the defensiveness. Then real forgiveness begins to deepen. Just as you turned away from God, so you begin to turn toward God.

The basic root of at-Tawwab has the meaning to face someone with your face. Turning your face away is considered extremely rude in most societies. So turning toward someone, actually turning your face, literally, toward someone else with a sense of forgiveness, with a sense of compassion, is probably the best physical metaphor that can be found for the stage of at-Tawwab. This is the very heart of repentance. In the last stages of *tawbah* you are repenting from repentance, from *tawbah* itself, as we saw earlier in the example of Saint Rabi'ah of Basra. At this point the divine forgiveness turns into al-'Afuw.

Ya 'Aziz, Ya Muntaqim

(yaa 'a-ZEEZ, yaa mun-TA-ḳim)

It is worth remembering that this whole discussion on degrees of forgiveness, working up to al-'Afuw, originally arose in the context of finding a balancing Name to al-Muntaqim, the great karmic force of reciprocity, which we more fully discuss in Chapter 7, Allah's Opposite Qualities. There we note that the strength that comes from realizing the divine Name al-'Aziz is a key to a person's needed transformation from a revenge-oriented ego structure.

Al-'Aziz is God's power as a refined strength that is rare and graceful. Such a sense of power allows your ego to become detached from clinging to its presumed power, and then you can start to forgive. Remember, to forgive is a kind of *fana*, or dissolving of self. You must give away the vengeful and spiteful stuff. You must give up the illusion that you possess power over somebody in order to allow the healing to emerge.

It is helpful to invoke Ya 'Aziz because the ego's ultimate power is what is being tested in life's crucible. What the ego tries to do is to take command, and replace God with itself. That is its ultimate stand. "Since there is no God, I will be God, and I'll be the most powerful being in the universe." Actually that attitude is very exhausting, and, in fact, it weakens the ego because it thinks that it has to do everything. It doesn't let anyone else do a job. It is always afraid. That fear is the source of its grandiosity, of its claim, "I am the ultimate one." Such a predicament can be deflated by invocation of Ya 'Aziz.

It makes sense that the way to at-Tawwab and al-'Afuw is to go through the relinquishing of the ego power. That's why Sufis say *'astaghfiru-llaah* so much. In the first stages in *'astaghfiru-llaah*, the "I" imagines it has the power to forgive, or some existence to forgive, and it gradually learns to give that power away. You encourage this self-effacement by conscientiously calling on Ya Ghaffar and Ya Ghafur. Such practice will address both your deflation into depression and your inflation into grandiosity.

Al-'Afuw is the station of the divine. It is the divine being that is doing everything. With at-Tawwab, a person still has some ego personality existing because there has to be an entity that is turning from something to something else. With al-'Afuw there is nothing that is turning and nothing to turn toward. There is just smooth sand, so to speak. Curiously enough, with al-Muntaqim, there is no more turning either. But with al-Muntaqim what is needed is to give up the revenging sword of your ego and surrender fully to the divine presence that will balance and correct conditions.

One presence erases the hurts of the wound—that is al-'Afuw. And one presence, al-Muntaqim, erases the imbalance of the energies, the imbalance of the passions. Al-'Afuw heals the wound on the emotional level, and al-Muntaqim addresses the wound on the level of primal impulses or passions. To realize al-Muntaqim is to get beyond the feeling that events have targeted you personally. Then you ultimately surrender to God as the balancing force. (For a more complete discussion of this from the psychological perspective, see Chapter 7, Allah's Opposite Qualities.)

Now we have talked about the four stages of forgiveness as reflected in the invocation of four divine Names: Ya Ghaffar, Ya Ghafur, Ya Tawwab, and Ya 'Afuw. We recommend doing all four sequentially over the course of time. Don't rush through the stages of duality. If you are still identified with your wounds it won't help to just touch lightly on Ya Ghaffar and Ya Ghafur. Doing that won't help you to realize the higher stages. You need to bring up the wound and give it proper attention.

When you progress to the stage of reciting Ya Tawwab, it is like a state of perpetually remembering to gaze at the face of the Beloved. You are continually being moved to release the hold that your wounds have on you and turn to the face of the Beloved. Al-'Afuw is more like a station of realization than it is a passing state. Realizing al-'Afuw is to become stabilized in nondual clarity of heart. All that is left is the Beloved. With at-Tawwab, the false self has been overcome so it doesn't grasp any more. In al-'Afuw there is no false self to grasp. Allah is awakened in you without boundaries or individualism.

There is a wound that some human beings bear that evidences a similar feeling of hopelessness but which is wider in scope. It is not experienced as the result of an individual incident. It is a deep despair, a despair that is seen everywhere. Such people see devils wherever they look—communists, fascists, terrorists, and so on. There is nowhere to turn. Persons like this are often prone to suicide. Invocation of Ya Tawwab directly addresses this misery and brings relief.

Our human life leaves behind it a trail of our wounded condition. There are different levels of woundedness. We find that the human psyche is generally constructed upon three fundamental wounds or "holes" of awesome magnitude, which we refer to as the family hole, the self hole and the divine hole.

The wound we call the family hole is the result of a feeling of deficiency and failure. Deficiency is used here in the sense that when you are faced with an inner hurdle, there is a missing piece that you cannot find. This missing piece is in the core of the human personality structure, and the ego has no idea of it at all. That is because that hole, or that absence, was generated before the ego was born.

Such a hole was generated in the womb and in the first weeks of birth. That absence has to do with a missing aspect in the family. A soul is born into a family in which there is a collective absence of a certain quality. Some families are missing heart, some missing intelligence, some missing will, and so on. A soul then gets born into that misconnection. The misconnection leaves an imprint on the body of the child and on the soul.

Later on, this imprint, or the absence of the activity of this particular quality, leads to the birthing of an ego centralized around the presence or absence of this quality's activity. If love was missing in the family, the ego later is born around the questions: What is love? How to get love? How to avoid love? How to run away from love? How to throw out love?

So the whole ego centralizes around an aspect that the ego itself is blind to in a crucial way. It is really an aspect of God that is missing because it was blocked in the family. This creates a feeling of deficiency in the ego. The ego always feels wounded, feels like a failure, when it wants to heal this deficiency.

Al-Ghaffar brings healing to the woundedness we carry because of our inability to heal what we are calling the family hole. It pertains to what the ego is always trying to heal, but the ego cannot heal. Only the divine can do this healing. As a result, the ego is bound by a sense of deficiency, a sense of failure, and a sense of being wounded. This is the first layer of a kind of narcissistic hurt.

There may come a time when you feel you have healed the wound of the family hole or that you have become disengaged from the family hole, and yet another deep wound now arises about the uniqueness of your soul. This wound is based on the feeling that you have not been seen as you truly are. You were asked to do something and to be something for the family, but you were not really seen.

The family ignored exactly the uniqueness and the blessedness of what your soul had come to contribute to existence. This leads to a devastating wound—that the very self, who I am, is not good. "My ego is not good. My personality is not good. My actions are not good. My mind is not good. My behavior is not good."

When that has been addressed, what is revealed is an even deeper hole, a deeper wound. "My very soul must not be good enough because nobody saw it, nobody acknowledged it." Your narcissistic self-identification has left a layer of shame, a layer of deficiency around your very soul. Such a condition calls out for the penetrating depth that comes from invocation of Ya Ghafur.

Here you are facing real existential angst. There is a fundamental crisis of authenticity. "I don't feel my very soul is good enough." By sincerely calling on Ya Ghafur, a veil is removed. Then you begin to see that your soul is God-made. It's the best there is. How could there be anything better? In these ways, al-Ghaffar and al-Ghafur can heal this secondary narcissistic woundedness, especially when used in conjunction with Ya 'Aziz.

At this point you may feel, "Here I am, I find my self is good, but I don't find God. Where is God? If I am good, if I am a good soul, why has God forsaken me?" This has been called the "Dark Night of the

Soul." This kind of wound is deeper, even more primary. It's almost like you have been healed at one level, and then you find a deeper wound that you sink down into. Each layer has its own wound. "If I am really a good soul, where is God?"

This dilemma is addressed at the level of at-Tawwab. In other words, "Show me your face." *Tawwajjuh*, the Sufi practice of exchanging a glance of complete oneness, means "to face." At-Tawwab also means to face. It simultaneously entails that you are looking toward the beloved, and the beloved is looking toward you. It is said the face of the beloved never turns away.

We have a description in the scriptures of the Prophet Moses at this stage. Difficulties were finally getting healed, and the Pharaoh didn't destroy him. Good things happened. He had quite an adventure getting married, and so on. Then he said to God "Show me something. Show me even a little *tajalliyyat*." Moses is looking for the divine face when he says, "Where are you?"

The stage of *tawbah* is the facing. You turn toward Allah. You discover that you had turned away because you were looking for Mom, or you were looking for Dad. You were looking for humanity to recognize you, to acknowledge that you are a good soul. You want to be seen as a good child. And when that wound is healed, you discover that you really are good. You see that goodness is the very nature of your soul, of your creation. Then you say, "Where art Thou?" We turn toward God. And the moment we turn toward God, there is the meeting, and the facing, and that is like recognizing the absolute and being recognized by the absolute. There is ecstasy.

Through God's love then you may be led to the stage of al-'Afuw where there is no more the distinction of lover and beloved. That thin barrier is removed. It is a very thin veil. At the end of the classic Sufi tale of human and divine love, after a journey of many years Layla finds Majnun entwined with the tree and she says, "Majnun, Majnun I'm here. It's Layla." And he says, "No, I'm Layla." She replies, "Majnun, come to your senses, I am Layla." "If you're Layla," he says, "I am not." At that moment Majnun has become the beloved. He has become one with Allah. There is no other, and no otherness. As Rumi writes, "The beloved is all in all; the lover but a veil."

When a human being reaches the dark night of the soul, which is terrifying, the wounded beast inside comes out. On the first day it comes out with a layer of hate, which can be directed at the physician of the heart. "I hate you because you are taking me to my shame, you are taking me to my humiliation. You are taking me through my woundedness. You made this happen. Why did you make this confusion? My life was fine."

At this stage the physician of the heart should say, "Good, good, we're making progress. We finally got to this." The wounded beast rises with the layer of hate because it must defend the wound from being touched. But beneath the layer of hate is a layer of shock. They feel deeply shocked. "How did God throw me into this existence? I can't believe that. I come from Allah; I come from the source. And look what happened to me! I am disconnected. I am not in alignment with the source."

So there is a layer of shock and trauma. This is the ripening of the psychological process. When you have uncovered the trauma in this way, it can be released. What comes out now is no longer the aggressiveness of the beast within or the numbness of the shock, but a deep despair, a deep tenderness, and a deep woundedness. The one who reaches this stage will now engage in real self-questioning. "What have I done to make God turn away from me?" There is deep tenderness and deep remorse inside the soul. "What happened between me and God that God turned away?"

Eventually you realize that in actuality it was you who turned away. God didn't turn away. Finally, at this stage you can truly make the turn of the heart. Then *tawbah* occurs. When this happens it can be said that you have repented from repenting. You repent from your own action of creating duality in the process of repentance. The duality is resolved, and you enter the realization of al-'Afuw.

What we have just described exposes the layers of the psyche and the depth of the ego structure that has been created as a defensive response to humanity's inner woundedness. We have linked this structure to the activity of the cluster of divine Names of forgiveness.

Each of us must face the confusion engendered by these three major wounds. There is a vacuum of self-isolation and disconnection in each wounded layer. We call these layers of confusion the family hole, the self hole, and the divine hole. As the emanations of divine forgiveness seen in this cluster of Names are conscientiously brought to encounter the layers of the ego, what is revealed in the process is a path for healing our deepest and most ferociously defended wounds.

qahhar
jabbar
qawiyy
aziz
dhal jalali wal'ikram
qadir
muqtadir
matin

Chapter 9

Modalities of Omnipotence

—The Names of Power and Strength—

There is little value in searching for different English synonyms for divine omnipotence as a way of seeking understanding of this cluster of sacred Names. To call one Name "strength" and another "compelling," and so on through all the Names in this family, does not tell us what we need to know. All these Names could be translated as strength or omnipotence, but how do we gain insight into their particular meanings? Their linguistic roots, and their relationships with one another, will provide the key.

By exploring the whole cluster as different modalities of divine omnipotence, relationships between the Names are uncovered.

A relational approach allows us to better address specific ways each Name can be used as a *wazifah* to help overcome human limitations and difficulties. An important aspect of all the divine Names is that their reality is manifested in relation to human beings. We are relational creatures who need to find divine truth and self-knowledge within the fabric of our relationships.

There are six divine Names we will consider as members of this primary family cluster. At the end of the chapter, we will discuss two close relatives to the strength and omnipotence family.

Ya 'Aziz

(yaa 'a-ZEEZ)

First, let's look at the structure of the word al-'Aziz. The sound code informs us that al-'Aziz is a kind of omnipotence that God gives to each and every atom in the universe, without distinction, without preference. Al-'Aziz has an innate quality of giving. It also has a root meaning of sweetness. It is precious and rare, like a baby eagle among birds.

Al-'Aziz is a fascinating combination. On the one hand, we have strength, and on the other hand we have adjectives such as sweetness, cherishing, rarity, and preciousness. The experience of the divine power is felt to be sweet and precious at the same time. Because of this rare combination of qualities, al-'Aziz plays an important role in relation to the other divine Names, and an equally important role in illuminating human relationships.

In the context of the pharmacopeia of divine Names, al-'Aziz is the ability of the power of God to take us from a sense of guilt, powerlessness, and shame to an experience of genuine self-worth. The divine Name al-Mu'izz, which has the same root, implies causality, and consequently can be seen as the agent of Al-'Aziz. In other words, Allah sends something or someone to accomplish the action of self-transformation. But as the power itself, al-'Aziz is more primary, even though it may seem more abstract.

Al-'Aziz is the power of God itself. It is Allah, through al-'Aziz, who is the real actor in the invisible world. When you realize this, you discover a source of strength that is not dependent on what the world does to raise you up or put you down. When this Name is realized you can recover from the habit of continually relating to life from the vantage point of seeing yourself as "the lowest of the low." You experience *'izzah*, the root of that Name of strength, within all the inevitable fluctuations of your life. Al-'Aziz allows you to bring the quality of perfection directly into all aspects of your life.

When al-'Aziz is viewed from the psychological perspective, it brings up a particularly important crux theme for the ego structure. The human ego structure is made of many layers, layers that ultimately defend against major wounds. There is a major wound of humiliation, a wound of shame, which most people carry. It is the result of the experience of your life in relation to others. And at another level there is a wound of shame also caused by our relationship with God, because many of us feel abandoned by God.

The biggest enemy here to psychological growth is the act of fixing onto the sense of an isolated, small self, when you actually need to identify with a much bigger reality. The instinctive narcissistic identification with a wound-engendered construct of self is what leads to our entrapment.

Al-'Aziz demonstrates what can be called pre-eternal value or strength, a strength that existed before time began. It is totally independent of any circumstantial state that we might go through in our lives. True value comes from a pre-eternal state that is totally independent of outer conditions, no matter how it might appear externally.

Seen in this way, al-'Aziz is the strength that gives each one of us a real inner sense of value. And at the same time, it is an inner sense of value that gives us strength. Our essence, our soul, is precious. To understand al-'Aziz, both qualities—self worth and strength—must be married. You feel you are made of the most precious elements of God's heart, the gold of God's heart.

From within your being you come to know that the human soul is divine essence. In this way, through the recognition that you are made from the fiber of the inner essence before time began, you free yourself from identification with a wounded self-grasping ego, and you experience a kind of transformation.

Those who are surrendered to this quality, and thus known as *'abd al-'Aziz*, can go through pain or through honor and not be centered on the ego-self, because they are not identified with the small self. They know true value. They do not subserviently look up to people with power over them or imperiously look down at people over whom they have power.

They look inward toward the divine light in the heart and as a result they know the source from which true value and power comes. This is discussed in more detail in Chapter 8, Divine Forgiveness, where al-'Aziz plays an important role. Al-'Aziz is also a quality to call on when dealing with certain pairs of divine opposites, such as al-Mu'izz and al-Mudhill, and al-Muntaqim and al-A'fuw.

Al-'Aziz is the true worth, the inner value or strength that comes directly from God without an intermediary. If you have no sense of value, you don't feel strong. Without this realization, the strength you are able to manifest is a kind of posturing, a fake strength. But when you know that your essence is rare and precious and undying, you have the strength to be. Then strength arises spontaneously from within.

Al-'Aziz is a wonderful combination. It has the qualities of being engaged with life, having a sweet nature, and being strong at the same time. It allows you to discover that you have been caught up and trapped in the fixedness of ego when, in reality, your true nature is a condition of continuously flowing from the source of all. When that realization breaks through, fixedness breaks. The ego releases its grasping and comes into a continual influx with true being. In this way, the ego can become an image of God and not an image of the parents or an image of internalized authority. Union, or remembrance, in al-'Aziz, produces fluidity.

Ya Qahhar

(yaa ḳah-HAAR)

The sound code tells us that because of the doubled middle consonant, al-Qahhar (and al-Jabbar, which we consider in the next section) must involve perpetual, continual action. Whatever else we arrive at about the meaning of the words al-Qahhar and al-Jabbar, we know these divine Names must convey the reality of continuously becoming. (See Chapter 4, The Sound Code, for a more complete treatment of how such forms work in the Arabic language.)

Al-Qahhar has suffered from some of the worst translations into English of any of the 99 Beautiful Names of Allah. A physical-plane root meaning of al-Qahhar is the searing effect that fire has on a piece of meat to get the juices flowing. That image gives a good sense of the kind of power we are talking about. It's the fire of longing, of yearning. Such passionate yearning is the fire of love. It acts on the piece of meat, which we should understand is the heart. In essence, all yearning ultimately relates to Allah.

The presence of al-Qahhar affects you with a yearning passion, a burning. Regardless of everything else that may be present in your life, you continuously long for God in your heart. No amount of drugs, sex, alcohol, or anything else will extinguish this yearning. It is continuous.

The manifestation of such power and omnipotence through the invocation Ya Qahhar has an effect that is like the heat of a fire that burns without burning out. You burn with passion, with yearning, with the heat of love. It is a quenchless flame that the Sufi poets go on and on about. It is the fire of love, which is also called *'ishq*. Things may fall apart, but you are still going to burn with this fire. It may even look like hell on earth, but there is a kind of a strength that overwhelms everything.

Another meaning of al-Qahhar is "that which is continually overwhelming everything else." But this overwhelming element is the feeling of yearning or passion or longing. It just burns and burns and burns away. Invoking this Name will certainly warm up the feelings. Ya Qahhar can work as a remedy for a cold heart. It will help a person develop great passion for life. But because of its intensity, the physician of the heart should be very careful to wait for a properly ripe moment to prescribe it.

Invoking Ya 'Aziz, we saw already, can serve as a remedy for shame, guilt, and worthlessness, because it develops the strength that arises from true self worth. With al-Qahhar the beautiful thing is that the self burns up, but the light is still there. Only the false has been extinguished. There is nothing left but the divine flame. The personality shell dissolves. The egoic identification with shame and humiliation is consumed by divine fire. A shift of identity occurs, and the spiritual wayfarer becomes the flame.

We can clearly see this in the story of Moses and the burning bush. In the end, the small self is consumed. There are several stages of Moses' relationship with this fire of God. First he hears about a burning bush, and this is called *'ilmu-l-yaqeen*. Then he sees the burning bush.

That is called *'ain-'al-yaqin*. It is when a person actually sees and experiences with the essence of certainty. Your essence communicates with *the* essence, *'ain*. The third stage, as seen by the Sufis, is that

Moses jumps into the flame and is consumed, and in being consumed, he becomes the flame. That is the final stage, which is called *haqqu-l-yaqeen*. It is becoming the flame.

A story about the great Tibetan saint Milarepa comes to mind. A gigantic demon shows up in his cave to bother his meditation, but Milarepa ignores him. The demon continues to linger around and finally announces, "I'm so hungry!" Milarepa says, "All right then. Okay," and he jumps into the demon's mouth! Milarepa, like Moses, has realized his essential ever-becoming nature, so there is no chance of diminution or augmentation due to outer conditions. There is a powerful inner sense of al-Qahhar overwhelming everything else and thus overcoming all attachment.

Al-Qahhar is a burning power that transcends time. It simply is. It doesn't have a beginning or an end. There is no extinguishing of it and no kindling of it. It is a continual flame of passion and yearning. We think this is a beautiful way to describe al-Qahhar, and we feel confident that such a rendering is at least more accurate than the way al-Qahhar has generally been translated into English.

Al-Qahhar overwhelms and annihilates all other attachments except your inherent relationship to the One. After such dissolution, all that is left is the unity. In Sufi terminology, it is the process of going from *fana* to *baqa*. Allah shines through the blackness. It conquers the beast within the ego that is trying to be the conqueror. The beast gets brought to its knees without being broken. Al-Qahhar overcomes by showing the beast that it is already defeated!

This Name of divine omnipotence takes us right to the breaking point to reveal our undefeatable essence. In this way it redefines what we are. The raw meat is now cooked. In one poem Mevlana Rumi describes hearing a knock on the door. The Friend says, "Who's there?" and hears the answer, "Me." The Friend then replies, "Go away! There's no place for raw meat at this table." A year later after undergoing a process of transformation the man returns and knocks again. "Who's there?" "You." "Come right in."

The process of al-Qahhar actually can be gentle, but it is relentless and continual. It has a compression force to it, a force sometimes experienced as a conquering force descending on you, compressing you. When people experience such pressure descending, it is natural to feel depressed. You feel as if you are being crushed. But when you surrender to al-Qahhar then you feel resurrection and exaltation. Metaphorically, we could say that the compression is like what turns coal into a diamond over the course of millions of years. The physician of the heart should be quite circumspect in prescribing this extremely powerful *wazifah*.

Ya Jabbar

(yaa jab-BAAR)

Al-Jabbar brings a very different quality of omnipotence. It is the power to do things, or to act upon the world. Al-Jabbar sets things straight. It is a healing strength. This is perfectly expressed in one of the variations of its root: the act of setting a broken bone to heal it. It is that kind of strength. As mentioned earlier, al-Jabbar has a grammatical form that, according to the sound code, makes it a continuous activity. So we can say that al-Jabbar is the strength to continuously heal all things all the time.

Al-Jabbar is the mender of bones, but it also means to set the backbone as a chiropractor might do. It is divine strength but a strength, first of all, to act on the world, and secondly, to act on the world with a specific purpose and effect, which is to heal. And it is the kind of strength to do this healing again and again, continuously. It never loses heart. And that means, no matter what comes up in the news, you continue to heal that. It is the power to fix whatever is in need, to heal what is broken.

Many well-intentioned people experience frustration and depression because they feel like they need to fix what is wrong, but they are too weak to do it. They don't have the strength. It is like a fundamental exhaustion. Then they get depressed. They always feel unhappy because every time they hear about something they want to go and fix it, but it's beyond their personal capacity, so they get over-extended and fall flat.

The repetition of Ya Jabbar addresses this endemic condition. This *wazifah* is an invocation of an all-pervading mending force. It gives the power to heal. The element that mends the bones, in a spiritual sense, is a quality of essence, a very refined substance that we could call brilliance. It is like when the sun hits the water and the water shines. It is as if white light atoms condense together and become an eloquent substance that shines with dense luminosity. This brilliancy of essence is found at the very foundation of existence. It is a basic element of will.

Al-Jabbar is not an all-compelling force in the sense of forcing you to move in a particular direction. It is compelling in the sense of stabilizing you in the direction of your focus. It empowers you to be stable so you are mighty in nature. You have the sense that, like a mountain, nothing can shake you. From this vantage point, when there are broken bones, it is the essential substance of liquid light that flows into the bones, fills in the cracks where the breakage is, and enables the physical body to mend.

Al-Jabbar is a power that aims at integrating all the domains of the universe. If you do not have it, you resort to splitting life into many pieces: good/bad, high/low, God/humanity. In short, it is a fractured existence. But when al-Jabbar comes, a unified existence comes with it, and all the fields are integrated and brought together in a unity.

Prayerful repetition of Ya Jabbar is a remedy for fractured human beings leading a fractured existence. It is a sacred Name that connects and mends the fabric of our self. It helps each of us overcome the disconnections in our personality structure that are caused by primary and secondary narcissistic wounding.

The essence of light, luminosity itself, is the divine Name an-Nur. When luminosity differentiates itself it comes as a wave of tidal light. And this tidal light, if it condenses, becomes brilliant substance. Al-Jabbar is the strength of this substance that flows out in the universe to mend the disconnections.

It is a common human condition to experience your own body as being disconnected. But when this healing substance comes, you experience body, mind, and heart as one unified field. A complete integration takes place. That is the jewel we discover in al-Jabbar.

Each Name has a *jawhar*, a jewel. It is like an essence. With al-'Aziz we find self-worth and strength. With al-Qahhar there is a burning power that transcends time, an unquenchable fire that cooks and makes one juicy, and that ultimately consumes the ego identity and transforms it completely. Al-Jabbar brings this brilliant flowing strength to continuously heal and integrate our fractured existence.

Ya Qawiyy

(yaa ḴO-weeyy)

Al-Qawiyy can be translated as divine strength or omnipotence, but as we have seen with the other members of this family, there is a unique way it will manifest. Al-Qawiyy is an internal strength. It is the strength to not use the power that you may feel surging within. This is quite different from al-Jabbar, which is always pouring out, always mending and fixing things.

Al-Qawiyy gives the strength to resist. It is the strength not to act on impulses. It is a strength that can be clearly sensed, though it is almost as if you are no longer there. You overcome the sense of needing to engage in a personal act of will. You are simply witnessing, but not acting upon, the power that you feel. There is a root meaning for al-Qawiyy of "emptying a house." At the spiritual level, the house is empty of the sense of ego-self, and that ultimately allows you to let the divine act.

The *'arsh* (Heart) throne is the empty, still place at the center of the universe. When we talk about the power and strength necessary to approach this place, the verb for it is *'istawaa*, which means to settle in perfect emptiness, to not act. You are guided to find this place through not using the power you may feel surging in you.

By settling into emptiness in this way, you discover an inward strength that is all-powerful, and yet not used in an outward way. Al-Qawiyy is a strength that comes from emptiness, a strength that arises from total peace, absolute silence. It is rooted in the place of no place.

Directing our attention to the human dilemma, there is a substance, an essence, that is juicy like wine, and when it runs in the body it fills the body with ecstatic passion. It has the sense of wine running in the blood. When the wine is running in the blood a person gets intoxicated, gets passionate, gets strengthened, gets full of power. We'll call it pomegranate essence. The image of the pomegranate is of a fruit that is inward, its juicy strength contained by its rough skin.

The pomegranate essence in its perfection is a wine that brings intoxication without drunkenness. That is because there is sobriety in the passion. When it is awakened in your system you feel very strong. The blood of the spirit is running through you. The body gets filled with life and energy, the spirit fills with courage, and the mind fills with a sense of ecstasy. In these ways we can see the liberated aspect of this quality.

The negative counterpart of the pomegranate essence is expressed as a passion that does not have any sense of sobriety. It is drunkenness. It is led by desires, led by power, led by revenge and destructiveness. It indulges the instincts and also uses the power of the instincts. It is a nihilistic, libidinal force that runs in the system. There is madness to it. It is like tainted wine. Underneath, or within, this force there is so much power that it drives people insane. They lose inner control and become destructive. It brings jealousy and the deepest desire for revenge.

This force, this desire, this powerful libidinal energy, is the strength that got suppressed or distorted when the child's desires in the Oedipal stage were not met. A suppression or distortion occurred when the son was madly in love with the mother, but the mother didn't find the appropriate way to reciprocate, or the father made it a competition. Perhaps the daughter was madly in love with her father and the mother got jealous, or the father didn't reciprocate.

In these instances, the tiger within gained control, but then was put in jail. However, every now and then a strong desire comes to break loose from this jail. Then human beings unleash the tiger, which comes out in the form of destruction. It destroys relationships, starts wars, and wreaks all manner of havoc.

Gradually you find the means to deal with the Oedipal rage and the Oedipal rejection and engage with the Oedipal power that is there. Then, instead of acting it out, you control it and direct it toward the divine source, and this power becomes divine intoxication. It becomes an ecstatic passionate love that has the inner strength to love everyone. When this divine intoxication manifests, you want to strengthen and empower others rather than destroy them and take revenge on them. The Oedipal power becomes restrained, and it is controlled.

It is here that we find the true omnipotence of al-Qawiyy. It brings the strength to overcome the distorted passion! With this realization, inner strength takes on a compassionate and ecstatic condition. You may know that human beings are weak, yet you don't destroy them. You know that creation is beautiful, and consequently you don't damage it. You are filled with love and strength to help heal all creation, to strengthen it, and to enjoy it. You are madly and ecstatically in love with God, with God's creation.

This negative counterpart is not real in Allah. It has been generated at the ego level, and what is needed is to find the strength to properly address it. The Sufi Hazrat Inayat Khan writes "I am the wine of the divine sacrament. My very being is intoxication. Those who can drink of this cup and yet remain sober will certainly be illuminated. But those who cannot assimilate it will become objects of ridicule in the eyes of the world."

A problem arises when spiritual teachers use their position as an excuse for taking personal license. They have an experience of spiritual power within, but they lack the means of containing it. So it spills out on their followers in the form of abuse and manipulation of all kinds. They need to discover the power of al-Qawiyy, which brings control, and which allows one to be full of strength yet empty of ego attachments. When that happens you have power but no personal agenda. Acts are spontaneous, effortless, and full of life. You are not self-conscious or self-grasping at all.

Al-Qawiyy is the strength that comes from the emptiness of self. This strength is held in the heart, in the most hidden place, in the *'arsh* throne. It is an inner empowerment strong enough to defeat the superego, the lower impulses, the lusts, and all the desires that have command upon us. Al-Qawiyy commands and disarms the commanding self, which is the most primitive expression of self.

The blaming self is more sophisticated than the commanding self; the blaming self is developing a conscience. But the commanding self is very primitive and adamant. You want something and you want it now. It has to do with the desire for the Oedipal stage and the breast. When you take the breast you feel entitled. You claim the breast in a most basic way, for survival, so it comes with an awesome power. And when we hear the justifications for wars, past and present, we often hear the aggressors say they are doing it for self-defense, for survival.

Al-Qawiyy involves giving up the need to cling to survival, and that means conquering death. With the realization of al-Qawiyy, we conquer death and fear, and we are strong. It is the exact opposite of surrender. The experience is dominated by the divine power acting through emptiness of self. This defines the path of the master.

The path of the master is a mirror image of the path of the saint. Saints surrender to death in the same way they surrender their attachment to anything else, physical or otherwise. Through such surrender the saints harmonize their will with all. The master, on the other hand, orchestrates all in accordance with the divine will.

In addition to Ya Qawiyy, there are other divine Names that can be used in recitation when facing your fear of death. Elsewhere we will speak of Ya Hayy, Ya Mu'id, Ya Muhyi, and Ya Mumit as resources in this same context. There are several kinds of fear of death that may be experienced. The particular one we are talking about in relation to al-Qawiyy is a kind of weakness that is felt in the face of death. You are overpowered by the fear of losing the "I am." For that fear the remedy is Ya Qawiyy. In such a way, the experience of death is transformed. This is the real *via negativa*.

Ya Matin

(yaa ma-TEEN)

Some might question whether al-Matin fully belongs in the divine omnipotence cluster of Names, but al-Matin brings an important kind of power that deserves consideration here. Looking first into the sound code of the Arabic language, al-Matin expresses the meaning of a divine strength that is functioning in all circumstances and in all situations, without exception. It brings consistency, firmness, and rhythm.

Human beings often go forward for a little while and then lose focus. You stop practicing what you have begun, or you go from one thing to another. Al-Matin is the strength to keep on keeping on. Consider how you learn to play a musical instrument. You can't pick up a violin or a vina and just practice when you feel like it, perhaps a few days at a time, and then stop for six months. If you proceed this way, you definitely will not gain any mastery.

Mastery is another word for al-Matin. Without the consistency, firmness, and rhythm manifested by this divine quality people lose strength and heart; doubts creep in, and you are very likely to fail. You become very susceptible to moods, to mood swings, and changes of heart. There is no consistency. Such a state is just the opposite of al-Matin.

There doesn't seem to be a lot of consistency in most of our lives. Many of us feel weak or helpless in the face of events. News of war, or the stock market, or anything dramatic just sweeps us off our feet. And since most of us have no control over political events or over ourselves, it feels like everything is awash. It is more a kind of despair than it is fear.

There is no quality of al-Matin or anything truly stabilizing in most of our lives. Something definite is needed, any regular spiritual practice. It could be as simple as a daily yoga practice or silent sunrise meditation. Invoking Ya Matin begins to cure the affliction of lacking stability in life. Al-Matin helps us attune to the essence which sustains incarnate being, since our focus often drifts in the midst of internal and external forces.

You may sit and try to meditate, but your mind and your emotions take over instead. What is needed is to engage a specific will to counter the internal forces. Sometimes the need is to become stabilized in relation to your experience of external forces. Even the weather may set you off. When anything takes you away from your intended direction, you need to activate another power to sustain your will amidst the influences of the world.

When you feel al-Matin in the system, the experience is very compressed, very solid. It is as if all your loose and spacious atoms got pulled together, and you become compressed like a solid rock. The Bible says, "Peter is my rock." You become the rock; you become the mountain; you become the anchor. You are grounded. No matter what the forces around you may be, they cannot take you out of your being.

The quality of al-Matin has to do with the strength of will to be in the world. It brings the capacity to be in the world. Many spiritual practitioners are able to feel grounded within their selves. They can sit in meditation and do their practices, but when it comes to being in the world, they often feel unfocused and fragmented. They are not well grounded in the outer world, though they may be grounded within.

The meaning of al-Matin is to have a solid foundation. A compressed, dense foundation gives something to build upon. It brings a rootedness to our activities on the spiritual path. No fear or temptation will take you out. You feel relaxed, grounded in the world for yourself and for others.

Lacking this groundedness often has to do with not having a father that took our hand as a child, introduced us to the world, and made the world feel safe. At the end of the stage of merging with the mother, a child needs help moving into the outer environment with ease and stability. If your mother is fearful of this, for example, then you have no counterbalance, and you are always susceptible to the mother's fear.

This gets internalized as an inner wound from your family. It operates as a kind of hole. There is no ground underneath you. Instead there is fear, and there is nobody to take you out of that hole. Some families, on the other hand, give you a feeling that no matter what happens you can weather any storm. Al-Matin has to do with the capacity of functioning. You have the foundation to call upon the resources of your being and apply these inner qualities in the world.

No matter what happens, you maintain balance. You can always recover after a fall. The absence of al-Matin in your self or in your family leads to pessimism. There is always the fear that you are going to lose everything in the next sweep of time since you lack a firm foundation. You may get this foundation in your childhood—or on the path of the mystic you may be graced to receive it from Allah.

Rhythm and health are synonymous. Rhythm is also the source of all music. The power that comes from rhythmic existence is expressed by al-Matin and is itself a kind of health and balance. Considering these divine Names as a pharmacopoeia of cures for certain ailments, we recommend recitation of Ya Matin for those who are not consistent, or who lack the foundation to function well in the world.

It could also be given to those who have become a slave of consistency and have lost spontaneity, or to those who easily get stuck. Embodying this divine quality brings balanced progress, and so the invocation of Ya Matin will work in both directions to bring such balance. The *wazaif* often can be applied toward excesses in both directions. This is indicative of how these divine medicines operate.

Ya Dhal Jalali wal 'Ikram
(DHAL ja-LAA-li WAL 'ik-RAAM)

This extraordinary divine Name has a most unusual form. Its sound offers a triple opening because of the linking together of three long vowel sounds. It is a form whose intensity has been emphasized again and again. Thus it is especially powerful in its repetition as a spiritual practice. Another unusual thing about Dhul Jalali wal 'Ikram is that it packages together two Names, Ya Jalal and Ya Karim, power and boundless generosity. What is mysterious is that these two Names, at first glance, do not appear to be naturally harmonious.

In the Qur'an,[44] Allah gives *takreem* to Adam. This quality combines both Jalal and Karim. *Takreem* has to do with the powerful manifestation as well as the heart-filled generosity of giving a gift. The gift is 'Ikram, a particularly emphatic form of al-Karim, and it is given to *al-'insaan kaamil*, the complete or perfect human being, the prototype of whom is Adam. Some illustrative root meanings of al-Karim are dignity, honor, and respect.

The Jalal part of this divine gift to humanity is in the incredible force of the divine manifestation that is continuously offered every moment. God is seen in the adamant core of the powerful essence of what is bestowed, and its emanation generously goes into everything and everybody, without exception. When, as a spiritual student, you perceive the continuous activity of Dhul Jalali wal 'Ikram, you are inwardly empowered to contemplate *takreem* in each and every human being. In doing so, you give ultimate respect and honor to mankind.

Giving such ultimate respect and honor to mankind is what Allah asked the angels to do upon the creation of Adam, because Allah saw the divine essence hidden in this archetype of humanity. The angels literally fell on their faces in prostration *(sajdah)* because their legs could no longer support them when they saw the mystery incarnated in Adam.

But the ultimate *takreem* is to see this divine manifestation continuously in all human beings, notwithstanding their composition of mud and water and their history of ignorant inter-relationships. Then you live in the reality of seeing the face of God everywhere because of the generosity, or the *karim*, which is continually being given.

Imam al-Ghazzali explains Dhul Jalali wal 'Ikram by focusing on the *dhal* (or *dhul*), which means "that." It is the same word as *dhat (zat)*, the absolute essence beyond name and form. Majestic power is at the core of the transcendental source that continually manifests. In accord with Arabic grammar, when using the vocative form "Ya" we say Ya Dhal Jalali wal 'Ikram; without the "Ya" the name is slightly different: we say Dhul Jalali wal 'Ikram.

The *jalal* is the strength inherent in the source. Al-Karim is an infinite receptivity of heart that allows you to be aware of this generous flow of strength. If you are fully aware of the continuous flowing of *takreem* in your heart, you are engaged in the sublime contemplation practice of *mushaahidah*, which is sometimes translated as "awe-filled witnessing." It is a way of actively witnessing all human beings and the whole creation.

Freely speaking in a visual way, with Dhul Jalali wal 'Ikram your heart is in the golden condition of generosity, yet there is also black radiance, which shines from the ultimate source where all mind and manifestation cannot be said to exist. This radiance is the black luminosity of al Jalal. It activates the power to seize the distracted mind and focus it entirely on the realization of absolute truth.

At the same time, on the heart level there is a realization that this power is a manifestation of utmost generosity. The heart feels the preciousness and value within the source itself and extends this to others. Truth becomes condensed in the heart and becomes golden. Your real self is brought to witness in this way. The word *dhal* (or *dhul*) in this divine Name also means the one who owns these qualities of al-Jalal and al-Karim.

Invocation of Ya Dhal Jalali wal 'Ikram brings a needed balance to the condition of being overly attached to the acquisition of power. And it also brings balance to your being when you are attached to a concept of kindness while at the same time being fearful of power. Its repetition is useful when you are caught in trying to choose, "Shall I administer loving-kindness or righteous power?"

While repetition of Ya Dhal Jalali wal 'Ikram is helpful for awakening generosity, it also enables you to overcome the experience of deficiency of power, fear of power, fear of being overruled by power, or fear of misusing power. With realization of this divine Name human beings can move to a full blending of heart and head.

Power is subject to outrageous abuse unless there is awakening of heart and development of the ability to see with the eye of the heart. For this reason, we have chosen to emphasize this divine Name in the discussion of the omnipotence family. Ya Dhal Jalali wal 'Ikram ultimately leads you to a sweetness, softness, and surrender that is filled with an easeful flow of awesome power.

Ya Qadir, Ya Muqtadir
(yaa ḲAA-dir, yaa muk-TA-dir)

As we know, primary families often have close relatives. This is true of the strength and omnipotence family of divine Names. We have been looking at Names that express the power to direct or control all actions. It becomes quite natural now to direct our attention to the related qualities of strength of divine purpose or will, and thus to al-Qadir and al-Muqtadir.

Qadar is the common core in both Names. It is the strength of divine purpose, the power behind God's purpose. When *qadar* is awake, you experience the power of divine purpose in life. This purpose acts directly on everything.

What enables you to say that there is meaning in your life is al-Muqtadir. The sound code tells us that al-Muqtadir acts directly on us. The source of its meaning, however, is transcendental, and that is al-Qadir. It is beyond our particular personality, genetic inheritance, and any conditioned situation.

Al-Qadir is a divine purpose, and it also means unlimited capacity. We have our own expectations about the course of events, but we should understand that one of the meanings of al-Qadir is "the overall course of events." With al-Qadir, there is a feeling that all real strength in the universe is one. Everything in the universe is connected by this power.

By awakening to this unlimited power, we realize that there is both a path and a specific destination. This divine quality gives meaning and real purpose to everything in life. Realization of al-Qadir brings a great confidence that all things are possible. It naturally expresses power, spaciousness, endurance, proportionality, and value. It offers both the power to manifest and to contain manifestation.

The basic verb, *qadara*, means to measure cloth with the hands, and it conveys the idea of appropriate value. This idea of worth and merit has both a cosmic and physical feel to it. A person who embodies the quality of *qadar* is competent and knows the true worth of things.

Some interesting territory is opened up with the root word *qudrah*, which is the common noun of al-Qadir and al-Muqtadir. It means to equalize, and it also means ability, courage, and prowess. There is a second set of meanings: natural, innate, and instinctive, as well as the idea of worth, merit, and value.

Al-Qadir explicitly makes reference to death and life, or what in Sufi terminology are the states of *fana* and *baqa*—the stages of return, going toward the one. These are states we have to go through repetitively, as it is part of the divine plan to return everything to God.

Now al-Muqtadir is the One who places you on a particular path to God, enables you to firmly put your feet on that path, and keep going on that path, step by step. It brings the ability to actualize the divine purpose in your life. The power that is guiding you put you in this very specific situation, here and now. There are no mistakes, and nothing is ever wasted or lost.

Each soul is unique, with a unique purpose in life. That is the meaning of al-Muqtadir. Where all this leads is that each of us needs to recognize al-Qadir and lovingly engage our ability to fulfill it. The lover makes use of whatever power the Beloved has granted and uses it in the same wise and beautifully proportioned way that it came.

When you have truly surrendered to al-Qadir, you are able to do to your utmost capacity what wisdom requires to fulfill your destiny. Al-Qadir and al-Muqtadir both have to do with fulfilling or discovering your destiny. Al-Qadir makes you aware of the cosmic power behind all purposive activity. Al-Muqtadir puts your feet on the path of the particular activity that you need to fulfill your purpose. It is a process of discovery and fulfillment that recognizes and embodies divine strength.

Invocation of Ya Qadir, Ya Muqtadir together as a pair offers an antidote to feeling worthless and powerless. Prayerful repetition can quite effectively and powerfully lead a spiritual wayfarer to the realization of their purpose in life.

kabir
'azim
wasi'

allahu akbar

'aliyy
muta'ali
waliyy
mutakabbir

chapter 10

Awakening to Infinite Presence

No subject could be more immediate for human beings than the infinite presence of God. A cluster of sacred Names invites us to dive deeply and directly into omnipresence. These Names manifest complementary pathways for realizing infinite presence. Their relationships with each other are a revealing way to gain insight into this mysterious subject. We will examine this family of divine omnipresence through studying the Names' dictionary meanings and roots, and by using the sound code embedded in the structure of Arabic grammar.

Ya Kabir, Ya Mutakabbir, Allahu Akbar

(yaa ka-BEER, yaa mu-ta-KAB-bir)

Al-Kabir and al-Mutakabbir can be described by English synonyms such as big, great, vast, and so on. This doesn't help us very much in understanding them individually, however, because such epithets can similarly be applied to all the Names in this cluster.

What is more helpful is to note that al-Kabir and al-Mutakabbir share a common root in the word *kabura*, which carries a meaning of magnitude in both space and time. *Kabura* means to grow old, and it also means to grow big. In modern Arabic, *kabir* can mean older or bigger. This combination of concepts may be familiar from our contemporary idea of the space/time continuum.

Al-Kabir is pre-eternal, and it is timeless. Al-Kabir is oldest in time and largest in space. If we think of the first event in the universe, perhaps the big bang, al-Kabir or Allah is even older, infinitely older. And if you think of the biggest extent of the universe, al-Kabir is yet bigger. The common Arabic word *akbar* is a different form of the same root. Theologians say that if you think of the smallest thing in the universe, the same incomparable quality of al-Kabir still applies, and thus al-Kabir is going to be even smaller. If you think of the nanosecond of a moment al-Kabir is going to be even newer.

'Ibn 'Arabi says that we cannot really compare God to anything because comparisons don't apply to God. He suggests that we read the signs of God in the universe as "take-off points." It is almost as if the whole universe is made of poetic metaphors. Thus, by poetically evoking the notion of incomparable greatness or vastness, we try to compare without making specific comparisons. We use the finite to experience something of the infinite in order to try to describe the indescribable. Mystics and poets perpetually engage in this sort of hopeless and wonderful activity.

The easiest and best way to understand al-Mutakabbir is to look at in relation to al-Kabir. But first, it will help if we look at another example in Arabic of a similar relationship between words. *'Alima* means to teach. The form of the word *t'alim*, which is similar to the form of *mutakabbir*, means to become learned. The sound code also tells us that words that have this particular form all have as part of their meaning "ever-becoming." Al-Mutakabbir thus means always moving beyond the limitation of the present experience, whatever it is. Al-Mutakabbir is always going beyond. It is ever becoming vaster in time and space.

Kabura embodies dignity, nobility, and excellence, and Mutakabbir is always beyond, always transcends our understanding of any those experiences. Remember, in seeking to understand the divine Names we are trying to understand relationships, not things. No matter what one's relationship to Allah is, Allah is beyond that. In fact Allah is infinitely greater. It is like the Hindu practice of reciting *"neti neti"* for every thought that arises. "That's not God. That's not God." You used your mind, and your mind brought forth a thought. But God is beyond that; it always transcends conceptualization.

Regarding the root meaning of al-Kabir and al-Mutakabbir, both words are related to *al-'istighfaar*, which is a word for arrogance and pride, a word that literally means inflating the self. *'Istighfaar* is the classic term for this affliction. In fact, al-Mutakabbir in bad translation is often rendered as the one who disdains being described by the *sifat*.

These shadowy aspects in the meanings that occur in various forms of the roots of the sacred Names are important to us in our inquiry. Given our orientation toward applying the Names as curatives for diseased and disconnected human conditions, when we come upon associated meanings such as arrogance and pride we immediately think that it is precisely this kind of problem to which that particular sacred Name should be applied as a medicine for healing.

Al-Kabir is a vast presence that is none other than Allah. In certain states of ecstasy, the world is a vast theater in which every atom is a sign of God. No matter where you might try to go, you can't escape from that consciousness. You can go into the spiritual world, the physical world, the metaphysical world, but in every direction, in every world, what you face there is al-Kabir. You see the face of the beloved in every drop of water, in every grain of sand. It is vast. It is wonderful. There is no escaping it.

There's a story about Mevlana Jalaluddin Rumi and Shams-i-Tabriz doing a *khalwah*, or spiritual retreat. While engaged in this practice, everything spoke the name "Allah" to them: the birds in their singing, the frogs in their croaking, and so on. Such a perception is not an overlay or an interpretation. It is a reality experienced everywhere as an infinite presence.

In a sense we should say that infinite absence is also al-Mutakabbir, because if we assert presence, then we must also assert absence. However, not to get stuck in dualism, the unity of being at this stage requires that there must be something that combines presence and absence. If that were not so, then our notions of presence and absence would be limited.

Mahayana Buddhists have a teaching called *sunyata*, the infinite emptiness of any so-called thing. Another way of describing this teaching is through the terms "interdependence" or "co-arising." Nothing has its own separate existence; in existence everything depends on other factors. As a consequence, everything is insubstantial, as nothing rests on its own independent basis. Everything is empty of its own independent existence. It doesn't truly exist except in a relative way.

So Buddhists often say that nothing exists, and by that they mean that everything is insubstantial. When they go on to speak of the absolute, *sunyata* is equated with the absolute as an infinite absence or void. At the same time, they say the clear light of illumination, *bodhi* or Buddha nature, is one and the same as this void. Here we have another way of describing both infinite presence and infinite absence.

We understand al-Mutakabbir as the path to vastness. It is going beyond, constantly going beyond limitation, just as the Buddhist Prajna Paramita mantra says: *gate, gate, paragate, parasamgate, bodhi svaha*. It is a process: beyond, and beyond that, and beyond that. . . Al-Mutakabbir has the sense of a continual action. It is not like a state. When you reach an apparent boundary, it always goes beyond.

On the other hand, al-Kabir is more like the state itself. There is no more beyond it. We are in the beyond. The Kabir itself includes presence and absence simultaneously. It goes beyond time and space. When we are in time and space, we are in the process of Mutakabbir. We are going through one dimension after another to transcend all. Time and space are conditioned within a certain frequency of existence and only exist within that band or frequency. Beyond this there is no time and no space.

Al-Kabir is the station beyond time and space, beyond expansion and contraction. It is incomparable vastness. Al-Mutakabbir is an ultimate transcending process. And al-Mutakabbir, since it is dynamic, can lead outside and then go back into the time and space continuum. If we think of al-Mutakabbir as an activity that leads to vastness and transcendence, by invoking Ya Mutakabbir a spiritual practitioner will be actively engaged with the boundaries of mind and indeed the overall structure that their personality defines.

To explore divine omnipresence, we need to let go of our boundaries and realize that God exists beyond these boundaries as well as within them. One way to experience the absolute is through our willingness to let go of our own definitions, our own boundaries, and our own comfort zone, whether these boundaries are in the mind or the physical reality.

Invoking Ya Mutakabbir is undertaking the continual action of dissolution of the boundaries. Whenever we reach a boundary, an irresistible wave will gently erase that boundary. And then comes another expansion and another boundary. So the continual action through al-Mutakabbir is that it will not stop at any boundaries or any comfort zone. When we come to al-Kabir there are no more boundaries. There is no more time. Time and space are themselves boundaries, but al-Kabir is like a boundless ocean.

Al-Mutakabbir also means the one who exceeds the actions of all others in goodness or excellence. The actions of the divine exceed all other actions. It continuously goes beyond. Because of this, repetition of Ya Mutakabbir or Allahu Akbar would be an excellent medicine for those who have a very low self-image.

Allah is vast, and that vastness quickens practitioners to overcome smallness. Repetition of Ya Mutakabbir can be given to those who feel insignificant or who feel enmeshed in limitations. The oft-repeated phrase "Allahu Akbar" means God is greater, not as a specific comparison, but in exactly the sense of incomparability we have just been talking about.

If we think "what I am experiencing is the ultimate power," then God is a greater power. If we think "this is ultimate love," then God is a greater love. Whatever we think, in doing so we have set a boundary. So if we expand it, then we keep breaking down all the limitations that are within our mind, and that can enable our mind to be free.

This kind of practice is particularly indicated whenever a person is caught up in a whole complex of security issues, a sense of being bound up, a sense of physical limitations, or an absorption in the denseness of the earth. Such absorption is evidence of a belief that this life is all there is. When that occurs, the repetition of Allahu Akbar, or of Ya Kabir, Ya Mutakabbir, is a key to exposing the limitations of the mind.

Usually these boundaries, or these limitations in the mind, are a defense mechanism against a sense of deficiency. The ego feels deeply deficient in its core, and the core of this ego deficiency cannot be resolved by any actions that the ego itself undertakes. The resolution of the core problem of the ego deficiency comes through awakening to the presence of Allah.

Our ego structure is based on deficiency. Human beings contrive a defense system because they feel that some core element is lacking. Underneath it all you feel really small. So when your inner structure has been inflated or deflated as a defensive reaction to such a core feeling of deficiency, then invocation of Allahu Akbar begins to open up that structure and overcome those boundaries. This process leads to becoming aware of and engaging with your deficiencies in an open and undefended way.

In prescribing Allahu Akbar, physicians of the heart are aiming to dismantle the totality of the defense structure, and in this way make space for the experience of the infinite presence of God. Repetition of this *wazifah* does not leave you helpless. On the contrary, it is often offered as a powerful practice of protection in all circumstances. The ultimate aim of the practice is the dissolution of the entire defensive structure in the personality, which means sooner or later the spiritual traveler will encounter the absolute.

Such an encounter evokes al-Kabir. The ego deficiency directly opens to the absolute. It is actually through the ego deficiency that there is entry to the absolute! And the encounter with the absolute then allows for real progress in relation to the ego deficiency. Through such a process there can be a true kind of inflation of self. One may actually become al-Kabir, the greatness of the divine presence. This is very different from a false inflation, which comes from the defensive act of creating an ego structure of grandiosity that is based on a core feeling of deficiency.

When invoking Ya Mutakabbir you take each individual thing and do a kind of comparison until you get to the ultimate absolute stage. For example, you begin with your limited notion of kindness, and invoking Ya Mutakabbir you ultimately understand unlimited kindness. Ya Mutakabbir, as a practice, would be for a person who is very much absorbed in the process of unfoldment. Invocation of Ya Kabir is more for the person who has already been touched by the experience we have been describing, one who has reached that station of boundlessness. It is a full emptiness. When al-Kabir enters there is presence and absence simultaneously.

Allahu Akbar seems to be a key for the problem of self-identifying with the experience of lacking al-Kabir and al-Mutakabbir. It can be a medicine for artificial inflation of the ego and also a medicine for feeling small and insignificant. There is a deflated way of being grandiose. To think, "I am the least of the least" is very grandiose.

Al-Kabir is more a station than a process. Allah is neither the process nor the station. Whenever we put a Name on the nameless, it takes a certain frequency. So even al-Kabir is still an activity within the cosmic field, an attribute. Erase it, and what will remain is the reality that we cannot put any Name on, the nameless.

To reach the boundless, we first have to go through the activation of something, and for this we have al-Mutakabbir. An inner dialogue might be: "I am beyond this boundary; I am beyond that boundary. Now I feel the infinite. Now I am beyond infinite because infinity is still a concept. Still, I am experiencing the universe within certain limits. It's great, it's mighty, it's peaceful, and it's full of love." It is experienced as infinite but still within a lens. The lens is a Name of Allah, which is a very subtle lens, but the Name is still a Name. That means it is an attribute. The physician of the heart at this ripe time may want to introduce the recitation of Allahu Akbar to invite transcendence of even this exalted state.

In summary, when we want to induce growth in students who are either inflated or deflated, we recommend Ya Mutakabbir. When they ultimately reach the reality of al-Kabir they appreciate the greatness of God's existence. There is a "full emptiness" that is awakened in the remembrance of Ya Kabir. It is neither static nor dynamic. In another sense, there is an "empty fullness" in al-Mutakabbir because in every stage of the implied journey of "becoming," a certain amount of attachment comes. When the ego gets attached to any of those stages, either to the fullness or the emptiness, it becomes trapped. For example, it then needs to come toward fullness by emptying out.

Getting ensnared by your attachments to the limitations of the journey can be resolved by realizing al-Mutakabbir. The cure for being attached to the goal of the journey, the limitlessness of the goal, is through realizing al-Kabir. So invocation of Ya Kabir is both for the person who feels very small, to experience vastness, and for the person who feels grandiose, to recognize that Allah is the most grand, and so to not be attached to the ego. The need is to overcome the habit of identifying with the activity of ego, identifying with the isolated self.

From the standpoint of these two Names' therapeutic applications, al-Kabir appears to relate to qualities and al-Mutakabbir seems to relate to actions. However, both Ya Mutakabbir and Ya Kabir can be prescribed to overcome pride. These Names complement each other, which invites us to recite them as a pair.

Ya 'Azim

(yaa 'a-ḌHEEM)

It is quite remarkable that al-'Azim comes from *al-'adaam*, which means to grow strong in the bones. In fact its meaning actually has to do with bones, literally hip bones. "Growing strong in the bones" becomes an inward experience of omnipresence. For the one who realizes al-'Azim, each and every sign of God gives the experience of a vast and infinite presence that can be felt in your bones.

There are other root meanings of al-'Azim that help fill in the picture: numerous, vast, the middle part of an open road. Another cluster of meanings is grave, severe, awesome. There is an awesome or overwhelming feeling connected with this Name. And there is also the meaning of magnitude. On top of all this, we can't talk about al-'Azim without at least mentioning the word *'ism*, which is implied within the word *'azim*. *'Ism* refers to the legendary hundredth Name, the greatest Name, which is unknown.

A verse in the Qur'an expresses this quality of penetrating into the bones.[45] In particular, it speaks of following a deep inner contentment in relation to Allah: *Dhoo fadl(in) 'adheem. Dhoo* means "that," but it has the sense of inwardness, a feeling of blessing, of inner contentment in the bones. It is a deep inward feeling of the infinite presence of Allah. It is not pointing us toward a journey and it is not orienting us toward the goal of the journey. What this Qur'anic passage really affirms is sacred presence pervading to the depths—to the very marrow of our bones.

Awakening through the process of invoking Ya 'Azim is actualizing the divine presence. You experience this presence right in the midst of life. It is an experience of the infinite in your deepest, essential self. Ya 'Azim is a *wazifah* for accomplishing extraordinary aims, the most extraordinary aims. Its quality is more the highest actualization, rather than the highest realization. This is an important distinction, to which we will return in a moment.

In the Qur'an there is mention of all the spheres of manifestation in the heavens and the earth.[46] These can be seen through the qualities of al-Mutakabbir, al-Kabir, and Allahu Akbar. All the spheres of manifestation are called the domain of the *kursiyy*. They are all included in al-Wasi', which is called the infinite container of all those realms.

Now al-Wasi' in that sense still doesn't include the Heart Throne: the *'arsh*, that center dot. The *'arsh*, however, is contained in the most sublime name of divine omnipresence, al-'Azim. Al-'Azim includes all of the spheres of manifestation plus the source, the *'arsh*. We can initially compare al-Kabir and al-Mutakabbir, and then compare that to al-Akbar, all of which are included in al-Wasi'. But the largest inclusive omnipresence is al-'Azim. It includes *'arsh* and *kursiyy*.

In a number of Qur'anic verses *'arsh* is related to al-'Azim.[47] These verses talk about the seven heavens and connect these spheres to the *'arsh*. This shows that al-'Azim includes not just the center, the *'arsh*, but also the manifestation of the essence. Al-'Azim's intensive form in the sound code indicates its outpouring into all things. The concept of al-'Azim is most closely related to Allahu Akbar.

Kubraa is the feminine form of *akbar*. *Ayat-ul-kubraa* is called the greatest sign, the one seen by Moses. From the standpoint of the 99 Names, the greatest sign is the greatest Name. And the greatest Name would be the elative of al-'Azim. There is a reference for all this in the Qur'an.[48] Here the words Allahu Akbar and al-'Azim appear in the same verse. This offers some textual evidence of their relationship. The main thing to notice here about Allahu Akbar is that there is a relationship between it, al-Wasi', and al-'Azim.

It is important to realize the absolute, but realization is only the beginning of awakening, the beginning of liberation. We then need to bring the absolute "into the marketplace," or to use a metaphor from the Zen Buddhist tradition, to "chop wood and carry water" instead of simply being on the mountaintop. On the mountaintop, we may realize the absolute. There is freedom. But once we start actualizing, we have to go through the process of embodiment in both worlds. Actualization means the descent of the absolute into the physical plane and the flesh. It means transforming the body, the nervous system, and ultimately the bones.

Moses coming down from the mountain is a picture of actualization. Many people attend to realization, but they cannot actualize it. It is difficult to function with one's realization amidst the currents of daily life. Actualization ultimately means the transformation of the physical, and the psychic as well.

The most difficult part is reaching the stage in which one doesn't get ruffled or knocked off-center. The practitioner who has actualized al-'Azim is always anchored. This state is not so much associated with the *hara* center, as taught in many yoga systems. You are fully anchored when the absolute descends into your bones.

One stage of this descent of the absolute is that it begins to meld the crack of our being, a crack that is stored in the bones. Unless the crack is melded, we go out to meet humanity with bones filled with a sense of pretense, falseness, and fear. Consequently, when the experience of the absolute comes, the brittleness in the bones releases an awesome amount of terror. It is the fear of being alone in existence. It is the fear that this universe can be destroyed, or that it can destroy one and all. As a result, when divine omnipresence has not been brought thoroughly into the bones, there is no empowerment.

When such fears dissolve, the bones become soft. The second stage of actualization is a stage of suppleness and vulnerability. The bones are like cartilage. They are supple, soft, and pliable. It is not that they have solidity; they have freedom. They can breathe again. Literally, we can now breathe in the bones. We can breathe in the marrow of the bones and expand the marrow of the bones.

In time, the soft bones begin to jell and transform into what might be called diamonds. The bone levels are like compressed salt diamonds. They physically contain in them a divine presence. This is seen in some of the great relics of enlightened beings, such as those treasured by the Tibetan Buddhists. Some of these bone relics are like pearls, and some of them are like diamonds. Al-'Azim demonstrates the actualization of the infinitude of the divine in our bones.

When students need expansion, when it is felt they can break the boundaries and expand outward, then we recommend starting them out on the repetition of Ya Mutakabbir. However, for those who have achieved some expansion but still feel small inside, we would prescribe Ya Kabir. There comes a time when, from that al-Kabir state, spiritual travelers need to return down the mountain, so to speak, and actualize their realization in daily practical life in a solid and consistent way. Then we would offer recitation of Ya 'Azim.

This is embodying the divine presence in a complete way, right into the bones. In the Qur'an, the Verse of Light[49] says that there are people who buy and sell in the marketplace and yet constantly re-member the Name of God. These are the ones who embody their realization in daily life. They actualize it right in the midst of the world.

Ya Wasi'

(yaa WAA-si')

The word al-Wasi' straightforwardly suggests the infinite omnipresence of the divine essence or face of God. This comes from two Qur'anic verses. The most famous verse affirms that wherever you turn, there is the face of God.[50] We can call Al-Wasi' an infinite surrounding presence. The verse says "The presence of God, the love (*rahma*), surrounds."

The word translated as "surrounds" is al-Wasi'. The physical image here is that of a womb. It is encompassing, comprehending, and surrounding. There is also a well-known prayer, "Oh Allah surround us with your compassion." Once again the association of al-Wasi' and the *rahma* (loving compassion) is emphasized.

Al-Wasi' is an all-surrounding embracing expansion. What an amazing combination! It is embracing but without narrowing, because it also expands. It is like a feeling of a huge embracing womb that is ever expanding. We experience this expanding space curving and becoming the womb. Modern physicists have said of the universe that space curves back on itself.

It is as if Allah takes space itself into this infinite womb. You cannot put a boundary around it, yet it is embracing. It does not become embracing *because* of a boundary. It is the vastness that embraces. Other dictionary meanings of the word *wasi'* are ease, opportunity, capacity, spacious, and pleasant.

From a psychological perspective, we should examine how much this image of al-Wasi' involves the idea of feminine and masculine. At first we may only be able to experience al-Wasi' through the female, because when the absolute descends in the female her experience usually becomes womb-like. And when the absolute descends in the male, it generally becomes for him an expansive feeling like fifty million sperm shooting to infinity.

So in practice we see that the human vehicle may dictate the nature of the experience, even though the experience transcends male and female. Still, it can be experienced in the male as an infinite emanation, and in the female as an infinite embrace. Understanding how space curves back on itself in such a cosmic way is a turning point for integrating the male and the female. Prior to this understanding, the embrace of male and female can be frightening because it brings up psychological issues such as the fear of being smothered or swallowed by another. This may arise from fears of being enveloped by the mother.

The practice of Ya Wasi' will be helpful for those who have fears of envelopment, fears of having a relationship, or fears of surrendering. Through invocation of this sacred Name they can overcome feeling smothered, and instead allow themselves to be truly embraced.

Men's fear of a certain kind of intimacy is overcome by surrendering to the feminine within or without. Many males in the journey are stuck on emanation. They just want to shoot their sperm to infinity. They just want to arouse this animalistic force and expand to infinity. And they suffer a great deal when the force turns around and comes back to them. When the force starts to descend, our bones soften, and often a deep fear arises for men—the fear of losing their gender identity.

This is a common psychological fear. There are two such nightmares for a man: fear of castration and fear of losing the gender identity and becoming a vagina instead of a penis. So men hold themselves together tightly and rigidly. They become aggressive and assertive. Most of this pose is the result of a forced identification with the penis that they are afraid to surrender.

When the absolute descends, the stages of surrender descend. In the surrendering, at one stage the man melts and suffers. Softness and mushiness translate into the unconscious as losing the penis, the hardness, the drive, the male identity, and so becoming a female. Castration is scary but at least then one can still think of himself as a man who has been castrated. But this experience of the absolute seems to remove the gender identity.

A counselor can warn them in advance: "You're going to be a vagina; you're going to be a sissy. You are going to be everything that you are afraid of. Go ahead and be it. Don't be afraid of that. Melt down. It's only a meltdown." And when this meltdown happens, the debilitating psychological associations are released, and then there usually comes a jelling, or integration. It jells again into a male or female psyche.

Many women who identify with the penis have the same problem that we just described for men. They can be called phallic women. They are hot, and they are driven and insecure. So for men, and sometimes for women, when the meltdown comes, it is a very nightmarish state, not to be underestimated in the journey. In therapy a counselor might encounter it almost every day. When the absolute descends to the final stage in the genitals, in the pelvic floor, then a terror arises that must be dealt with.

Invocation of Ya Wasi' carries a feeling of safety in the womb. It is the feeling of being softened and embraced. It is a beautiful practice to make the universe as safe as possible. All is within the womb of God, and we are all in it together. We are surrounded by the oneness. Everywhere we turn, there is the face of the Beloved. So no enemy is there. There's no "other." Every face is the same face. Every name is a Name of Allah. It is beautiful, safe, and full of ease. This is the station, or *maqaam*, that comes with the realization of al-Wasi'.

Al Wasi' also manifests as the antidote for tightness in the body, and this is equally true for men and women. Such tightness is very common around the spine and the neck. For many women the tightness appears around the womb. This layer of weakness comes from a false kind of pulling oneself together that arises when we are faced with the fear of disintegration. The fear is that to allow disintegration is to allow a vague mushiness. It might bring an experience of what happened in the womb, even though there is no ego memory in the womb because impressions happened on the soul level and on the biological level.

When a physician of the heart takes students to that dimension, egos panic. They hit a ring of terror. They become very scared to go there because the ego does not know what exists in that domain. The ego itself didn't even exist at the time of our formation in the womb. There is only an impression that comes from merging with the mother and from merging with the physical environment.

No matter how difficult it is to relate to this dimension, nevertheless there are many impressions that were imprinted in our body and our soul during its time there. So when you usher a person to the place we have been describing, you usher them to a stage that is pre-ego. Be careful about that. Terror might arise, and the guide needs to warn them that they might become terrified. The ego is afraid of losing its familiar containment even though it means entering into a much greater container.

It also makes sense that since al-Wasi' embodies the capability of holding, what might arise for a woman is the fear of not being able to properly hold or make a proper container for the baby in the womb. Repetition of Ya Wasi' could, in such cases, help avoid miscarriage. Invocation of Ya Wasi' is also a very useful meditative practice for expanding the container of the heart and clearing away impressions that obscure the light of one's soul from shining through the globe of the heart.

Ya 'Aliyy, Ya Muta'ali

(yaa 'A-leeyy, yaa mu-ta-'AA-lee)

The divine Names al-'Aliyy and al-Muta'ali have a similar relationship to each other as what we saw with al-Kabir and al-Mutakabbir. We will first examine al-'Aliyy. Al-'Aliyy is the one who is beyond, completely beyond. It is the one beyond whom there is nothing. Looking at a physical form which is a variation of the same root, we find the word *al-'aliyah*, which is a she-camel that has sufficient strength to bear a burden. Al-'Aliyy also has the meaning of being beyond nobility, rank, or dignity.

The word *t'aliy* is very unusual; it means one who is beyond or who is completely transcendental. But it is used to call someone and say, "Come to Allah." Or "Come up here." It's like the invitation of the divine. It is as if God is saying, "I am high so that you may reach this high station. I am transcendental so that you may reach Me. Come up to my station." Consequently, this form is used as an approach to the divine infinite presence. You approach God while understanding at the same time that God is always beyond what we think we are approaching.

God is an infinite station of realization. That is al-'Aliyy. And yet God is always approaching this imminence, and that is al-Muta'ali. There is an instructive use of this particular grammatical form that occurs in the Qur'an.[51] Here it appears in an ecumenical context: "Let's join together in what we can agree on." It's like an invitation. Come on, different people of religious persuasions. Come on and let's get together and see what we can agree on.

No matter how high one goes, or how much one attains the absolute, there is something more absolute or higher than that. Invoking Ya 'Aliyy allows for high aspirations. It seems to be a vision of the highest. Allah's work is the highest. And with al-Muta'ali there's an action: it is an invitation to transcendence. There are many ways to ascend to Allah. The approach is like Jacob's ladder, the ladder of light. Al-Muta'ali is how you approach or how you are lifted.

These two members of the omnipresence family, as we shall see later, offer a wonderful counterpart to al-Waliyy, which is the intimate quality in which God is experienced as being closer than our jugular vein. There is a beautiful Qur'anic verse about the *'arsh* throne of Allah being suspended above oceans of mercy. The familiar word Subhanallah carries the meaning "to swim." And that is how we are thinking of Muta'ali. There are pathways through this water-like medium, through the oceans of mercy.

It will be beneficial to return to the word *al-'aliyah*. Al-'aliyah is like Allah with "iya" in it. It can take the form of the word *'illat*, which has the meaning "got sick." *Aut al-'Ali* is the one beyond sickness, the one that transcends sickness. Al-'Aliyy is the one who takes away all sickness. What is the particular sickness that this quality addresses in us? Initially, we notice that it may be felt as a sickness in the stomach.

Invocation of Ya 'Aliyy brings compassion to men and women who are in an environment that is hostile and dangerous. It is recommended for those of us whose specific expectations for situations never actually work out. Such people often get deceived. They are victims of bait and switch. In general, they have core issues around the experience of betrayal. All these kinds of things are often experienced as a queasy feeling in the stomach.

The sickness we really are dealing with, at the root, is caused by an ultimate attachment to ego-self. And such a sickness must be worked on directly. It is not symbolic. We need to learn how to face our jealousy and arrogance. The ultimate sickness is putting our ego-self above God. When the self is put prior to God, the ego is put on the divine throne. Invocation of Ya 'Aliyy reverses that order! God goes above the self.

Take the famous case of the 12-year-old kid, Pharaoh Ramses II. Here's how you could express his point of view looking at the historical situation in which he finds himself: "For 12 years all of these ministers have been telling me I am God." We shouldn't think he is a bad person. He is sort of surprised. "I've never heard this before. I am God. Isn't that something!" If anything could be called evil here, it is simply the evil of false identity. He is affirming what the world constructed around his ego. And we do this again and again in our lives when our experience of the world reinforces our sense of an isolated and separated ego-self.

At this stage of a person's experience, the physician of the heart is dealing with narcissistic inflation or deflation. They are the same. Invocation of Ya 'Aliyy is the healing agent of the inflated/deflated ego. It all has to do with what you enthrone in the sublime Heart Throne of God. Is it the ego that you enthrone in the sacred altar of your heart? Or is it the one, beyond whom there is nothing?

Al Muta'ali can be seen as a pathway for transcending every layer of ego identity. The personality is like an onion with many layers, and each layer has a certain identity in it. There are many gradations of the "I" until the core is reached, or what is called the ego identity. The ego identity is the crystallized sense of self. Here there is a totally isolated feeling. The ego exists, and it is alone. It's the one running the show. It is sitting right on the throne. There is no one else. We call that narcissistic. It makes the false claim, "I am God."

To make this claim is not exactly arrogant. Actually, it is just a naïve attitude. It is as if we are saying, "I really believe that the universe revolves around me because that's my experience." We have these expectations that everything is going to go exactly our way. It is a sort of expectation that is vested in the ego itself.

Psychologically, there is a stage around age 1 or 1½ in which children experience themselves as the center of the universe. They cry and they get the breast. They want something and they throw a tantrum to get it. When a spiritual traveler begins the stage of actualization and individualization, they may feel they are the center of the universe, but at that stage it is not from a narcissistic viewpoint.

Prayerful repetition of Ya 'Aliyy and Ya Muta'ali is the antidote to narcissism. It leads to overcoming our clinging to an egocentric view. The most precious thing in accomplishing this reorientation of perspective is experiencing the universe, or God, as fully embracing you.

The narcissist needs to be special, to be loved, adored, worshipped. In the spiritual process, the physician of the heart needs to fully expose the deep narcissistic wound. The narcissistic wound originally arose from the child's feeling of being different or special. Now we expose the wound, and we enter the wound to heal it.

In the final stage, we begin to feel the need to be special and loved is being met. Only now, at this stage, the need to be seen and to be loved is being met by God. We offer our self to God and God gives it back to us. This is a very beautiful healing of the narcissistic wound. And it occurs because we are intrinsically connected to God, connected to our origin.

There is a difference between al-'Aliyy and al-Kabir. And there is a difference between al-Muta'ali and al-Mutakabbir. Al-Kabir and al-Mutakabbir embody the path to transcendence and omnipresence. They deal with the boundaries of time and space. Al-'Aliyy and al-Muta'ali also embody the path to transcendence and omnipresence, but they deal with the boundaries of identity.

Ya Waliyy

(yaa WA-leeyy)

Al-Waliyy is a much-loved Name. Its root, *walaa*, means intimacy. The intimacy that is meant here is total intimacy. It is a quality that can be equated with *'uns*, the root of the word for human being. What it means to be a human being is *'uns*, or total intimacy, a quality that is the same as *walaa*, the root of al-Waliyy. God is the most intimate friend.

The thing that is the most human about us, our most human attribute, is our intimate link with the divine. And we should remember that this means intimacy with ecstatic love, total passion. "Allah is your lover, not your jailer," as many Sufis have said. Al-Waliyy is the most intimate connection possible.

This intimacy is expressed in the famous Qur'anic verse that says Allah is nearer, more intimate than your own jugular vein.[52] *In Allah, 'aqrab 'ilayhi min habl-il-wareed. 'Aqrab*, the nearest or nearer, is a synonym for al-Waliyy. The meaning conveyed is nearness, intimacy, and closeness.

God is your best friend. It's the nearest friend. Ya Waliyy. This is pure intimacy. Al-Waliyy is right at the essence of everything that Sufis wish to communicate.

Al-Waliyy is the strongest word for union with the beloved. *'Aw 'adnaa* is another synonym for this union. But *'aw 'adnaa* can also carry the meaning of *dunyaa*, or the world. In Surah 53 of the Qur'an, *al-Najm* (the Star), there is a famous passage that describes the closest you can get to the full embrace of the beloved. The verse says, "Two bows' lengths or closer."[53]

Even closer than this intimate distance of two bows' lengths is what is conveyed by *'aw 'adnaa* and by al-Waliyy. 'Ibn 'Arabi takes two bows' lengths, or two arcs of a circle, to delineate the arcs of ascent and descent. Viewing the human being's intimate relationship with God, in the arc of ascent we approach God walking, and in the arc of descent God approaches running toward us.

This is the relationship. It is all based on love. A hadith *qudsi* says, "My slave comes to me walking and I respond by running to my lover." Still we have the trace of twoness. But *'aw 'adnaa* means even closer. "Two bows' lengths, or closer." 'Ibn 'Arabi says the trace of that division between the two arcs' length disappears and becomes *hu*, the ultimate essence of essence of essence.

Hu is the ultimate syllable, the breath of divine self. In a sense it is the Name that can't be pronounced. Yet all beings, enlightened or unenlightened, are pronouncing the greatest Name of God constantly. It is the sound of the breath! This is wonderful. Some people know they are doing it and some people don't, but everyone is breathing this ultimate seed syllable. It is the most intimate possible expression of unity with God.

In one sense, we could see the quality of al-Waliyy we have just been describing as the opposite of Al-'Aliyy. Al-'Aliyy is transcendental, and it seems to imply rising above something down there. From that perspective whether you make the journey or not may appear to be immaterial. Twoness, or distance, appears to be suggested as part of its meaning. But with al-Waliyy there is not even a sense of merging into the one. It is simply total unity, simply *wataa'*.

How can contemplation of Ya Waliyy be applied to address human needs? We see various layers in the ego structure of the personality. In one inner layer is stored a deep sense of loneliness, alienation, disconnectedness. This is generated by the absence of intimacy in the home. When children don't get enough intimate rapport with their mother or father, they experience reality as a desolate, lonely place.

This particular layer gets imprinted in childhood. And usually it has its own defense mechanism. People who are self-identified in this layer often are labeled as schizoid. They have the characteristic of isolation, withdrawal, and disconnectedness. This isolation is expressed by the habit of unleashing themselves in an aggressive way. Either they attack fast or they quickly withdraw and disconnect. In such people we find splitting and isolating, and they generally have no resiliency.

In the middle of their ego structure is a deep loneliness, a deep isolation in which they don't experience the universe as an intimate place. When such a person is able to work through their defense structure of aggression or withdrawal, then the deeper feeling of loneliness really begins to open up. And through feeling the depth of the loneliness, there arises a kind of spaciousness, a field through which sheer intimacy is experienced.

It is as if the love of God is arising and drawing the person into itself. God is the most beloved, intimate, close friend, and from that emerges a deep sense of loyalty, because now they have begun to feel the closeness with the beloved one that they were vainly seeking before.

A person needs to approach the experience of sheer loneliness by exploring the defense system around their ego's self-identification with this isolation. You should soften the structure and then melt it. Then there can be a gradual discovery of the undefended sheer loneliness and isolation of being disassociated in the core.

When this is realized, most often this whole layer of the ego-structure will open up, and that allows you to experience the space of intimacy with the divine beloved. It manifests as an infinite ocean of intimacy, an infinite field of intimacy. It is a very subtle and delicate space, filled with gentleness and delicate luminosity. And it is vast. The whole universe is an intimate field.

With al-Waliyy we have omnipresence with an intimate flavor. Intimacy is a very delicate transparent space. The lover is closely interrelated with every part of the universe. Everything is held in a very intimate way. God is intimate with everything: the good, the bad, the high, and the low. As human beings, we are healed by fully entering the depth of this feeling. Such an experience usually melts away our sense of isolation and softens the schizoid structure.

Everyone has a schizoid layer. You feel so lonely. No one is close to you. Nobody. In this deep layer your experience is that you are all alone and that even God has left. But at the stage of the journey we have been describing, you are able to uncover and accept the experience of being alone in the universe. When that happens what had been experienced as isolation gets filled with the space of intimacy. You were all alone. You were a hidden treasure. Then you opened up out of a deep yearning for intimate love.

Each of the divine Names we have discussed in this chapter offers a unique pathway for awakening to the infinite presence of Allah. They all carry the meaning of vast embracing divine omnipresence. As we began to view them as a family, we were drawn to see how their relationships with each other help reveal more about God's all-embracing presence.

Throughout the course of the narrative, we have recommended particular applications of the Names as a healing for certain ego-engendered structures of human disconnection, sickness, and isolation. In general, though, we can say that prayerful invocation of any of these Names opens up our experience of omnipresence and makes this divine reality less conceptual for us.

wakil

muzit

razib

hafiz

wali

mani'

muhaimin

chapter 11

The Matrix
of Divine Protection

The theme of divine protection evokes a vast field of Names, a field that can be illuminated by exploring its interesting configuration. One Name in particular arises at the center of the matrix of these qualities. It has the richest and most inclusive meaning, and it contains within its various meanings all the specific qualities of the other Names in the cluster.

Al-Hafiz presents itself as the most fitting Name to be translated "O Protector" in the deepest sense of all this phrase may imply. It can be viewed as a lens through which to understand the other divine Names of protection. Moreover, each of these Names is enhanced by being paired with Ya Hafiz in recitation.

Al-Muhaimin, al-Muqit, al-Wakil, al-Wali, ar-Raqib, and al-Mani' focus on specific aspects or dimensions of protection, while al-Hafiz covers them all. It is in the center of the mandala. We will start with the more particularized Names and examine the aspects of divine protection that they each emphasize. Then we will talk about al-Hafiz in its own right, and show how each Name's qualities fit into al-Hafiz.

An important underlying theme of our exploration of these divine Names is to enter into the realm of the human psyche where a person's issues of being wounded exist in relation to the quality of protection. Some terrifying terrain may be exposed when the physician of the heart goes into this subject. We refer to this inner landscape throughout the chapter and particularly in the final section, where we offer suggestions for how to move toward psychological healing.

Ya Muhaimin

(yaa mu-HAI-min)

There has been a spirited debate among scholars about the proper root of al-Muhaimin. A grammar book of the Proto-Semitic historic derivations of the Beautiful Names of Allah[54] has enabled us to settle this question to our satisfaction and to determine that al-Muhaimin is not a quadraliteral with the root *hayamana*. In Proto-Semitic *'af'allah* is *haf'allah*, which means the "h" in Muhaimin is not a part of the root.

Consequently, it becomes clear that Muhaimin comes from *'amana*, which is also the root for the sacred Name al-Mu'min, the one who is ultimately trustworthy. To say *'aameen* (or "amen" in English) is the meaning of the root that both these divine Names share. This derivation is also confirmed by 'ibn 'Abbas.

Ya Muhaimin may be viewed as an invocation of the trustworthy guardian in whom one can have full confidence. Other earthly forms of the word are "nurse" and "caregiver." The meaning derived from this root is to be secure and safe. An exact physical-plane meaning is to put oneself in front of other people to protect them, as the guards in a caravan would do.

When travelers on the spiritual path annihilate their ego-personality structures by annihilating defensiveness and boundaries, they awaken to self-effacement or *fana*. Then they are able to feel held by the most sustaining of presences, and there is no more fear. There is a feeling of safety, *'amaan*, and anything that comes into their field with the aim of a destroyer is instead dissolved. It is easy to see how this aspect of divine protection in the everyday practice of Sufism is found in the *barakah*, or atmosphere of magnetic blessing, of the *shaykh*, or spiritual guide.

Manifestation of the divine protection through the *shaykh* and the lineage of teachers, which is called the *silsilah*, is the activity of al-Muhaimin. In a famous sacred tradition, the Prophet Muhammad, speaking in the voice of God, says "the saints (or friends) of Allah are under my domes; none knows who they are except me." The divine protection is through the saint because the student is under the dome of the saint, just as the saint is under the dome of Allah.

At the personal psychological level, the spiritual counselor often uncovers a deep fear in the student that comes from a lack of trust that the universe is a safe place. It is a feeling that the material sphere does not provide safety or sustenance. This fear can be aroused very early, even in the prenatal period. Perhaps the mother was unable to properly nourish the fetus. In a general way, the weaknesses of the earthly mother and father are internalized.

When a child in this condition tries to navigate the world of adults, he or she feels there is no support. Feeling lack of support engenders anger and then grief. Ultimately, through the dissolution process, a gentle dark abyss-like state takes over and embraces the spiritual traveler. This state is like the feminine face of God, and the radiance within it is like the masculine face of God. Nourishment and protection are combined in such a realization of the heavenly mother and father.

Often when you begin to deal with this process you feel swallowed by the dark. You fear that you will become lost in this darkness because you will have no sense of self and no direction. But when you fully trust and surrender, then there is no more abandonment. In this kind of darkness, there is nowhere to get lost. It is an ocean of potentiality, an ocean of grace and peace and presence that has no content.

Because they share a common root, we recommend pairing Ya Mu'min and Ya Muhaimin in prayerful recitation to face foundational issues of protection and safety in the world. Such repetition addresses both the sense of "being lost" that you may have in the world as well as its opposite—the cynicism about the world that comes as an ego-defense against becoming overly gullible and trusting.

Ya Muqit

(yaa mu-ḴEET)

Al-Muqit offers a somewhat different aspect of divine protection. The sound code tells us two things about its meaning: It is intensive, and it entails a particular kind of manifestation that goes into everything without exception. An earth-plane variation of the root meaning of Al-Muqit is to provide a measure of grain as reliable nourishment to someone to retain life and protect from death. Al-Muqit emphasizes the All-Powerful's unlimited ability to provide for everything.

Al-Muqit is a trusted, reliable source of sustenance. It has the same kind of energy that we find in al-Wahhab and ar-Razzaq, which are discussed in Chapters 16, 18, and 19 on divine abundance. With al-Muqit, the divine protection comes in to feed and nourish for the sake of survival. There is also an earthly meaning of "the fat of a camel's hump."

But man does not live by bread alone, and a well-known treatise by the Sufi al-Makki, called *Qut al-qulub*,[55] draws out the meaning of al-Muqit. *Quloob* is the plural of *qalb*, or heart. *Qut* is the same as Muqit, the one who provides and nourishes. The title of this Sufi text could be translated as "The reliable sustenance for the hearts."

Reliable nourishment is what we all trust to protect our hearts from dying. So al-Muqit can be seen as the one who feeds or nourishes our spirit, breath after breath. Every breath nourishes and protects us from dying, *qaa'it-un-nafas*. The breath itself is a kind of nourishment from God that protects from the death of the heart.

At the personal level, mother's milk is the first thing children rely on for sustenance. It is filled with nourishing love. And there is another essential milk that flows with the milk of the mother. It has a honeyed taste and comes pouring from the upper palate, especially when the pineal gland is open and relaxed by connecting to source. That essential secretion descends in the palate, goes into the heart, into the center of being to provide nourishment for the heart, *qut al-quloob*.

However, there are other factors that arise here. The relationship with the mother's breast can bring up deep issues of entitlement. Babies are born with a strong sense that they are entitled to certain things in life. One of them is the mother's breast and the milk. It is built into them. As soon as they are born, their eyes know where to look, their mouth knows what to do, and they reach out. They know it by smell, by sight, and they go for it.

This is true in the animal kingdom and in the human kingdom. The baby knows if it goes to the breast it will get nourishment, it will get connected to a reliable source, and it will get safety. In short, it will get everything it needs.

A fundamental sense of entitlement says, "I belong and this belongs to me." If this sense gets violated or interfered with, or if the milk that was coming was not sweet because it was mixed with the mother's fears and resentments, then a shadow falls over the sense of entitlement. This leads to a lack of basic trust in the source as the provider.

Instead of feeling "I am entitled to connect to source and to derive nourishment from source," it transforms into, "I am entitled on a personality level to fulfill my personality needs in whatever way my ego dictates." You embark on a journey in which you begin to feel a distorted kind of entitlement: "I want to get what I want to get whenever I want to get it, and however I want to get it."

Such disconnection is filled with the lack of deep trust in the divine sustenance and manifests in immense issues of deprivation that must be addressed. So the ego, the deepest core in the ego, wants to go back to that breast. And it knows if it goes there, it will get deep nourishment.

The problem is that the ego is now relying on an object that is intrinsically unreliable; it is an image of the past. Every time you want to rely on something, your unconscious is saying to you that what you are looking for ought to be your mother. In the unconscious, mother is the source. She is the provider. She is the one you should orient toward. All this is mistaken reliance on a false source in the unconscious.

Students at this stage are unfulfilled, and they don't know why they are not fulfilled. The physician of the heart needs to help them disengage from their unconscious drive and consciously redirect their search to reconnect with reliable sustenance. By offering the invocation of Ya Muqit and Ya Muhaimin, the physician of the heart can start students on the way to the presence that is sustaining, to the source that is fully nourishing.

Ya Wakil

(yaa wa-KEEL)

Tawakkul, for Sufis, means complete trust in Allah. It is a *maqaam*, or established station of realization, and not a *hal*, or passing state. *Tawakkul* is a form of the word *wakil*. A basic linguistic meaning of al-Wakil is to entrust someone else with property, reputation, or important affairs. In traditional Islamic cultures, if you wanted to deliver a message to someone, especially a proposal of marriage, you would find a wakil—one who has this trustworthy nature—to deliver it.

With the sacred Name al-Wakil, you are relying on God entirely, because God is the only one who is worthy of complete trust in every affair. In that sense, God—the being that is completely reliable—protects you. The one who trusts in this way is guided to nothing but Allah.

Someone asked Imam Qushayri, "What is the one who has complete trust in Allah?" Qushayri replied that one who trusts completely in Allah is like an infant who knows nothing but to resort to the mother's breast. This complete trust is described in the Qur'an with the phrase, "those whose hearts cling to Allah."[56]

There are three stages of trust, of *tawakkul*, and each stage is associated with one or more divine Names. The first stage is associated with al-Qadir. Your feeling that you are in the hands of Allah is like that of a slave. You are a corpse in the hands of the one who is washing your body in preparation for burial. The corpse washer turns you however they wish, while the corpse has neither motion nor self-will. In this stage you are passive and humble.

The second stage is called *tasleem*. It is associated with al-Kafi, the one who satisfies all needs. Al-Kafi is another divine Name that isn't included on the official lists of 99 but which is extensively practiced, often as part of a prayer for divine healing. From the Qur'an: "If you really trusted in Allah you would be satisfied with what Allah has given you."[57]

The part of this quotation that means being satisfied is in the word *kaafee*. *Kaafee* is a quality that is found in *an-nafs ul-raadiyah*, the perfectly content gradation of *nafs*. That perfectly content self is discovered in invoking "Ya Kafi." You call out to the quality of God that satisfies all needs, and you are content with the response of the source, whatever it is. In this stage of *tasleem*, there is peaceful trust and surrender.

The third and highest stage of this journey to complete trust in Allah is called *tafweed*. It is dissolving of self in Allah (*al-fanaa'u fi-llaah*). The traveler on the path abandons merely human qualities and embraces the divine qualities. There is complete and absolute trust in Allah.

At this point, the traveler can only find and experience the divine qualities. The divine Name al-Khaliq is associated with this stage. When we say Ya Khaliq, it points to when the human quality passes away and what remains is a divine quality.

This process of transformation, which is an aspect of al-Khaliq, holds true for all the divine qualities. The whole process is called *takhalluq*. It proceeds in a serial way. The lower self passes away gradually. It slowly abandons its identification with denser qualities of *nafs* and embraces the divine qualities in the same process.

Qur'an: "In Whom do you trust to always provide you with sustenance and to protect your property?"[58] To Allah belong the treasures of the heavens and the earth. By abandoning the clinging of *nafs* and trusting in the protection of Allah we experience the fullness of Ya Wakil.

Several forms taken by the root of this sacred Name have negative aspects. In line with our general psychological approach, we always view these as suggestions for addressing human dysfunction and deficiency in a homeopathic way.

Tawaakala is a sixth form of the word and means to abandon, to desert, and to not help someone in need. It comes from a kind of passive quietism or fatalism. The attitude of fatalism is a pronounced problem in Middle Eastern culture. It is this which the Prophet Muhammad addressed when he said, "Trust in Allah, but tie your camel's leg."

A *wakarun* is an impotent person, and in modern Arabic a *wakil* is a lawyer. While, of course, many lawyers are trustworthy, there is a shadow side of al-Wakil here too. The Sufi Samuel Lewis said in one of his poems, "Beware of wolves in sheep's clothing telling you to beware of wolves in sheep's clothing."

Tawakkul means in all things to develop your inner relationship with God, the only One who is utterly trustworthy. Repetition of Ya Wakil is particularly appropriate for those who have profound issues in trusting others to be responsible.

Ya Wali

(yaa WAA-lee)

We can appreciate the protective quality of al-Wali by understanding how those who are close friends protect each other quite naturally because of the quality of their intimate mutual relationship. *Waliya*, the root of al-Wali, has a physical meaning of turning back toward someone in familiarity, friendliness, connection, and closeness. At the same time it means to turn away from hostility, anger, alienation, and loneliness.

We saw the same dynamic process of turning in the invocation of Ya Tawwab, as discussed in Chapter 8, Divine Forgiveness. However, Ya Wali has the added feeling of Ya Sahib, the intimate friend. *Saahib* means companion, friend, or fellow, and is related to al-Wali in meaning. Because of great intimacy in your relationship with someone, you feel protected in their presence. It is compared to the protection of the family bed.

On a grander scale, there is a kind of relationship between lover and beloved, between God and servant, which deeply establishes the experience of feeling safe. There is uninterrupted friendliness and intimacy. Nothing can feel better than this kind of relationship. A person who has realized this feels deserving, worthy, competent, and fit. You feel protected because of your close loving relationship, and God feels protective of such a lover because of the intimacy that is shared.

The other sacred Name with the same root, al-Waliyy, is more in the divine love category than al-Wali, and the element of protection doesn't play the same part. Al-Waliyy totally emphasizes the omnipresence of loving intimacy. Al-Waliyy is the name Sufis have chosen to mean "saint." It emphasizes the love/friendship with God.

With al-Wali, while there is also intimacy, protection is emphasized. Putting these two Names together, we could say that in the presence of al-Wali, the friends of God, the 'awliyaa, are protected and provided for. It is natural to pair Ya Wali, Ya Waliyy in repetition.

In modern Arabic, *wali* means governor, and *wilayat* means the place from which one derives spiritual authority. There is no presupposition in the word *wilayat* as to whether the authority is legitimate. Thus there is the sense in certain forms of al-Wali of an authority that may be used or misused. Following our psychological approach, we take these kinds of ambiguities and shadows to suggest that repetition of the sacred Name is a remedy for the inequities and deficiencies involved in human relationships.

One who has realized al-Wali will conscientiously protect and provide for those for whom they are responsible and who may be dependent on them. It is a personal kind of activity based on an intimate loyalty to God. Such a one will not sell out for any reason. Consequently, repetition of Ya Wali may be indicated for human beings who have a deep personal entanglement with betrayal.

Modern psychology speaks about developing healthy attachments that help children find the qualities they need in life. At a personal level, those with a wound that was caused by betrayal may have never felt that there was somebody at home who was on their side or who was loyal to them. The very people who were supposed to have protected them ended up betraying them.

To find the protection of al-Wali is to find a pearl-like substance. You are intimately connected with life. When children have this quality they feel embodied in worldly existence and grounded in their own bodies. They don't feel empty. Its absence results in their acting out from the schizoidal plane. That is to say, they act from an experience of isolation, and with disconnection from their minds.

Those who have overcome this disconnection are embodying who they are, embodying essence, which is a feeling of fullness. It is a feeling that you exist as an individual person who is capable of being in touch with your deepest truth, and in touch with the reality outside.

If there is good attachment, if there is contact, if there is bonding, if there is belonging, and if there is protection, this essence will grow. That quality, that pearl, is the station of the true Wali. He or she is embodied and has connected the two worlds of the absolute and the relative.

Because al-Wali and al-Waliyy share the same root of divine intimacy, we find them to be a very natural pairing, and we highly recommend prayerful invocation of them together. Invocation of Ya Wali, Ya Waliyy is a means of overcoming the schizoidal disconnected ego identity that all human beings have in varying degrees.

Ya Raqib

(yaa ra-ḴEEB)

The next member of this cluster illustrates divine protection through the specific quality of protecting by watching over someone or something. Ar-Raqib means to protect, to preserve, to guard, and to watch over, especially at night. There is an extremely great desire (*riqaab*) to do this, which is an important part of its meaning.

Put another way, a tremendous love or concern gives ar-Raqib's protective oversight an intensive focus. It is a kind of watchfulness. Earthly forms that its root takes are suggestive of these qualities. You wait for your companion alertly because you love what you are waiting for. A mother watches over her helpless, sleeping child. You are particularly alert because of how deeply you care. These are good images of how such divine protection can operate.

This kind of loving attentiveness is the basis for the Sufi practice of concentration, called *muraaqabah*. Realization of ar-Raqib is a key to advancing on the demanding path of concentration. The relationship between ar-Raqib and *muraaqabah* is the same as that of al-Hasib and the Sufi practice of *muhaasibah*, a method of inward self-accounting.

Realization of ar-Raqib is an active contemplation. In other words, it is done with eyes open and taking everything in. One form of the word is *'irtaqabah*. It means to ascend to an elevated place called *marqabah*, a place of observation. You ascend to that place to pass the night and watch the stars. The word for stars is *raqeeb*. It is exactly the same as the divine Name.

Raqeeb means a star that you watch, observe, and concentrate on. You watch some stars rise and some stars set. Staying awake in the night from an elevated place with a concentrated power of awareness to watch the stars is called a vigil. Those who are called *raqeeb* would then be the leaders of contemplative life who sit through the night meditating: literally watching the stars descend. From this original source, it is easy to see why ar-Raqib came to mean meditation itself.

Raqbah is a slave, male or female, and a form of the word, *raqoob*, means a poor old man who has no way to earn a living and no one to provide for him. Forms of the divine Names that reflect negative characteristics are always suggestive in terms of homeopathic applications to the human condition. Neediness and dependency are inner structures that recitation of Ya Raqib can address and heal.

Ya Mani'

(yaa MAA-ni')

The strongest meaning for this Name is found in the phrase "*mana'a al-haseen.*" It means to defend a fortress and to resist against encroachment. This is a very specific aspect of protection, but it is the one that, as a first reaction, most people think of as protection's primary meaning. Al-Mani' is to make a fortress inaccessible, unapproachable, impregnable, and therefore secure. *Haseen* in the phrase above means to make it inaccessible.

Al-Daafi' is a synonym of al-Mani'. A practice that can be done is Ya Mani', Ya Daafi'. These Names are synonyms, and it adds emphasis to the specific quality when they are done together. Daafi' has the earthly meaning "to defray a hail of arrows by means of a rhinoceros-hide shield."

It is important to note that al-Mani' has an opposite divine Name, al-Mu'ti. Al-Mu'ti comes from *'ataya*, which means to accept a gift. Accepting a gift is very different from establishing an unbreachable fortress. In its approach to divine protection, al-Mu'ti is truly an opposite as well, because it means accepting whatever may come as coming from God.

In line with the importance we place on the divine opposites and the relational approach to the 99 Names, we strongly recommend recitation of Ya Mani', Ya Mu'ti as a pair. The joint invocation of these two opposites addresses two psychological conditions that mirror each other.

First, there are people who have a need to over-protect themselves. Such a condition arises as an extreme personality structure of ego-defense. Second, there is another kind of imbalance that comes from not being sufficiently individuated to discriminate properly and thus being unable to protect oneself from harm. Pairing these two opposite divine Names addresses both these poles of human imbalance. In each case, such a paired recitation mediates toward inner harmony and integration.

Al-Mani' has a deeper meaning than just protecting or guarding one's fortress against attack from without. It means to resist, turn away from, or abstain from your inclinations of indecision, doubt, guilt, or weakness. It also means to withhold or hold back from using your power or ability to carry out revenge, or to act out anger. In a general sense, with the invocation of Ya Mani' you are protecting yourself from your own inner self-destructive inclinations as well as from outer forces.

Ya Hafiz

(yaa ḥa-FEEḌḤ)

The sound code informs us of the intensive quality of al-Hafiz. Everything in the heavens and earth is in the protection of Allah right down to *dhurrah*, which literally is millet, a metaphor for atoms. The protection reaches to the smallest particle in the same way as the loving mercy of ar-Rahim, which has the same grammatical form in the sound code.

What is especially noteworthy about al-Hafiz is the richness of its many layers of root meaning. First, it is to be mindful, conscious, considerate, aware, and careful; to respect, to honor, to revere. The second set of meanings is to keep in your heart, to be mindful, even to memorize. All this is the meaning of *haf*. This state of *haf* is compared with its opposite, which means to forget. *Haf* is an exact parallel with *dhikr*, which means to remember.

We aspire to be among those who remember Allah rather than among *ghaflah*, those who have forgotten. A famous Qur'anic verse reads, "Remember me and I will remember you."[59] Allah is protecting/remembering everyone, especially when such remembrance is reciprocal. Invocation of Ya Hafiz incorporates mindfulness, consciousness, and remembrance, as well as the usual idea of protection.

Another specific quality of al-Hafiz is that of preserving the order, timing, and sequence of the whole universe in a constant and dependable manner. That's called *nidhaam*. Allah will preserve the order, sequence, and timing of the universe, and we don't have to fix everything. This is yet another way of seeing divine protection.

Al-Hafiz has another extraordinary meaning in this constellation of divine protection. It means to save from decay and preserve the eternal quality in a thing. God is a preserver in the sense of saving from oblivion and destruction, keeping things from adulteration or unnecessary change.

The Preserved Tablet—*mahfoodh*—the eternal source from which, according to the Qur'an, all the scriptures of the world, in all the different languages, have been derived, has the same root as al-Hafiz. *Mahfoodh* is also translated Protected Mother of Books.

The Qur'an says "this book will not change; it will remain incorruptible through time, translation, and addendum."[60] The passage may be seen as a literal theological assertion. However, considering Shaykh Junayd's affirmation that what passes away never was, and what remains always was, is, and will be, we may get a glimmer of how it is that the eternal in a thing is protected from temporality.

In Sufi language, the eternal in a thing is called the *malakut* of each thing. In fact, this is precisely how all the divine Names in their immutability work through material things. In that way, God protects the essence, the eternal light or spirit. To invoke such protection we recommend chanting Ya Hafiz, Ya Baqi.

It should be mentioned that the meaning of al-Hafiz reaches outside of the protection cluster. It means to know or be mindful of the secret. *Hafidha as-sirr* is to know the secret, and to keep the secret. In this we see an important relationship between al-Hafiz and al-Khabir, the knower of the inner knowledge or wisdom.

The great fullness of meaning that is found in al-Hafiz makes it the most inclusive divine Name of protection. Such fullness allows it to act as the matrix for all the Names of divine protection that we have thus far considered. Moreover, this matrix-like connection with the other Names of protection is evident in very specific terms.

We will now briefly demonstrate how al-Hafiz underlies, or includes, the other Names of divine protection.

Al-Muqit has been described as "reliable and nourishing." Al-Hafiz also means someone who protects, who has the ability to provide for, nourish, or take care of. The other meaning of al-Muqit is found in another form of the root of al-Hafiz, which means to be careful of, mindful of, attentive to needs and desires, and considerate.

It is to be watchful over, mindful of, and heedful. This points to a kind of super awareness. And here we see the connection with ash-Shahid and ar-Raqib, both of which embody being especially attentive and aware. This level of meaning should also be seen in al-Muqit.

Al-Hafiz is like al-Wakil, too, which we described in the context of being able to trust someone with one's property. Al-Hafiz, the dictionary suggests, means to keep from destruction, to keep one's promise, to keep one's word. In this way, al-Hafiz also reveals the characteristic of being trustworthy, or worthy of trust, and this is just like al-Wakil. They are even similar in their nuances. And this aspect of placing one's trust in God and God's representatives also relates to the quality of al-Muhaimin.

With al-Wali we saw that trust of people may occur because you are intimate or friendly with them. Protection is based on that relationship of intimacy. Al-Hafiz is like this too. "*Hafidha hurmanta saahibih.*" This translates, "He protected the honor, the name, and the respect of someone out of regard for his close friendship or relationship with that person." Out of respect for his friend, he was careful or mindful of preserving their relationship. The quality arises out of social relationship, respect, and love.

If you fully realized al-Hafiz, it would mean to constantly be aware of every need, want, and request, even to provide for these before they are requested, and to do this assiduously. *Hifaadh*, the noun form of Hafiz, has that meaning. It also means keeping or fulfilling a promise, and, equally important, when you do this, you do it with love and affection.

One last example is *haafidhu-l-'ayn*. It means not to go to sleep; to watch over the ones you love while they sleep. This is a good definition for both al-Hafiz and ar-Raqib. Al-Hafiz also has the same quality as al-Mani', which is like defending a fortress, as well as meaning to restrain and to withhold.

We see an excellent example of this in relation to the *nafs*, or lower self. *Fulaan yahfadhu nafsahu lisaanah*: to restrain one's *nafs* and one's tongue. This power to restrain the impulse guards our soul against the wear and tear caused by frequently burning with anger. Those who have realized this sacred quality guard against wearing out their tongues through thoughtless and frequent taking of God's Name in a habitual way.

We want divine protection against angry impulses and thoughtless speech. Such protection comes in two forms. Compassion specifically protects the soul from getting worn out from anger, and *dhikr* protects the tongue from getting worn out from the abuses of language. The way to accomplish this protection is by engaging the *nafs* in compassion and the tongue in conscious remembrance of the sacred Names.

Pairing Ya Hafiz in recitation with each of the other Names of divine protection is a good way to enhance and emphasize the specific qualities of protection of each Name. Thus we could see Ya Hafiz, Ya Mani' as a way to protect yourself from the poison of revenge when you have the power to exact it, because the giving up of this impulse in the remembrance of the divine power is cooling. It is a wonderful curative for burning anger.

There is one culminating meaning of al-Hafiz, and we find it in the Qur'an in what is known as the Throne verse, which is frequently recited as the great verse of divine protection: "Allah's protection extends over everything that is in the heavens and the earth."[61] *Wasi'a kursiyyuhu-s-samaawaati wa-l-arda wa laa ya'ooduhu hifdhu-humaa*. The word for protection here, *hifdhu-humaa*, is a form taken by the root of al-Hafiz.

This verse is etched on copper and put on prayer beads. There is a tradition that the Name referred to as the "greatest name" is buried in the verse, and so recitation of the Throne verse as a whole is thought to have powerful protective qualities.

Some Psychological Reflections

By way of concluding this discussion of the divine protection family, we want to paint a general picture of some overarching aspects of divine protection, viewed from a psychological perspective. We begin by speaking in broad terms about divine protection, using some visual imagery.

There is a certain emanation of the absolute that has to do with what could be called black essence. Black essence brings protection. It resolves all attacks that come at the person. Anything that comes dissolves in black. Black essence erases it, disintegrates it. It gives a certain kind of protection. Nothing touches the core of your being.

If you are graced to receive this quality you don't react impulsively to threatening situations. At such times, you know yourself as individual, and that you cannot be damaged or harmed at the level of being. That makes you feel at ease and be more present and more able to manage situations instead of impulsively resorting to the fight or flight mechanism.

On another level, the topic of divine protection has something to do with what can be called "the citadel." The citadel is the aspect of essence that gives you support, or the capacity to be unwavering in your soul's direction in life. No matter what comes to your world, this citadel protects and preserves you in the direction of the truth.

You feel solid, strong, and sufficiently rooted to continue the *dhikr*. You continue the remembrance that you are connected to God, that you are part of God, and that you are preserved and protected by the great being. Then, no matter what is thrown at you, it will not cause you to falter. You can maintain this connection even through anger, temptations, or fears.

You see the presence of this citadel in the story of the infidels who wanted to throw Muhammad off his path. They started threatening him, attacking him, tempting him. And he said to them, "If you put the sun in my right hand and the moon in my left hand, to influence me to leave this spot, still I will not. No temptation, no threat will take me away."

Divine protection in this aspect we are calling the citadel is rooted in an inner certainty, and it preserves your integrity of being through all tests. It is a quality that both protects you from negativities and gives you perseverance in the direction of truth. The lack of this quality is often connected with a psychological complaint about the absence of a father to take the hand of the child and to walk with him or her in life.

What is needed is a father who says, "I know that you are a precious human being, and I am here to protect you, develop your capacities, and at the same time introduce you to the world in a protective way so you don't lose connection to the real source of your being." Where can you get a father like that except in the one and only being itself?

What happened with most of our fathers is that there was a missing quality in them, and it broke the continuity of our direction and perseverance in the truth. They were lost, and so we got lost. They were scared; that made us scared. We make this assertion simply to register it, and not to point a finger of blame at the fathers.

They simply didn't have the perseverance or protection that would have encouraged the child to move from a state of coziness with mother in the house out into the world, to meet all the world's assaults and distractions and still persevere, so that the child still feels its self, its real self, and feels also the connection to the great being. Such a quality allows the child to learn the skills and the means to deal with the world without losing his or her fundamental connection.

Counselors who deal with an experience of a father's absence often encounter a great deal of anger and indignation: "Why weren't you there? Why didn't you help me?" After the phase of anger comes the depth of sorrow and compassion. They didn't have anybody to hold their hand, to walk their walk with them. And after that stage comes a sense of loss. "I don't know how to walk that walk. I don't feel protected by the universe."

There is a hole here. And subsequently, as adults, they go back to their homes at the end of the day feeling the absence of this quality of protection. And they want to fill this hole. Usually students try to fill this cavity by developing perseverance and steadfastness, which is fine in the beginning stages of the journey. But there comes a time when they reach the end of their perseverance. Then they need to fully turn to God: "I cannot do it. You have to preserve me in the direction of the truth."

At this point, perhaps what we called the black essence comes and erases the fear, or perhaps the citadel lands. And the citadel, when it lands, is often connected to the adrenal glands. Those who have trouble allowing this citadel-like protection to settle in often have trouble with their adrenal glands. They are plagued by fear.

The citadel, in whatever forms it comes, takes away the fear. You feel that the deepest place of essence protects you here and now, right in this relative realm. The highest realm is protecting you in this realm. Such an experience releases the fears from the adrenal, and it releases the fear from the spleen. And then the fear often lands in the perineum.

There is a center at the lowest center of the base of the spine, between the anus and the genitals. That center is plagued by fear. The instinct of survival in humanity is here, and it is distorted by fear. And the deepest fear is that you will experience the absence of a force greater than you that will protect you. You fear that force doesn't exist, or you fear that you have lost your connection to it.

There is a program playing in the perineum that says you are all alone in the universe, and you have to make it by yourself. One reaction to this fear, which is typical of American culture, is to act as if nothing is important but you, just you, when taking care of your own interests in the world.

Human beings are led to a place of fear by the desire to become self-reliant, which is a worthwhile motivation. But something in our experience of what we call self-reliance falls short of a true feeling of peace and safety. Individuals and nations, exaggerating this desire for self-reliance, can come to view the world from the place of survival and self-interest. This pattern is intrinsically destructive.

Such nations and individuals think they can promote strength by maintaining fear. If you let up on the fear, then you don't feel strong. In this false citadel, fear and strength have to go together. That's why terror is now in fashion! The system is based on the false citadel, on walking in the direction of survival and fear.

On the other hand, the real citadel is to walk in the direction of truth. You feel the courage, the support, the stability, the ease, the relaxation, to walk in the light, to walk toward the truth, and to bring the truth to people. It is a preservation of life, a preservation of the light on Earth, instead of a destruction of life in the name of what is feared. The holy citadel ultimately lands in the perineum. The citadel opens there and takes away the ring of terror, the fear of survival that became lodged in the perineum.

At the present time, human instincts are distorted. We often sit in houses that are safe, and yet we are afraid. We live in gated communities, surrounded by protective devices, and we are terrified. Our world is a vivid external picture of the ring of terror that is surrounding us within. And much of it has to do with the psychological issues of seeing our incomplete relationship with our father. For example, we see government as a father who professes to protect but who actually misleads.

The personality contains the structure of a ring of terror. It is also carried in the cells, in the DNA. For early humanity and some peoples today there was or is a fear of not surviving, of being attacked by animals, of being unprotected from the elements. Modern times have brought even greater and more distorted terrors. And this ring of terror keeps being perpetuated right into the cells and the marrow of the bones.

The terror in the perineum dries people up because it brings fear of existence. It leads to an existence without support, without the preservation of light. And yet, the terror is created as a defense! Even though it is a terrifying presence, it is a defense against absolute helplessness. As long as we are terrified, desperately holding ourselves together, we think, "at least I am preserving myself."

But if you actually melt into your inner terror, simply surrender into the terror, something deep awakens. Underneath the terror, you become fully aware of a feeling that you were very adamantly defending against being exposed. It is the feeling of being lost in the universe.

When you actually allow yourself to go to that place of being lost, instead of reacting to fend it off through endless fear-filled patterns, then blessings descend or unfold. What is necessary is to let down the defenses, to surrender, and become fully vulnerable. Having done that, from the place of lostness, you can remember your connection with the source.

The fear-based personality feels unsafe in existence. It is not protected, not preserved, not guided, and it is petrified of being shattered or broken. So it builds up enormous complex systems of defensiveness. It builds a false citadel. It wants nerves of steel, and takes that metaphor as a mark of those who are brave. Actually, such nerves of steel don't do much except defend against encroachment, and they deteriorate in time.

There is nothing shameful about feeling fear and relying on the greater source in the God reality to deal with it. If you block fear you become defensive and this kind of defensiveness actually makes you defenseless. "Defensive" here means you don't feel anymore. You are just blocking. Such defensiveness manifests as hostility and anger.

Real courage is not an activity of ego. It arises from an inner sense of divine protection and it has much more power than does anger. Such a one is standing for truth, flowing in the truth. It may come as a kind of divine wrath that is not angry but that burns away ignorance.

This whole topic is difficult to discuss because our egocentric predicament makes us want to name as divine our anger, our hostility, and our indignation. We want to hallow our own process of *nafs* by coloring it over with the concept of God. That's what a great deal of the so-called foreign policy of nations often does. It claims to eliminate evil in the name of God, but there is no real God in the phony citadel that is at its core.

According to Abdullah Ansari, who wrote a *tafsir*, or interpretation, on the phrase *Ghayri-l-maghdoobi (madzub)* in the first surah of the Qur'an, there are people habituated to form, who keep following the same ritual over and over while at the same time getting angrier and angrier about the world. He compares it to chewing an iron peanut. People who walk the path of anger may have the appearance of outer form, but outer form, if genuine, ought to awaken the inner form.

The *nafs* becomes attached to certain forms out of fear. This is actually a fear of the formless. The forms are being clung to as a defense against that fear. Consequently, because you are angry, your anger is usually taken out on people who don't follow your particular form. The Qur'an says "No fear is upon them. Neither do they grieve."[62] The definition of intimacy with the beloved is the *waliyya*.

The spiritual process needs to be more than simply invoking a protective Name. It somehow needs to deeply address the fears that human beings have. The idea of having a protective Name that we can just put on like a kind of armor is an extremely rudimentary kind of thinking. Still, it can be a first step.

We should not lose track of the beginning stages. At first it is necessary for the student to blame others. It is necessary for them to see the problem as outside of themselves. That's how the unconscious operates. It sees what is within it as being outside. They will be blaming the father, the mother, and the society. They will be blaming their counselor, blaming their teacher, and just generally blaming.

Then they go on to blame themselves for not being worthy, because how could they have been treated so miserably unless they were somehow deficient? After going through all this, they can go into the deeper stage in which they begin to face their deficiencies calmly and with confidence.

What can be accomplished through recitation of these Names should not be seen in a mechanical sort of way. You need to engage and interact with your ego-centered reality through the prayerful and introspective repetition of the sacred Name.

Turning our attention one final time to al-Hafiz, we want to emphasize that, according to the sound code, the divine protection offered by al-Hafiz reaches every situation and every thing. You are divinely protected. There can be no dangerous situation where you are left without protection. This basic meaning in the structure of the word is extremely important.

As a matrix, al-Hafiz can be usefully combined with each of the other divine Names of protection. In each case, the fact that al-Hafiz also contains within it the quality being invoked by the other Name, allows for a strengthening of the effect of this combination.

Thus, invocation of Ya Muhaimin, Ya Hafiz would strengthen trust in the preservation of essence through time. Calling out Ya Muqit, Ya Hafiz would enhance the sense of divine sustenance in our lives and our hearts. Ya Wakil, Ya Hafiz would deepen our trust in God in all situations. Ya Raqib, Ya Hafiz would deepen our caring attention. We already recommended combining Ya Mani' and Ya Mu'ti, as well as Ya Wali and Ya Waliyy, and others, but in all of these cases as well the Names of protection could also be effectively paired with Ya Hafiz.

Having seen the amazing interplay of relationships of the divine Names within a cluster, as we have in this chapter, allows us to awaken a greater understanding of the prevailing and overarching quality of divine perfection that is embodied in each Name, and in the whole cluster of Names. It also broadens our awareness of the multi-faceted activity of Allah.

wasi'
qabid basit
khafid rafi'
ghaniyy mughni
ya-fattah

chapter 12

The Secret of Ecstasy

—The Ecstasy of All That Exists—

Allah ('al-LAAH) is the first Name of ecstasy as well as the first Name of love. This wedding of love and ecstasy found in the basic root of the Name Allah is discussed in Chapter One. The meaning of Allah is rooted in an ecstatic love beyond the powers of mind to formulate. The secret ecstasy of Allah is a fundamental mystery of essence itself.

This family of divine Names particularly reveals the presence and expression of God's boundless ecstasy in a variety of ways. But to properly understand this ecstatic cluster, we must once again consider the particular form of the Name of God in Arabic: Allah. Everything begins with the treasure hidden within it.

"Hu," the aspirant, breathy sound made at the end of the word Allah, is a sound that is hidden as a divine Name within each recitation of Allah. The relationship that Allah and Hu have with each other describes the nature of ecstasy. It does so by conveying that there is a secret within the secret. The subtle way the sound "Hu" arises at the end of the invocation "Allah" also suggests an infinite process of essence of essence of essence...

Hidden ecstasy is called *suroor*, which means "secret" as well as "ecstasy." *Suroor* can manifest as an ecstatic sound, a secret essential joy that penetrates into the deepest levels of the heart and brings inner delight and happiness. It is not an expanding ecstasy such as we will explore in the divine Name al-Basit. In fact, *suroor* is found within al-Basit's opposite: al-Qabid, the contractor.

Hidden ecstasy is contracted into the secret place of the heart. On the practical level, it is an ecstasy that has no external signs such as laughing or crying. It is so internal or quiet the ecstatic might not even know that he or she is experiencing it. *Suroor* is *sirr*, a secret. And there are two more meanings of *suroor*. One meaning is to produce fire. This fire, *'ishq'allah*, is an ecstatic, all-inclusive fire of love that burns but doesn't consume. Another form of the root of *suroor* is *surrah*, the umbilical cord.

A final meaning of *suroor* points to the secret that the lover shares with the beloved. It is a kind of pillow talk, called *munaajaat*. There is an intimate conversation between two lovers who trust each other with the deepest secret of their hearts, a secret that is preserved by the intimacy of union.

There is another reason for beginning this discussion of the ecstasy family with the Name Allah. Allah is the perfect Name to set forth with on a voyage to the ecstasy that is identical with all existence itself, because it is totally inclusive. It is the essence of all the *jamali* and *jalali* Names—the Names of beauty and the Names of power.

In very general terms, by contemplating the divine Names of beauty, lovers are led to ecstasy. This voyage to ecstasy calls on all the senses. Beauty is contemplated through hearing, tasting, feeling, and so on. The spiritual traveler is thus taken into a realm of divine intoxication. On the other hand, contemplation of the divine Names of power takes the lover toward sobriety. As one's path continues, it is ever more evident that intoxication and sobriety are inseparable.

The great love that is at the core of all existence loves both intoxication and sobriety, just as it loves both the beautiful face and the wrathful and powerful one. *'Ishq'allah* cannot separate its love of ecstatic states from its love of sober states. It is an all-consuming love that has no limits and that includes all possible aspects of being.

By way of summation, in *Allahu* the ecstasy of the essence is both hidden and evoked. Everything is aflame with that essential ecstasy and love.

We have now set the stage for the appearance of the other divine Names that manifest the secret ecstasy of all that exists. The various members of this cluster each have unique characteristics, as we shall see. But what is equally interesting is that each Name acts in ways that complement other Names, and this makes for a much better understanding of the whole range of divine ecstasy.

Ya Qabid, Ya Basit, Ya Khafid, Ya Rafi'

(yaa ḲAA-biḍ, yaa BAA-siṭ, yaa K̲H̲AA-fiḍ, yaa RAA-fi')

We begin with two complementary pairs of divine Names. Both pairs express opposites. As can be seen in Chapter 7, Allah's Opposite Qualities, there is a dynamic process inherent in the relationship of such opposite Names that is quite transcendental. Understanding al-Qabid, al-Basit, al-Khafid, and ar-Rafi' will illuminate the opposite states of ecstasy and sobriety.

The divine qualities that are expressed by these Names expand, contract, raise, and lower all human beings in their states and stations. Al-Qabid is sober. Al-Basit is ecstatic. Al-Khafid contracts our spiritual station and ar-Rafi' exalts our spiritual station. Looked upon as a whole, these four divine emanations can be regarded as the regulators of all spiritual states or conditions. Having said this, we need to look into what is meant by states and stations, and what is involved in their regulation.

Al-Basit, the divine quality of expansion, and al-Qabid, the divine quality of contraction, directly relate to *ahwal*, temporary states of ecstasy. This is sometimes referred to as "entering a *hal*." States such as these are always contracting and expanding, which demonstrates their transiency quite clearly.

When viewed from the standpoint of human beings, al-Basit expresses the vast expansion of self and its ultimate absorption into the one and only being, like a sugar cube in water. But this state of absorption is transient. As the state departs, al-Qabid expresses itself into the limitation of individual selfness through contraction. These oscillations are the repeated experiences of those who have set forth upon the spiritual path.

Al-Khafid and ar-Rafi' are different from the previous pair. They do not relate to states (*ahwal*); they refer to stations (*maqaamaat*). Allah alone raises or lowers the soul in its spiritual station. To truly receive the benefit of reciting Ya Khafid, Ya Rafi' we need to give up our resistance to Allah being the one and only actor behind the process of the raising and lowering of our levels of spiritual realization.

When spiritual practitioners are so graced to give up their ego's perspective, they can then observe God's activity, through these Names, in unveiling the inner workings of their souls.

God lowers the wing of protection on your soul through the action of al-Khafid. The lowering of your station is in no way like a letdown from a temporary high. That experience would be in accord with the activity of al-Qabid, just as al-Basit evokes various degrees of spiritual intoxication.

Nor is reciting "Ya Rafi'" a technique for becoming elevated in your spiritual state. Ar-Rafi' means that God is the exalter of spirit and the only one who raises humanity through the spiritual stations.

Ya Basit, Ya Qabid, Ya Wasi'

(yaa BAA-siṭ, yaa ḲAA-biḍ, yaa WAA-si')

We will look more deeply now at al-Basit by examining some of the ecstatic states that are an important part of the meaning of this Name. *Nashiya* is to be drunk, to be enraptured. It is to drink in and inhale beauty to get to an ecstatic state. *Tarab* is to be enraptured or transported to extreme ecstasy with the beauty of music. In these states you become astonished, stunned, and dazzled. In such rapture there can be supernatural events ranging from healing the sick to calling down rain.

What we will see throughout the progression of states is a continuing refinement of the ecstatic process. Through its unfoldment, Allah comes more into the picture and ultimately breaks forth on the scene. The spiritual traveler begins to see the beauty of the beautiful one that is constantly unveiling and revealing aspects of divinity. In the stages we have described so far, laughter and tears abound.

As you begin to look within and see the beauty of a deeply intense ecstasy, you start to shine. The spirit begins to rise. It actually floats and expands with an intoxicating, light feeling. You fly toward Allah. Everyone and everything receives ecstasy from you and falls in love with you. Mevlana Rumi writes, "Everyone was drawn to me to become my friend, but no one knew what it was that drew them."

After these phenomena comes a stage where the ecstasy becomes truly beneficial for all. You disappear in the ecstasy and are totally absorbed. You are drowned in beauty. It wipes out the self; it is *fana*. You become absent of self in the beautiful. Divine beauty, al-Jamil, is progressively realizing itself in all these states of ecstasy. The state is temporary, but while it lasts, you awaken from within to God's presence and you experience your own absence.

When the transience inherent in the expanded state eventually becomes apparent, the activity of al-Qabid draws you back into a limited self-awareness. The nostalgia, the hunger, and the clinging that you now have for the expanded ecstatic state, as well as the aversion you have for the contracted state, become stumbling blocks for the ego.

At this stage, the divine Names come to your aid. By repeating Ya Qabid, Ya Basit as a pair, you begin to see the action of God in both contraction and expansion of heart. You can then easily adjust your inner feelings more and more in the direction of equanimity throughout all conditions of life. What makes achieving this joyful inner equilibrium difficult is the stubborn belief that you are in control of this process of expansion and contraction.

What is needed is to practice seeing God acting through both expansion and contraction. Such practice leads to a unifying and transcendental realization. Ecstasy comes with balance. What is opening for you through this process is the pathway of balance, a pathway that is called *siraat-ul mustaqeem* in the opening chapter of the Qur'an.

Prescription of these divine Names is an antidote for the ego's attachment and aversion to the passing states of awareness. These emotional reactions of attachment and aversion easily become defining shadows in your ego structure that then cause dysfunction and disconnection from the source.

We recommend recitation of Ya Qabid, Ya Basit, until the practitioner experiences the dawning of some equanimity about these extremes and begins to see God working through both. At that time we suggest invocation of the transcendental Name, Ya Wasi', as this directly evokes the infinite container which includes both these opposites. (For more on this Name see Chapter 7, Allah's Opposite Qualities.)

Ya Khafid, Ya Rafi'

(yaa K̲H̲AA-fiḍ, yaa RAA-fi')

The typical experience of humanity, and the experience of all beginners on the spiritual path, is that of being stuck in time. You have hope for the future and you have grief over the past. Or perhaps you have fear of the future and nostalgia for the past. In any case, such emotional casting back and forth traps you in time.

But of the lovers of God the Qur'an says, "No fear is upon them; neither do they grieve."[63] In other words, your happiness is not subject to outer conditions. This is the nature of the higher stages of ecstasy.

Al-Khafid and ar-Rafi' do not happen in time. They do not even happen in the moment. They manifest in God's time, which is eternal. God raises the soul in its station, ar-Rafi', and God lowers the soul in its station, al-Khafid. You are the passive slave of God, and God is acting in you to reveal reality. When you become aware of this, nothing essentially changes even though things appear quite differently.

Allah's secret is perfection. *Sirr* is *Birr*. *Sirr*, or secret is related to *surir*, hidden ecstasy. *Birr* is a cognate of the divine Name for the completeness and perfection of love, al-Barr. The *kamali* condition, the perfection, which is a balancing of *jalal* and *jamal*, is both hidden and revealed within the processes of ar-Rafi' and al-Khafid.

And while the condition of ar-Rafi' may be the measure of the degree of ecstasy, it is also true that al-Khafid is shaping the heart to grip the infinite and make it finite. A sacred hadith says, "The heavens and earth cannot contain me but the heart of my loving servant contains me." The heart is infinitely spacious and containing (gripping) at the same time.

The heart's particular focus of feeling allows it to incarnate or individuate the all-pervading reality. As another sacred hadith has Allah say, "I am as my loving servant imagines me to be." The water takes on the quality of the cup. Blue cup, blue water. Square cup, square water.

God is in whatever shape the heart is in. Even if the heart is dead, God takes that shape. And the heart is the treasure house, the perfect accommodation, for the discovery of all the divine Names. In the most natural condition of heart, all the divine Names are balanced. None predominates.

We have pointed out the need to find ways to achieve balance as an answer to the dilemma the spiritual traveler has been put into in their journey through the stages of divine ecstasy. Having tasted delectable expanded states, you easily form an attachment and cling to them. At the same time you may find yourself gripped by great emotional agitation, even active aversion, toward a whole variety of ordinary, mundane, and contracted conditions that your state returns to after having been expanded.

These divine Names are invaluable in the process of seeking balance in the midst of life's vicissitudes. When you recite them from the heart, deeply contemplate them, and allow the reality of their presences to be felt. Then your ego—which is clinging to some states and pushing others away—has a realization that allows it to let go and release its hold. A new perspective dawns as to who is actually the actor.

Even though we have said that the heart takes the shape of the moment, and in so doing allows God to manifest, the heart's innate nature reveals an essential egalitarianism and equality. If we put this principle of equality into the theological context of trying to identify what is idolatry, it would say: the mistake idolators make is not in saying God is in *that* stone, but in saying God is *not* in all other stones as well.

Recitation of Ya Khafid, Ya Rafi' draws us into ecstatic wonder by means of an awe-filled witnessing of the undiminished activity of God as manifested in and through all stations of realization. Now we are ready to turn to al-Wajid, the most inclusive divine Name in the ecstasy family, and a Name that contains all the stages of ecstasy.

Ya Wajid

(yaa WAA-jid)

During our discussions of the previous Names in the ecstasy family, we have in passing briefly described some of the transient stages of ecstasy. One constant about all these stages on the path is that divine beauty, al-Jamil, leads you into them all. The final ecstatic stage, described by the Name al-Wajid, reveals the all-encompassing ecstasy that is the intrinsic nature of existence itself.

Al-Wajid affirms that ecstasy is the essence of existence. At this culminating stage of ecstasy, you are absent of self in God's beauty. However, when you come out of that absorption you become conscious of existence and see that its essence is ecstasy itself. Both of these phases are equally filled with joy. It is as if you are witnessing God playing a game of hide and seek.

Al-Wajid is the most complete Name to use in a general discussion of divine ecstasy. As all forms of ecstasy are included in its various meanings, it is the natural take-off point for the whole family of Names that express divine ecstasy. Since al-Wajid's meaning includes a complete picture of divine ecstasy, we will take some time to go into it systematically.

Al-Wajid is the divine ecstasy where you come to know that the very essence of existence itself is ecstasy. The root of the word *wajid* (W-J-D) equally means ecstasy and existence. The grammatical sound code of the Arabic language tells us that al-Wajid has a unique intensive quality. All this clearly points to a basic meaning: al-Wajid is the unique source, the only cause, of existence and ecstasy.

There are distinct types of ecstasy that can be described. The first is pure expansion, *bast* (as in al-Basit). In the darkest night of the soul great lights of ecstasy may appear. These ecstatic moments are experienced as spontaneous gifts. They have been described as gleams, as glimmers, and as shining stars. When you are in these states you think you are in eternity, but the experience quickly vanishes, and generally there is no lasting effect. The *nafs*, or lower self, is quite armored against change.

But these surprising and wonder-filled moments move you forward, and due to even such fleeting appearances, you now may become a seeker of truth, a *talib al-haqq*, a seeker of the real. A desire for renewed ecstatic union leads spiritual travelers to the door of the next type of ecstasy. They pray for a way to achieve such great joy without the bitter aftermath of remaining stuck in their craving for the repetition of that glorious state.

They must realize that, after all, they did not cause this state to occur. Then they may search for a *tareeqah*, one of the various Sufi orders. Ecstasy is deliberately evoked in these lineages by the use of a wide variety of practices and techniques. Such practices may frequently produce a *hal*, a transient state of ecstasy as has been referred to previously. Diligently proceeding along the path of a *tareeqah* in such ways may turn you into a *salik*, a true spiritual wayfarer.

There is a hadith that says, "When you are in prayer, cry, and if you can't cry, make yourself cry." This teaching suggests that it is appropriate to use techniques to get into deeper spiritual states. Then through these techniques you begin to balance the expansive and contractive states. The discovery of this inner balancing is called *mukaashifah*.

The next stage is called *mu'ayyinah*. It involves deeper discovery and deeper ecstasy. Now the eye and ear of the heart are opened wide. God becomes the eye with which you see and the ear with which you hear. Everything becomes transformed. For example, the sound of crickets might be experienced as a chorus of angels. What is occurring is a piercing of the veil. It is a discovering of the eternal within passing phenomena.

In the chapter devoted to her in the Qur'an, when the beloved one of Allah, Mary, is pregnant and in birth throes with Jesus, she actually hears the voice of the palm tree offering guidance from God. Many visions also occur in dreams, and the face of divine beauty manifests in this way. Passionate love can also bring forth an ecstatic vision of the eternal beloved, as in the Qur'anic story of Yusuf and Zulaykha. In short, the eye of the heart opens, and you see reality.

There are methods offered in the *tareeqahs* that emphasize visualization, silent meditation, and practices with light. In India, the spiritual environment that the *tareeqahs* were able to create to invite ecstatic experiences such as we have been speaking of is called a *sam'a*. There is music, rhythmic movement, and turning, along with recitations of *dhikr*, Qur'anic verses, and Sufi poetry. There are many techniques in many *tareeqahs* that are intended to encourage *mu'ayyinah*.

A third level of al-Wajid is called *mushaahidah*. The *shahid*, or inner witnessing in the stage of *mushaahidah*, is a witnessing of all your senses simultaneously and continuously. Now, you are continuously aware of God's presence through all possible changes of conditions. Such continuity of awareness completely balances contraction and expansion.

The perceptive reality that is spontaneously arising and dissolving in the sacred altar of the heart reveals itself in and through a continuous awe-filled awareness. At this stage, the lovers of God have become fully established in an ecstasy that is stable and consistent. When you are in this stage, for example, you are able to witness the raising or lowering of all spiritual stations, including your own, as the activity of God.

'Ibn 'Arabi says, in reference to the process of becoming established into a spiritual station (*maqaam*), that the key to realizing that station's ecstasy comes through a kind of coupling process. The two extremes of being raised up and lowered down must be equally embraced. Consequently, when you experience yourself being either raised or lowered, you are never oblivious of the other side. And you have no preference about the raising and the lowering.

There is a similar equalization of *jamal* and *jalal*, the manifestations of beauty and power. You have no personal interest in being somewhere other than the state you are in. You naturally come to see how the one extreme contains the other. The expanded state is within the contracted state.

It is the same with ar-Rafi' and al-Khafid. Everyone wants to be raised to a higher station in intimacy with Allah, but, the desire of our ego notwithstanding, there may be great wisdom in the opposite experience coming to pass. We may even come to see the action of Allah embodied in the lowering of our station. It is al-Khafid, the only one who lowers beings in their spiritual station.

It turns out that al-Khafid is used in two specific ways in the Qur'an. One place is in the image of a mother bird lowering her wings over her chicks. This is given as a specific image of God offering loving compassion—Ya Rahman—through a protective, covering gesture. Simply to contemplate this image should raise one's appreciation of the spiritual depth of al-Khafid.

The other usage of al-Khafid in the Qur'an again shows it as a kind of protection. Children lower the wing of protection over parents in their old age. It is interesting to note that recitation of Ya Khafid may actually be a remedy for students who have come to a place where spiritual practices don't work for them, or who have become burned out around spiritual practice and prayer.

Repeated together as a pair, Ya Rafi' and Ya Khafid offer protection to the traveler on the path against his or her own spiritual greed. You are protected from going too high or too fast when you are not prepared. This lowering, as it turns out, comes from a loving protective concern for the soul of the wayfarer. Sometimes being unseen, being lowered, is the best medicine for growth.

What evolves along with the process of more fully realizing al-Wajid is that we are led to being completely content with whatever *maqaam* the continuous activity of God puts us in. Such a beautifully developed condition of self is called *radiyyah*. (See Chapter 17, The Seven Levels of the *Nafs*.) You are content with where God has placed you. And God responds with contentment for that soul who is content. There is a continuous presence of contentment.

Ya Ghaniyy, Ya Mughni

(yaa GHA-neeyy, yaa mugh-NEE)

Looking at divine ecstasy through a slightly different lens, we will now examine the Names al-Ghaniyy and al-Mughni. They share the same root meaning: an incredible, inexhaustible treasure house of riches. The boundless riches that are found in both these Names, as we shall see, are divine ecstasy, al-Wajid. And we now know that al-Wajid is a Name synonymous with existence itself, *wujud*.

If your sense of isolation has brought you to a joyless condition in life, invocation of Ya Ghaniyy, Ya Mughni can provide the antidote. Repetition of this pair of Names will serve to activate your realization of a hidden treasury of joy within. For the *salik*, the whole-hearted and conscientious traveler on the spiritual path, realization of al-Ghaniyy means knowing that the great treasure is found in all space and every space, and in every particle of existence.

Al-Ghaniyy is actually a state of the effulgence of Allah in every atom of the universe. The hidden ecstasy is not different from existence itself. Already we are talking as if there were two separate conditions when we say, as a way of trying to express this, that all existence is suffused with divine ecstasy.

This emanation, this effulgence of God, ecstatically flows forth from its infinite treasure house to all of creation. It flows from existence to that which has no existence. What we receive from its innermost quality is the answer to the existential question "Why do I exist?"

In the Qur'an is the passage: "We found you in want (*fuqaraa'*) and then gave sufficiency (*ghaniyy*)."[64] This is saying that human beings are full of poverty and neediness, and to this condition Allah responds with richness and fullness. When Ya Ghaniyy is repeated it can have a transformational, even alchemical, effect on the situations in your life where you find yourself stuck. Your existence may seem to be joyless and empty of meaning, but al-Ghaniyy transforms it and awakens what is hidden within.

When you recite this *wazifah* there should be an alchemical feeling about it. For example, you should not be trying to ask that some outer thing should happen to alter circumstances, such as the opening of a door, or increasing a channel for expression. Instead, something inherent, something that is present but hidden in whatever situation you are facing can transform it from within. It is more about being than doing. In realizing your own real poverty or emptiness, including the emptiness of your idea of your self, al-Ghaniyy is revealed.

This insight leads to a deeper understanding of the Qur'anic passage quoted above. By a process of *fana*, you give up the desire of the ego—its need to somehow fill the hole of what you don't have. Then you are able to enter the true richness of the all-sufficient state of Allah, as al-Ghaniyy.

The teaching here is in the same vein as the beatitude of Jesus, where he teaches that the poor in spirit, those who are filled less with a sense of self, are joyful and are the inheritors of the bliss of the kingdom of heaven. No wonder many Sufis took this Qur'anic passage as an encouragement to become *faqeer*s, thoroughly without personal possessions.

Recitation of Ya Ghaniyy is also indicated as a remedy for those who reject help because they have isolated themselves in a false individuality. With such people there is an insistence that "everything is fine; I don't need anything." They are unable to accept the fact of the necessary interdependence that life shows us throughout creation.

In psychological terms they may have rejected the object relation because of the experience of being rejected by their parents. They either find that the universe is utterly barren of value, or it is full of an abundance that it is impossible for them to have. In our culture there is a tendency to concentrate on outer wealth, on the façade of our houses, so to speak, and to ignore the interior.

If you do not feel it is safe to show your needs, repetition of Ya Ghaniyy is recommended. You may discover that the universe is truly abundant. Al-Ghaniyy challenges the game of fake humility that is actually a way of trying to cover over the need, a way of denying to yourself your real neediness.

It is a mistaken idea of spiritual pedagogy that tells aspirants they shouldn't want anything. If you acknowledge the wanting and the greed, you may find that what is intrinsically within that desire may lead you to what you really need: love, joy, and peace. Yearning is in every cell.

This yearning, this thirst, is the universal activity of *'ishq*. Instead of continually struggling to deny this desire, it becomes engaged in your practice. As you call out to the essence of al-Ghaniyy, every part of your being is restored to integrity, the distortion caused by material coarseness is overcome, and you find the richness that God has made.

Because Allah bestows al-Ghaniyy on temporal creatures, it becomes possible that a temporal creature can temporarily act as the embodiment of al-Ghaniyy's infinite and inexhaustible reality. This is an important metaphysical point about manifestation itself.

The source and primary cause of the richness of existence is al-Ghaniyy, and the causal manifestation of this richness is al-Mughni. We can clearly see this in Chapter 4, The Sound Code, where, as a member of the fourth form, the causal nature of al-Mughni is shown.

Every individual existence is a vessel. Al-Ghaniyy is the treasure of divine ecstasy put into the treasure house of all existence. Al-Mughni is the one who causes that ecstasy to be bestowed in particular ways on particular beings. Their relationship is suggested by the passage in Exodus that says the light of God alighted on a bush, which began to burn, but which was not consumed by the flame.

Repetition of Ya Mughni is a remedy for your experience of dependence and neediness on another. Realizing al-Mughni is to become constant in your love and affection. You can do this because you are rooted in the infinite stillness of the reality from which all multiplicity gains its existence.

Al-Ghaniyy and al-Mughni are so linked together in meaning that to bring fullness to the process of realizing and embodying the divine ecstasy, we recommend combining them in recitation: Ya Ghaniyy, Ya Mughni.

Ya Fattah

(yaa fat-TAAH)

We will end this chapter with al-Fattah, a sacred Name for opening and for beginning. We treat this divine Name elsewhere as part of the family of abundance and blessing. But it should also be seen in the context of the ecstasy family. What al-Fattah specifically has to do with love and ecstasy is that the opening that it offers is an opening of the heart. Repetition of Ya Fattah opens the heart to love and ecstasy, to the inner light of the soul.

You open the heart with the key, which is al-Fattah. The double "t" tells us this opening activity is continuous. It is continuously opening, opening layers of the heart deeper and deeper. The journey never ends. You are opening up the veils of darkness over the heart to uncover the light of the soul within the heart's globe. Recitation of Ya Fattah sets up the dynamic process of going deeper and deeper in your opening.

Al-Fattah is a very powerful name. Even in the midst of despair, it offers the possibility that you can open to love and ecstasy. Because its opening power is continuous, and because the secret of ecstasy is hidden in all existence, you can have confidence that by calling on this great Name, there could always be a breakthrough, regardless of any prevailing condition or circumstance.

jami'

awwal akhir

mu'akhkhir muqaddim

batin zahir

muhdi' mu'id

quddus

chapter 13

The Arc of Ascent and Descent

—Continuous Creation and Assimilation—

There is a process we can trace in the universe that is continuous and circular. Sufis call it the arc of ascent and descent. That which is hidden through stages becomes manifest and then, again through stages, returns to the unmanifest dimension, only to manifest again. There is creation, dissolution, and assimilation, a cycle that continues endlessly.

The view of the universe that this model offers is very different from the linear view of a first creation in time that occurs out of nothingness. The reality referred to as Allah is described in the Qur'an as "Never born and never giving birth."[65]

In this chapter we will look at some of the divine Names in the context of the arc of ascent and descent. In particular we will concentrate on Names that illustrate the dynamic inner structure of the process of manifestation and infinite return. Several sets of paired Names, when considered in this context, help reveal the two arcs in operation, and point toward the reality of the *'arsh* throne.

The throne of God, called the Heart Throne or *'arsh*, should not be viewed in an anthropomorphic way. A simple definition can be given on the physical plane. When we explore the root meanings of the word *'arsh* we see that it refers to a shady, cool bower over a well that affords refuge and safety. There is a sense of living waters that give *barakah* or blessings.

In more abstract terms the *'arsh* represents a relationship between the infinite and the finite. It turns out that an infinite line in both directions is not really a straight line; it is a curve. Whatever we see is a finite unit of an infinite circle. One of the Names of God is Da'im, or circle. A form of this word, *dawwaam*, means the movement of that infinite flow continuously in a circle without beginning or end. This is a key to how God can be described: as a circle with a dot in the center.

The notion of that still point, or dot, gets close to the meaning of the *'arsh*. It can be said to subsist in the center of the infinite circle described by a continuous flow that moves through the arcs of ascent and descent. We will come back to this paradigm a bit later in our discussion.

We are exploring the family of divine Names that directly relate to creation/manifestation and dissolution/absorption. It will help to begin with the finite realm. Simply put, something is finite if it has a beginning and an end.

Ya Muhyi, Ya Mumit, Ya Hayy

(yaa MUH-yee, yaa mu-MEET, yaa ḤAIYY)

There is a whole cluster of Names that function in a finite way. Al-Muhyi and al-Mumit are excellent examples. That which brings life, when something begins, is al-Muhyi. And that which ends life, when something ends, is al-Mumit. Al-Muhyi is an expression of the arc of ascent. As life arrives, al-Muhyi is its only cause. Al-Mumit expresses the arc of descent. When death comes, al-Mumit is the only cause. These Names describe the reality that is behind the everyday experience of living and dying as we know it in this finite realm.

Al-Hayy, on the other hand, expresses the undying, ever-living nature of Allah. This transcendental Name is not affected by birth and death. Its ever-living nature includes both al-Muhyi and al-Mumit. Both death and life, as finite phenomena, begin and end continuously in al-Hayy, the ever-living. Al-Hayy, as a divine Name, can be said to be in the eternal and infinite category.

Following this example, it is not difficult to see the infinite circle of the arc of ascent and descent. It is of particular importance to see how contemplation of this divine circle, of necessity, intuitively leads to recognition of the undying, eternal state. We saw how al-Hayy includes both al-Muhyi and al-Mumit in its reality. Later we will see that the transcendental relationship al-Hayy has with al-Muhyi and al-Mumit is very *'arsh*-like.

Ya Qabid, Ya Basit, Ya Jami', Ya Quddus

(yaa ḲAA-biḍ, yaa BAA-siṭ, yaa JAA-mi', yaa ḳud-DOOS)

Aspects of the arc of ascent and the arc of descent become clearer when we consider the qualities of love and ecstasy and how love and ecstasy develop. In the arc of ascent, the lover pursues the beloved until union is attained. Here we see the lover as active and the beloved as passive. But in the arc of descent the lover suddenly understands God as the active pursuer. Then the lover becomes *'abd*, the passive, empty server of God.

There is a famous hadith that says if you walk toward God, God comes running toward you. When, as a lover, we pursue God actively we pursue *bast* (Ya Basit), expansive ecstasy, and we feel close to God. An idealization process is taking place where we are shaping a greater and greater God ideal.

At this expansive ecstatic stage we may view *qabd* (Ya Qabid) as a restriction, and doing so, consequently, may feel far from God. At the top of the arc, a reality is experienced where expansion and contraction merge. It is al-Wasi'.

Subsequently, when we enter the arc of descent all of the belief systems and ideals that we built up on the arc of ascent are dissolved, and we passively experience the action of God untying and gradually loosening the knot of our beliefs and experiences of the beloved. As our belief systems become untied, we start to see God in every form. And again this is the all-inclusive heart quality of al-Wasi'.

Al-Jami' and al-Quddus offer further insights into the mysterious process of the arc of ascent and descent, especially when seen through the lens of divine ecstasy. Al-Jami' has the quality of gathering everything together into a whole, and al-Quddus has the quality of leaving behind everything but the essence. They appear as opposites. Sobriety enters after ecstasy is experienced.

The ecstasy of al-Jami' comes in the arc of ascent. You begin to integrate aspects of your *nafs* (lower self). There are many stages of ever-increased merging with the utter fullness of being. Finally the lower self joins the *ruh* (soul) and real ecstasy dawns. There is great joy in the union of this embrace.

As this fullness dissolves, in the arc of descent, varying aspects of *ruh* manifest and merge into different aspects of the *nafs*. Now, for lovers to join with the beloved, they see the need to separate from everything other than Allah. The call of the purity of the soul gives birth to the willingness to let go of habitual patterns in the *nafs*. So the lover is joining with the one, as in al-Jami', but also separating from the world, as in al-Quddus.

In the arc of descent, for the beloved (God) to pursue and join with the lover, God constantly manifests in separate containers, through the emanations of the divine Names. It is almost as if the beloved, out of the love to join with the lover, manifests in a mode of separation. These containers (*dharf*) each contain the divine manifestation while existing on the plane of multiplicity. This divine activity of al-Quddus is continuously happening in every single time and place, as evidenced in the sound code by the double "d" in Quddus.

It is quite beautiful when you see both Names operating at the same time. The divine mystery obliterates the distinction between joining everything together and separating out everything but essence. Joining and separation become as one. These apparent opposites are aspects of the same thing. According to 'ibn 'Arabi, the culmination of the whole process is the grand synthesis, *Jaam'i-ul-jawaam'i*, the joining of all joinings, beyond the arcs.

Ya 'Awwal , Ya Akhir, Ya Mu'akhkhir, Ya Muqaddim, Ya Batin, Ya Zahir, Ya Mubdi, Ya Mu'id

(yaa OW-wal, yaa AA-k̲h̲ir, yaa mu-'AK̲H-k̲h̲ir, yaa mu-ḴAD-dim,
yaa BAA-ṭin, yaa D̲HAA-hir, yaa mub-dee', yaa mu-'EED)

The arc of ascent and descent is the perfect orbital map to orient us in looking at the family of Names that describe the divine action of creation and assimilation. There are Names that relate to the metaphysical structure of this process, and there are Names that describe the process at the level of physical causation. These all need to be viewed together.

When we considered al-Muhyi and al-Mumit earlier, we saw we were looking at a circle continuously moving from al-Hayy, the ever-living, and back to al-Hayy, the ever-living. The beginning is the end and the end is the beginning. Al-Muhyi begins with al-Hayy. It infinitely approaches al-Mumit through the stages of life, and then releases again into al-Hayy.

That is how it looks from the finite perspective. From the eternal perspective, the life caused by al-Muhyi, and the death caused by al-Mumit, are themselves nothing but aspects of the eternal life of al-Hayy.

The process of moving toward the one, toward union with Allah, is the arc of ascent. Its apex is the point of *liqa'*, or reunion with the beloved. It is at the top of the breath, so to speak. Then the arc of descent begins along with the letting go of everything including self, and culminating in absorption in the infinite. This process traces the stages of what in Sufism is called *fana*, the soul's return to God, and *baqa*, the soul's awakening to the real self.

Al-Muhyi and al-Mumit can easily be seen to follow the general pattern we have described above. This suggests that it might be beneficial to see if the same kind of thing holds true for all the opposite Names, that in their circle of causal expression they continuously pass through a transcendental quality outside of time and space.

This brings us to the core of our discussion. We want to explore the inner nature of the divine processes of creation and dissolution. The first thing we should understand is that the processes of creation and dissolution occur in both time and eternity. This is illustrated by the following divine Names.

Al-'Awwal means God is the first. Al-Akhir means God is the last. But al-'Awwal is the first without a second, and al-Akhir is the last without a penultimate. They are eternal qualities, outside of time. They can only be infinitely approached as limits, as in calculus.

The divine qualities al-Muqaddim and al-Mu'akhkhir allow us to move forward and backward in time. As al-Muqaddim moves awareness forward in time, you infinitely approach but never actually reach al-Akhir, the last. And as al-Mu'akhkhir moves awareness backwards in time, you infinitely approach but never actually reach al-'Awwal , the first.

Turning our attention from time to space, two more divine qualities present themselves, al-Batin and az-Zahir. Al-Batin means completely hidden and az-Zahir means completely expressed. The idea we may have of going from nothing to something is not exactly it.

In the realm of the divine Names, manifestation is going from al-Batin to az-Zahir, from the hidden to the manifest. The arc is completed when that which is fully manifest returns to the hidden condition. Reflecting on this process allows us to see creation, or manifestation, as a process of becoming more and more visible. When we try to approach al-Batin and az-Zahir from the finite perspective, just as described before, our approach continues without end.

Al-Mubdi' is the one who begins a process, but it is not the absolute beginning. It is a beginning in time. Al-Mubdi' brings invisible essence into visible manifestation, and continues to do so in various stages. As this process progresses forward in space, we finally get to az-Zahir.

Al-Mu'id is the one who brings a process to an ending or a return to the source, but it is not the absolute end itself. It is an end in time. Al-Mu'id returns the visible manifestation to invisible essence. In stages, al-Mu'id infinitely approaches al-Batin, moving backward in space, so to speak.

Al-Mubdi' and al-Mu'id are important in terms of framing our discussion. Al-Mubdi' names the process through which all the divine qualities manifest from the source. Al-Mu'id names the process through which the divine qualities all return to the source. Let's take some time to look more deeply into these divine Names.

We'll arbitrarily begin with al-Mu'id, the one who ends. A relevant root form of Mu'id is 'aada. It means to return to a place after having left it. But though you might think this is an ending, actually nothing ever ends in this infinite universe. It is a place of return for a new beginning in an endless circle. A form of the word 'i'taada means to repeat a thing over and over again.

Another meaning of the verb 'aada is to efface, which is the same as *fana*. It could be used in a sentence like this: The winds and rains effaced the houses until they collapsed. *Naqada*, another variation of Mu'id, is to undo a knot after it has been tied. It has a physical meaning "to undo," which is another way of saying *fana*. *Fana* is loosening the knot of the mind.

Al-Mu'id is returning to Allah in the process of *fana*, through either physical or spiritual death. It also means that, as you return time and again, there is the alternation of *fana, baqa, fana, baqa*. Al-Mu'id would be *fana*, and al-Mubdi' would be *baqa*. They go together. They need to be understood together. For this reason, as is generally the case with the opposite Names, our recommendation is to recite them together: Ya Mubdi, Ya Mu'id.

Mu'id means to return, in stages, until you get to some ultimate place. If Allah is *baqi*, the real self, everything else is *faa'in*, the impermanence of composite existence. Shaykh Junayd says, "What passes away in *fana*, never really was; and what remains always was, always is, and always will be." The states and stages of this process are called *darajaat* and *maqaamaat* in Sufism. In this way they describe a *tareeqah*, or pathway, to the ultimate source.

The sound code tells us al-Mubdi' is causative. It means to cause to begin. It carries the meaning of making a precedent, an original beginning. In contrast with al-'Awwal , it means to do the first thing first, and begin again with the second, and so on. Al-'Awwal is more transcendental; it is the first without a second. Al-Mubdi' is the beginning of everything else.

There is a physical-plane form of the word, *'abda'a*, which means to grow a second set of teeth after losing the milk teeth. The more abstract meaning of al-Mubdi' is to cause a thing to come into existence. It causes anything to be found, *wajada*.

The phrase *baadi'-ur-ra'yi* means the first idea, the first impression of what is perceived. It is the first creative thought—what appears before any judgment or analysis takes place. *Badiy'* means "made or brought into existence." But it also means something wonderful, extraordinary, amazing, unique, and new. *Badiy'ah* means an unexpected surprise. We become enthralled at the first appearance of a thing.

These are important extensions of the root meaning of the Name because they take us into the psychological realm. Reciting Ya Mubdi' may help us to reignite childlike wonder, to get out of a plodding state and become fired up. It can be used to rekindle yearning or desire for God realization. It is causative, the first to get things going. But just as it is difficult to start things, it is difficult to end them.

God brings existence forth, *yubdi'u khalqa*. That's the Mubdi' part. Then God brings it back or returns it to its source, *thumma yu'iydu*. That's the Mu'id part. In a nutshell, that may be the best way to present these two divine Names.

Al-Mubdi' and al-Mu'id show up as pairs all over. A good example is: *bada'a thumma* [66] (you begin a thing), then *'aada* (you repeat it). In this case *bada'a* means to do something for the very first time that has never been done before, initiate a thing, begin a thing. Every time you begin something with consciousness, al-Mubdi' manifests into that time and space, and every time you consciously complete something, al-Mu'id manifests in that time and space. Beginning and ending are like manifesting and then returning to the beginning where one started in the first place. The path is circular: *qaaba qawsain*, a link of two bows or two arcs.

Al-Mubdi' is moving from al-'Awwal, the first. Its direction is from the timeless into time. It is moving in this great direction from the infinite to the finite. In a similar manner, al-Mu'id journeys from the infinite to the finite when it moves from al-Batin, the utterly hidden world, to az-Zahir, the visible world.

The mystery of the process of continuous creation from the infinite to the finite can be seen in great detail by examining the three pivotal divine Names that constitute the primary cluster of the creation family: Ya Khaliq, Ya Bari', and Ya Musawwir. That is the subject of the next chapter.

khaliq
bari'
musawwir

chapter 14

God the Creator

—Its Manifestation in the Universe and in Humanity—

We need to look much more deeply into what it means to call God "the creator." While it is quite common to call God the Creator, little effort is usually made to be clear about what being a creator means when applied to God. How does the infinite become finite? How does the hidden treasure become known? Is there any way to intellectually approach the mystery of such creation?

One approach is suggested by study of the 99 Names of Allah. Three Names in particular, Ya Khaliq, Ya Bari', and Ya Musawwir, constitute a cluster that describes the metaphysical process of divine creation. By concentrating on the inner meanings of these qualities, we think that some of the confusions around the idea of God as creator may be dispelled.

Ya Khaliq
(yaa KHAA-liḳ)

Let's begin our discussion by looking at meanings on the physical level. There is a metaphor from leather making that illustrates the relationship among the three divine qualities Al-Khaliq, al-Bari', and al-Musawwir. In fact, the word *khaliq* means a leatherworker. In one of the root forms of al-Khaliq, we find the meanings of measuring a piece of leather and of conceiving a design that is beautifully proportioned.

The extension of the metaphor of leatherworking to this cluster of Names is irresistible. Al-Bari' could be seen as the activity of cutting the pieces of leather using the design that has been conceived. Al-Musawwir would be to sew the individual pieces together and complete the form. But how does this metaphor help in understanding the divine process of creation?

Begin by imagining that the uncreated boundlessness of infinity is the mind of God free of all impressions. Within that apparent nothingness, self-awareness dawns and an activity begins of imagining an infinity of hidden possibilities. This activity is al-Khaliq. God is the imaginer of the infinite possibilities of being. All manifestation begins with this creative leap.

The imagination of God, *al-khiyaal*, is not exactly "creating" as we ordinarily understand it. It is imagining what could be created. We might say it is the dawn of creation. The phrase *rabb-il-'aalameen* in the opening chapter of the Qur'an refers to God imagining all the infinite possibilities of universes upon universes.

When we speak of ideas in the mind of God, this is not to imply that any such ideas are separate from God—or identical with God, either. Such ideas, or activity of mind, are identified with God in one sense but not another, just as we are identified with our ideas in one sense but not another. *Khuluq* is the stuff God dreams. Shakespeare must have sensed this when he had Prospero say, "We are such stuff as dreams are made on."

Khuluq is an innate characteristic of the mind or soul. We are constituted by nature to dream the dream of God. *Fitrah* is essentially the same as *khuluq*. *Fitrah* is the innate or natural disposition of the mind to know God. Following this direction, we come to the astounding conclusion that the natural disposition of everything is to relate to the infinite.

We focused first on the divine perspective—God's imagining of possibilities—rather than the human perspective, but the meaning is the same. From the human perspective, the lover imagines the beloved. It is called *thanaa'*, the soul's natural ability to imagine the beloved. A sacred hadith has Allah saying, "I am as my lover imagines me to be." We see the dynamic relationship of the attributes of divine creation on the arc of descent—God's creation of the human being—and on the arc of ascent—the human being's imagination and realization of the God reality.

Since it is the innate disposition of the formless and eternal God to imagine the universe, it is actually impossible to say the universe begins. After all, in one very real sense, it is always there. There is a word *khilqah* from the same root as al-Khaliq. It means something created or made in the mother's womb. *Khaliqah* means a well of water formed by nature and not a dug well.

In both of these physical-plane forms of the word we get the same sense of a disposition being created by what was already present in its natural container. It is noteworthy also that Al-Khaliq is deeply related to al-Qadir, and thus it expresses both destiny and natural disposition. Al-Khallaaq is another form of this divine Name equally used in the Qur'an. The very form of the word tells us that this creative quality must be repetitive and continuous.

Everything's creation can rightly be attributed to Allah, the one and only source of existence. If al-Khaliq describes ideas in the mind of God, *al-Khallaaq* explains their inner workings. There is an expression *khalq jadeed* that is found in the verse of the Qur'an where the Queen of Sheba's throne is made to appear out of thin air.[67] There are hidden possibilities within the *khalq jadeed* that allow for such an occurrence. Both *khallaaq* and *jadeed* mean beginningless and endless.

There was never a time when God was not beginningless and endless. Indeed, time itself should be viewed as a part of what is created. God brings time from nothingness into existence. *Jadeed* means ever-renewing and constant, but it is not repetitive in the sense of doing the same thing over and over. The realm of infinite potentiality constantly brings forth freshness. Every emanation of ar-Rahman, ar-Rahim is qualitatively different.

In the Qur'an we read, "Every moment God is manifesting."[68] God's glory is manifesting every single moment. This mystical view of a continuity of divine creation is very far from the deistic notion of a God who retires after initiating the first cause. Every moment we are seeing al-Khaliq in action. And we are seeing, as well, what the ongoing results are from that initiating action.

Using spiritual practice to slow down the moment in which God is manifesting is called *talwaaniy*. What is then seen is that in each such moment God is simultaneously destroying and creating the universe. Both *fana* and *baqa* are present in each moment. *Talwaaniy*, then, is a way of slowing down time to see what time essentially is. What is exposed is the endless dance of time and timelessness, emptiness and fullness.

Another reason to drop the conventional linear timeline from our mental map is that a better way to graph time is as part of a circle. Time is not well described as a line stretching out, because we can't say time has a beginning or an end. It is a continuous arc that can be pictured as a circle. We name the arbitrary segments of this circle for reference and measurement only.

A second important meaning for al-Khaliq is "beautifully created, shapely and well proportioned." It is made smooth, like a stone or gem without cracks or fissures. It is fit and apt for every circumstance. Another root form of the word offers a physical metaphor: She rubbed her body all over with saffron perfume (*khalooq*). Here we have beauty, pleasing to the senses, and well proportioned nicely bundled together. These are all aspects of al-Khaliq.

But now we should again turn our attention to the mind of God at the stage where al-Khaliq appears. We already talked about how the leatherworker comes to see the possibilities of a beautifully proportioned design in the leather. Another way of describing this stage of the creative process is that it is like imagining the letters hidden in the inkpot.

There are infinite possibilities in the ink, but there are not yet any defined things. There is not even the distinct possibility of things appearing. What has occurred in al-Khaliq is that the infinite consciousness of God has concentrated itself into self-awareness and has fallen in love with its hidden possibilities of self-knowledge and realization.

Ya Bari'

(yaa BAA-ri')

Al-Bari' is the sacred Name that describes the next phase of God's creative process. At this stage there will be distinct possibilities of things appearing. Going back to our original metaphor: The individual pieces of leather are now cut out according to the whole design that was originally imagined. In abstract terms, what we have here is the beginning of individuation, while still in the undifferentiated condition.

Al-Bari' is not infinite possibilities; it is inexhaustible potentialities. They are delimited, *ta'ayyun*. They are separate potentialities in the sense that now they are individuated from one another. Multiplicity begins here; we become aware of multiple essences. This is still well before what is generally called manifestation, but now what before was possibility has a definite potential to manifest. 'Ibn 'Arabi calls it *'a'yaan thaabitah*, the essences in pre-eternity which exist in the pure awareness of Allah.

Such is the realm of the divine Names. It is how they exist. They are separate potentialities formed from the ocean of infinite possibilities. They could be called archetypes. They are individuated ideas in the mind of God. This is the realm where the sacred Names exist in essence before they are seen to manifest into things. In classical Sufi terms this realm is called *jabarut*.

Al-Bari' picks up where al-Khaliq leaves off. As you will recall, when al-Khaliq's activity begins, nothing is visible. The dawn of creation is thoroughly hidden. Reality is so thoroughly and completely unseen that it would be correct to say the activity of al-Khaliq is *creatio ex nihilo*. In an important sense, something is being created out of nothing. Yet that nothing, out of which all creation comes and to which it returns, is not different from the everlasting uncreated nature of God.

Hidden in the silence of God's absolute nature is an innate disposition toward self-knowledge. It is God's loving inclination to more fully know what is hidden in the formless reality that gives birth to the dreaming of universes. It is God's inherent nature that makes al-Khaliq rise. Al-Bari' then fashions what comes out of this initial creative impulse into something else. In other words, the pen has been dipped in the ink well, and now there is a dot of ink on the point of the pen.

Let's take some time to explore a few main meanings and some extended meanings of al-Bari'. We will look at different forms that the root of al-Bari' takes, especially forms that express its quality in physical terms. This is a literal, even earthy, way to expand our understanding of any divine Name.

A set of words that come from the root of al-Bari' all have the meaning "to become free of" or "to remove yourself from." For example, we find words that mean such things as: to free the penis from urine by shaking, to separate legally from one's husband or wife, or to assert yourself as free and clear. The intellectual consequence that we draw from such roots is a definite encouragement to explore the extended meaning of the concept of "becoming free from."

First, from the standpoint of the divine creator, what is created is free from all fault and imperfection. What God makes is well proportioned and free from inconsistencies, defects, and imperfections. The nature of al-Bari' is to make the universe like that. At the human level, everyone can free themselves from deep-seated guilt because the creation of humanity is free of all blemishes.

It is also necessary to discover a more profound sense of what it might mean to free yourself from some unclean thing. This is especially so since it is now clear that uncleanness is not innate. Such a freeing of self means a process of inner transformation. Through real processes of purification you are freed from the tyranny of the ego and become fully in touch with the intrinsic purity of your soul, which is your real self.

Indeed, healing is a primary meaning frequently seen in al-Bari'. It is appropriate to invoke Ya Bari' as a Name of divine healing, as well as a Name of divine creation. The sound code tells us that al-Bari' as a healing Name would mean "the only one who causes healing to occur." *Bara'a al-jurh* means "the wound healed." *Bari'a min al-marad* means "recovering from disease." *Bari'a* is "becoming sound and healthy, to have a real convalescence."

In other words, al-Bari' also means to heal. Repetition of Ya Bari' may be done as part of a prayer for divine healing, and accompanied by visualization of this healing taking place. Some varying forms of al-Bari' have the meanings "to be safe and secure, to be free from harm or from the fear of harm." For this reason al-Bari' can be seen to overlap into the protection family as well.

There is a tenth-form expression of al-Bari' that means to persist in searching out knowledge that is hidden in the divine secrets until they are realized with clarity and you are free from doubt and uncertainty. It is to keep up the activity of discovering or uncovering the essence of a thing until that essence is rendered free from obscuration. When we are engaged in the activity of contemplation upon the beautiful Names of Allah, it is al-Bari' that is manifesting when we discover the essence of any sacred Name.

Ya Musawwir

(yaa mu-ṢOW-wir)

Al-Musawwir is the completion of the activity of divine creation that began with al-Khaliq and al-Bari'. Of the three, it is the Name that comes the closest to material objects in the universe, but it doesn't actually fully manifest into the visible, sensible world, the world described by az-Zahir. Al-Musawwir continuously and increasingly goes toward that final manifestation. It can be described as a movement from the infinite to the finite. It is also a journey from the hidden to the fully visible.

The form of the name al-Musawwir itself expresses all the stages of unfoldment. It is a continuous causal movement from infinity to finite embodiment. The form of the word totally mirrors the word *tasawwuf*, which is the process of moving in stages toward absolute purification—in other words, the path of Sufism.

In contrast to al-Bari', where there are multiple essences, in al-Musawwir these potentialities move toward actualities, toward individuated things. And each thing has fully realizable multiplicities. In just such a way, God, in the inner world, creates Adam, or the human being, as a cosmic prototype. We will examine the significance of this a bit later.

For now, let's look at some physical-plane forms of al-Musawwir. *'Istaara* means to bend something or to fold it. For example, we fold a piece of leather into a three-dimensional shape. *Sawwara* means to make into a shape or form. It draws from exactly the same well of meaning.

We reach another level of abstraction when we look at the fifth form of the root, the form of the word that actually renders it as al-Musawwir. Here it departs somewhat from the metaphor of leatherworking, because the meaning is "I fully picture it to my own mind."

In this construction, we can see how al-Musawwir is not actually completely manifest on the physical plane. It is ever emerging toward az-Zahir. It appears to the mind or imagination as a completed picture or image. That is what *tassawwur* means: to fully conceive of a form of a thing. It is the completion of the activity of the divine imagination!

Surah means the form of a thing. The form of the things that are made by al-Musawwir is *musawwaraat*. What is the form of the one who continuously forms? It is the things formed. The particularity of divinity is explained in al-Musawwir. We can explore this particularization by looking at four different levels of meaning in the definitions of *surah*.

At the first level, *surah* is just a shape, *shakl(un)*. There is a second meaning, *mithaal*, a likeness. A likeness is formed from other things that previously existed in the process. A third meaning of *surah* is a mental picture conceived or formed in the mind; it is a word for idea.

The last level of meaning of *surah* is the most important. Here *surah* means both the essence and the attribute. The essence of a thing, its true inner reality, is *haqqiqah*. The aggregate of qualities is *siffah* or *sifat*. What God the creator makes is both. This meaning of *surah* as both essence and attributes is a significant clue. It leads to the ascent back to the source. It also demonstrates how the universe can be looked at with both eyes open: to the essence and the attributes.

All the names have clues like this, but it shows up strongly and grammatically here in al-Musawwir. So *surah* means a form that is both an aggregate of qualities (*sifat*) and also the Face or essence itself (*dhat*). The meaning of *surah* embodies both the divine mystery and its particularization. And both essence and attribute are implied in the word Allah, as we saw in Chapter 1.

What we have presented thus far is a rather abstract description. Let's look at a few examples of this process in the Qur'an and the hadiths. In the Qur'an it is stated that Allah created Adam in His own image (*surah*). There are a number of recorded sayings of the Prophet Muhammad that relate to this, such as: "God came to me last night in a most beautiful form (*surah*)" ('*ataaniy rabiyy fi 'ahsani surah*). And Muhammad goes on to describe the vision to be in the shape of a young man.

Another hadith says that Muhammad saw the *hu*, the transcendental essence, through a particularization. That transcendental essence is inconceivably rich and effulgent in its emptiness: It is constantly manifesting forms, and in the process, revealing the purpose of forms as they change in time and space.

'Ibn 'Arabi directs us to understand what is being formed as the mechanism for the accomplishment of the process of *tasawwur*, the vehicle for the completion of the activity of the divine imagination. He says this mechanism is one of going from the infinite to the finite. Cosmically, al-Qabid, or the quality of divine contraction, allows the infinite to become finite. By such a process, for example, we come to have a particular individuated religion. But then an expansive process, described by al-Basit, takes us from that particularization to the one essence of all religion. And so on. The arc of ascent and descent again makes its circular manifestation.

The name al-Musawwir itself, being the so-called final stage of manifestation downward, contains hints or seeds of the journey of return back to the essential source of everything. Even though it describes the downward manifestation, it suggests the circle, the return. Just as the formless is innately constituted to imagine forms, the formed is made so as to imagine the formless.

A first dictionary entry for form one, *saara*, is: "He made himself lean toward—inclined his neck to face toward." The specific example given for this form of the root of al-Musawwir is "the hearts incline themselves toward Allah." You have a loving inclination or desire.

This meaning demonstrates al-Musawwir perfectly as the mechanism for the descent of the divine creation. As a famous sacred hadith says, "I was a hidden treasure. I fell in love and that loving yearning was to know the heaven and earth, so I created them by the breath of infinite compassion." *Mahabbah*, the most ordinary name for love, is used in this passage, while *rahma* is the loving compassion conveyed by the divine spirit or breath. Al-Musawwir is the mechanism of creation. It is the one who has this loving inclination.

The Qur'an says, "Allah loves them with pre-eternal love predating the universe, and the sum of human love is the refraction of this unlimited eternal love."[69] God loves them: It unfolds in the activity of al-Khaliq, al-Bari', and al-Musawwir. When the created ones love God, again it is through the activity of Khaliq, Bari', and Musawwir. There is a natural disposition that draws the finite to come to know the infinite. It is the basis for the whole Sufi path. And we see the same mechanism of divine creation operating on the journey of return.

In the Qur'an it is reported that Abraham asked God to teach him the secret of life and death, so God told him to take four birds and put them on the four mountains at the four corners of the world, and to train them. *Sawwar* means a homing pigeon. Abraham is to train the birds so that they love him so much that when he calls them from the four corners of the world, they will come.

So Abraham did this; and when he called, all the birds returned.[70] The divine secret communicated to Abraham is the training of hearts. Hearts can be tuned so that they will be inclined to fly to the source when the call comes. Knowing this secret makes Abraham a great model of the spiritual guide.

The inner structure and process that God uses to create the world is recapitulated in our hearts, and this allows the imagination of God to become real in human terms. 'Ibn 'Arabi describes the human being as the created creator.

How These Divine Names of Creation May Be Applied to the Human Condition

To complete the picture of al-Khaliq, al-Bari', and al-Musawwir in accord with our purposes in this book, we should look at how a physician of the heart could skillfully use their contemplation and invocation in conjunction with the psychological stages in a student's development. In some way that will involve looking at how each of us has become disconnected from the eternal source of continuous divine creation.

We can find some clues about that disconnection in the negative connotations, or what we sometimes refer to as the shadows, that appear in certain forms of the divine Names. *Khaliqa* means "to forge, to fabricate, to lie in speech or fantastic stories." It also means "to feign or to pretend to do something that is not really in one's heart." The dual meanings in the English word "fabricate" are an exact parallel.

In just this sense of illicit fabrication, at the time of its revelation the Qur'an was called by some to be full of fanciful tales of the ancients, *khuluq-ul-'awwaleen.* The Prophet Muhammad's words were called the imaginations of a madman, merely the repetition of some ancient superstitions about the unseen world.[71]

There are infinite possibilities in the creative imagination, called *khayaal*, which is another variation of the root of al-Khaliq. In fact, there is a whole style of Indian classical *raga* called *khayaal*, which expresses creative possibilities.

From the standpoint of human creativity, a deep relationship with al-Khaliq leads to the development of the Sufi practice of contemplation, sometimes called *tadhkeer*. Accomplishment in contemplation is possible because the practitioner mirrors this very aspect of the mind of God, with its infinite potential.

And this process continues. In relation to al-Bari', these potentialities become delimited and individuated. Now, all the things that could be manifested are there as well as things that would be impossible to manifest. However, when the contemplation process takes us to al-Musawwir, the potentialities are ripe for manifestation.

There is also a shadow side in certain forms of al-Bari.' *Bari'a* means to shun, to avoid, to keep aloof, to separate oneself from. *Bara'ah* means a covert place of hiding. In such a hiding place a person separates and keeps aloof from others. It is how the ego makes a shadow even in its notion of purity and healing. It comes with thoughts like "We are pure from the impure ones," or "we're healthy and not like the ones who are ill." There's that shadow. And it has a beginning in how we separate out of the essences in al-Bari'.

When the quality of al-Musawwir is used in the contemplation process, the direction of moving from the unlimited to the limited is completely reversed. You begin with the shape of the manifestation, contemplate the divine Name behind it, and then move to the essence of the essence. There is a continual and unending process of divine creation. It is encoded in the double "w" in al-Musawwir.

There is an opposite meaning in certain forms of al-Musawwir. *Saara-hu* is to demolish it, to pull it down to the ground, to fall apart." And in one form of the word it means to crack like a mountain and split apart. This is an important clue into a human condition that al-Musawwir may address.

But it is also an effect that al-Musawwir may have at a certain stage on the whole ego-structure. This potentially demolishing aspect should be taken as a warning for spiritual counselors that giving repetition of these three sacred Names too early in a student's process may have an unintended shattering effect. The spiritual wayfarer may not yet be ripe enough in their process to attain to the body of bliss.

Here's a way of looking at the overall process. Within the great field of the 99 Names, the creator, the generator, the actualizer is an entity that constantly differentiates the absolute and generates from it dimensions of reality. Those dimensions of reality jell and manifest in more forms. A structure of being is discovered here. It is a stage of embodiment, a level of evolution, in which you are in touch with the total body of bliss, and you become capable of embodying a truly grand structure. We sometimes call this inner structure a *stupa*.

The goal is God individuated: complete individuation. And that total embodiment of who we are in essence is the aspiration of all humanity. In even our most selfish aspect, we all want to be God or Goddess. Nobody wants to be less. Those who say they want to be less than God or Goddess are really pretending. They are fabricating an image. In no time, the ego will come out again and want everything in the universe. So human beings get trapped because we are really trying to give our ego everything, and still our ego is not happy. It can never be happy on its own terms.

When you look more deeply at the core of what your ego really desires, it makes sense to say that God must want that for you because the ego is part of the divine creation. You are created in God's image, so that must mean that somewhere in your essence is a hidden treasure wishing to be known. God's process of self-knowledge will express itself in your own process of realization.

In the basest of terms, in following the ego-quest we are following what has sometimes been called Satan. The ego wants to be God, to have it all, and to be totally superior. The problem is that the ego is defined by its narcissistic isolation, and this isolation must be melted—for it inevitably thwarts the discovery of the real self. The real question becomes, "What does it mean in the deepest sense to want to be God? What would that look like?"

We suggest that it means having an identity that truly feels "I am God," but not in a separated way. It means having a structure that is capable of doing what God does in activating and manifesting the process of continuous creation. It means entering and merging with the field that is always yielding and flowing with the ecstatic, loving impulse to fully know the hidden treasure within your true self.

There is a jeweled structure in the universe, a *stupa*, that is available to us. All who reach it feel they are reaching God the creator. In the heart of the absolute there is a giant dynamo transforming the absolute into infinite universes. It is like a prism, and this prism may be made of jewels, and perhaps those jewels are the 99 Names of Allah. This aspect of the jeweled structure corresponds to us, individually. We have just such a structure within us.

However, most of us are caught up in our limitations, and the structure is hidden. It is submerged. It has been replaced by the totality of the structure of our personality: ego, super-ego, conscious, unconscious. There are so many pieces. If you lump them together, they constitute the totality of the personality. This constructed entity has an identity, and the identity is the ego.

The ego is constantly losing touch with the submerged jeweled structure—the divine image, as it were—to generate what it knows as its familiar domain. All human beings are generating their own reality within which they then live. Separating it out from the world, they name it as their own manifestation.

But along the journey of life, there comes a stage when you see that the ego is representing reality in a certain way and the mind is also representing reality in a certain way, but the underlying structure is representing something else entirely. As the journey unfolds, your identification with the ego and the mind gets replaced by finding your self-identity in the reality of the individuated soul.

Then the totality of one's personality structure gets replaced by this jeweled structure we have called the *stupa*. Christian mystics have called it the Holy Grail. Muslims and Jews may name it is as the reality of the Holy Temple. The Tibetans call it the wish-fulfilling gem. It is the totality of blessed individuality.

If you reach that station, as the agent of God's creativity you can generate and manifest and actualize anything that the great heart of the universe desires. This is the wish fulfilling jewel: "Be" and it becomes. *Kun fa-yakun.* It is the ultimate body of bliss that generates blessings. It is what all humanity longs for.

When you are in the body of the personality, you are constantly generating what is familiar. You just keep doing it again and again. The familiar body is quite small. But from the embodiment of the *stupa*, you can function beyond the limitations of what we have already known, and in a blissful way. In this grand sense, we all are creators, generators, and actualizers. It is all an expression of the unlimited abundance of divine love.

To fully engage with al-Khaliq, al-Bari', and al-Musawwir is awesome. But for the physician of the heart to try and rush into it with a student prematurely is dangerous. Giving students the invocation of Ya Khaliq, Ya Bari', and Ya Musawwir, with inner contemplations such as we have just been describing, is usually left for the last stages of the journey.

By that time their vision has expanded, and their capacity to see the totality of their identification of the ego-structure has been enhanced. They know which parts are their mother, which parts are their father, which parts are the identity they have created as their own. They know which parts reside in the body, in the head, in the chest, and so on.

At this stage, students see the structures created by the ego's clinging, and they also understand the incompleteness of just dissolving into the absolute. They want to jell into being present and accountable, to fully actualize what spirit may bring. They have done so much scanning and so much knowing that it becomes easy to let go of the old form and to allow the new structure to come. That new structure constitutes the body of bliss, a great jeweled body of blessings.

Our process with al-Khaliq, al-Bari', and al-Musawwir is always going on, whether we are creating from the false personality or from the absolute. But in the final gradation the absolute descends, washing you all over, dissolving you and jelling you in the body of bliss, the jewel of enlightenment.

There is a prominent term in Sufism, *'inkisaar-al-'awaa'id*, the breaking of the familiar. When we do so we awaken to a huge limitless container (al-Wasi') of love/ecstasy that is called *rahma*. It is the gate to all the Names and the breath of the whole of creation, as described by Allah.

The warnings about premature invocation of this family of Names should not be taken to mean that use of these Names individually might not be valuable at earlier stages of the spiritual path. Someone who has been so broken apart by life that they don't have any way of pulling together a structure to work with could be given Ya Musawwir. Some people have a great deal of solidness and practicality but lack vision and creativity. Repetition of Ya Khaliq could be beneficial for them, but such repetition wouldn't be helpful for one who lacks a working structure.

Ya Bari' could be of value for people who are stuck in the middle between vision and manifestation. They have difficulty moving from the visionary realm to doing something with it in the world. You see a lot of it, nowadays. People are facing computers and games all the time, and their minds are filled with ten million visions. But when they come to worldly existence, they feel helpless and incapable of fashioning anything from that.

To briefly summarize the theme of this chapter, as it relates to mankind's overall condition: Allah made Adam in the shape, the divine *surah*, the divine form. This act reveals the truth about all human beings. What it means to be a complete human being, *al-'insaan kaamil,* is to actualize the reality hidden in the depth of the heart of all.

It is a continuous process. Every day, our emptying and filling is the creative activity of the living God. From the perspective of its inherent perfection, the human being is a kind of archetypical container in which can be found all the Names of all the divine perfections—all the jewels, the complete list, however vast that may be.

samad batn azaliy

daiym·dahr

'awwal 'arsh zayyum

'allah akhir

hayy bari

abadiy ahad

zahir

chapter 15

Temporal and Eternal Aspects of the Divine Nature

Alarge cluster of divine Names displays hidden facets of time and eternity. It may surprise some readers to hear that the Names lead us into different kinds of eternity. Some of the Names that we consider here don't appear on official lists of the 99 Names of Allah, but all of them can properly be considered Names of God.

This cluster of sacred Names describes pathways for understanding the temporal and eternal aspects of the divine nature and for accomplishing specific purposes in an individual's spiritual evolution.

Ya Dahr, Ya Azaliyy, Ya Abadiyy
(yaa DAARR, yaa AZ-a-leeyy, yaa AB-a-deeyy)

The most general term for time itself is *dahr*. There is a famous hadith in which Allah is reported to say, "Do not blame time or despair of time, because I am time" (*Tasabur ad-Dahr fa ina Dahr walaa*). In this light, ad-Dahr is clearly a Name of God, although it is not on any of the official lists of 99. Most human beings experience time simply as the passing of manifestation, but the hadith reminds us to see God right in the midst of this commonplace reality. And, as we shall see, there are many other ways of experiencing Allah through the medium of time.

One important view of time and eternity is manifested by the Name al-Azaliyy. The Orientalists translated al-Azaliyy as "pre-eternity," but that philosophical term doesn't fully express it. We will begin with a form the root of the word takes, a concrete Semitic meaning: to straighten, to narrow, to confine. *Azalu malahum*: "They restricted their cattle from grazing in a certain place."

How does this root meaning connect with the overall meaning of the divine Name? The answer is actually quite poetic. Al-Azaliyy is a time so ancient, so old it has no beginning, and the mind cannot conceive of it. Faced with this, the mind senses itself under restriction and recognizes its inherent limits. The mind cannot conceive of or understand a time without a beginning. Because the mind cannot conceive of beginningless time, philosophers like Aristotle and Thomas Aquinas posit a First Cause or First Mover as a necessity. This perceived necessity is their proof, or definition, of God.

Contrary to this notion, al-Azaliyy is the eternity before the first cause. And the moment you say "before the first cause," your mind has to stop. That is the Zen-like meaning of al-Azaliyy. The mind must stop because time without a beginning is inconceivable to the rational mind. The cattle have been stopped from wandering in that pasture. However, if the mind is restricted from understanding beginningless time, then what can understand it? That is a stimulating question we will want to explore.

Having looked at the root meaning of al-Azaliyy, let's look briefly at the word as a noun, *'azaliyy*. It means the continuance of time without respect to beginning, or without respect to a limit on the beginning. *'Azaliyy* captures both these concepts: time without respect to beginning, and ever-continuing in time.

We are talking about the existence of a thing that is not preceded by nonexistence. Such a thought is far removed from our ingrained, everyday concept of things in time. However, in many spiritual traditions there are descriptions of events happening in pre-eternity. For example, the angels and Adam have a discussion in the Qur'an.

The *'a'yaan thaabitah* are in pre-eternity. They are like ideas in the mind of God—pure possibilities. This realm is ontologically prior to manifestation. We might be tempted to say that this is before things are fully manifested, but as we are seeing, there can be no "before" *time*. In actuality there are different *azaliyyah*, different pre-eternities. One of these eternities has to do with the existence of God. Another has to do with ideas in the mind of God. And another can be viewed in relation to physical manifestation.

We started this discussion at the level of the existence of God, the existence of God that is not preceded by nonexistence. The existence of God as al-Azaliyy means that there is no such thing as time. Understanding that there is a reality that is not preceded by nonexistence exposes the emptiness of the concept of time.

There is still another kind of eternity, called *khalq jadeed*. *Khalq jadeed* means that every moment the universe is simultaneously created and completely destroyed. That is something that happens every indivisible moment (*al-wakt*). Between the moments that the whole universe is simultaneously destroyed and created, a thing exists in al-Azaliyy. It exists in a time outside time.

The rational mind balks at this notion. It conceives from one moment to another. However, what is conceptualized as a thing existing in time is a mental construct, an illusion. The mind jumps from one moment to another in time, and that is how we can even conceive of a thing lasting in ad-Dahr—lasting in time as we perceive it. The view of *khalq jadeed* invites us to think of things as returning to Allah in the moments between creation and destruction. That is a kind of eternity that occurs between the moments.

It will help us in our investigation of time and eternity to consider the companion Names to al-Azaliyy. Al-Azaliyy is freed from the limit of a beginning. Its mirror-opposite is al-Abadiyy. Al-Abadiyy is freed from the limit of an end. The divine Name al-Baqi, while often translated in a way to make it synonymous with al-Abadiyy, actually will be seen to include the meanings of both al-Azaliyy and al-Abadiyy.

Al-Abadiyy is another Name that appears in the Qur'an but is not on official lists. It has been translated as post-eternity. It is fruitless to try and compare pre-eternity and post-eternity. Al-Abadiyy is "time without respect to an end," and Al-Azaliyy is "time without respect to a beginning." Mind is unable to perceive time without an end or without a beginning. We have no empirical experience of that condition through the five senses.

Ya Azaliyy, Ya Abadiyy are an excellent pair of divine Names to be invoked together. Then the third Name, Ya Baqi, can be added as the transcendental Name that includes both.

All of the Names of the eternal are called *ad-dahr ul-mutlaq*, which is translated as absolute time. The word *mutlaq* means freed from limits. It is presence that is absolute in its nature. There is no beginning to it, no end to it, and no frequency in it. It does not go into the frequency of time and space.

It is in relation to this absolute state that God says, "I was a hidden treasure." "I yearned to be known" is the next level. It is a second kind of eternity. At this further level we find ideas in the mind of God, angels showing up in preexistence, and that kind of phenomena. The next layer of eternity is the eternal continuance of what is called physical manifestation.

With the act of differentiation, the absolute, the hidden treasure, begins to manifest, and appears as divine substance. At this point we enter essential time. Essential time is time that has a depth and dimensionality that is very different from the relative time that we ordinarily experience. The familiar mundane realm of relative time also is a frequency existing as a potentiality in the absolute. Relative time is where we measure and count the ever-continuing phenomena.

The Prophet Muhammad went on the entire heavenly journey of the *miraj* in a few minutes. It occurred in essential time. His whole mechanism slowed down. He entered the nonconceptual mind. Occurrences in essential time have a magical quality. The atoms of time and space expand.

There is a wonderful teaching about when time stops, which is called post-eternity or Abadiyy. In several places the Qur'an makes references to this that have been interpreted to mean "There is a post-eternity within post-eternity."[72] This comes from frequent instances of *khaalideena feehaa 'abadaa*. The juxtaposition of *khaalideena* (dwelling forever) and *'abada* has the force of repetition of *'abadan 'abadan*.

Scholars use these references as a basis for speaking about the experience of a state such as the paradisial realm, which may not be the ultimate, but which is not like the material world, either. Souls experience a hell or heaven state as if it were forever. Then "forever" stops, which is an ultimate paradox. However, it's not that time or forever that stops; rather, existence in that plane comes to an end.

Al-Azaliyy and al-Abadiyy are not only beginningless and endless—they are unquantifiable. They cannot be divided into parts. You can go through regular time into an aspect of timelessness, into Abadiyy, Azaliyy. In fasting, such slowing down (*talwaaniy*) starts to happen. It is perceptible.

Breath practices, spiritual retreat, and meditation are standard ways of slowing down time. Once you stretch time out, it creates the possibility that you can actually split one of these time atoms and go right through it to al-Azaliyy, al-Abadiyy. That, and not asceticism, is in fact the purpose of such practices. Such a process must be a universal because it is used by Yogis and Sufis, and in all spiritual schools. Beyond rational theorizing, the mind definitely stops.

How are the Names of God for the eternal and the Names of God for the infinite related? One connection is to see how al-Azaliyy refers to the infinite and al-Abadiyy to the eternal.

A concrete meaning of the root *'abada* is "dwelling in a place permanently, without quitting or leaving it." Another concept for the root meaning is "to be wild" (*tawahash*). It means to shun or flee from others as wild animals do when they see people coming. Once again, we see that the mind runs from the notion of an indivisible time without an end. It disappears. Here we have a beautiful mirroring of what we saw with al-Azaliyy, through a different root. The mind has to stop. But the unspoken mystical truth is that the mind may run from the reality of that inconceivable condition, but the heart does not. That is what makes the heart the heart.

It makes no sense to describe eternity as "a long time." To speak of long or short duration implies an end. It is better to call it absolute time. Such time is continuous and cannot be divided into specific segments. This realization is liberating. Absolute time is everlasting and eternal. The "everlasting" part really expresses al-Abadiyy. It lasts. It is duration without respect to an end.

The two Names, al-Baqi and al-Abadiyy, both have the linguistic meanings of continuous, duration, remaining, staying, abiding, constantly, permanently, without end or terminus. The essence of this is everlasting time. This is nicely indicated by the phrase *'Ad-dunyaa 'abadin wa al-'Akhiratu 'abadin*, which translates as: "The world has a limit on time, but the next world has no limit on time."

Azaliyyah is the plural form for different kinds of eternity. This is not just a subject for metaphysics. In mathematics, there are different kinds of infinities that can be worked with very practically, and the logic is quite precise.

To recite "Ya Azaliyy, Ya Abadiyy, Ya Azaliyy, Ya Abadiyy" sounds and feels very natural. They exactly mirror each other, even including the double "y" sound at the end. This can be followed with Ya Azaliyy, Ya Abadiyy, Ya Baqi. And it may be natural to continue on with the invocation Ya Hayy, Ya Qayyum.

There is a suggestion of the infinite in the number 99, referring to the number of the divine attributes of Allah according to a hadith of the Prophet Muhammad. The number's meaning goes beyond the idea of 100 minus 1 and suggests that the absolute nature of God is beyond the attributes. The number 99 is also a metaphor for the infinite, because the repetition of 9's suggests an infinite series. The number 100 signifies completion. With 99 we seem to be looking at a finite set, but its symbolism is to point toward something that does not end.

Psychological Implications

Some people approach the material realm with a belief that it will be constantly around, that it is eternal. They are totally caught up in their material possessions and absorbed with the goal of consolidating objects. Their view of inner reality is full of objects, and their external reality is full of objects as well. They are preoccupied with objects.

Such people would benefit from reciting Ya Abadiyy. Realizing the essence of this Name will help them to see there is an everlasting place. Through al-Abadiyy, those who are fixated on objects can recognize the eternity of space.

Others are pressured by or attached to time. Like the white rabbit in *Alice in Wonderland*: "I'm late, I'm late, for a very important date. No time to say hello, goodbye, I'm late, I'm late, I'm late." With such people, the problem is not about objects. It is their relationship with time that is pressuring them. This is how they demonstrate their disconnection from God, who is continual in time. When you realize al-Azaliyy you recognize the eternity of time.

In Western culture especially, we feel an immense pressure of time and space. Invocation of these divine Names can break that cycle. To combine Ya Azaliyy and Ya Abadiyy in repetition will break the total limitation of time and space and open up the concept for those who are stuck there. By inwardly consolidating time and space through the repetition of Ya Azaliyy, Ya Abadiyy, you may be led to an image which, when preserved inside, enables you to become more capable of beneficially altering your approach to a multitude of daily problems, such as your work responsibilities.

When a physician of the heart administers Ya Azaliyy and Ya Abadiyy, they are not simply focused on breaking the limited view of time and space. Contemplating these Names will also enable practitioners to consolidate their self-image by incorporating a more accurate perception of time and space. If you have the right perception of time and the right perception of space, it will give you a good sense of who you are and where you are. Al-Abadiyy and al-Azaliyy break the boundaries and break the images in the mind.

Through time and space you break into the *mutlak*, the absolute. Many of us think we will be successful if we can compress time and space. We are obsessively busy with occupying our time and trying to achieve. Thoreau said about this, "The mass of men lead lives of quiet desperation."

All this desperate activity is an attempt to cure a deficient self-image. Deep inside there is a deficient image that is based on believing, "I am supposed to be God-like, but I am not up to that job." So we think that if we accomplish more, achieve more, and make the most efficient use of every second, maybe we will reach the pinnacle.

Our sense of self is deficient because there is a fundamental disconnection from God, from source. With the help of these practices, under guidance, the concept of time and space begins to break, and we begin to reach down into our narcissistic deficiency. Instead of trying to perfect our limited view of self—along with all those entanglements of speeding up inner time and space, congesting inner space, and speeding up inner time—now we are able to diffuse time. There will be spaciousness. The self-image will dissolve into Ya Azaliyy, Ya Abadiyy, Ya Baqi.

Such an approach is not quietism. It doesn't mean to go slower. Space and time open up for you. The mystic feels God is doing the work, and this takes the pressure off the limited disconnected ego. It is giving up ownership, giving up attachment to the false sense of self. And this actually allows you to fully experience the moment. You make time and you make space. In fact, you must do this because you need time and space to consolidate a self-image.

When the inner compression is released, you have immense inner time and space, and you may actually move much faster than an ordinary human being because the obsession with securing the future has not taken hold of you. There is inner spaciousness that allows you to plan better. So it doesn't mean just slowing down in a simple-minded way. Ya Azaliyy, Ya Abadiyy are a perfect pair.

The root of al-Baqi means "to remain." It relates directly to the classical Sufi description of the spiritual path in terms of *fana* and *baqa*. *Fana* is the dissolving of the limited, disconnected self, the *nafs*. *Baqa* is becoming established in the real self, the *ruh*, and thus becoming fully connected with the God reality, which is the true source of our being.

The great Sufi Shaykh Junayd defined *fana* and *baqa* in a wonderful way. He said that *fana* is what never was, and what never was is what dies. *Baqa* is what always was, always is, and ever shall be. From this we can clearly see that al-Baqi includes both al-Azaliyy and al-Abadiyy. Of necessity it must include both to take in the now, all of the past, and all of the future.

Qur'anic verses such as the long passage 28:88 say that everything undergoes a dissolution process except the face of Allah. "Everything will perish save His countenance. His is the command, and unto

Him ye will be brought back." Total *fana* leads to *baqa*. In this way each of us is forced to go to *huwa*, the face of Allah. The face of God is synonymous with *dhat* (*zat*), absolute essence.

In the Qur'an we read: "Everything upon the face of the earth is annihilated (*faa'in*) except the face of Allah."[73] In this stage, *fana* cannot be contemplated without *baqa*. They cannot be separated. *Fana* and *baqa*. They have to go together. The rest of the Qur'anic verse describes the face as Dhul Jalali wal 'Ikram. The emphasis is on the *dhul*, the *dhat*, the essence of everything: that which always was, always is, and always will be.

Ya 'Awwal , Ya Akhir, Ya Batin, Ya Zahir

(yaa OW-wal, yaa AA-khir, yaa BAA-tin, yaa DHAA-hir)

There is a grouping of four divine Names that are important to explore at this stage of our investigation—sacred Names that express the essence of time and eternity.

Al-'Awwal is usually translated "the first," and al-Akhir is usually rendered "the last." The mystical paradox is, how could God be a first or last if God is infinite? The answer given by 'ibn 'Arabi is that God is the first without a second, and God is the last without there being a next-to-last.

It would be just as accurate to say that God is a first without a before, and God is a last without an after. "Without a before" is a definition of al-Azaliyy, and "without an after" is a definition of al-Abadiyy. So these two new Names fit into our previous discussion. God is al-'Awwal, a first without a second, but also a first without a before. Anything that is understood by the rational mind has to be in time, because the rational mind is temporal. All these Names are tools to uncover a condition before mind and after mind.

The way of speaking about infinity, using negative qualification, is just a metaphor for that which cannot be described. In the English language, the concepts "infinite," "absolute," "ceaseless," and "endless" are all expressed through the use of negatives: not finite, not ending, and so on. The negative, or erasing, function of these attributes helps us to enter something beyond the mind, to experience a unity and infinitude that is beyond the mind.

Beyond the knowledge of the mind is the knowledge of the heart, which Sufis call *ma'rifah*. What we are seeking is the realm of omnitude, the everythingness of Allah. Of necessity, it must be direct experience beyond conceptualization.

If we look at al-'Awwal and al-Akhir in their dynamic aspect we find a guideline for the process of awakening. To everything that arises, there is something before it, al-'Awwal. And that reality is the absolute. And to everything that ends, there is something after it, al-Akhir. And that reality is the absolute.

So with every activity that you are going through or processing, if you tune into the One that is before the activity, and the One that is after the activity, you will maintain your continuity of being in the absolute. You never leave it. You don't get stuck in time and space. You see time and space arising in a field. This is a way for your limited self to annihilate its false view of its own nature, which is based on disconnection and alienation, and to let essence arise.

What al-Batin means is the "hidden treasure." Another way of putting this is to say God is the inward, without being inside of anything. This is not in the sense we are accustomed to thinking of something as inward as opposed to being outward. God is the most hidden, but not hidden in something else, something other than itself. God is veiled, but in plain view. Allah is *Sirr-ul-'asrar*, secret of secrets.

Al-Batin's opposite is az-Zahir, the manifest. In these two divine Names we are confronted with the apparent opposites of the unseen and the seen. Az-Zahir is the outward, without being outside of anything else. One translation of az-Zahir is that God is the most outward, the most manifest. Allah's presence is so evident that you don't see it because there is no otherness to see.

In all these ways, inner investigation leads us to an understanding that goes beyond the mesh of the mind, which is precisely what the four divine attributes al-'Awwal , al-Akhir, al-Batin, and az-Zahir are pointing toward.

Ya Hayy, Ya Qayyum
(yaa ḤAIYY, yaa ḳaiy-YOOM)

Traditional Sufism focuses on the phrase Ya Hayy Ya Qayyum to describe the whole glorious family of all the Names that direct us toward the infinite and eternal. It is an enormous and important *wazifah*.

In Chapter 7, Allah's Opposite Qualities, we considered al-Mumit and al-Muhyi, the One who brings death and the One who brings life. We said that by contemplating on these qualities, the Name al-Hayy, the ever-living, comes forward to suggest itself as the transcendental essence of both.

Al-Hayy is the life that is beyond the cycle of life and death as we know it. It is what everyone is longing for. Al-Hayy expresses the ever-living, the always-living. What is called the cycle of life and death fades away into that reality. Discovering it enables you to deal with the experience of loss. What remains is al-Baqi.

The other attribute of this famous pair of sacred Names is al-Qayyum. The root means to stand, instead of falling down or falling apart. The similarity with al-Baqi—that which remains—is unmistakable. The sound code makes it a continuous activity due to the doubled inner consonant. According to 'ibn 'Arabi, the formulation of sound in al-Qayyum shows that it continuously, without a single break, bestows existence (or *kun*) to everything else. He says the very fact that anything else exists, including being itself, is because of the nature of al-Qayyum, which is beyond the passage of time.

Things come and things go. They are forming and emptying constantly. That's *fana*. But al-Qayyum says they continually exist, even after death, in God. So the flow of existence beyond created and uncreated being is this *kun*, which is continually bestowed by al-Qayyum. *Kun* is a different kind of word for existence. In contrast, *wujud*, another aspect of existence, is not bestowed or given.

The Qur'an affirms, "*Kun fa-yakun.*" Allah has only to say, "Be," and it is.[74] Al-Qayyum is an existence beyond being, appearance, form, or continuance of form. Things go up, things go down, things are built, and things fall apart, but, even so, the essential existence of a thing is maintained through al-Qayyum. This divine quality keeps things going even when you can't perceive continued existence.

The 99 Names of Allah are designed to break through the barriers of the mind, to reach the source and know the nature of the source, yet at the same time they also describe the attributes of the absolute. There is dynamism in them. Each Name plays on two levels. The level of describing the nature of the absolute puts the mind into cessation to experience that reality. But we can take al-Qayyum, for example, also as a process that the personality can go through daily.

You are guided into the absolute and out of it. You are resurrected in the absolute and through the absolute. If you connect to the absolute, then this connection leads to the disintegration of the personality, and as the personality disintegrates, the other phase of the divine Name comes through, which is the resurrection.

You resurrect and regroup, but not in the personality. You regroup in your essence, your essential structure, your higher self. There is a continual process of disintegration/integration, disintegration/integration that each of us goes through in our unfoldment. Cessation of the activity of the mind, of the ego, and of the personality is not enough. There is also *qiyaamah*, resurrection in the body of light.

Your essential being emerges as attributes of love, or attributes of clarity, or whatever quality the source of being is bringing forth. So al-Qayyum also means the process of resurrecting, or integrating, from the level of the absolute. It is as if the absolute regroups the person. Here you can see the level of the absolute in its suchness and the level of the absolute in its individuation.

Ya Da'im

(yaa DAA-im)

Let's consider time as it is named in its various forms: *dawwaam, da'im, dayyoom*. All these divine Names for time in Arabic relate to circles. They all imply movement around a circle and the circle's relationship with a point that doesn't move. This is the most important thing for us to understand.

'Ibn 'Arabi looked at the circle of time in terms of different dimensions. One dimension is the dimension of opposition: the horizontal disc of first and last. Another is outward and inward. He noted these dimensions because God's manifestations are always changing. He thought that through these two axial orientations, we could understand the whole idea of change through the manifestations of cycles.

In the center of the circle 'ibn 'Arabi places *'arsh-allah*, the Heart Throne of Allah, the fixed point that doesn't change. This is the immutability of God. You can find his discussion in *Fusus al-Hikam*, Seals of Wisdom. This transcendental absolute can be reached through contemplation of any of the opposite Names of God.

Ad-Dayyoom or ad-Da'im really describes the process of reaching the transcendental absolute. The word Adam comes from ad-Daim. *Adama* in Hebrew is the earth, the ground of being. In the Semitic languages "*dam*" means the blood. In Arabic, as in Hebrew, the word "Adam" can be derived from plowed earth. *Atin* is earth and '*ad-daam* is time. Into the earth, God breathes the breath of life.

Ad-Da'im means always present. But movement is implied here, so ad-Da'im is present in movement. It is present in the very change that we tend to abhor so much when we become emotionally and philosophically attached to the changeless. Ad-Da'im is an excellent way to connect the concepts of physical manifestation and time. It can be seen in circles, in the circle of the breath. *Da'im* and *dayyoom* are constantly moving without a break. Constantly moving in time is a way of describing the Eternal. Continuously moving in space is a way of describing the Infinite.

Such a description should not be confused with drawing a timeline. A circle doesn't have a beginning point or an end point. The main emphasis here is continuous movement in time and space: *harakah barakah*. Movement is blessing. So many of us find ourselves stuck, bogged down from loss, and trying hard to transcend the problems of birth and death. In spite of this common experience, it is an amazing thing to discover that in the continuous movements of life, God is revealed.

Much investigation in physics centers on the age of the universe, but more interesting questions may be, "Does the universe have a beginning? "Does it have an end?" The Buddhist view is that it doesn't have a beginning or end, and this view can be a major point of difference between religions, because many Buddhist scholars don't think that Western theology grasps this concept. The notion of a timeline is very strong in many Western religious interpretations. But when we say *dayyoom*, we have to draw a circle.

It is not only the universe that does not end. Spiritual realization does not end either. Enlightenment doesn't mean the process of realization is over. The great bhakti yogi, Swami Ramdas, responded to a question about his state of realization with these words, "Like the sacred river Ganges that has flowed and become one with the ocean, I continue to flow into the ocean."

The equations of time in physics point in both directions, forward and backward, but physicists tend to only pay attention to those that they can work with in the forward direction. They have to include both directions, because the formulas don't work unless the negative direction is also included. And the Sufi shaykhs say that the beginning is the end and the end is the beginning.

Dayyoom is a good way to think about the whole process because there are no breaks in it. Abu'l Qasim Junayd, founder of the Junaydi school, said that there are never-ending cycles. Some people in his time thought that after attaining *fana* in Allah the process should be complete. But *da'im* is discovered in the never-ending cycles. In impermanence we find permanence.

Ad-Dayyoom is movement without a beginning or an end. We can conceptually segment it, but there are no minutes or degrees in this circle. We might perceive the cycle of life and death, but ad-Dayyoom doesn't. In the center there is a point that indicates peaceful rest, centeredness. It is pure emptiness, the heart of silence.

Some of the divine Names emphasize the absolute nature and the transcendent element and others emphasize the immanent or dynamic nature as a doorway to discovering the absolute. These are referred to as *tashbeeh* and *tanzeeh* in *Fusus al-Hikam*. What all this leads to is the inseparability of the relative and the absolute. The 99 Names of Allah have great dynamism. You can take them from the relative into the absolute, and from the absolute into the relative, or into manifestation.

There is *dayyoom* and there is *dayyamoom*: continuity into the absolute and continuity into the relative. It is a nonstop process, so it would be a serious mistake to fix on a preference between the two. If a person gets stuck on the absolute, void of all Names, it can be a dangerous state. And to get lost in the attributes may also be dangerous.

In the first instance we may despise this world and embrace a kind of asceticism. The other pole of attachment leads to a kind of spiritual materialism. If we don't disintegrate, we cannot be reborn in a new form. Every day we need to dissolve in the absolute whatever form or images or ideas arise. Then we can resurrect in a different form, a different state, with different feelings and different energies.

The river never stops flowing. It is a great meditation: "What is forming, that is emptying; what is emptying, that is forming" is how this realization is expressed in one translation of the Heart of Perfect Wisdom Sutra of Mahayana Buddhism. Meditating in this way, students don't get fixated on either form or formlessness.

Approaches for the Physician of the Heart

When a physician of the heart is counseling students, questions often arise in connection with the student's disintegration or reintegration. We need to locate in the student the two domains of the absolute and of the manifestation. If the student is actively engaged in dealing with the absolute, then we should focus on the divine Names as a doorway to the absolute or as a description of the absolute. If they are most actively engaged in dealing with the relative, then the focus should be on the process of reintegration.

In general, our approach is that it is wise not to interfere with where they are actively engaged. For example, if their engagement is in the relative reality, we encourage them to watch this process and to see that the absolute is the force behind it. They need to see that the process of integration/disintegration is an expression of the absolute state. In this way they may be able to lodge themselves in the permanent, which is underneath the relative sphere. When this is accomplished, then they can fully disintegrate, and subsequently integrate within the permanent field.

Both domains can be invoked with the divine Name. For example, when you say Ya Qayyum, if you take the most refined meaning, it is about the absolute. If you take it as the process, it applies directly to what is happening in your daily life. So the counselor needs to be careful about where the student is. It is not so much about directing them to where they want to go. It is more about grounding them in where they already are moving.

Ya Samad, Ya Ahad

(yaa ṢA-mad, yaa A-ḥad)

As-Samad is one of the most untranslatable words in the Arabic language. Roughly speaking, it means that everything depends on Allah, but Allah doesn't depend on anything else. We find as-Samad paired with al-Ahad in the Unity Surah[75] of the Qur'an, and their similarity in sound emphasizes the strength of this pairing.

The eternal continuance of a thing is called *samadiyyah*. This is part of the meaning of as-Samad. However, we can't properly grasp the whole meaning of as-Samad without looking at it together with al-Ahad. Taken together they mean the One and the Infinite at the same time. The singularity of al-Ahad is the dot at the center of the continuous effulgence of the infinite circumference, which is as-Samad.

Must an infinite singularity that is at the same time one and infinite include each and every possibility without exception? Intuitively speaking, the answer is yes. And that would include even apparently contradictory possibilities such as the possibility of not being, or the possibility of the infinite being finite. This direction of inquiry again makes it clear that we should not reject the relative as illusory and unimportant, as it is clearly and directly a part of the God reality.

The reverse of the question we posed above might be stated: "Does the totality of all possibilities necessitate a singular and infinite oneness?" If so, that would posit the one as the source of all. This way of posing the question appears to be a kind of reformulation of the ontological argument for the existence of God first presented by Saint Anselm and generally expressed as: "I have an idea of a being than which no greater can be conceived; therefore God is."

Al-Ahad describes a state of being. It is a single, transcendental, and infinite singularity or oneness. This oneness of being is called *ahadiyyah*. *Ahad* and *ahadiyyah* refer to states, and *samad* (and *samadiyyah*) refer to processes. From the point of view of al-Ahad there is just the One.

Samdah, however, means to return to a place of origin. From its perspective, there is the continuous process of returning or reconnecting to the one. It is a perpetual movement toward the one, an activity that never ceases. Al-Ahad means a unity that has no "toward the one" in it because there's no journey, there's no separation, there's no traveler, and there's no path.

One surprisingly good thing about all this paradox-filled philosophical discussion is that you can sing it! We, the writers of this book, feel that none of the sublimity of these teachings truly penetrates without ecstatic chanting. Each of us should use the invocation of the sacred Names as a kind of a stepladder to the realities behind the words. A ladder is of no value if you just admire it but don't use it.

There is another kind of unity that is called *waahidiyyah*—the mystical and transcendental oneness that underlies not only all forms but each and every form. Everything is a mirror for God's face. That is called *waahidiyyah*. So the totality or infinite can be perceived within each and every finite element. It is the vision of infinity in a grain of sand. Every speck reflects the infinite. Consequently, you can see a thing as finite and you can see a thing as infinite at the same time.

God-realized beings can do this all the time with no effort, but the rest of us have to manipulate the symbols to perceive or unveil the infinite. The way this is done with time is called *at-talwaanee*. It basically means slowing down the flow of time, stretching it out using various techniques such as music, chanting, ritual prayer, dancing, and meditation.

The effect of these practices is to manipulate the experience of time itself. Using these ecstatic techniques, the units of time may be metaphorically perceived as beads on a string. Then, at one point, you may be able to slip between the moments to perceive timelessness. It is called *'ibn al-waqt*, the "child of the moment."

The moment, in some states of consciousness, is timelessness itself. It is a moment and yet it is not a moment because it contains all moments. It is like the metaphor of Indra's net in Hinduism: a net with a jewel at each intersection, each jewel reflecting all the other jewels of the net. In *waahidiyyah*, every Name is the greatest Name of God—because it is a Name, and thus contains all the rest of the Names.

As-Samad expresses a complementary process in which each and every thing returns us to the One. Every Name, every plurality, is another opportunity to realize the *waahidiyyah* underneath it. By contrast, *ahadiyyah* is like the field of Oneness. It is all-inclusive, and there is no place where we can make distinctions, such as that a thing is other than Oneness.

A spiritual wayfarer may be going through the process of experiencing the divinity of their embodiment as an individuated soul. Before reaching the cosmic unity, they reach personal oneness. The personal oneness is experienced as a point of light. It is an inner being of light within them. In this sense, al-Ahad is the individuated identity, the individuated God within, the dot within the circle.

As-Samad can then be seen as the continual process of this individuality flowing into union with the infinite, pictured as the ever-expanding circumference. It is a continual sensing of unity, but you exist in this unity as an individual rather than existing in the infinite as the infinite. You become uniquely responsible for creation in the universe you embody.

Everything exists in the absolute, but there is a unique individuality. Ar-Rahman, for example, can refer to God not only as an oceanic loving mercy but also as an individual who is made of divine love, who actualizes it.

We strongly recommend the recitation of Ya Ahad, Ya Samad as a pair. We also recommend invocation of Ya Wahid, Ahad, Rahman. This latter practice emphasizes the individualization, or realization of one's true soul essence that is the doorway to the oceanic. The ocean exists, but a unique fish is swimming in it. In doing this practice, vocalize "Ya" only before Wahid.

When you progress through your own narcissistic issues of hurt and lostness and disconnected identity, al-Ahad enters the picture and you experience your self as a unique entity. In a complementary way, as-Samad makes possible the constant communion or interaction between the fish and the ocean. What manifests is your own unique mandala or divine configuration. Seeing the whole picture enables you to awaken more as an individual, to become aware of the personality that you have composed in particular, and to understand how to transmute it.

hamid
shakur
mu'ti
subhanallah
alhamdulillah
allahu akbar

chapter 16

The Names of Gratitude and The Gifts of God

The Names of gratitude, abundance, and blessing constitute a very large family of divine manifestations. The cluster that bears these qualities is so vast that we have found it necessary to break it down into four separate chapters.

Because a central purpose of this book is to suggest how the beautiful Names of Allah can help humanity in its development, it is appropriate to begin with the qualities of gratitude and thankfulness. This is the place to which we as human beings should return in order to begin our journey to wholeness.

In the discussions about these divine qualities it is important to notice that what is always occurring is a mutual relationship or two-way flow, a giving and a response. It is not simply essence giving to the multiplicity of manifestation, which is to say, God giving to created beings. Divine gratitude, for example, is also expressed by created beings giving gratitude to the source.

The place to begin our consideration of this family of divine emanations is with al-Hamid and ash-Shakur, two sacred Names that embody gratitude and thankfulness.

Ya Hamid, Ya Shakur

(yaa ḥa-MEED, yaa s̲h̲a-KOOR)

Al-Hamid is a manifestation of infinite gratitude into each thing and all things. This much is clear from the sound code embedded in the word. Viewed as an emanation from the unique divine source, al-Hamid flows from essence toward multiplicity. However, in the familiar form Alhamdulillah—where the "il" indicates directionality—all gratitude goes to Allah. So the quality of divine gratitude also flows from multiplicity back toward essence.

This dual directionality in the quality of gratitude demonstrates a truth that is necessary to our understanding throughout this cluster of Names. Allah is not only the perfection of a particular quality that penetrates all existence, but Allah is also the emanation of that same quality which all existing things give back to the infinite source. At a deeper level, these two are one and the same.

While there are some important, subtle differences between the two Names, al-Hamid (from the root *hamd*) is nearly synonymous with ash-Shakur (*shukr*). Both could be simply translated "divine thankfulness." However, we can say that *shukr* is a more specific sense of gratitude and *hamd* is a more general sense. Al-Hamid tends to manifest more as gratitude for divine qualities along with the feeling of gratefully returning it to Allah. Ash-Shakur manifests more as thankfulness for specific blessings.

We also need to ask the question, "Who is thanking whom here?" We see with al-Hamid that all and everything is thanking Allah. With ash-Shakur, according to the sound code, we understand that divine thankfulness penetrates to the very core of the densest thing. *Ash-Shakeer*, which is a different form of the word, means Allah is also emanating thankfulness to each and every one.

In the family of Names of abundance we will continuously uncover the intimate connection of blessing, blessed, and blesser. Our process will demonstrate how this triad is inwardly present in each of these sacred Names.

Al-Hamid and ash-Shakur are certainly more similar than they are different. The obvious place to differentiate them, as we have already suggested, is through their grammatical form in the sound code. Al-Hamid emanates from the ultimate source, Allah, out into every single thing. That is the emphasis or intensity specified by its form. Ash-Shakur is a somewhat different intensive. It emanates into the deepest place. It reaches all the way to the hardest place in the heart, into the deepest wound.

There are physical-plane meanings of other words formed from the same root as al-Hamid that express an intense, flaming fire and a day of fierce heat. Understanding that such layers of extended connotation inform the rich meaning of all words drawn from a common root, we can say that al-Hamid manifests into each and every thing in creation like a burning heat or a burning love.

Ash-Shakur is the one who emanates gratitude into the hardest and densest place in the heart. The lover will strive to find it there! Several forms of ash-Shakur's root have physical meanings that refer to udders or breasts filling up, and to the incredible sensation a mother has when her milk lets down. Ash-Shakur means to turn your attention with thankfulness toward inner perfection.

Repetition of Ya Shakur is an antidote for dissatisfaction with the falseness or incompleteness of the world. Thus you feel gratitude in your heart and direct your gaze outward to the signs of Allah in the world. Several stages are described in this process in which gratitude is manifested and returned to Allah.

In the ultimate stage, the heart overflows like a fountain onto the tongue, the limbs, and all the actions of the thankful servant. That is how the Prophet Muhammad described himself to his wife: "Am I not *'abdun shakurun* [a grateful servant]?"

Hamd and *shukr* are combined in the recitation of many *dhikrs*. Invocation of Ya Hamid, Ya Shakur helps overcome the thought patterns of the lower self, or *nafs*, by expressing gratitude to God. The benefit of this practice is enhanced by our recognizing that Allah has gratitude for everything that is.

The very last line in Hebrew in the Psalms of David is "*Kol haneshamah tehalel Yah. Hallelujah.*" It is often translated, "Everything which has breath shall praise God," or "The universal soul of all that is shall praise God." The translations cannot touch the quality in the original Hebrew. Mystics are always struggling with language to try to approach and evoke the inner reality. That is why inspired poetry often communicates more effectively than philosophy.

In contemplative and prayerful repetition of Ya Hamid and Ya Shakur, there is both a sense of submerging in an ocean and a sense of the activity of the waves of the ocean. The feeling of Ya Shakur seems to evoke more the aspect of divine activity and Ya Hamid more the sense of the ocean of divinity itself. This distinction is somewhat arbitrary because the ocean is not different from its activity. However, the feeling of an ocean of gratitude is very important because it evokes a multidimensional reality.

One of the most interesting things to explore about these two divine qualities of gratitude is what they both address in the structure of the dysfunctional egos of human beings. They relate most directly to the continual complaining and dissatisfaction of the *nafs*, or lower self. (See Chapter 17, The Seven Levels of the *Nafs*.)

At a certain level of ego we experience a part of our self that constantly complains about everything. Nothing is ever right. Always we are finding fault. This attitude of the ego blinds the soul from perceiving the great abundance and richness of what is present in the inner or outer kingdom. As long as your ego is trapped in a pattern of complaint, you are incapable of appreciating reality, God, or yourself.

When a spiritual student begins to actually see how much they are constantly complaining, they are suddenly in touch with a deep layer of their own woundedness. Further investigating this layer often discloses that the ego itself has constellated around a wound caused by not being seen for who you are by your parents. Because we were not seen or recognized or appreciated by those close to us, we sustained a deep hurt in our heart, and because of self-pity we narcissistically identified our self with this wounded condition as our ego-structure developed.

When the level of the narcissistic wound is reached by spiritual wayfarers in their process, they come to realize how much they always are complaining, and also how much this complaining colors reality. Then a kind of remorse opens up, a sorrow, because they understand that they have blinded themselves.

Such remorse leads to repentance, or inner turning. You feel, "I am my own obstacle on the way to grace. I am an obstacle on the way to realization." When this awakened understanding is nourished through the experience of being touched by divine gratitude, a kind of ego death is engendered.

The ego dissolves, and a state of sweetness is born in the sacred heart. The quality is honey-like. Whatever the universe has done to you before now, or whatever humanity has done, generated only bitterness within and made an obstacle in your way. Now there is a great and profound sweetness, and when it arises you simply want to return home. You just want to melt. And when that melting takes place, the honey opens up the heart, the mind, and the body.

Such an experience is true gratitude. It is a profound death of the ego, even if it is not the ultimate ego death. The ego dissolves and, returning, becomes like a drop of honey. Its structure had been made of separation from God and separation from the sweetness of the heart. It had become a grain of sand, causing pain and bitterness.

When this grain of sand melts, the profound state of gratitude with all its many attributes is born. A feeling of sweetness spreads in the heart, which brings with it the power of transformation. It is the very essence of gratitude. There is gratitude for everything because it is experienced as coming from Allah.

In every aspect of life you are receiving abundance. The tree is giving you oxygen. The water is precious. It is as if the whole universe has become a breast that has been created to nourish you physically, mentally, and emotionally. And it is as if the divine breast lets down its milk within us, and this wonderful feeling of ash-Shakur washes away the distinction between the ego-self and the divine reality.

The veil that has made this universe into a place of deprivation, a place to be constantly complained about, has been removed. The whole universe becomes an oceanic goldenness. It started as a drop of honey and it becomes a golden universe. The heart is opened, and there is sweetness and gratitude for every moment you breathe.

Prayerful invocation of Ya Shakur, Ya Hamid can be an invaluable tool for awakening gratitude. These sacred Names work well when paired together. The emanation of Ya Shakur penetrates to the deepest, most difficult place of heart, and Ya Hamid touches everything without exception. There is also the dynamic interplay of merging in the ocean and individuating in the activity of the waves.

When students are going through their own personal woundedness, ash-Shakur may be the more useful Name. "Nobody loved me, nobody saw me; I was all alone in childhood and I had to work so hard." When they are dealing with feelings like that, engaged with a personal sense of being wounded, working simply with repetition of Ya Shakur can be very useful.

Invocation of Ya Shakur can be a remedy for the most intimate, personal wound, and that would include the wound that comes from the way you constantly betray your own self. Intellectually, we know so much about how to take care of ourselves, and yet we don't do it. Ya Shakur will help you face the pain of how in everyday life you really sabotage your own journey.

On the other hand, when students begin to feel their woundedness in a more general way, recitation of Ya Hamid may be more effective for healing. At this time the feeling that is dominant in you is that the universe itself doesn't seem to be really nourishing or supportive. It is not just the parents or the childhood traumas that are your main issues.

The ultimate anguish comes when you see that you yourself are your own obstacle. Nothing else but the stubborn condition of your ego is between you and the experience of divine abundance. So invocation of Ya Shakur can directly hit the most personal anguish, and Ya Hamid can deal with the impersonal aspect of the experience of disconnection.

There's a verse in the Qur'an much quoted by Sufis, "We will show you our signs in yourselves and the horizons, and we will show you the horizons in yourselves."[76] Here we see a clear reference to the two modes of gratitude, the mutuality of giving and receiving that is an essential part of a deeper understanding of divine abundance.

To perceive the signs of Allah deeply in yourself, for instance, and thus to experience gratitude, would be ash-Shakur. The ability to contemplate the signs on the horizons would be al-Hamid. It is a more outward ability. Inner gratitude is ash-Shakur, and all-pervading outer gratitude is al-Hamid. The expression *al-hamdu lillah*, as we shall see, captures both the inner and outer aspects.

The Three Wedding Gifts: Subhanallah, Alhamdulillah, Allahu Akbar

The story is told of how Fatimah, the daughter of the Prophet Muhammad, came to him shortly after her marriage to Ali. She said that the marriage required continuous work at home, and she requested that her father give her the gift of a servant as her dowry. He declined but said he would offer her a much better wedding present. He then gave her the daily practice of repeating Subhanallah, Alhamdulillah, 33 times each and Allahu Akbar 33 (or 34) times.

A historical consequence of the Prophet's generous action can readily be seen. His gift to her has been gratefully received and beneficially practiced by millions of people over the centuries. It caused the creation of the *tashbeeh*, or prayer beads. Subhanallah, Alhamdulillah, and Allahu Akbar are called the three wedding gifts, and they deserve prominent treatment in any chapter on divine gratitude and abundance.

We will first complete our discussion of Alhamdulillah and then focus on Subhanallah and Allahu

Akbar. After that, we will turn our attention to the divine Name al-Mu'ti, which carries the meaning "the gift of God." Not only is al-Mu'ti connected with the wedding gifts, but it also will provide the perfect transition to taking up the full cluster of all the sacred Names of divine abundance.

Alhamdulillah

We have already briefly mentioned Alhamdulillah in the opening section since it comes from the same root as al-Hamid. The name of the Prophet himself, Muhammad, also comes from this root and means "the one who is the source of all praise." Understanding this, we come to see that the word "Muhammad" implies all of the Names of God.

Taking the reciprocal side of this, in the Qur'an Allah applies two divine attributes—Ra'uf and Rahim—to Muhammad.[77] Describing the Prophet as being graced by these qualities strongly suggests that these two kinds of love are the most necessary for a complete human being.

Alhamdulillah's movement is continuous, as can be seen in the word al-Muhammad, which has a double m, an indication of continuous activity according to the sound code. This continuous activity refers to both inward penetration and outward manifestation. Inwardly it is al-Mahmud; the outward manifestation is al-Hamid. Seen together it is the unending activity of gratitude embodied in what is called the arc of ascent and descent.

One of the meanings of Alhamdulillah is directional—all praise goes to Allah, toward the One. The "il" indicates this. It goes from multiplicity back toward essence. There is a further clue here that the mystics take from a second meaning of this Name. Alhamdulillah doesn't just indicate to go toward Allah; it means "owned by Allah." There is no verb in Arabic that specifically means "to have," and, as a result, possession is represented by a preposition. So all gratitude belongs to Allah even though there is no verb for "belongs to."

What this nice ambiguity, or quirkiness from the point of view of English grammar, describes is that Allah is both praising the many, and the many is praising Allah. In the famous Sufi text by 'ibn 'Ata'llah, the *Kitab-al-Hikam* (known in English as *The Book of Wisdom*), it is affirmed that when we say Alhamdulillah, it is Allah praising Allah through us.

It calls to mind Mevlana Rumi's saying, "The Beloved is all in all, the Lover but a veil." In our language we have the concepts of love, lover, and beloved, and that is certainly one way of thinking about the nature of love. However, when we deeply contemplate Alhamdulillah these veils may be lifted, and our entire way of conceptualizing love, gratitude, blessing, and abundance may be unified.

The Qur'an says that in rows upon rows of birds, each one knows its own mode of *hamd*, its own mode of gratitude or praise. Each bird that sings shows the diversity of *hamd*. This phenomenon is described in diverse ways, such as the way trees cast shadows into water. In truth, every single atom of the universe says Alhamdulillah in its own way.

Subhanallah

To get deeply into the meaning of Subhanallah, it may serve best to begin by studying a form of the word, *subbuh* (sub-BOOḤ). This word appears in the chapter of the Qur'an describing the *'arsh Allah*, which is also called the essence of God or the Heart Throne. *Subbuh* means to swim. The description of this encircling of the divine center can be found in the Qur'an.[78]

In this verse we read that the angelic realm is always revolving (*subbuha*) around the center, around the throne of God, which is the pure essence. It is an activity of continually encircling, continually swimming. This activity is mirrored in the physical world by the planets encircling the sun, and the sun with the whole solar system encircling the center of the Milky Way, and so on. As they continuously spiral around this center, the angels are saying "Subhanallah," whose meaning expresses their loving devotion to God and their surrender to the divine essence.

Another verse uses the words *nu-sabbihu* and *nu-qaddisu* (a form of al-Quddus).[79] The root of the Name al-Quddus has the meaning "to return to one's true home." So the continual activity described here is a classical spiral that involves both a circling motion and a movement back toward the center.

The concluding syllable of *subbuh*, with its emphasized "oo" sound (sub-BOOḤ), means that its activity is ever penetrating into the deepest center. Subhanallah is both a return to the source as well as an infinite or continuous circumambulation of the center. And it also carries the meaning of a deeper and deeper penetration to the source of all, which is called *dhat Allah*. Such an image of the heavens is very like what you find in Dante's *Paradiso*.

Subbuh and quddus mirror each other, as they are intensified in the same way by the sound code. The doubled middle consonants imply continuous movement, and the final "oo" sound implies penetration to the depth of the heart.

We read, *Tusabbihu lahu-s samaatu-s-sab'u wa-l-'ardu wa man feehinn. Wa 'in min shay('in) 'illaa yusabbihu bi-hamdih.*[80] This is saying that the seven heavens and the seven earths, and everything in them, do this Subhanallah. The number seven is a symbol for the infinite.

Everything is revolving in love around God. There is not a thing in all the universes, heavens, and earths that doesn't say Subhanallah. That is what is meant by "Everything in the seven heavens and the seven earths do this Subhanallah." Even inanimate objects do this. There is a famous story where the Prophet Muhammad picked up pebbles and heard them saying "Subhanallah" in their own language. He was attuned to the sacred manuscript of nature.

Subhanallah often is paired with Alhamdulillah. The phrase is *subhanallah wa bi-hamdih*, which appears in the Qur'an in several places.[81] Allah is Subhanallah, which means it is totally above or beyond, any conception, attribute, form, or qualification. But by adding *wa bi-hamdih* to Subhanallah, what is expressed is that, notwithstanding being beyond all form, Allah is in all forms as well. God is both transcendent and immanent. *Al-hamd* invokes this relationship between essence and attribute.

Subhanallah can be compared with al-'Aliyy in that it is infinitely above. And there are two more Names that are associated with Subhanallah. They are al-Halim and al-Ghafur. These Names are discussed in Chapter 6, Love's Mysteries, and Chapter 8, Divine Forgiveness. The great Sufi saint Abdul Qadir Jilani recommended pairing Subhanallah with 'Azim. Al-'Azim is the name of divine omnipresence that includes in its meaning not only all the circles around the *'arsh*, but also the *'arsh* itself.

Let's look into the question of how the invocation of Subhanallah might be used by a physician of the heart to promote inner healing. We see that its recitation applies directly to the condition of splitting yourself off from the source because of the pulls of daily life. There is too much focus on the immanence, so to speak.

Extreme immersion in anything leads to a kind of automatic conditioning. It often comes up in therapy. People feel that to focus on some new issue that is arising they have to leave behind the whole field of their being, even though this field includes great gifts and blessings. They should be encouraged to continually remember that, regardless of whatever issue is coming up, it is also true that they intrinsically and constantly have the relationship of orbiting around the essence, around the true source of all.

Repetition of Subhanallah can be helpful in dealing with schizoidal defense. This is where a person feels alone and, as a result, splits off from everything and everyone. They can learn that it is possible to constantly orbit around source, connect to source, and still be able to deal with the relative realm at the same time. The Qur'an says, "No matter where you turn there is the face (essence) of Allah."

Our discussion of Subhanallah begins to suggest the grandeur that is offered by this, the first of the wedding gifts. It also clearly demonstrates how Subhanallah is intrinsically linked with the second gift, Alhamdulillah. The transcendent reality of Subhanallah is balanced by Alhamdulillah, which is fully immanent.

The opening of the Qur'an, *Al-hamdu li-llahi rabb-il-'aalameen* dramatically demonstrates God's immanence. *Rabb-il-'aalameen* means, "Sustainer or Cherisher of all the worlds." So what is being affirmed is that all possible manifestation is included in the divine *hamd*.

Allahu Akbar

The third wedding gift is Allahu Akbar. Allahu Akbar and the sacred Names al-Kabir and al-Mutakabbir share the same root. Al-Kabir is the static state of being infinitely large. Al-Mutakabbir is the process of becoming ever larger, which we compared to an infinite approach to the state of al-Kabir. Both al-Kabir and al-Mutakabbir refer to the manifestation. Al-Akbar is beyond the greatest state, and it is beyond the infinite progression of ever-greater spheres.

There is some confusion about the translation of Allahu Akbar because *akbar* is what is called an elative, which has no equivalent in English grammar. In English grammar it must be translated as either comparative or superlative. But neither the translation "God is great" nor "God is the greatest" quite works. What is said about it in theology is that Akbar is not comparative, because what can God's greatness be compared with? It is incomparable.

Akbar is beyond the infinite approach to infinite greatness of *mutakabbir*. Allah is both the infinite static state (al-Kabir) and beyond the infinite static state (Akbar). Allahu Akbar means God is incomparably great. When we observe any instance of a particular manifestation of greatness, Allahu Akbar reminds us that God is incomparably greater than that. But this quality of being ever greater also means it is ever smaller. Thus, it can be said that al-Akbar infinitely approaches the center state, called the *'arsh*.

How do we know that Allahu Akbar has the meaning of incomparably smaller as well as incomparably greater? The proof has to do with the word *fawq*, which appears in a Qur'anic verse that says Allah isn't ashamed to use the similitude of a gnat or something smaller.[82] A group of people had been making fun of the various similes in the Qur'an. The word *fawq* means both greater and smaller.

In the Qur'an there is mention of all the spheres of manifestation in the heavens and the earth.[83] These can be seen through the qualities of al-Mutakabbir, al-Kabir, and Allahu Akbar. All the spheres of manifestation are called the domain of the *kursiyy*. They are all included in the embrace of al-Wasi', which is called the infinite container of all those realms.

Now al-Wasi' in that sense still doesn't include the Heart Throne: the *'arsh*, that center dot. Al-'Azim does. It is the largest inclusive omnipresence, as it includes *'arsh* and *kursiyy*. Al-'Azim is a word that includes not just the state of the center, the *'arsh*, but also how the essence manifests. To understand al-'Azim is closely related to understanding Allahu Akbar.

Kubraa is the feminine form of *akbar*. *Ayat-ul-kubraa* is called the greatest sign of the presence of God. It is the one seen by Moses. From the standpoint of the 99 Names, the greatest sign is the greatest Name, which would be the elative of al-'Azim. One reference for all this is in the Qur'an.[84] The words Allahu Akbar and al-'Azim appear in the same verse.

Briefly summarizing, Alhamdulillah can be seen in the phenomenon of the arc of ascent and descent, how everything returns to the source, and how boundless gratitude from the source flows into all of creation. Subhanallah offers us the image of swimming around the central still point in spiraling circles of light. All beings and all realms of being constantly circumambulate and interpenetrate that heart center. Allahu Akbar appears to be even greater than the other two because it leads our process to go beyond concepts. The mind falls away and is led into essence. There is not a trace left of the conceptual.

Ya Mu'ti

(yaa mu'-ṬEE)

Al-Mu'ti comes from the word *'ata'ullah*, which means "gift of God." It will serve as a perfect transition from the wedding gifts and the whole discussion of gratitude in this chapter to the very large family of the Names of divine abundance, which is the subject of subsequent chapters. Later in this section, we shall see that al-Mu'ti opens the door to a psychological approach that a physician of the heart can take to address the ego-dysfunction of narcissism.

What kinds of gifts are given by al-Mu'ti? They are truly infinite and abundant. These gifts come without a break and are given to everyone—saints and sinners. When we look at how al-Mu'ti is used, we shall see that what it brings are predominantly spiritual gifts. What especially distinguishes al-Mu'ti from al-Karim is the definite sense that al-Mu'ti carries of the Cause behind all of the multiple causes of manifestation.

In the Qur'an it is taught that the gifts of God are both general and particular in nature. "Allah is the one who gives everything its created form and spiritual guidance."[85] God's gifts are also quite particular. "We have given you *al-kawthar* [abundance]."[86] *Kawthar* also has the meaning of camphor, a substance that infuses anything else with its essence.

The all-inclusive word for God's gifts, al-Mu'ti, clearly implies abundance and endless, inexhaustible supplies of gifts. Al-Mu'ti's form of giving is that of an infinite infusion of gifts. "Except as Allah wills, the flow of gifts from al-Mu'ti is uninterrupted." And "The way that God explains giving the gift is stretching out the hand with gifts upon all."[87] The gifts of God are not closed to anyone. They go to the deserving and the undeserving. So al-Mu'ti, in addition to being the cause behind all that is bestowed, has the quality of manifesting gifts to everyone without interruption.

An intensive form of al-Mu'ti means "to stretch the hands upward or outward both to give and to take." *'Ataa'* means both the thing given or taken. Some of the variations of root forms of al-Mu'ti have an ambiguity around giving and taking. In the actual particular form of the divine Name, al-Mu'ti, the meaning is to freely give gifts, but the ambiguity we have referred to is important, as it illustrates the interrelatedness of giving and taking.

This ambiguity is humorously expressed in a Sufi story. A very self-centered Imam had the misfortune of falling into a freezing vat of water set aside for ablutions. He floundered around in it and looked like he was going to drown. A man nearby repeatedly shouted to him, "Give me your hand, give me your hand," but the Imam ignored him. A Sufi who was standing nearby said, "You don't understand these people." He then went up to the vat and said, "Take my hand," and the Imam gladly obliged.

While these ambiguities can be seen in variations of the root in form 1 of the sound code, when al-Mu'ti appears in other grammatical forms, it is differentiated. For example, in forms 3 and 4 it only means "to give." In form 6, we find the word *t'atin*, which means standing on the tips of your toes to take something. *'I'tw(un)* means a gazelle that stretches itself toward the leaves of a tree to take.

The fourth form variation, *'a'ta*, is the verb form. This word is used a great deal in the recorded traditions of the Prophet. It means "what God gives." It is a free gift without any expectation of return. Al-Mu'ti is the nominal form of *'a'ta*. Another word, *'i'taa'*, indicates the situation in which one is obliged to give as a duty and thus could expect something in return. An example of this is the 4th pillar of Islam, a tithe. It is a duty to give that away, and any reward would come from God.

The most interesting variation of al-Mu'ti is *'ata'ullah*, which means "the gift of God." This gift is freely given in the absolute sense of the word. It is given from such a one who is truly generous, liberal, and bountiful. It is motivated by unconditional love. So al-Mu'ti is the one who gives *'ata'ullah*. The gift itself is *'ata'ullah*, and the one who so gives has these qualities as well.

Al-Mu'ti is the ultimate source, the ultimate cause, which is an unconditional love. The *al-*, or definite article "the," both distinguishes it from every other kind of conditional giving, and characterizes what is given by al-Mu'ti as the only true gift.

The activity of both giving and taking is extremely important, as we find in variations of al-Mu'ti in the second and third grammatical form. Through this we clearly see that both giving and taking are ways of serving or benefiting. What is being emphasized is that the concept of the divine giver necessarily implies someone to accept the gift. They go together. *Yu'attiyniy* means "out of a sense of generosity, he served me and he benefited."

Al-Mu'ti mostly appears in the Qur'an in the form *'a'ta*. However, we read, "By the night when it overspreads, by the day when it shines forth, by the mystery of creating male and female, each one [male and female] hurries to different ends except the one who is *mu'tia* and *taqwaa*."[88] Let's look at these two qualities.

Mu'tia has a feminine meaning. It is like a bow supple to the one who takes the string. It bends but does not break. Its strength and function are best when it is bending, but not bending so far as to break. *Mu'tia* is docile, yielding, supple, gentle, meek, mild, and giving. All these are straight translations from the dictionary about how a bow is when you take it.

The Qur'anic metaphor points to the give and take of the mutual relationship of men and women. When someone truly takes this relationship to heart, they bend yet don't break. The same is true of night and day. When the day predominates, the night doesn't disappear, it is just obscured. This verse is a very striking metaphor for men and women, and it also shows our relationship with God.

Taqwaa, which is included along with *mu'tia* in the verse, is virtually untranslatable, and is often mistranslated as fear of God. It can perhaps best be approached with an illustration: the baby is asleep in a room with the door closed; when you want to go in and get something from the room you have heightened awareness of every step. You have *taqwaa*, or ultimate consideration. Saying that you are afraid you would wake up the baby doesn't fully express this. *Taqwaa* is mentioned frequently in the Qur'an. This passage is saying that all men and women are just busily rushing around in the world except those that have these two qualities of *mu'tia* and *taqwaa*.

If we achieve a heightened awareness of other peoples' feelings, we are properly sensitive to the effect of our actions in the relationship of male and female. We are asked both to be flexible in the give and take of the relationship, and to be highly aware and super considerate of the other person's inner and outer state. As the rest of the verse explains, when this happens your inward state does not remain hidden, and is gradually unveiled.

We are always interested in the variations of the roots of the divine Names that express negative qualities. We view these as indications of opportunities where the sacred Name may be applied in a homeopathic way to address particular human shortcomings. Such a form of al-Mu'ti is *at-tayyaa tuah*. It means "I rushed him, I hurried him." *Ta'atta* means to be in a big hurry, a mad rush, and not to have abundant time because of being too busy. A 10th form variation of the root is *'ast'ataa an-naasa bikaffih*: "he demanded that people give him a gift or present by stretching out his hand."

One last shadowy form is *ta'aatin*. It has several negative meanings: to make bold, to venture into something without hesitation or consideration or *taqwaa*; to rush into something that is a bad or foul activity; to take by the hand that which is not right or just or due; to conquer, to overcome and take by force; to vie with one another, to compete and be contentious.

Prayerful repetition and contemplation of Ya Mu'ti can be a great cure for the blindness of the narcissist. Narcissists only see giving or taking as directly related to themselves. They do not see the exchange or reciprocity that is involved because the narcissist's ego has become split off from the nourishing source of unconditional love.

Narcissism has a wider meaning than the condition of being enraptured with one's own self-image. For the narcissist, giving is always conditional. What are they going to get for it? At no level are they able to give without strings attached, nor can they graciously receive a gift. The universe has a dynamic process. It dissolves and it creates. To be stuck in only one realm is quite an imbalance. It does not allow al-Mu'ti to unfold.

Narcissists are focused on themselves. They are caught up in the false sense of ego that feels, "I am the only significant one." A full-blown narcissist is so centralized in their sense of ego that they have no sensitivity or consideration for others. They are always calculating what they do and what they give. Even when they receive from others, they believe it is because of their own intrinsic merit. They negate the source and negate others who are likewise in the field of their experience. They get very isolated in thinking about themselves and feeling only themselves.

Narcissism is a dilemma for all humanity. It is the deeply hidden core of the original formation of the ego. But the one whom we typically identify as a narcissist is extreme in this regard. It can become pathological. The cure is *taqwaa*, which arises from the full realization of al-Mu'ti. It brings the awareness that is needed to be properly in relationship. This is what it takes for success in the relationship of male and female, or indeed in any relationship.

It should be understood that narcissism has many layers. One layer of our narcissistic self-identification with human deficiency is deeply engaged by the practice of conscientiously reciting Ya Mu'ti. However, narcissism must be continually revisited because there are so many layers of the ego structure, each subject to a distinct form of narcissism. Different Names heal at different levels.

Having been led in our spiritual inquiry to this condition of the ego, it will be very useful to summarize the seven levels of *nafs*. *Nafs* is a concept that needs further explanation. It can be variously translated as ego, lower self, self, soul, and breath. Through further investigation we will see that different divine Names directly address the condition of the ego, or *nafs*, in its different levels of manifestation.

What follows in the next chapter is a summary of such an investigation. It will be a brief treatment of a big topic. This material itself could be expanded into an entire book, but we will only touch upon some high points. After this excursion into the levels of the *nafs*, we will return to our more usual way of considering the Names in the family of divine abundance.

nafs
al·mulhimah
al·mutma'innah
az·zakiyyah
ar·radiyyah
al·mardiyyah
al·lawwaamah
al·ammaarah

Chapter 17

The Seven Levels
of the Nafs

The structure of narcissism in the human ego can be seen in the seven levels of the *nafs*. It is interesting to explore which Names from the divine abundance cluster and elsewhere might helpfully address which levels of the *nafs*. Then, by identifying the level of *nafs*, a physician of the heart could apply a cure by prescribing an appropriate divine Name. Our investigation might provide an interesting alternative to the conventional psychological approach to the healing of narcissism.

At the outset, we should say that different Sufi treatises variously identify three, five, and seven levels of *nafs*, and that the names given to the levels differ. We have chosen one such system.

What is most important is to get a sense of the gradations of the denseness and intensity of vibration in the ego that are revealed by looking into its various layers.

These layers represent developmental stages that may coexist. We have sought stories in the Qur'an that illustrate the gradations of *nafs* and that refer to sacred Names within a particular context.

An-nafs ul-'ammaarah

An-nafs ul-'ammaarah is the first, most dense, level of *nafs*. An excellent context to describe this level appears in the Qur'an in the story of Yusuf and Zulaykha. We are told, "*An-nafs ul-'ammaarah* drives toward degradation, except for the divine loving compassion of Allah, for Allah is Ghafur and Rahim."[89]

Even though this *nafs* drives toward degradation, it should be emphasized that the scripture immediately says "except for. . ." It describes the *nafs* of Yusuf (Joseph of the Old Testament) and the *nafs* of Zulaykha at the stage of their initial attraction to each other. The story is very specific about Zulaykha's attempt to seduce him.[90] It is important to understand that the *himmah*, or desire, which is the motivating force behind this *nafs* is not the problem. Desire can either elevate a person's humanity toward dignity and self-respect, or drive it toward degradation.

The Name *al-Karim* carries meanings of dignity and self-respect, abundance and generosity. This is an indication that recitation of Ya Karim may provide healing for this level of *nafs*. If *an-nafs ul-'ammaarah* drives your craving toward degradation, through calling on al-Karim the *himmah* can be transformed into craving Allah instead of your own self-degradation.

Each one of us has this *nafs* that is always running, but we have the choice of choosing, as Yusuf did, to elevate it through calling out "Ya Karim" instead of our version of "O baby, light my fire." At this gross level of *nafs*, there is a sexual addiction that never ends. Al-Karim's quality of divine abundance is here viewed in the context of addressing sexual craving. Such craving can only be satisfied with al-Karim. God is infinitely abundant; it is God that can fill you with self-respect, and you realize this is the only thing that can satisfy your craving.

A specific object of our craving will never fill up this inner hole in our sense of self. Among all the types of craving, sexual craving is gargantuan. People are driven by it all the time. The more one gets, the more one wants. Like junkies, people are willing to degrade themselves, abandoning themselves to the objects of desire.

It is the appetitive craving running toward self-degradation that is the quality of *an-nafs ul-'ammaarah*; sexual craving is simply being used as an example of this. When *an-nafs ul-'ammaarah* dominates, a person regards everything and everybody as merely an object of their desire, which only gets worse.

When you desire to elevate your humanity, dignity and self-respect, you focus desire in a quite different direction. The textual indication for the application of al-Karim to this condition is the heart of the whole story of Yusuf and Zulaykha. Zulaykha was told by her husband to make Yusuf's stay *'akram*, which is an emphatic form of *karim*. We are then told, "She, in whose house he was in, sought to seduce him from his *nafs*. 'Come here.' 'God forbid [Yusuf said], He has made my stay beautiful.'" *'Ahsana mathwaa.*[91] In other words, Yusuf is saying that the dwelling place of this *nafs* has been made perfect or beautiful.

Later in the surah, Yusuf is revealed as a prophet. God taught him the interpretation of dreams, and the surah says Yusuf grew in wisdom and knowledge of the unseen worlds until he became *'ahsin*, one of the perfected ones. In spite of these spiritual gifts, his *nafs* still was not under control. It is clear that he desired Zulaykha as well.[92] But he was able to counter his *nafs* by remembrance of al-Karim. In the context of this story, we also find Ya Rahim[93] and Ya Karim[94] as antidotes for the appetitive craving of *an-nafs ul-'ammaarah*.

An-nafs ul-lawwaamah

An-nafs ul-lawwaamah is the second level of *nafs* or ego. This level is specifically mentioned in the Qur'an, "I call to witness the *nafs*."[95] This gradation of *nafs* is our sense of self that is utterly devoted to self-reproach, blaming, complaining, and contrasting. The sacred Name al-Hasib is mentioned in the next verse as an antidote to this condition of *nafs*. It expresses the divine action of fully accounting for the meaning of everything. Al-Hasib is treated in Chapter 22, God's Omniscience.

Quite revealing is a key story that demonstrates the meaning of *an-nafs ul-lawwaamah*. It occurs at the point when time ends and post-eternity (*abadiyy*) begins. Shaitan (Satan) appears and speaks, and many souls reproachfully accuse him saying, "You promised us differently." He replies, "I don't have any power over you. I called you and you listened to me. I had no authority. Don't blame me; blame your own soul [*nafs*]."[96]

It is the blaming and self-reproaching *nafs* that is referred to here, and it doesn't matter whether you blame Shaitan or blame yourself; you are still blinded by this *nafs*, and unable to find the depth of your being. Shaitan essentially is saying, "You all listened to me to get your answer. You did not direct your attention to Allah, al-Mujib, who always answers every petition and prayer."

The true inner calling of *an-nafs ul-lawwaamah* is to listen to the voice of al-Mujib. Shaitan is speaking wisdom in this dialogue. There is an abundance to be found in al-Mujib, an abundance that answers the condition of the complaining *nafs*. This *nafs* can learn to listen to al-Mujib instead of being dominated by its habit of constantly complaining. In listening, it hears the response that is always abundantly there. When you call the Lover, the answer comes, "I am there." Then Shaitan's game is up, so to speak.

An-nafs ul-lawwaamah has this way of covering over the voice of God by its habit of listening to the blaming voice. The interesting thing is, once this covering is gone, the gratitude is there! Ash-Shakur is present. *Kafara*, the covering, is the opposite of *shakara*, thankfulness. Allah is present to answer every thought with abundant generosity. That is al-Mujib.

Recitation of Ya Mujib should be used when there are deep abandonment issues, which is a very common theme on the journey. Abandonment issues are often a major cause of settling into the state of *an-nafs ul-lawwaamah*. Such a state often goes back to the deep feeling of being a child who is abandoned in the universe. There is nobody there: there is no mother, there is no father, and there is no God. What is present is a deep sense that this universe is vacant and empty and not responding. You blame parents, the world, or God, and you blame yourself for not being good enough to receive what was there. You may reach out, but nobody seems to answer. All this brings a sense of abandonment.

When the student feels abandoned by the teacher, abandoned by God, abandoned by the work, no matter what is done, they are not convinced. They have a very specific need, and that specific need can only be met by source. Even if the counselor mirrors it back, it doesn't do students much good. They have to go through this abandonment.

It is as if the teacher, and the teaching, and the work have taken them to the valley of no echo, no return. They are just looking at the void. They are in touch with their deepest, narcissistic interest and are self-indulgently identifying with this wounded condition. When they reach that place it is time to call on Ya Mujib, to call upon the only One who would respond, the One who always responds.

The healing powers of al-Mujib are more fully discussed in the next chapter.

An-nafs ul-mulhimah

An-nafs ul-mulhimah is the third level of *nafs*. Its meaning is connected with *ilham. Ilham* is considered to be direct guidance from God without an intermediary. God sends such guidance to your heart directly, but God does this through the membrane of the *nafs*. At this stage, there is less density in this membrane, and that is what allows *an-nafs ul-mulhimah* to be called the inspired *nafs* or the enthused *nafs*.

An-nafs ul-mulhimah is the place of the white light of spiritually ecstatic experiences. The *nafs* becomes inspired as a result of the intensity of such ecstatic experiences. It becomes enthused. How a person responds to the challenge of this enthusiasm or arousal is the crucial thing to understand.

If there is an inner harmony of soul—*nafs* and *ruh*, held in a balanced heart—then your experience is even, unbent, well-formed, symmetrical, and in equal proportion. This is called *sawaa'*. If the *nafs* is able to manifest this kind of harmony while it is ecstatically inspired, it can discriminate properly.

The *nafs* then can distinguish between *taqwaa* and *fujoor. Taqwaa* is to be conscious of the infinite presence of God in everything, all the time. *Fujoor* literally is a tear, or ripped place, in that God-consciousness. A well-balanced *nafs* is innate. It is a perfection we are born with as human souls. However, when the divine enthusiasm cannot be contained within the membrane of the self, there is what can be called a rent or tear, and reception of the direct stream of guidance from God (*ilham*) may become warped or distorted.[97]

If this level of the *nafs* is in good shape, it has discrimination or discernment. However, if it has become unbalanced, it can't distinguish between guidance and distorted perception. It will consider the *taqwaa* to be *fujoor*, and vice versa. Here is a straightforward but extreme example. A woman drowned her three children because, according to her, God told her to do it. The voice of God might have told her heart something, but because her *nafs* was torn and out of balance she couldn't properly discriminate what the guidance might have been.

It is obviously of utmost importance to learn how to address the challenges present for the ego at the level of *an-nafs ul-mulhimah*. In the Qur'an we read first about the innate perfection and harmonious form of *an-nafs ul-mulhimah*. "Then Allah balanced it, made it proportional and well formed, and God breathed his own *ruh* into it, his own soul."[98] It refers to all beings. No one's soul is left out.

And then the verse talks about *shukoor*, gratitude for our hearing and our sight and our understanding.[99] The healthy response to divine inspiration is gratitude. Gratitude is the response of a healthy soul. But how should you meditate on what should be faced and resolved, in order to arrive at such divine gratitude? A key is offered elsewhere in this surah.[100] We read that both spiritual and material gifts are being continuously offered by the divine abundance. Meditating on this reality helps generate gratitude, and true gratitude helps you avoid distorted versions of pride, suggested by the ego in its grandiosity.

To get more to the heart of *an-nafs ul-mulhimah*, the inspired *nafs*, it is necessary to differentiate three levels of divine guidance. This will prepare us to understand a most relevant narrative in the Qur'an that tells of the relationship between the guide Khidr and Musa (Moses), a narrative that throws light on the inspired *nafs*. Inspiration is a kind of divine guidance, and it is important to understand the three levels of divine guidance to understand the narrative. The first level is *al-hudaa*, the second is *al-rushd*, and the third is *al-'ilhaam*.

Briefly summarizing, we can say *al-hudaa* is divine guidance at the prophetic level. It is guidance meant for the populace as a whole. Such general guidance comes through the Prophets and Messengers. *Al-rushd* is for a more select group; it may come through a Murshid or spiritual guide who serves as a channel of guidance. It differentiates guidance and applies it to specific needs, and it mediates between extremes.

Ilham is the inspiration itself, and the word, as we have seen, is related to *an-nafs ul-mulhimah*. *Al-'ilhaam* is direct guidance to the heart from God, without intermediary. It is necessary to fully ripen in one's inner evolution to benefit from this stage of guidance. Such guidance is of the highest quality. *An-nafs ul-mulhimah* is shorthand for it.

This highest quality of guidance is illustrated in the narrative about Khidr and Musa (Moses).[101] Khidr is the prototype of the Murshid or spiritual guide; he is working under direct divine guidance. Khidr's *nafs* is perfectly realized *mulhimah*. Musa is the *mureed*, or disciple, in this case, and he is being taught *rushd* from the Murshid. These levels of guidance work together. In all complete formulations of Sufism, we are shown how all levels work together to confirm each other. No level contradicts another.

Musa has accepted Khidr's guidance, but he has been given the condition that he remain silent and not question Khidr about his actions. While we commend the whole narrative to your attention, we will focus on a few details within it and follow 'ibn 'Arabi's lead in the interpretation. Khidr is the archetype of the spiritual guide. As such he must manifest *rahma*, loving compassion, *'ilmu-l-ladoonee*, meaning knowledge directly from the divine presence, and *'ullimta rushda*, the ability to communicate and guide the *mureed*. Note that it is not sufficient to only have compassion and be divinely inspired; a realized teacher must also have the ability to engage effectively with the *mureed*.

The first incident in the story that leads Musa to question Khidr occurs when Khidr deliberately scuttles a boat. While this act has been variously translated, grammatical analysis clearly shows that Khidr sank the boat and did not order Musa to do so. Musa questions this destruction of property, thinking it to be a waste of resources and possibly worse.

What Musa doesn't know, but Khidr does, is that a ruthless tyrant had turned to piracy to enslave the population. Khidr buys a boat from a large family about to go bankrupt and then destroys his own property to save the family from bankruptcy, prevent the piracy of the ship, and ultimately prevent a war. That is the loving compassion. He scuttled a huge cargo boat with all the money and treasure, but it was his own property, and no life was destroyed.

Khidr doesn't answer Musa at the time, but after two more incidents when he is questioned he does explain. Khidr's actions, which seemed wrong to Musa, actually demonstrate the three qualities of the Murshid mentioned earlier. The incidents demonstrate the student's mistake of being judgmental without knowledge.

Khidr's action parallels the enlightened action of Musa's mother, who put him in a flimsy boat of reeds and pushed him toward an Egyptian princess who was bathing. To an unknowledgeable observer, it might have looked like she was abandoning her child to drowning, but it was a bold act to save his life and allow his ultimately prophetic mission to be fulfilled. The mystery here, according to 'ibn 'Arabi, lies in the realization of the quality of *sabur*, as in the Name as-Sabur— steadfast perseverance with confidence in God and without reactivity.

In the second incident where Musa questioned Khidr, it appeared that Khidr had killed an innocent soul. How could this be an act of loving-kindness or *rahma*? What Musa didn't know and Khidr did, according to the explanation of 'ibn 'Arabi, is that the youth was the head of a gang of highway robbers who were starving out a walled city. No one could go in or out, and anyone in the vicinity was in great jeopardy. No one was willing to try to interfere with this ruffian because they were afraid of his violence. Khidr risked his own life trying to capture him but inadvertently killed him in the process.

It is important to see in the Qur'anic story that Khidr performed the actions himself. He didn't ask his student to do it. Teachers who are tempted to go beyond proper bounds in what they ask their students to do should take this to heart. Each of these incidents served to remind Musa about his own life.

It is *rushd* on Khidr's part to teach Musa about his own actions. An overseer was about to kill one of the Israelites when they were in slavery and oppression. Musa, striving to prevent this, killed the guard inadvertently and was forced to flee into the wilderness. In exactly this way, a *mureed* comes to understand his or her own life through the actions of their Murshid.

The context of the third occasion when Musa questioned his teacher's inspired action requires us to understand the fundamental etiquette in the desert that one is supposed to offer food and water to the traveler. Khidr and Musa arrived and weren't offered any sustenance even when they asked. This would be seen as a huge moral failing. Khidr's response was to repair a breach in the wall of the city. Musa questioned Khidr about it saying that at least you could have asked these people for payment since you are doing them such a favor.

What he didn't know was that repairing the breach in the wall was not only preventing an army that was heading that way from overrunning the city but was also preventing the self-centered people in the city from eating up the inheritance of orphans. He buried this inheritance in the wall so that it could be properly dispensed at a later time.

This particular incident illuminates the episode in Musa's life when he encountered Jethro, who became Musa's guide. Some scholars have said Jethro was the Khidr in the Qur'anic story. Jethro promised that if Musa served him for seven years, he could marry one of Jethro's daughters. Not only did Musa fulfill that pledge, he then worked three more years for no additional payment.

Reflecting on all this, we see that *an-nafs ul-mulhimah*, when in perfect harmony, manifests divine compassion and enlightenment directly from the source, and fits it into a context of practical spiritual guidance, or *rushd*. It is also clear how easy it is for the *nafs*, overcome by divine inspiration or enthusiasm, to become unbalanced and delusional.

An-nafs ul-mutma'innah

The fourth level of the condition of the soul is called *an-nafs ul-mutma'innah*. It is generally translated as a *nafs* that has become serene, calm, and peaceful. In the Qur'an it is described as "O soul in complete rest amidst trials of extreme hunger and extreme anxiety."[102] This is the opposite of the typical condition of impatiently rushing about full of stress and harried. Such people are always complaining that there is never enough time.

In the Qur'an there is another reference to this state along with an interesting parable. "O thou, human being, who has attained to inner peace, Allah sets forth a parable: A city enjoyed peace and quiet and serenity, abundantly supplied with sustenance from every place, and yet it was not thankful for the gifts that God had favored it with."[103]

This parable of the city is the classic symbol for the *nafs*, the self. This is also true in dream interpretation. *Mutma'innah* is how the city is described here. It is also described as *'amminah*, protected and secure. The *nafs* maintains serenity and well-being. In the passage we are told the city was supplied and sustained, and so on. That is the quality of ar-Razzak. Indeed, a whole subgroup of the family of divine abundance is invoked, which demonstrates how the serene *nafs* is constantly supplied from all quarters. We find here the sacred Names al-Wahhab, ar-Razzak, and al-Fattah.

In the Qur'anic parable, the city is suffering from hunger and fear. This evokes the endemic problems of the consumer society of today. You can be in the richest country in the world and still suffer constantly with hunger for goods and the extreme fear of losing what you have. This shows a weakness in the *nafs* that is the opposite of ash-Shakur. *Mutma'innah* is the serenity that overcomes that weakness.

A person who has reached this state experiences being sustained from everywhere by boundless abundance. In the conclusion we learn, "From a serene soul comes this onrushing feeling of deep gratitude for all the delight, blessings, and gifts of God. So eat and enjoy the sustenance which Allah has given you, good and very good, and offer thanks for all the delightful gifts that God has given you."[104]

The Qur'an says, "O soul that is *mutma'innah*, return to me [Allah]."[105] A soul at peace has become unveiled enough to feel its closeness to God; now it can truly feel drawn back to the infinite source. In this passage, God is speaking directly to our *nafs*. It is a strongly emotive verse using the language of lover and beloved. Mevlana Rumi expresses this at the beginning of his *Masnavi* with the story of the call of the flute, the empty reed plucked from the reed bed that longs for return.

There is a famous passage that describes the process for attaining to *an-nafs ul-mutma'innah*: "Those who have attained a certain degree of certainty, their hearts have found peaceful serenity [*mutma'innah*] by means of *dhikr Allah* [remembering God through recitation of the Name]. Certainly in remembrance of Allah all hearts find *mutma'innah*."[106]

Mutma'innah is an inward joy that is difficult to describe in words. This passage is quoted by all Sufis. It really explains how the soul gets to a stage of inner peace. Within Sufi orders, the Murshid gives the *mureed* what is called *bayat* (initiation) specifically, and then instructs him or her in *dhikr*, so that the heart and the soul can become *mutma'innah*.

Another famous passage in the Qur'an describes the Prophet giving *bayat* to his followers. At the time, the companions of the Prophet Muhammad's army thought they were going to be led back to Mecca and be completely wiped out by their enemies there. Actually the ultimate outcome was harmonious, but that is another story. Now they were at an oasis called Hudabiyyah and they convened a community meeting (*khas*) under a tree.

At this *khas*, all the companions took *bayat*. That is to say they each joined hands with the Prophet and made an oath of trust and allegiance. This *bayat* ceremony took place under the tree and, it is believed, involved some kind of instruction in verbal *dhikr*. There was a powerful variety of responses on the part of those who participated.

Hazrat Ali took a single step, called the *qadam*, the step of Ali. All the sacred dances of Sufism come from this single step. It expresses both a kind of ecstasy and a kind of serenity. As a historical footnote, in the 1920s so-called fundamentalists cut down this tree, but its seedlings have spread around the world. It was the place where the institution of *bayat* began.

In the Qur'an, we read, "It is Allah's good pleasure on those who have attained this degree of inner certainty when they took *bayat* under the tree."[107] Allah knew what was in their hearts (this *mutma'innah*) and sent down upon their hearts *sakeenah*, which also means peaceful serenity. It is the result of this *dhikr* that so affects hearts. The end of the verse reads, "*A fathan qareeban.*" This phrase means two things—outwardly it means that Mecca was opened in a bloodless way very soon afterwards, but from *fattah* it also means an opening of heart.

Their hearts opened due to their intimacy or nearness to Allah. That is the outcome of the *bayat*, the *dhikr*, and the ecstasy. Its effect is to open hearts to the immediate presence of the divine. This passage is a wonderful summary of the essence of *an-nafs ul-mutma'innah*.

The whole chapter is called *Fath*. In the second verse we read, "We have opened for you a clear opening. Ya Ghaffar, Ya Ghafur." In the fourth verse we find, "It is Allah who has sent down the *sakeenah* to the hearts of those who have attained certainty." But the core of this transmission is expressed in 48:10 where it refers to the *bayat*.

In reality, the *bayat* is truly made with Allah. It literally says that the hand of Allah is over the hand of the Rasul, or Divine Messenger. This is the mystical reason why *bayat* is so valuable and can have deep consequences. This inner meaning is felt flowing through *bayats* in all traditions everywhere.

An-nafs ul-raadiyah **and** *an-nafs ul-mardiyyah*

The next two grades of *nafs* are related linguistically to each other. Level five is *an-nafs ul-raadiyah*. Level six is *an-nafs ul-mardiyyah*. We find these levels mentioned together immediately after the reference to *an-nafs ul-mutma'innah* in 89:27 (see above). Verse 28 talks about these next two levels together.

Radiyyah means contented or well pleased. *Mardiyyah* is well pleasing and manifesting contentment. They are discussed in Surah 88, called *Al-Ghashiya*—the Overwhelming. Verse 9 describes "their joyful, delighted, ecstatic, faces [*na'eem*]," and goes on to *an-nafs ul-raadiyah*. "You are contented, satisfied, nourished, and enriched."

Such contentment can be compared with the opposite condition of the *nafs*, described in verses 1-7, where it is said that their faces are humiliated; they are laboring and weary. There is a parable about a tree that has gorgeous fruit and smells wonderful, such that you become very hungry. You salivate and want it, but it doesn't nourish you or satisfy your hunger. The more you eat, the hungrier you get. And it causes humiliation because of what you have to do to get it. It is a picture of the suffering caused by the lower self, *an-nafs ul-'ammaarah*. Then the next verse contrasts this, by saying on the other hand there are these others who are well nourished.[108]

In the Qur'an we read of those who follow the *ridwaan Allah*, the path of drawing close to Allah.[109] This word *ridwaan* captures the meanings of both *radiyyah* and *mardiyyah*. Those who follow this path are in varying degrees of nearness to Allah.[110] Some are *mutma'innah*, and some more *radiyyah*, and some *mardiyyah*. Their desires are satisfied but not from their grasping for the fruits. "Allah did confer a great favor on them when he sent a Rasul from among themselves reciting the signs of Allah, purifying them and instructing them in the Book and the wisdom of the Book."[111]

This is an important verse because it shows what is the result of following the *ridwaanu-llah*. One is able to follow this path because of a continuous and unbroken stream of abundance. That is why those who follow this path become *radiyyah*, why their faces radiate this deep contentment and satisfaction.

Ya Mannaan, another divine Name of abundance not on official lists, occurs in this passage. It is related etymologically with *manna* from heaven. Al-Mannaan is being content, thankful with the divine gifts. It is like al-Mu'ti. We appreciate the giver by appreciating the gifts. We are continually fed by al-Mannaan, by al-Mu'ti. The uninterrupted gifts of abundance deeply satisfy the soul's yearning for contentment.

Also contrasted with *radiyyah* is *sakhita*. It means to despise. It is to deem a gift as little, to not appreciate. There is a hadith: Appreciating and being well pleased (*mardaah*) with divine perfection is from Allah, and deeming it little or insignificant is from Shaitan.

Lastly, *radiyyah* has to do with love. An illustrative narrative occurs in the Qur'an where there is another instance of *bayat*. It is an individual initiation. Here we read of Allah pouring down the *sakeenah* upon the Prophet Muhammad and strengthening him with angelic forces. But one companion, Abu Bakr, is also involved. "They two were in the cave," (referring to Abu Bakr and Muhammad). It is a story of the silent *dhikr*; soldiers were coming and the two had to be quiet and remain hidden to complete their flight to Medina.[112]

Abu Bakr thought they were both going to die. But a spider spun its web at the entrance of the cave, and the experienced desert trackers, noticing the web, assumed no one was inside. At this time the Prophet initiated Abu Bakr into the silent *dhikr*. *Sakeenah* poured down upon them as a result of that silent practice and the *nafs* became *radiyyah*, despite the extremity of the outer circumstances. The Prophet said, "Have no fear, God is with us."

There is a little more to add about the stage of *mardiyyah*. These two stages are like the two different sides of the same coin. Linguistically they are related, and they appear in the Qur'an together. The same moment the *nafs* becomes well pleased with God, God is well pleased with that soul. That is what *mardiyyah* is. It is the same reality looked at from two different viewpoints.

There is a type of person who gives his or her whole life yearning for *mardaah*, the good pleasure of Allah. Literally, they devote their whole soul (*nafs*) to yearning for the pleasure of Allah.[113] That really expresses the nature of this sublime level of the *nafs*. They give their all, and Allah is well pleased with that soul. Allah is *ra'uf* (full of gentle loving-kindness) for such lovers. God gives *ridwaan* to them. We all strive for all this and only attain it when we are well pleased with Allah. *An-nafs ul-raadiyah* and *an-nafs ul-mardiyyah* should be treated as a set, as two sides of same coin.

An-nafs ul-zakiyyah

The seventh stage is called *an-nafs ul-zakiyyah*. As we have previously seen, the Qur'an speaks about the person upon whom Allah confers the abundant blessing of *mannaan*.[114] Then it speaks of such people and uses the word *feehim*, which can be translated, "the messenger was among them," or "the messenger was within their souls." The messenger in their souls recites, rehearsing the signs of God to them, and purifying them.

An-nafs ul-zakiyyah means a pure soul; it is the highest and last grade. "How happy is the one who purifies her [the *nafs*]."[115] The verb here means to purify, and also to increase blessings from Allah, and enjoy a state of abundance. This leads us to al-Ghaniyy, a Name associated with this stage. The boundless joy in such a state of abundance of the soul is al-Ghaniyy, which is an infinite treasure house of blessings. Al-Ghaniyy comes in the passages 35:15-18. "Whoever purifies himself purifies his own soul, and to Allah is the final destination of all the ways."[116] The soul is purified of all selfhood.

Purification of selfhood is a synonym for *fana*, the dissolving of the egoic condition. *Fana* leads to *baqa*, realization of the real self, which leads to *liqa'*, the final meeting, the final union of all ways. This process of purification is called *tasawwuf*, or Sufism, as the word is translated in English. The one who is purified is called a Sufi, so some books refer to this seventh stage as *an-nafs ul-soofiyyah*.

An-nafs ul-zakiyyah is referred to as *faqeer*,[117] which is another word for Sufi. It means the one who is content to be empty of self in relation to God. The purified soul realizes al-Ghaniyy. "O people, you are *faqeer* toward Allah and *Allah huwa al-ghaniyy al-hamid*."[118] In other words, Allah is the richness of the treasure house of eternal joy and abundance. This is the goal of the Sufi path: to be this empty, to be *faqeer*, toward Allah who is *ghaniyy*.

All the prophets have this *an-nafs ul-zakiyyah*. The purity of the messengers is referred to in this way in Sufi sources. Examples are Musa at the burning bush and Muhammad in the *Miraj*. Musa hears of the bush, talks to the bush, throws himself into it and is totally consumed. This demonstrates a realization of pure oneness, *tauheed*, unity. This stage has been described by saying that none may enter the garden of the self, but the self. What enters is nothing—and that nothing is God's selfhood.

An-nafs ul-zakiyyah, or purified self, is called the greatest sign, *ayat-ul-kubraa*. The Qur'an says, "So that we may show you the greatest sign. . ."[119] In the Surah *an-Nazi'at*, Musa is talking to the bush. He is told to go back to Pharaoh even though he doesn't want to, and say to Pharaoh, "Would you be purified?"[120] To be purified is to attain *an-nafs ul-zakiyyah*. Musa is to show him the greatest sign—meaning to show him *an-nafs ul-zakiyyah* from his own soul.[121] To hear the greatest Name, a form of which is given by God to Musa at this time, it is necessary to have a purified soul.

The *Miraj*, or journey through all the heavenly realms by the Prophet Muhammad, is the context for this same teaching. "Truly he did see the greatest sign of God."[122] The narrative here tells of Halimah, the wet nurse of Muhammad when he was just a toddler. They were going down a road with a ditch on either side; he ran ahead and fell into the ditch. She ran after him. Two angels came down. One had a dagger of pure light, split Muhammad's breast open, washed his heart in pure light, and sealed him up. Then the wet nurse took him out of the ditch.

This represents the purification that his *nafs* underwent to be able to pass a line described in the *Miraj* story as the lote tree that divides finite reality from infinite reality. This is the line that the Archangel Gabriel couldn't cross. As the angel said, "I took you through the six heavens, but I couldn't pass this tree lest my wings burn." The rational mind cannot pass this barrier, but the *nafs* that is entirely purified can. It is purified even of the rational mind.

Muhammad beheld the divine reality on another occasion near the lote tree, beyond which none can pass.[123] The lote tree is the tree of nothingness that stands near the Garden of the Abode—the highest heaven. "Behold the lote tree was shrouded, covered with the greatest sign."[124] The greatest sign is the *nafs* that isn't there, because it is dissolved in the reality of the divine self. As the sacred hadith affirms: "I become the eye with which one sees." The question of who is seeing whom is not really answerable. The seventh heaven is the garden of unity. This is the culmination of the *Miraj* story.

An-nafs ul-'ammaarah begins as greed. That yearning is built into every cell. But the flame of greed can ultimately become transmuted and spiritualized. The paradox is to be able to stay with the passion for the goal when the quest isn't yet fulfilled. All yearning ultimately directs you toward the light, the source of all, the treasure house of all existence and ecstasy. The journey through the seven stages of the *nafs* leads the soul to the realization of Ya Ghaniyy, the divine Name that expresses the infinite treasure house of being.

In the process of this purification we have specifically noted a number of sacred Names that can be instrumental in addressing the issues of *nafs* at each level. Because the Names that arise in this context all have a deep resonance with divine abundance, we have included them in the text at this point, even though it may seem to be a bit of a departure from the general form of our approach. In the next chapter we will return to consideration of divine abundance in our usual way.

dhal
jalali
edal
ikram

Jamil

sabur

karim

majid mujib

chapter 18

The Treasure House of Divine Generosity

We have just begun to explore the inexhaustible treasure house of divine abundance. We examined the attributes of gratitude and thankfulness, the three wonderful wedding gifts, and al-Mu'ti, the gift of God. The question then arose how to apply the qualities of divine abundance in ways that might address the full range of human psychological conditions.

In line with a classical Sufi approach, our first way to answer this question was to view the human soul through the lens of the seven levels of *nafs*. The ego, or *nafs*, has a self-identity in each of these seven layers of soul, and the divine Names serve to address the nature of the ego in each layer.

We now turn our attention to other important members of this family. The great scope of this cluster of Names that are emanations of divine abundance, and the importance that these sacred Names can play in human psychological growth, require us to devote two more chapters to properly do justice to this rich material.

Ya Karim

(yaa ka-REEM)

It is natural to begin with al-Karim, a Name for divine abundance with a most inclusive meaning. As we have seen throughout, in Semitic languages word meanings are deeply enriched by considering the family of words that branch off from each root.

Some of the forms taken by the root of al-Karim, K-R-M, convey the reality of the earth. *Karumat ardu-hu* is a name for a fecund, productive soil or earth. *'Ardun makroomatun* means generous, well-tilled, and irrigated land that yields abundant produce. These are very evocative images for the divine attribute of al-Karim.

The more abstract meaning of a source of abundance that is generous, liberal, and giving naturally presents itself when such an image of the land is extended to human beings. There is a second meaning of al-Karim, which goes beyond our usual notion of generosity. It is to be rare and precious, to be valued, to be excellent, like a good, well-bred horse.

The divine quality named by al-Karim is a manifestation of abundance; it emanates abundant gifts that are rare and precious and which have the best quality. This manifestation reaches everything in creation, leaving not a single thing out. It is important to note that the gifts brought by al-Karim are both material and spiritual in nature. It is a universal kind of bounty, or generosity, that is not restricted in any way.

Al-Karim is frequently paired in the Qur'an with another Name of divine abundance, ar-Razzak. *Rizq* is the noun form of this sacred Name. From the divine perspective, *rizq* is an endless source of material bounty. *Rizq(un) kareem* is seen several times in the Qur'an.[125] What is strongly implied by the combination of these qualities is the inclusive nature of al-Karim. One of these references specifically makes it clear that women are equal recipients of this universal bounty.[126]

Karamaat is a form of al-Karim that is often mentioned by Sufis. It refers to great spiritual gifts or powers. The principal description of such gifts is the story of King Suleiman and Bilqis, the Queen of Sheba.[127] A friend of King Solomon causes the throne of the Queen of Sheba to be transferred from Yemen to Jerusalem, literally in the twinkling of an eye. The last words of this description are *rabbiy ghaniyyun karim*. Such an event is considered one of the *karamaat*, or miracles, that come from al-Karim.

We now begin to see the inclusive role that the quality of al-Karim plays in the cluster of divine abundance. In the Qur'anic passages noted above, al-Karim is combined with two other Names in the abundance family, ar-Razzaq and al-Ghaniyy. Al-Karim manifests material gifts in its union with ar-Razzaq, and spiritual gifts in its union with al-Ghaniyy.

Popular forms of Sufism have often been much associated with purported miracles, and exaggeration of the powers of Sufis in these stories has caused *karamaat* to acquire a somewhat pejorative association. It has even led some believers to frown on miracles as such.

These negative connotations, however, arise because of a mistaken understanding of the source of abundance. All abundance comes from al-Karim. If grace results in material prosperity or in spiritual gifts of powers, the important thing is to fully understand that this grace is the activity of God. It is not a quality of the assumed virtue of your own ego.

The real *karamaat*, the greatest spiritual gifts, are not such things as turning lead into gold, reading minds, transporting thrones, or even healing. The three greatest gifts described in the Qur'an are *qawl*, *kitab*, and *qur'an*. We will consider each one of these in turn.

The Prophet Muhammad calls Surah 36 the Heart of the Qur'an. In this chapter there is a verse dedicated to the heart itself. *Qawl* means "a word from Allah that is the essence of al-Karim"—and that word is "peace."[128] Everyone yearns for this word of peace that is coming from Allah. That it comes is considered the ultimate miracle.

The second miracle is *'umm-ul-kitab*, the mother of all the books or messages. It is called the preserved tablet. It is the ultimate source of all divine revelation. Every sacred book in all periods of time is drawn from this one source.[129]

The last of the three greatest examples of *karamaat* is considered to be the Qur'an itself. One passage combines al-Qur'an and al-Karim.[130] In the cosmic sense, what Qur'an really means is that the book of nature, within and without, is a kind of divine song. Such is the cosmic nature of the Qur'an as it is in the mind of God, in all the possible worlds. Once you have seen and acknowledged it in its universal sense, you can then think of it as the specific recitation, the divine song that is celebrated and recited in the religion of Islam.

Al-Karim is gifting this divine song to us from the boundless realm of abundance. The great miracle here is present in the very essence of this boundless realm of divine abundance, and how this essence is also manifested as a specific text of revelation in the world of multiplicity. The goal of contemplating any sacred text should be to read the transcendent universal message inside the manifest one.

When Muhammad was challenged by skeptics to prove his status by performing miracles as Jesus had done, he said that the Qur'an itself is a miracle. One reason it is a miracle is that the Prophet himself, being illiterate, could neither read nor write. But it is likewise a miracle because al-Karim sends it forth from the transcendental reality of *al-kitab ul-maknoon* or *'umm-ul-kitab*, the preserved tablet.

There is one message, but there are many messengers and many manifestations of different scriptures. All these are emanations of al-Karim, because they are truly of benefit in every way. When it is taught that none can touch the Qur'an except those who are pure, the deeper meaning is that you cannot touch the inner meaning of any spiritual book unless you have a purified heart.

To summarize, the greatest spiritual miracles are the word of peace, the Mother of the Book, and the particular manifestations of that transcendental reality that can be recited. Viewed from its context in the sound code, al-Karim is the source of boundless generosity that manifests into all creation everywhere and without exception.

There is a famous verse in the Qur'an: "We [Allah] are surely continuously ever-generous [*karramnaa*] and honoring of the children of Adam [*banee Adam*], giving special favors beyond the rest of our created being."[131]

What is the mark of special favors that Adam was given? Specifically, humanity was given all the divine Names in the pre-eternal covenant. The heart of the complete human being has been seeded with all of the Names as a hidden treasure to be uncovered in every soul. It is a great sign of al-Karim. Al-Karim goes everywhere, but when it gets to Adam (humanity), it is superabundant.

God demonstrates through every Prophet what it means to be a complete or perfect human being, a perfect reflection of the divine essence, endowed with all the sacred Names. This state is described in the Qur'an where the term *rasul karim* appears.[132] It is not only Adam, or the children of Adam and Eve, that have been given this treasure, but the function of *rasul* has been given this gift, this *qawl*.

Qawl means "the word," and "word" here is used in the sense of all the divine Names. The *rasul* becomes al-Karim, and al-Karim breathes the breath of the word into *rasul*. It is the apotheosis in the *qawl*. "I call to witness the planets that recede, that hide, the night that dissipates, and the dawn that breathes away the darkness, that this is a word (*qawl*) from *rasul karim* endowed with the essence of power from the possessor of the throne."[133]

This passage strongly emphasizes the gift of the miracle of the word inside the messenger, and the power of the beautiful names of God. What is given is a universal gift from a universal giver. There is no high and low in it. Allah is honored in giving the gift of abundance and Allah honors the one who receives the gift of abundance. That's what *karramnaa Allahu banee Adam*[134] means.

As a consequence of this essential divine generosity, it is possible for any human being to be a complete teacher, because every heart has all the divine Names in it. Buddhism gives this teaching in a parallel way. It is reported that Gautama Buddha at the moment of his enlightenment said, "I see now all sentient beings are enlightened; they are simply unaware of it."

Honoring is present in both giving and receiving. This truth is most important to understand when the physician of the heart is asked to deal with the psychological issues that arise from distorted notions of abundance and poverty. True abundance cannot thrive when we function in the mode of separation and ego-isolation.

A shadowy form that the root of al-Karim takes also gives us a clue for its homeopathic application to the human condition. *Karramnaa* means "to stay aloof from." It has all the bad connotations of nobility, of disdaining others and separating oneself from them. It manifests as elitism. The *'an* means from, separate from, thinking of yourself as superior.

By thinking of yourself as superior, you lose sight of the fact that all the gifts you have received come from al-Karim. This shadow state can be a stumbling block for spiritual teachers and a trap for those who are materially wealthy. Since such people are richer in a certain sense, they may think they are wiser and better. Prayerful repetition of Ya Karim addresses the assumed superiority of this ego condition. We refer the reader to Chapter 17, The Seven Levels of the *Nafs*, where al-Karim is discussed as a divine remedy for the first and coarsest level of ego, *an-nafs ul-'ammaarah*.

Continuing to investigate what is paired with al-Karim we find, *rabb-ul-'arsh il-kareem*,[135] lord of the throne of generosity. This reference points directly to the next divine Name we will discuss, Dhul Jalali wal 'Ikram.

The first element to grasp about this complex Name is that both the essence and the manifestation of divine generosity are designated as Karim.

Ya Dhal Jalali wal 'Ikram, Ya Jamil, Ya Sabur

(yaa <u>DH</u>AL ja-LAA-li WAL 'ik-RAAM), (yaa ja-MEEL), (yaa ṣa-BOOR)

Dhul Jalali wal 'Ikram is a very complex and important Name, but the simple Name al-Karim is essential for understanding it. In the whole list of the 99 Names, Dhul Jalali wal 'Ikram is the most complex. We should not be surprised to learn that this one Name provides a key for understanding all the rest. This was discussed previously in Chapter 9, Modalities of Omnipotence, where it served as a culminating way to understand strength. Like *akbar,* it is an elative.

Dhul affirms the essential reality (*dhat*). That reality goes beyond the particular qualities of all the *sifat*, beyond all the 99 Names of Allah. It is their source.

'Ikram, which is the form al-Karim takes in this Name of God, is an intensive in the sound code. It is especially generous. In particular, what is intensified in *'ikram* is its strong combination of two aspects of al-Karim's full meaning: it is both the source and the manifestation of generosity. Moreover, *'ikram* is very close to the quality of divine beauty, al-Jamal. And, of course, divine power, al-Jalal, is specifically named in Dhul Jalali wal 'Ikram.

The absolute essence (*dhul*) is thus affirmed as being both *jalal* (all-powerful) and *jamal* (all-beautiful). These divine attributes should be understood in a dual sense. Each Name is the only source of a particular quality's emanation, be it al-Jalal or al-Jamal, and each Name is also the emanation of that quality into all things. *'Ikram* includes both these aspects of al-Karim.

When the qualities of power and beauty (*jalal* and *jamal*) are balanced, we get *kamal*, which is perfection. This process becomes a key for the student on the path. It is a hidden code, if you will, for how to actively contemplate all the divine Names.

As seen in the sound code, the use of the grammatical form *jalal* (rather than *jalil*) and *jamal* (rather than *jamil*), specifically points to "the only source of power and beauty." Since they specifically relate to source, *jalal* and *jamal* can be said to be closer to the essence. In contrast, in the sound code the forms *jalil* and *jamil* show the divine quality expressing itself throughout the whole of manifestation, leaving nothing out.

This naturally leads us into the subject of sequential steps of contemplation. Such steps move from reflection on superabundant beauty to a similar reflection on essential power, and ultimately to the realization of pure essence itself.

The first step of active contemplation of divine beauty is in observing the signs of God in the heavens and the earth, including the signs in one's own *nafs* or self. It starts with the manifest aspect of the beautiful, al-Jamil. Such signs are present everywhere to the one who has the eyes to see. A story is told of Jesus walking with his disciples and passing by a dead dog with a putrid odor. The companions held their noses. Jesus did not react in that way, but instead directed them to see what beautiful teeth the dog had.[136]

The second step is contemplation of the beauty of the divine essence. That is al-Jamal. It is the face of divine beauty. You are not yet contemplating essence itself, but you are seeing the beauty of the essence. Ecstasy and intoxication are present in both of the stages of *jamil* and *jamal*.

The third step is active contemplation of the signs of divine majesty or power everywhere. That is al-Jalil. And the fourth step, al-Jalal, is contemplation of the majesty of the divine essence. In contrast to the first two stages of contemplation, these are both stages of sobriety and clarity, rather than stages of intoxication and ecstasy.

The fifth step is contemplating both the *jamali* and *jalali* sacred Names at the same time. It involves balancing both the beauty and majesty of the essence. That is al-Kamal, which means completeness, as well as perfection. This stage involves a balancing within divine essence itself, without any consideration of the manifestation.

The sixth step is union with, and balancing of, divine manifestation in contemplation. Divine manifestation is called *tajalliyyat*, a word that comes from the radiance of the day. If the Sun didn't exist as the source of light, there would be no day. Manifestation is dependent upon essence in the same way that daylight is dependent upon the sun. Complete balancing in contemplation is both *jalil* and *jamil*. It is continuous abundance.

A story of Moses illustrates this sixth stage.[137] Moses says to God, "Let me see you." God says, "You cannot see me." "Then give me a sign." God then sends his *tajalliyyat*, or manifestation, upon a mountain. The mountain is reduced to dust and Moses swoons. Later some Bedouins asked Muhammad how much did God send down to bust up the mountain, and he replied about as much as the size of the moon that you find on the little fingernail.

The story of Moses also illustrates the need for balance. Both *jalil* and *jamil* are manifested in a balanced way in God's Prophets. The seventh and last step of this contemplation process unifies what is described in the fifth and sixth steps. It is the union of divine essence in the balance of beauty and majesty, combined with the union of divine manifestation in the balance of beauty and majesty. It is the union of all unions.

It may be satisfying intellectually and metaphysically to describe these seven stages, but the process only begins to become clear when we fully take the first step. There are literally thousands of Qur'anic verses where we are shown *tafakkur-al-jamil*, the manifest signs of God's beauty. We are enjoined to see the signs on the horizons and in our own selves.[138] Sufis therefore are interested in music and art and an infinite variety of ways for realizing the divine superabundance by contemplating divine beauty in this world.

Travelers on the spiritual path are asked to actively cultivate awareness of the inward signs of divine beauty no matter how difficult the situations they may be facing, and even because of such difficulties. At the culmination of such a process is a realization of what is called *sabr jamil*. *As-Sabur* brings a depth of perseverance, which is the quality that allows you to fulfill your contemplation of the divine beauty in manifestation, even in the face of great difficulties.

It should prove helpful to look at a few notable instances where *sabr jamil* is mentioned in the Qur'an. It is used twice in the story of Jacob and Joseph. *Sabr jamil* is a quality that was realized by the patriarch Jacob. It allowed him to see through the outer form of situations. When he is shown a shirt dyed in blood and told by his errant sons that wolves have eaten Joseph, he replies to them that their *nafs* has made up the story.[139] Through *sabr jamil* he sees this truth in his own self.

Later, near the end of the story, this quality is mentioned again. His youngest and new favorite son, Benjamin, has been detained in Egypt, and Jacob's other sons tell him that it is because Benjamin was caught stealing. Again he responds by saying *sabr jamil*, and affirming that this tale too has been constructed by the *nafs*.[140]

Another outcome of contemplating the signs of exquisite beauty in one's own self is to overlook all human faults with a beautiful forgiveness. This is called *safah jamil*. According to the highest standard of Muslim ethics, one does not cut people off for bad behavior. In the Qur'an, during a period of tension between the emerging Islamic community and the Jews and Christians of the time, the Muslims are told: "Even if they have cursed you, forgive them and overlook their misdeeds because God loves those who do this."[141]

The Qur'an again speaks of *sabr*, to return harsh words with good words, harsh action with good.[142] To act in such a way is considered *jamil*. *Al-Jamil* is a quality that is identified here with *al-Karim*. To arrive at the state of *sabr jamil* is to be generous in your view of humanity and to overlook individual faults. Many more examples could be given.

The Qur'an is filled with references to contemplation of the divine beauty and generosity in manifestation. The signs of God are the divine Names inscribed in the soul of humanity in pre-eternity. This is our birthright as human beings. What is called *tafikkar* is thoughtfully contemplating the inner aspect of the divine generosity and beauty on the breath while in the midst of crisis and the rough events of the world.

The ultimate stage of *sabr jamil* fully manifests the attribute as-Sabur, which is completely consistent in all situations. By grace, the traveler on the path of contemplation of the divine abundance may ultimately penetrate to the essence of beauty itself. Such a being walks gently on the earth and has loving gentleness toward the outer manifestation. Through heightened insight into reality, he or she sees the infinite worth, or *karam*, of every individual. God is all in all.

Ya Mujib

(yaa mu-JEEB)

Allah is al-Mujib, the one who answers all prayer. This bountiful quality places al-Mujib in the family of the Names of divine abundance. In Chapter 17, The Seven Levels of the *Nafs*, al-Mujib is recommended as a remedy for the condition of the *nafs* at the second level, *an-nafs ul-lawwaamah*. Now we will dig further into the inner meaning of al-Mujib and find out more about the true nature of prayer.

In some of the forms that the root M-J-B takes, we find examples of a kind of reciprocity. It is the quality of call and response, which is a good way to understand the internal dialogue of prayer. The form that the root takes as al-Mujib is a causative in the terms of the sound code. In the context of prayer, this quality means that each person's prayer will be answered at a particular time, and in a particular place and manner, according to God's knowledge.

Many teaching stories illustrate how human beings err by failing to recognize the divinity of causative qualities. A familiar example would be of the man who is stranded in a flood but is convinced that God alone will save him. Because he is waiting for God to do it, he rejects the boat that comes by, as well as the helicopter. The causatives direct us to see God working through what appear as secondary causes.

At the outset we would like to say that any discussion of prayer should consider the dilemma posed by some form of the following question: Since God has knowledge of all things, and God must already be aware of what we need, then why pray?

What is the purpose and nature of prayer? The answer to this emerges as we look at the root meanings of al-Mujib. *Jaaba* is a first-form root of the word. It means to bore a hole in a rock to get water. The eighth form, *'ijitaaba*, means to dig a well. *Jawwaba* is the name given to an excellent well-digger, one who always finds water.

Jawwaba, a second form, means to penetrate the blackness of the night like the light of the moon, which when it rises illuminates the darkness and renders clear what has been hidden. A second meaning is to travel through the night and penetrate the blackness like a bird in flight. *'Injaaba*, a seventh-form variation, means to become clear, open, and unobstructed.

In contrast, the form of the word as a noun is *jawbah*, which means a shield. *Jawwaba alay-hi* means to be shielded or protected.

Taking all these root meanings into consideration, we can now look at the question we posed earlier: Why should we ask anything of God if God already knows what we are asking? The act of asking is like shining a light that penetrates our inner darkness of confusion. It shines light upon our own *nafs* and allows us to know what we really want and what we are really asking for.

That is quite a different way of looking at prayer. It is not a letter to Santa Claus. The purpose of asking is to penetrate the darkness, to dig through obstruction and reach water. In a parallel way, we don't praise Allah because Allah desires to be praised, but because the act of gratitude transforms our condition and opens us to God.

Al-Mujib appears in the Qur'an in conjunction with the word *qareeb*, which means the one who is near.[143] The *muqarraboon* are the ones who are near, or who continually draw near. "There are companions on the right and left hand, and those who are beyond heaven and hell; they are the ones who draw near."[144] A sacred hadith goes on to say that they become ever nearer to me until I become the eyes through which they see, the ears through which they hear, and so on.

Al-Qarib means truly listening, and not simply desiring an answer to your request. Such a standard of listening implies that if you, as a lover, are caught up in paying attention to the distance between you and the beloved, you are not in a position to be close enough to get the answer which is there.

Qareeb also has the superlative form *'aqrab*. *'Aqrab* appears in the famous Qur'anic passage in which the nearness of Allah is vividly named. "It is We who made you in the first place and We know the dark whisperings that your own soul [*an-nafs ul-lawwaamah*] whispers to you, for We are nearer to you [*'aqrab*] than your own jugular vein."[145]

Other forms of the root of *qareeb* mean "to harmonize." What can be seen from this is an increasingly intimate relationship with God in which the internal dialogue is harmonized. Those of us who are stuck in *an-nafs ul-lawwaamah* are caught up in the internal voice of blame, criticism, comparison, and judgment. This voice brings up all the past regrets and future fears. These worries all come from listening to the dark whisperings of the *nafs*, rather than listening to al-Mujib, who is answering our deepest need.

'Ibn 'Arabi says that if you are not listening deeply to deep internal dialogue in your prayer, then you are not really praying. This intimate dialogue, or pillow talk, is called *munaajaat*. *Munaajaat* describes the inner dialogue of the lover, the call and response. The one who responds to the lover's need is al-Mujib.

The Qur'an says that we will be tested by outward conditions and by our own personal selves, *an-nafs ul-lawwaamah*. There will be much that grieves us. It goes on to say, "When my servants ask you concerning me say that I am really very close. I answer every call when anyone calls me, so listen and seek an answer from me."[146]

An elegant aspect of this passage is that the word "to answer" is the fourth form of al-Mujib and the word "to listen" is the tenth form of the root. In his commentary on the Qur'an, Yusuf Ali writes, "Only those who will listen with their hearts will hear God's answers. As for those whose hearts are dead, Allah will raise them up from the dead, where they will finally all return to Him."[147] To raise from the dead, al-Ba'ith, is to revive dead hearts so that we may be open and listen to the answers.

Another point to the Qur'anic passage is that the lover calls the beloved and the beloved listens; then the beloved answers the call of the lover, and now the lover who is near to Allah is able to hear and listen. We can fully see in this the operation of the principle of reciprocity, an important factor to properly understand in contemplating the divine Names of abundance. What is transpiring is not just a one-way stream of propitiation. It is an intimate dialogue.

In a variety of ways, prayer, al-Mujib, is paired with nearness, al-Qarib. The intimacy of al-Mujib is described in a slightly different manner in the Chapter of the Star.[148] What is being recounted here is the night journey of the Prophet, in which he approaches the divine presence. It is an intimate conversation conducted in the manner of two turtledoves.

We read, "Call to me and I will answer you."[149] We are given an imperative to act, to call, but we should not be attached to receiving an immediate response. Not knowing the time, manner, and place in which al-Mujib answers is really a protection, or shield, for the one who asks.

We have already seen how repetition of Ya Mujib directly addresses the tendency of our lower self to blame and complain. This is a most important function from the standpoint of purification. There is also a shadowy form of the root of al-Mujib, in form 6, that means to use our supposed intimacy as an excuse to argue or dispute, and to use rough language in our relationships. Invoking Ya Mujib should therefore also serve as an antidote for such excesses of ego.

There is another major area where repetition of Ya Mujib will be most useful: when a person is going through a process of dealing with abandonment issues. What is uncovered at such a time is the child's deep feeling of being abandoned in this universe. There is nobody there for them: there is no mother, there is no father, and there is no God. Consequently, there is a deep sense that the universe is vacant and empty and does not respond to their needs.

The student can ask and reach out, but there is no answer, and that brings up the sense of abandonment. When the student is feeling abandoned by the teacher, or by the work, or by the guidance it is a good time to invoke Ya Mujib. At such a time students are looking at the void, and they are also in touch with their deepest, most narcissistic interest. But there is nothing and nobody to respond. There is not even an inner source within them that they can find.

When they reach that stage, it is a beautiful opportunity to call upon the only source that can respond and meet them precisely, al-Mujib. To call on Ya Mujib is to call upon the one who will always respond, who will always answer. Deep abandonment issues are a very common theme on the journey. At a certain time, the student feels abandoned by the teacher, abandoned by God, abandoned by the work. No matter what the teacher does, the student is not convinced.

The student has very specific needs, needs that can only be met by the source. Even if the teacher mirrors back what they need, it doesn't help much. The student has to go through this feeling of abandonment, the feeling that their basic need is not being met. The stage has been set to turn to al-Mujib.

There is a substance called colostrum that may help to illuminate our relationship with abandonment, and with al-Mujib. Colostrum is the liquid that comes through the mother to the baby in the first two or three days of life and before the mother's milk arrives. If at that earliest stage there is interference with the fulfillment of receiving the colostrum, the baby's need to be deeply nourished is not met. What arises in the child is a feeling that there can be no satiation of their needs in this universe.

The child calls, but there is no response. Because there is no response, a very deep hunger comes, a deep, deep starvation. And that starvation usually is centralized at the solar plexus. When that person goes deep within and opens up their system, this deep hunger appears. It is a hole they will often try to fill up with food. It is a very common occurrence that whenever this hunger comes, they eat. They are narcissistically trying to get love, trying to find relationships, trying to get acknowledgment, and in general trying to fill up this deep hole of starvation.

When the student is allowed and encouraged to go through their deep hunger, then al-Mujib begins to awaken. The student is able to recognize their deepest longing from day one, their basic need for love. The absolute manifests as love, and this love comes to the mother for what has been created. Physically it comes first as colostrum, and later as milk. It is coming from the most abstract realm, to a feeling, and then to a substance.

Emotion is not enough for a baby; they need a depth of love. The absolute may be viewed as a field. As it manifests, it gets denser and denser, until it meets the child's need with utmost love. If this basic satiation doesn't happen, deep inside around the stomach, there is a gut-level feeling that this universe cannot fulfill them. Usually there is deep despair in the psyche. The student is sure that their need will never be fulfilled.

This impression is so strong because the feeling of being abandoned was imprinted in their guts when they were babies. Whenever a student is saying, "This will never be met. This will never happen," or "I will want this forever and ever," it inevitably reveals they are responding to an insatiable place of abandonment.

Their state may be calling for invocation of Ya Mujib and Ya Majid around the diaphragm. These Names can readily be paired because they both respond directly to the deepest needs. Consequently, if the spiritual students do a lot of breathing, relaxation, and calling out in prayer, a most wonderful transformation may occur. When they get in touch with their place of starvation more and more, they become able to call, "Ya Mujib, Ya Majid." (Al-Majid is treated in the following section.)

Now the center begins to open. It opens first as an infinite hole that feels it cannot be satisfied by anything. It is like a hungry ghost. You can eat and eat and take in whatever you like, but there is no response and no satiation. Intense dissatisfaction is burning in the center, around the diaphragm. In their unconscious, this feeling is very powerful.

Now, the engagement with the center has been accelerated, and along with their opening to feeling, they are fully opening into the experience of deprivation and abandonment. At this stage, the center begins to secrete abundance. It is infinite abundance. It becomes the mother to whatever the soul, the psyche, thirsts for. It is the giver, the responder, the supporter, and the nourisher.

All such qualities of abundance now open from this center. Ya Mujib in this way answers our prayers from the place of abandonment. It is the abundance that pervades everywhere, the *kawthar*. Now the center of abundance secretes sweetness, and inner milk start to flow in the system. A person feels complete satisfaction. You feel that the whole universe is really very giving, very responsive to your deepest wants and needs. You begin to secrete a kind of honeyed gold. When the center of infinite abundance opens up, a fountain of abundance secretes whatever the heart desires, and manifests the quality that you need in your daily life.

Ya Majid

(yaa ma-JEED)

"The outpouring of the sublime" is a simple phrase in English to express the divine quality of al-Majid. "Glorious" is a reasonably good synonym. The basic picture in the sound code is that al-Majid is a manifestation of a particular kind of superabundance into each thing and every thing. The Qur'an refers to the *'arsh*, or divine essence, which is also called the Heart Throne, as *majid*. Al-Majid must therefore include in its meaning the transcendental source of this sublime quality as well as its manifestation.

There are several particularly fecund references to al-Majid in the Qur'an that throw great light on its sacred quality, but before we look at these passages, we should lay some groundwork by examining various forms taken by the root of al-Majid (M-J-D) to get at some very physical aspects of its meaning.

The phrase *majadat-il-'ibl* reveals a physical-plane meaning: the camels fed on luxuriant, abundant pasture land so that they completely filled their bellies and satiated themselves in a way that allowed them to fully know it. The main point to be drawn from this usage is that the gift here is luxuriant and superabundant, and the one who receives the gift is fully conscious of it.

The noun form, *maajid*, simply means full satisfaction or satiation as a result of eating and drinking. Al-Majid, in all its roots, emphasizes both abundance and full knowing satisfaction. With al-Majid we are always conscious of the satiation that has been offered, but al-Karim is neutral on this point.

A second basic meaning of al-Majid can be found in the word *'amjada*. It is used in context in the following dictionary description: "In order to show them respect, honor, and dignity, the host entertained the guests with superabundant food, making sure they were completely satisfied."

An additional aspect is that it is part of your own honor to make sure that the guests are abundantly served and that they know you are respecting them. This is all part of spiritual etiquette or *adab*. Another form of this word, *'adaba*, means to invite to a banquet or wedding feast. For the one who has that manner, the whole world is Allah's banquet, and everyone is invited to partake of it.

There is nothing about al-Majid that is ambiguous. It is not accompanied by trial or by some hidden obstacle. It is fully apparent that the gift is coming from God, who is wholly good. The form that the word takes as a sacred Name, al-Majid, refers to the One who manifests flowing superabundance in such a way that all who partake of these gifts are consciously satiated by them. It also means bountiful, good, and beneficent.

How does the divine aspect of al-Majid manifest in the world? Presenting a few instances that have been described with this quality may help us to more deeply understand the gifts that this sacred Name brings. A first place to look is at the story of the two angels who arrive at the home of Abraham and Sarah. The angels bring a message from God that Abraham's wife, who is 90-something years old, will have a child.

Sarah laughs at this news, and it is for this laughter that her child, Isaac, is named. She says, "Shall I bear a child, seeing I am an old woman and my husband is an old man? This would be an amazing thing." The response from the angels is, "Are you amazed at what Allah does? His *rahma* and *barakah* (loving compassion and blessing) are gifts such that your future will be full of children. For Allah is *hamid* and *majid*."[150]

This extraordinary story reveals a fundamental quality of al-Majid. It brings gifts that amaze, astonish, and astound. They are wondrous and unexpected. God's compassionate nature reveals unexpected gifts that astonish the mind. That is the glory of al-Majid. Perhaps these gifts are ones that you would never even think to request because they appear so improbable. The result of this wonder-filled manifestation of al-Majid is the dawning of true gratitude, al-Hamid.

True gratitude is seen as we read the next verse in the Qur'an. It says that fear passed from the mind of Abraham, and the good news of that abundant gift fully struck him. One result of that amazing manifestation was that Abraham was able to discover previously unrealized attributes in his own heart, such as the incredibly gentle love of al-Halim, the quality of often turning to Allah, and others. These qualities were unveiled because of the astonishing gifts that came from al-Majid.

There is a second instructive Qur'anic reference to al-Majid.[151] In the first verse it is a description of the Qur'an itself. In the second verse it refers to the Prophet Muhammad, and says, "Are you amazed that someone came to you from among yourselves?"

Most of the commentators concentrate on the Qur'an itself being *majid*. But consider just how amazing it was for an illiterate shepherd to be the mouthpiece of this great ocean of wisdom. It is the most unlikely, uncanny, almost disturbing, wondrous, jolting event. Now that everything has become so institutionalized, it is hard for modern people to look back on history with the proper perspective. That a simple man from among the tribe, Muhammad, could come forth with this amazing recitation of the Qur'an, was a great reason to be lost in admiration and wonder.

Al-Majid is like the light of the rising sun. When it arises it illuminates your mental horizons and you are lost in admiration. Meanings become inexhaustible. The wider the horizon of your experience, the farther your spiritual eye can see. It is a beauty that none can tell who have not experienced it in their soul. It is an effulgence that manifests and enlightens. Sufis say that the meanings of the Qur'an are 70,000 in number, resembling the depths of the ocean, and to explore those depths one relies on the beauty of al-Majid.

The third Qur'anic reference is about the *'arsh*, the divine essence, which is also called *majid*.[152] This expands the meaning of al-Majid to include not only its manifestation but to point directly to the unique source of the quality as well. The gifts that are described as coming from this *'arsh* are very specific and particularly human: al-Ghafur and al-Wadud.

In this context, al-Majid is presented as the source of every instance of forgiveness as well as the source of the most human manifestation of intimate love. The transcendental essence amazingly shows up in these specific manifestations. In the next verse it is all connected with divine will.

These verses suggest all this transcendental superabundance amazingly acts continually in every time and place, without interruption. Without our even asking, and beyond our belief, we discover that the will of God is constantly manifesting the inexhaustible gifts of al-Majid from an infinite source.

There is another specific reference to the Qur'an that bears repeating, and which we discussed along with al-Hafiz in Chapter 11, Divine Protection. The Qur'an is called *majid*.[153] But where is the Qur'an located? *Fi lawhin mahfoodh*.[154] Its ultimate location is the inexhaustible source of all revelations, called "the preserved tablet."

The amazing source of the Qur'an is the transcendental source of all wisdom, whether written down or not. And in this instance, the Qur'an is just one historical instance of the superabundance of al-Majid. This passage strongly implies that the Torah is al-Majid as well as the Buddhist sutras, and so on.

Recitation of Ya Majid may naturally be given to those who are stuck in the mundane reality. They are overly literal, though they may style themselves as "realists." Caught in a life that is heavy and onerous, they fail to see the wonder that is manifesting in the universe. Prayerful invocation of this *wazifah* may help open the doors of perception.

A shadowy form that the root of the word takes, *tamaajada*, gives us another key for al-Majid's application in healing the human condition. *Tamaajada* is to attribute *majd* to yourself and your actions, and to the actions of your ancestors. In other words, *tamaajada* is to glorify yourself rather than God.

If people have this shadow, where they feel compelled to mention their own glorification, and be in competition to see who is the greatest, they most likely have serious issues of abandonment. They imagine that personal possession of great riches means they have been especially favored by God, and conversely that the lack of such riches by those in poverty means that such people are being punished by God.

Their attitude of competition is a cover over a deep wound of disconnection. One way that a person defends against the feeling of deprivation is by denying it, and that leads directly into pride. "I am better than you; I am of a better class." We strongly suggest pairing the two divine attributes Ya Mujib and Ya Majid in recitation, as an antidote for issues of abandonment.

Because the family of Abundance continues with more divine Names that deserve proper consideration, we will continue (and conclude) the subject in the following chapter.

wahhab

razzaq

ghaniyy

fattah

mughni

muqsit

chapter 19

Completing the Family of Divine Abundance and Contemplating it as a Whole

We originally thought to call this vast family of sacred Names the family of blessing, but we came to realize that abundance was a more inclusive term for the specific quality these Names all have in common. It then became apparent that more fully understanding divine abundance would give us a key for applying this whole cluster of Names to the specific needs of people suffering with feelings of neediness and isolation.

All human beings have issues of scarcity. Everyone goes through an experience of scarcity. At that time you may experience the universe as a place where there are no resources available to you, within or without. The different ways human beings come to isolation in their egos are caused by the particular kinds of experiences of scarcity.

Painful experiences of scarcity coagulate into a defining attitude of self, an attitude that is based on a sense of deficiency. There may have been scarcity in the environment you grew up in, or in your relationship with your mother, for example. This has led you to experience the universe as a place that lacks what you need. You don't know how to really be grateful because you are identified with being needy.

Contemplation of the whole family of divine abundance offers a great opening for all of us who have become caught up in identifying with neediness. Awakening to these generous qualities will challenge your habitual view of scarcity. By becoming aware of divine abundance, you can begin to bring your own personal experience of scarcity into a healing relationship with real abundance and generosity.

As written elsewhere, we recommend recitation of Ya Shakur as a starting point. By calling gratitude and thankfulness into your awareness, you start to shake up your habitual view of neediness. This is a good place to begin. However, it should eventually be followed up in more specific ways, as different Names in this family of abundance address scarcity with particular emphases.

A physician of the heart will know that anyone who feels the universe will not meet all their needs may react to this underlying wound by developing an attitude of feeling entitled to receive more than others. People whose identity is built around passionately believing that doors are not open to them sometimes choose to force entry and batter down these doors. On the other hand, the counselor will also encounter those who are bitter, shut-down, and resigned to do nothing about their state because they feel they deserve to be deprived and are unworthy of anything better.

Disconnection from the ever-abundant source can manifest in the personality in the form of grandiosity or depression. In both instances, the dysfunction and isolation of the ego are a result of the same thing—internalizing and identifying with your wounded condition caused by your experience of scarcity.

Calling forth the different Names of abundance allows isolation and alienation to dissolve, because the false self fades away in the light of the reality of the sacred quality. The spiritual counselor can be precise in the process with students by going into what happened in childhood and identifying at what stage of development they got blocked.

The child's soul, facing the confusing circumstances of incarnation, gets impaired or affected at different stages. The soul is bringing inherent qualities of abundance and blessing into existence, but this process often comes into conflict with the child's parents and home environment. When the soul faces daily conflict, the essential emerging quality that is expressing itself by bringing abundance to life subsides, and this retraction generates a vacuum.

The vacuum, or hole, that occurs when the soul is thwarted in some way attracts and invites ideas and emotions of scarcity, lack of support, lack of recognition, or lack of abundance to arise. The mind tries to fill up this gaping hole and, in the process, projects meanings—conceptualizations to which it becomes emotionally attached.

In general, human conflicts having to do with giving are connected with a person's inner relationship with the field of abundance. The answer to all such predicaments will come when one realizes that the divine source is generating and manifesting abundance continually and in a variety of forms. Such a realization allows you to consciously accept and connect with the source.

We hope that the kind of detailed investigation of each sacred Name in the abundance family that we have undertaken in this group of chapters will serve physicians of the heart to better identify the particular Names that could be most useful for a given person. What follows is a very incomplete list, to briefly offer examples of the kind of fine-tuning we are speaking about.

Invocation of Ya Wahhab is the antidote for the scarcity you feel when you believe nothing is flowing in your life. Ya Razzaq is the remedy for the feeling that the basic essentials of life are scarce. Ya Fattah is for the experience of everything being closed to you. Ya Mu'ti is the antidote for the feeling that the universe doesn't provide for all your needs.

Ya Karim answers where there is a scarcity of inner bountifulness or generosity. Ya Ghaniyy is the antidote for the experience that joy or meaning is missing in life. Ya Mujib is for the person who feels no one is willing or able to hear him or her. Ya Majid is an antidote for the scarceness of wonder in your life, and so on through the whole cluster of Names.

Six important emanations of Allah's abundance remain to be considered before we can complete our exploration of this vast and extraordinary family of Names. When we have done that, then we can address this entire domain of concentration and take a concluding overall perspective.

Ya Wahhab, Ya Razzaq, Ya Fattah

(yaa wah-HAAB, yaa raz-ZAAK̲, yaa fat-TAAH̲)

There is a wonderful inner and outer relationship between al-Wahhab, ar-Razzaq, and al-Fattah. These three embodiments of divine abundance appear sequentially in the lists of 99 Names and are inseparably grouped together, in part because they share the same form in the sound code. The first syllable has a short "a" sound, the middle consonant is doubled, and then a long "aa" is added after it. The sound code tells us that the activity of each one of these three qualities is repetitive, continuous, and unending. This is a very important similarity. Moreover, as we shall see, these Names naturally dovetail into each other.

One metaphor that has been given to express their meanings and interrelationship is to say that al-Wahhab is the free rain that is given to all, ar-Razzaq is the water that flows in irrigation ditches, and al-Fattah is all the fruit harvested from all the trees that have been irrigated. In other words, al-Fattah is the continuing action of all that will ever be accomplished. Images of rain and water are found in the varying root meanings of all three of these divine Names.

Another way of expressing the relationship is to say that al-Wahhab is like being freely given fish from a fisherman; ar-Razzaq is like learning the skill of fishing; and al-Fattah is like all the fish that you will ever get as a result. All three are ever-continuing gifts from Allah, but they embody a developmental sequence, and there are important nuances about the nature of each gift.

These Names offer a beautifully coordinated set of tools to address the human condition of felt scarcity. As we have seen in earlier chapters, in going deeper into understanding the nuances of meaning of the Names it is helpful to become attentive to the Names as words, in terms of their sound code, their grammatical forms, their roots, and other words formed from the same roots, including words that are associated with a disability or shadow. All of this information is a source of guidance that may suggest how to apply the Names as a remedy for human suffering.

Ya Wahhab

(yaa wah-HAAB)

Al-Wahhab expresses God's continuous giving of divine blessings. It is a giving that is without any attachment. The grammatical form of Al-Wahhab is an intensive, which emphasizes giving continually, universally, and without disruption. It is a free gift, with no expectation of recompense. There are no strings attached. You could say it is to give with the right hand without the left hand knowing.

The basic meaning of the verbal root of al-Wahhab is *wahaba*: to give or to bless, or to bestow something on someone freely with no intention of gaining compensation, recompense, or requital. The eighth form, *'ittahaba*, means to accept something as a free gift without any thought of an obligation to return something back. The fourth form of the root is *'awhaba*, which means to give a gift out of superabundance, fullness, power, ability, or capacity.

Some physical-plane forms that the root of al-Wahhab takes are also instructive as to particular aspects in the divine quality. *Mawhibah* is a cloud that rains freely on everything without distinction, because of its great abundance of water. *Mawhoob* is a child, or anything, that is given by Allah as a blessing.

A shadowy root form, *wahhibtu fidaka*, literally means "I make myself a ransom for you." In other words, I will sell myself into bondage and give away everything for your sake, in order to make you happy. In ordinary human affairs, this is indicative of a kind of codependency that generates martyrdom or self-sacrifice. It is also a product of a lack of felt abundance.

Another instructive shadowy form of al-Wahhab is *wanaan tu*, which means to delude oneself through the process of imagining. We can glean from this that repetition of Ya Wahhab may effectively deal with the mental plane. Often the crucial issue is a person's belief system rather than the actual facts of their reality. The problem may simply be that they believe there is scarcity and not that there actually is scarcity.

Here in America, we may think there is scarcity while our refrigerator and pantry are full of food. Yet most of us are constantly complaining or fearful about scarcity. We are conditioned to live in fear even when surrounded by relative abundance. Repetition of Ya Wahhab may help deal with the mental plane, with the obstacle to the experience of abundance that lies chiefly in our own belief systems.

Ya Razzaq

(yaa raz-ZAAK̩)

Ar-Razzaq may be used in connection with the actual reality of scarcity rather than our projections about it, which we saw with al-Wahhab. Many people really are poor and don't have food. Moreover, outward circumstances may be antithetical to people's needs in dramatic ways such as war, famine, and disease. One who realizes ar-Razzaq finds that God's continuing abundance is always a resource for them, regardless of outward conditions.

Ya Razzaq is the remedy for feeling that the basic essentials of life are scarce. Those in dire straits need to overcome the belief that because they don't have food, there is no abundance. When they invoke the quality of Ya Razzaq it gives rise to their God-given ability to find hidden resources to achieve success. A simple example would be finding the inner confidence and taking the initiative to draw water from the well, dig an irrigation ditch, and cultivate crops.

Calling on Ya Razzaq addresses our earthly condition of scarcity by realizing the quality of the One who continually sustains all. Through reflecting the quality of ar-Razzaq in ourselves we come to find that Allah provides sustenance for our physical needs. The straightforward meaning of ar-Razzaq is the One who continuously gives sustenance, who is always giving at every opportunity to benefit all people.

A shadowy form of the word, *rizqah*, means a wolf or bird of prey, a predator. Under the guise of giving sustenance, *rizqah* takes it back. Strings are involved in the giving, such as special interest lobbyists might employ. With such a wolf, or *rizqah*, there is no "free lunch." Their predatory attitude uses the quality of generosity as a cloak over ulterior motives. There is another shadowy form, *raaziqiyy*, that means to be weak and dependent on others. They think, "I don't have the capacity to make use of what opportunity presents to me, or I just don't know how to make use of it. Someone should do it for me."

As with the examples given earlier, when a word form of the root of a divine Name manifests a negative quality, we take it to suggest that that very Name is the remedy for such a condition. Through this kind of analysis, we understand that ar-Razzaq offers an answer to a more social kind of problem, rather than a problem that is particularly mental.

Repetition of Ya Razzaq addresses a kind of social codependence. You can experience being trapped in scarcity because of your social interactions. Then you feel you cannot have any resources that are independent from the scarcities of such a deficient society or relationship. Invocation of Ya Razzaq will be useful for one to develop skillful means of independence.

Ya Fattah

(yaa fat-TAAḤ)

Al-Fattah means both "to begin" and "to open." Through this Name, you begin to open your heart to the infinite possibilities of the divine presence. With al-Fattah, the opening is continuous. *Fattah* is the Arabic word for enlightenment. It is an enlightenment that is continuously happening.

Al-Fattah brings great power to clear the way of obstacles and open the path of your life for success. It is the One that opens the heart to love and ecstasy. A variation of the root, *al-Fatiha*, is the beginning or opening chapter of the Qur'an.

Al-Fattah refers to opening something with a key, and invoking Ya Fattah is a key to opening the heart to Allah and to finding the divine within. It is a very powerful Name, because even in the midst of despair it brings the possibility of opening up to love and ecstasy. Allah is opening up the veils of darkness over the heart to uncover the light within. The invocation of Ya Fattah sets up the dynamic process of going deeper and deeper in your opening.

A fifth-form variant of the root of al-Fattah, *tafattaah-an-nawr*, means to blossom. This is a beautiful image. Al-Fattah also means for buds to open up and blossom. The image of a bud opening, or flowers bursting forth, is a meaning that comes from the richness of the earth to enrich our understanding of this sacred Name.

Another good physical-plane meaning for al-Fattah is found in the divine invocation *ya miftah-ul-'abwaab*. God is called on as "the opener of doors." *Miftah* is a form of al-Fattah and *'abwab* means doors. The first doors to mention that it opens are the doors of Mercy and Compassion. They are universal and unrestricted.

The second doors are *ridwaan* and *sakeenah*—words that mean contentment, indwelling peace, and tranquility. They are mentioned in the Qur'an at 48:18. At 7:96, the third kind of door is mentioned. It is called *'abwab as-salaam*. That is the door of blessings (*barakah*) and complete peace. In invoking *Ya miftah-ul-'abwaab* you are calling on Allah to open those doors.

There is an eighth form of al-Fattah, *iftataha*, which means to invade, to conquer, to take or to win something by force. *Fattah* is an unusual word because it means to enlighten—literally to open up to light—but it also means conquest. And the tenth form variant, *'istaftaha*, is to demand to be opened. The yearning typical of the tenth form is intensified here into a demanding. When an army comes up to a city, they demand it to be opened to them. They *'istaftaha*.

Futhah is another form of the root of al-Fattah that shows the shadow. It is to boast, to brag, to make a vain or ostentatious display of what you possess of material wealth or of knowledge you have acquired. Parenthetically speaking, for a language without vowels, words like *fattah* and *futhah* are very problematical. Without the vowels being formally written, what the reader sees could be either word. That sort of thing is why 'ibn 'Arabi said that understanding Arabic is 90 percent context.

In the psychological realm, a person who has a lot of distrust and impatience must force things to happen. He or she feels, "I am entitled; I've got to have what is my right. If not, then I collapse, because if I don't get it, I feel like I must not be entitled, and therefore I am unworthy." Their response is to either force things to open their way, or collapse into self-pity.

This attitude can be seen in many travelers on the spiritual path. They react badly when the results they are looking for in their practice don't manifest, or when they don't get the outer recognition they seek. Entitlement issues arise, and they become pushy and aggressive.

It is essential for the physician of the heart to understand that the ego, because of deeply painful experiences, creates a separated and isolated identity. The deep pain is an occasion for self-pity, and, as there is the wish to avoid feeling the pain so much, it engenders a contraction into a defensive structure, which is expressed in different ways in the whole personality. The ego identifies itself with an idea of self it constructs because of self-absorption. It is a narcissistic identification with the painful experience, such as scarcity, which we are considering here.

The defense that is created can be based either on grandiosity or hopelessness. In both cases, the core condition of woundedness that is being defended is the same. What is needed for growth to occur is a positive realization of the divine quality—in this case divine abundance—that itself is the answer to their isolated condition.

When you specifically heal the woundedness regarding your own soul, a great personal enlightenment takes place. It is possible to speak of personal enlightenment and of impersonal or universal enlightenment. Personal enlightenment hits the specific constellation of the individual. It dissolves that individual constellation and then heals it. You begin to know your real self in this existence. You know it individually, and you can navigate life with balance, clarity, and grace. The other kind of enlightenment is cosmic in scope; it has to do with the absolute. Individual enlightenment has to do with the individuated soul.

Both realizations are very important, but—for cultural and psychological reasons—human beings often believe they can bypass the individual enlightenment, or they simply don't see it. In the family of divine abundance, many of the Names deal very specifically with the personal aspect, and with particular blind spots. It doesn't help to ignore this work, as these personal blind spots are major obstacles to the realization of cosmic enlightenment as well.

For example, from the psychological point of view, human beings who are afflicted in relation to al-Fattah want to force things to happen. They can be differentiated from those who are afflicted in relation to al-Mu'ti. This latter type is generally quite resigned and passive. They resist what is being offered, but it is the result of a passive state of disconnection.

Such disconnection occurs because of a belief and feeling that the universe is not open to them. For this kind of isolation, repetition of Ya Mu'ti is beneficial. Al-Mu'ti is a core Name for the whole abundance family, as it means the gift of God, and all the forms of giving can straightforwardly be known as gifts of God.

At one level, the feeling that the universe is not available may have originated in the feeling that one of your parents was not available. This evolves into a feeling that you are not entitled to anything, that no door will open for you. You have asked and been rejected. As a consequence, you have self-identified with that wound and feel hopeless and worthless. Calling on Ya Fattah turns this around and asks for the universe to open to you so that you can overcome difficulties.

Being in a hopeless state may also be a result of lack of trust, and Ya Wakil might be indicated. But, in the sense we are talking about in relation to the Names in the abundance cluster, we are looking at an attitude of entitlement that has arisen from the experience of scarcity. The physician of the heart is aiming for the student to realize that actually there is enough.

Ya Kafi is a divine Name that is often used in healing, though it isn't included on the canonical lists of 99 Names. In the Qur'an we read *'a laysa allahu bi kaafin,* "Isn't Allah enough for you?"[155] Al-Kafi is that abundance of God that is more than enough.

Let's briefly review some of the conditions to consider when prescribing Ya Wahhab, Ya Razzaq, and Ya Fattah. Ya Wahhab addresses a human disability that appears in the form of passivity, stuckness, and inertia, especially in the mental sphere. There is a belief and feeling that the abundance of the universe just isn't flowing in your life. Invocation of Ya Wahhab activates that flow. Your aggression toward the universe or God, which is a feeling that arises from a sense of entitlement, responds to Ya Fattah. And this is particularly true for students who feel entitled and are greedy in spiritual matters.

Ya Razzaq offers itself as a remedy to the pattern of exploiting people or constantly scheming to do so. The condition of ego to be healed is the habit of continually demanding from others. It is interesting that the bird of prey described earlier is a shadowy form of ar-Razzaq's root. Ya Razzaq also answers the condition of the person who is willing to wait for God to offer them the free gift of al Wahhab, but who is unwilling to marshal himself or herself to actively cultivate the resources that life is offering.

Grammatically, al-Mu'ti is a causative. It is the cause of all causes. All our shadowy responses to al-Wahhab, ar-Razzaq, and al-Fattah express blindness toward seeing the gift of God that is the cause behind all causes. In other words, when you are despairing that the universe isn't flowing for you, you don't realize what the cause of all causes is doing. When you are trying to manipulate people by scheming, you don't realize the true nature of the cause of all causes, Allah. And when you're trying to force the door open and storm the treasure house, again it is the same kind of blindness.

Therefore, al-Mu'ti is a core name that operates for the whole family of divine Abundance. It is discussed as the gift of God in Chapter 16, Names of Gratitude. There are two more very important Names, divine qualities that go right to the core, that we will discuss next.

Ya Ghaniyy, Ya Mughni

(yaa GHA-neeyy, yaa mugh-NEE)

Al-Ghaniyy and al-Mughni are central to the realization of the nature of divine abundance. Their sacred qualities directly address human alienation—the isolation of self that manifests as lack of joy and lack of meaning in life. These Names were discussed in Chapter 12, The Secret of Ecstasy, but they are important to understand in the context of abundance as well.

Al-Ghaniyy is the source of all existence or being, and it is the source of all ecstasy. Al-Ghaniyy is the treasure house or container of all existence, and it is manifesting existence to every single thing at all times. Its emanation is a flowing forth from the treasure house to all. Al-Ghaniyy is the One who gives existence to that which has no existence.

Al-Mughni is a fourth form, a causative. It is the ability of Allah to confer the state of embodying al-Ghaniyy to a person, so that they actually feel there is abundance and may become the instrument of its manifestation. Al-Ghaniyy is quite transcendent and al-Mughni is more immanent.

Invocation of Ya Ghaniyy is an antidote for the fixation that there are not enough riches or success in our life. It is a remedy for boredom and the experience of meaninglessness. It has an alchemical quality of transforming existence, uncovering the joy hidden within.

Al-Mughni has a metaphysically important and complex relationship with Al-Ghaniyy. Allah causes the state of embodying al-Ghaniyy to be bestowed on temporal creatures, who then can act as the embodiment of the infinite and inexhaustible reality. In this temporal way, Al-Mughni serves to give contentment, protection, and guidance to humanity from the essence, and that allows us to say that al-Mughni embodies the infinite and inexhaustible reality.

The source and primary cause of this core quality of divine abundance is al-Ghaniyy, and the manifestation of it is al-Mughni. Repetition of Ya Mughni is a remedy for the experience of dependence and neediness on another. We generally recommend repeating Ya Mughni paired with Ya Ghaniyy. With both Names there is a root meaning of dwelling in a place constantly. You have an essential place to be, and it gives you the comfort of being.

In repeating Ya Ghaniyy, there is a profound sense of spiritual alchemy. You're not trying to open any doors. You're not trying to make flow happen. You're literally not trying to do anything. The field you are concentrated on is transformed from within. There is a divine possibility inherent right in what the situation is offering that is the key, if only you can uncover the seed and transfigure it.

Realizing al-Ghaniyy is about being, not doing. Doing would suggest that you actually possess something. Unfortunately, what you think you possess is actually the fullness of your own nafs, or ego. Real being, however, requires you to realize the emptiness of your ego. Then the infinite richness of al-Ghaniyy can be revealed.

One set of meanings is very simple: Al-Ghaniyy means rich; Al-Mughni means enriching. Al-Ghaniyy is the one who gives riches. It is more like an oceanic experience, while al-Mughni is more like the wave experiencing itself.

In the Qur'an, "We found you in want and then gave sufficiency."[156] In the quoted passage, you are *fuqaraa'* (want) and Allah is *ghaniyy* (sufficiency). Al-Ghaniyy is richness and fullness. Your existence may seem to be empty of meaning, but al-Ghaniyy transforms it and fills it from within.

The Beatitudes of Jesus point to the same apparently counter-intuitive idea that to be empty of self is to be full of God, and to be puffed up in your sense of self is real poverty. The only way to realize wealth is to realize the inexhaustible treasure house of abundance. And to fully know that divine abundance, we need to realize the complete inner poverty of our own grasping ego-self. "Blessed are the poor, for they shall inherit the earth. Blessed are the poor in spirit for theirs is the kingdom of heaven."

There is a shadow form of the words in one of the variations on the root of al-Ghaniyy. *Wunyan* means self-satisfied and conceited. "He was made to feel as though he didn't need anybody else," which is a negative statement in a tribal society. It shows a lack of understanding of the truth of interdependence.

Following this lead, Ya Ghaniyy would be the antidote for the person who vainly insists, "Everything's fine. I'm just fine." Such a person cannot feel what they lack; they can't feel their own shadow. It is a phony kind of self-reliance, because you can't rely on the limited ego-self, the fabricated self. It will always let you down. It is easy to recognize it as a false individuality, because the individual sense you are experiencing is quite isolated.

In such a state, the centripetal force of the formulation of the ego is still revolving around woundedness, around what you need but haven't received. It's not safe to show your need. You have to say everything's fine. "I don't need anything; I don't need anybody." Recitation of Ya Ghaniyy, Ya Mughni helps all who are in that kind of wounded isolation to open up and see that the universe is really abundant. You can reach out and get what you really need.

There are people who are afraid to ask for help, even when they actually need help. They are afraid they will be rejected. In psychology, this is known as rejecting object relation. The child has the mother and father, and these beings appear to be abundant, but the child is feeling needy because he or she keeps being rejected. The child then feels weak and small, while believing the others are mighty. The child will sometimes deal with this by saying, "I don't need anybody. I'm going to make it on my own."

The child does this because the moment they reach out to others, they are bound to feel their smallness, their insignificance. So they deny their need. Or they might identify with their neediness. But in both cases they will not reach out. Their state has to do with being wounded around scarcity, and it is about entitlement.

Regardless of how the universe is experienced, as scarce or abundant, people who are marked by this wound don't know how to reach out and receive what is there. But the one who is comfortable with the emptiness and poverty of self is not afraid to reach out. The experience of wealth on the inside is different. It is like the hidden treasure of Allah. There is no need to show it off. It is enough to just be it.

The physician of the heart should always draw out the students who come with fake humility and fake poverty. Challenge them by saying, "You are so greedy! You have so much greed and you need to bring it out. But you need to direct it toward the right source. If you think you are contented in any way, check again. You are lying to yourself; you are lying to me. And you really need to see you are *so* greedy. Open the greed and want. Want as much as you can."

The counselor needs to do this because the student ultimately will not be satisfied with anything short of inheriting the Kingdom again. Unless you gain back everything, you will not be contented. What you gain is not much about material things. How much stuff do you actually need? However, every person wants the whole Kingdom! You want all the glory, you want all the love, you want all the freedom, and you want all the joy. So the physician of the heart should challenge them to desire.

Prayerful repetition of Ya Ghaniyy challenges the fake humility and the fake poverty, both of which are blatant ways for people to deny their own need. Their desire might manifest first as external. "I need this, I need that, I want this, I want that." At this stage, the traveler on the spiritual path begins to see these things as symbols of internal riches. At that point their wanting opens into truly wanting: "I want love, I want joy, I want peace, I want power, I want majesty. I want all! And only when I have all, will I be contented. Not when I deny it."

Contentment is reached when you attain the Kingdom. Less than that, and you are not contented because it is less than your divine inheritance. Your soul longs to realize and become the image and likeness of God, as affirmed in the scriptures. This very aspiration is a challenge to a certain concept of spirituality. Many try to be humble, but they achieve it by splitting off their sense of self from the source, which is certainly not spiritual, no matter how much they may argue that it is.

For the problems of false humility and the like, we recommend encouraging spiritual greed, and at the same time, calling on Ya Ghaniyy to transform this greed into greed for the Kingdom. It might be asked how spirituality could possibly be greed. Yearning is built into every cell, and yet we have failed to harness it and fulfill it. We need to be able to stay with the passion for the goal through all the un-fulfillment. We can awaken the flame of greed until it reaches the truly spiritual. When that occurs, we are directed toward the light of al-Ghaniyy, the source of all, the infinite treasure house of all existence and ecstasy.

That is what Sufi poetry often does. It tweaks that sense of desire and meets people where they are. So it speaks of drug-induced or alcohol-induced or sexually induced ecstasy. Speaking in the common vocabulary is a far more useful device than encouraging people to lie about their inner state and be in a state of denial.

Sufi poetry starts with human love, for example, and builds up to the portrayal of divine love. At the end of the story of the two greatest lovers, Majnun and Layla, he sees her and says, "You are not the Layla that I worship." In other words, the particular form is just a representation of the reality.

Greed and yearning are connected. Inherent in greed is the yearning. We have yearning and more yearning. There's a thirst in every cell. It is called 'ishq, the wine of love, and 'ishq is a universal attraction. Every cell is yearning to realize itself as God, and that is the full richness of al-Ghaniyy.

When every part regains its integrity, the wholeness of who you are connects with the richness that God has created in every particle that exists. To cultivate the inner richness, the paradox is that it is beneficial also to cultivate the material. When such integrity is restored, there is an experience of boundless bliss.

The root meaning of existence is ecstasy. The roots of both words are the same. What is most necessary for the spiritual traveler to do is to correct the distorted idea that the material realm is the source of the dispensation of richness. When you become empty of the clinging of self, existence is filled with the riches of al-Ghaniyy. Your heart becomes the real Aladdin's Lamp.

Ya Muqsit

(yaa MUK-sit)

Al-Muqsit is on the threshold between the Names of divine abundance and the Names of divine knowledge. It could rightly be placed in either family or in both. It will serve as a good transition to the knowledge family.

Al-Muqsit resembles two Names discussed earlier, al-'Adl and al-Majid. Al-Muqsit shares with al-'Adl the quality of being just, fair, and equitable, but unlike al-'Adl it is not viewed as an inherent quality. Al-Muqsit is a causative in the sound code; consequently, it pertains to being equitable, fair, and just in the giving or distribution of divine gifts.

Al-Muqsit is completely unlike al-Majid in one important respect. With al-Majid the receiving of the gift is immediately apparent to the one who has received it, as is its source. Al-Muqsit is completely the opposite of this. Here, you are usually quite unaware that you have received the bounty that emanates from God through this divine Name.

There is a cloud of unknowing around the equity of the gift you receive. That is to say, you can't see how what you received was really fair. This confusion is found in the first two forms that the root of al-Muqsit takes. These variations of the root can mean "a person distributed the property among them equally, fairly, and in a just way." But it is also true that the same words can mean the exact opposite, depending on the context in which they are used.

There is no ambiguity in *taqassata*, which is a fourth-form version of the word. Here it simply means they divided the thing among themselves with *qist*, which means with equity, equality, justice, and proportionality.

A second basic meaning of al-Muqsit is what can be called a person's lot in life. The way *qist* is seen here can be expressed as follows: Allah makes each one's lot in life to be a portion of the subsistence that is assigned to every created being. Such portion may be little or much. The point is that it is God who makes it the way that it is, and this essential quality of the giving is a subsistence that goes to every being. From our vantage point, however, the purpose is veiled as to why a particular subsistence is made great or made little.

We get an interesting clue to the mystery behind the way inequality is perceived when we look at two words from the dictionary. *Yakhfidu* means "makes it little," and *yarfa'a* means "makes it much." A hidden meaning connected with al-Muqsit is suggested by the fact that *yakhfidu* has the same root as the sacred Name al-Khafid, and *yarfa'a* has the same root as its opposite sacred Name, ar-Rafi'. These Names point to the mystery of how it is God's action that protects us by lowering us in our spiritual station, or *maqaam*, and exalts us by raising us in our spiritual station. These raising and lowering actions echo the mystery of greater or lesser subsistence.

A third basic meaning of *qist* is simply the balance or the scales. The basic image is that God's action is a raising and lowering of the scales. In the Qur'an we find, "O my people, give just measure and don't withhold from the people their due; and don't commit any injustice. That which is left to you by God is the best for you if you but believed."[157] In this passage, *qist*, which is the noun form of al-Muqsit, is used.

It occurs again where the whole universe—heavens and earth—is described as set up in a delicate balance.[158] It is a balance of the microcosm and the macrocosm. It applies equally on the scale of the whole universe and the scale of how people conduct their business, in the marketplace.

We read, "He sends down the Qur'an and also the balance."[159] The word for balance here is *furqaan*, which means inner discrimination. So the book itself is not enough. Inner discrimination is also needed. The heart's interpretive ability is required in order to receive the divine teaching.

After having warned against stealing the inheritance of orphans and enjoining believers to give full measure and weight to all that they do in justice, the Qur'an goes on to describe what that justice means.[160] This reference defines al-Muqsit. "This indeed is my way—symmetry, balance, and harmony." The conventional translation of *siraat-ul mustaqeem* has been "the straight path," but we think the words used above make the meaning more clear in English.

The universal application of *qist* can be seen in this verse: "To every people was sent a messenger, and when their messenger comes, the matter will be weighed among them with justice [*qist*], and not one of them will be oppressed."[161] All the messengers had this in common—they manifested a book with an inner and outer balance so that the people who received it might stand forth and embody justice.

Invocation of Ya Muqsit calls on the one who is the ultimate cause of divine gifts. All these gifts are apportioned in a just and equitable manner. This just apportionment is affirmed to be true, even though we can't always easily perceive the divine source in the particular forms that it manifests.

Doing everything in a balanced way applies to more than just the marketplace. Acting in a just and equitable way is motivated by mutual love and by love of wisdom. In the Qur'an, after another warning about devouring other people's property, we are told that when we are asked to make a legal decision between two disputants to do it with wisdom (al-Hakim) and equity (*qist*) because "Allah loves the *muqsiteen*," those who manifest this quality of al-Muqsit. "Do this for the love of Allah."[162]

This passage demonstrates the generosity and abundance of the divine quality al-Muqsit, and also shows universal love. The general meaning of al-Muqsit is a seeking of proper balance within the context of universal divine love.

From the perspective of human growth, al-Muqsit provides the perfect opportunity to go into some psychological issues that are based on getting your full share and are about fairness in general. In the family situation and in the student/teacher relationship it often seems that someone else is getting more attention, or is just getting more.

In the child's psyche, coming to make this accusation is the result of a wounded condition. Each child is a unique being and needs to be mirrored in a unique way. Each soul brings a constellation of qualities. One child brings a great feeling of power, another incredible sweetness. Different children have different soul inclinations. Often parents miss out on seeing and accepting the soul station of their child, or of their different children.

Not being seen, not being known, not being truly mirrored, makes for the formation of a narcissistic constellation. From the beginning, there is a deep wounded feeling from not being clearly seen. You feel that there must be something wrong with you or you would be seen, so out of self-pity you then narcissistically identify with your assumed sense of deficiency.

Regardless of how fairly love and attention may be given, the child is always feeling wounded in a certain way. Life is not fair, and they feel that they are not receiving what they specifically need. And what they really need is for somebody to see the uniqueness of who they really are, and to nourish that uniqueness so their soul can develop whatever capacity it needs.

Each soul comes into existence to do something. We might say it comes to heal a pattern of karma and to evolve certain aspects of divine perfection. But if there is a prevalent wound about things not being fair, not being distributed fairly, it gives birth to envy and jealousy. Such people always see that others get whatever they want, but, as for themselves, they do not.

Others have the "right" mother, the "right" father, and the "right" companion, but the wounded one never gets what they really want. The fundamental problem is that what they really want cannot be provided by any external thing. That is because, in a very basic way, they themselves were not mirrored from the beginning about the nature of their soul and about their basic needs. The result was a deep narcissistic wound around not being seen.

That wound cannot be met by any other mirroring. It can only be met when the wound is opened and, at the same time, when the necessary quality that they have lost touch with because of not being seen is reached. It is a quality they very much want to preserve their fractured connection with. And when, by grace, that quality is truly reached, you feel, "I have finally been restored to what I came here with, and from here I can start life anew." A determined yearning to know what you really need has led you to this point.

Now you awaken to the uniqueness of your soul, and when that happens, you feel justice has taken place. Nothing short of this will heal your fundamental sense of injustice. A spiritual practitioner learns to bring this whole constellation of feeling into their invocation of Ya Muqsit. "Where is my share in existence?"

By really bringing up this question, the intensity of feeling that comes from opening to your inner wound is brought into a process of relationship with al-Muqsit. As this relationship deepens, you see that what it means to discover what you call your share comes from truly connecting to your soul station, your core reality. It has nothing to do with getting some material thing or some outer recognition.

When you become aware of what your soul came in with then al-Muqsit provides you with a view of life that is truly balanced. The universe really is abundant. It meets everyone exactly in the way they need to be met. The universe is a giant mirror, and it will mirror back to each being specifically what they need.

There is an important lesson here for spiritual guides in their relationships with students. Unless you are absolutely abundant, and capable of mirroring back the specific core of that person at any moment—which is beyond the ability of most any teacher—you are going to run short, just as most parents do.

It is important for the teacher to accept that they may be unable to mirror back the student's inner core. When they understand this fact, it can assist with healing the teacher's own narcissistic need. The narcissistic need of the teacher is that they have to be seen as always having all the answers, as being all-mirroring. So they need to take an inner pause and say, "I really don't know. I cannot be that all-mirroring."

And when teachers let go of their attachment in this regard, they have pulled out from being the narcissistic supplier. Then the student is allowed to fall into their own hole. They fall into a place of deep woundedness about the loss of the specific quality they need but don't know how to reach.

The moment they fall in the hole, then al-Muqsit can begin to activate, bringing them the right emanation, the right connection. Allah, as al-Muqsit, is mirroring back exactly the very nature of their soul. This soul is golden; this soul is generous. It is the majesty of each individuated soul that is being seen and that shows itself.

It becomes clear that invocation of Ya Muqsit is beneficial for bringing inner harmony and balance to life. It involves acceptance of your lot, be it high or low, as being a gift of God. Its repetition may be particularly helpful for those who complain endlessly about the injustice of the distribution of divine abundance. Invocation of Ya Muqsit will help to bring awareness of the divine gifts that are offered but have been hidden by outer appearances.

It is natural for the question to arise: If everything is so equally and justly distributed in the universe, why does life often appear so unjust? There are many such questions of knowledge that will be addressed as we turn our consideration to the large cluster of Names that embody that divine quality. Al-Muqsit provides the perfect transition for this, but before we begin consideration of the Names of knowledge, we want to offer a vision of the whole cluster of divine abundance as an essential domain.

The Essential Domain of Divine Abundance

As we come to the last phase of our narrative about the cluster of divine abundance, we think it may be helpful to offer an overview from a visionary perspective. There exists what, for lack of a better name, we are calling ultimate source. It is an unlimited field. The field gets differentiated through various mechanisms, analogous to prisms and lenses. The underlying neutrality of the field is transformed, and it generates energy as well as all its structures and variations.

The vibrational emanations we are considering in this cluster of divine abundance are very powerful attributes of being. They reflect the birthright of the soul. A field in our hearts should be illuminated with them and allowed to radiate throughout every aspect of our lives.

It helps to visualize this cluster of seven or eight Names of divine abundance as a great chandelier. This gives you a way of feeling a whole gestalt of qualities as an illuminated field. Being able to light up the whole chandelier means beginning to function at another level. Holding such a full constellation of related qualities simultaneously enables you to have a more direct, immediate, and experiential realization of divine abundance.

These kinds of experiences allow for the emerging actualization of an archetype of divine abundance that can function in your psyche. Connecting with this archetype enables you to sense, and become actively engaged with, the totality of a whole domain. It moves you beyond just dealing with one attribute or another.

When the physician of the heart knows that a student is working within a particular domain—abundance or power, for example—they can hold the whole field for the student while the student deals with the different specific attributes of the domain. This is in line with the intention of the physician of the heart that students be encouraged to integrate the whole grand domain of God's being.

This stage of rising to the consciousness of an essential domain can be a great time of transition for the traveler on the spiritual path. An essence that has been mysterious and hidden is unveiled. You know in the most direct way that it exists. Before this happens, the 99 Names are seemingly ungraspable. Now you can see them all the time. The Abundance family shines as the light of a many-jeweled chandelier.

As soon as you begin seeing the Names as clusters, you begin the construction of a gestalt. In the beginning, the student may take one Name, or another, or a pair. Later the physician of the heart may encourage them to put the families of qualities together and affirm them as a constellation, as we have described with the domain of abundance. All the jewels are pulled together, and a kind of inner vehicle gels and becomes defined.

If the teacher and student can go through this process together, those vehicles will activate. This should not be rushed. Inner preparation and careful attention are called for at this stage. Putting the Names into clusters is one way of preparing students for this large leap, where they may feel the gestalt of a whole domain as their field of awareness.

chapter 20

In Quest of Wisdom
—Inner and Outer Knowledge—

Divine emanations of knowledge, omniscience, guidance, wisdom, and truth, seen as a whole, form one of the largest clusters of Names. In our investigations of this cluster, we discovered the quality of wisdom was always present as an essential element in each particular Name. Every one of this grand array of qualities leads us toward a wisdom that is both discerning and healing. The cultivation of such wisdom by those who would become physicians of the heart is a central intention of this book.

This vast field of knowledge/wisdom needs to be given proper respect, and not treated in a survey manner. The next series of chapters is dedicated to a systematic exploration of this family of divine Names. We will discuss the invocations of Ya Shahid, Ya Khabir, Ya Warith, Ya Ba'ith, Ya 'Alim, Ya Muhsi, Ya Hasib, Ya Raqib, Ya Sami', Ya Basir, Ya Hakim, Ya Hakam, Ya Nur, Ya Haqq, Ya Mulhim, Ya Hadi, and Ya Rashid.

Perfecting Inner and Outer Knowledge

We begin with two divine Names that many scholars and commentators say represent outer and inner knowledge. Ash-Shahid is knowledge of the outer world and al-Khabir is knowledge of the inner world. The interplay of these two Names will lead us to al-'Alim, a transcendent Name for knowledge that contains them both. Omniscience must embrace both the inside and the outside.

Ya Shahid

(yaa sha-HEED)

Ash-Shahid, the knowledge that arises from the senses, is a good place to start. One popular misconception should be addressed at the outset. In the Qur'an the two linguistic forms, SHA-hid and sha-HEED, are used interchangeably, and the differently stressed syllables are not significant. For example, in verse 12:26 both forms are used: "One of the witnesses [*shahida*] gave evidence [*shahid(un)*]."

In classical Arabic, SHA-hid means the source of all knowing through the senses, and sha-HEED means knowledge's infinite manifestation. In the verse above, the source is the witness, and the manifestation is the evidence. Neither form of the word means "martyr." Wild explanations have been given for why martyrs later came to be called sha-HEED, but regardless of what later occurred linguistically, we can unequivocally affirm that in classical Arabic the two forms of the word are roughly equivalent cognates.

Ash-Shahid immediately directs us toward outer knowledge. Let's look at some of the concrete forms that the root of this sacred Name takes. *Shahida* is a verb that means being an eyewitness and openly declaring that experience of witnessing. *Shahid* means a being who knows by seeing clearly with open eyes.

Another basic meaning is given by the form *shahud*. This means one who is present, and is opposed to *ghareeb*, which means one who is absent. The form *'ashhada* means to cause to be present, or to cause to witness with the five senses. Knowledge of the visible world, ash-Shahid, is related to *mashhood*, which means the present moment.

There is no need to belabor how easy it is to become trapped in the surface knowledge of the material world. This world is called *dunyaa* in Arabic, from *dun*, meaning whatever is near. Humanity does not make the best use of its God-given faculties of hearing, seeing, and intellect. Limited by the outward appearances of things, we don't use these faculties to seek a deeper kind of knowledge, and our lack of gratitude for the gifts we have received limits us still further.

Our limitation is naturally contrasted with Allah's unlimited knowledge of all surface things. The Qur'an says, "To Allah belong all the things of heaven and earth, and Allah is witness to all things without limitation."[163] In other words, there is no limitation to God's *shahid*, as compared to mankind's *shahid*, which is marked by heedlessness.

To become unstuck from the snares on the path of knowledge, the spiritual traveler needs to do some form of *shahaadah*: Each one needs to bear witness to God's reality. A kind of dissolution of the lower self, or *nafs*, is required to do this. Such *fana* may lead to complete union. After union, God becomes the eye through which one sees and the ear through which one hears, as described in the Qur'an.[164]

"Their hearts and eyes are transformed so that nothing diverts them from the remembrance of Allah."[165] Continual *dhikr*, or remembrance of God, is the method that transforms our hearts and eyes to see through the outer world into the inner world and so overcome the traps of outer knowledge. *Dhikr* transforms any heart and ear so that it gives witness, *shahid*, to the depths of reality.

Another method of transformation is called *ziyarah*, which is travel for the sake of knowledge, and usually involves visiting the tombs of saints. "Do they not travel through the land so that their hearts and minds may learn wisdom and their ears may also learn to hear? For truly, it is not the eyes in their head that are blind, but the eyes of the heart in their breast that are blind."[166] By traveling in search of knowledge, the eyes of the heart may open.

A last method of transformation is contained in the teaching "die before you die." The Qur'an refers to *khalq jadeed*.[167] Allah has the capacity to renew creation with every breath. This is both a suggestion about the nature of time and a teaching about dying before you die. What this dying and renewing of creation leads to is explained in the next verse: "After the dark suggestions of the nafs are quieted, one realizes the reality of 'We are nearer to him than the rope of the vein in the neck.'"[168]

These are just some of the methods for approaching God's shahid. The word for transformation, *taqallub*, and the word for heart, *qalb*, come from the same root. In fact, one of the Names of God is Ya Muqalib, al-Qulubi and it is said at the end of some prayers. Al-Muqalib is the one who transforms hearts and eyes.

The fruits of this transformation into God's shahid are great. Transformers, or angels, are described as ash-Shahid.[169] *Al-'insaan kaamil*, or complete human being, is also called ash-Shahid.[170] Finally, Allah is described as ash-Shahid.[171]

"On that day we shall raise up [ba'ith] from every religious community ['ummah] a *shahid*."[172] This is a universal statement, which is later repeated.[173] At 5:120, Jesus speaks: "I was a witness to my community when I was with them, but you [Allah] are the witness for all times and places."

In all this, we see ash-Shahid in its fully expansive sense. Allah witnesses (*shahida*) Allah's own reality. "We shall show the signs on the furthest horizons, and in themselves, until it is clear to them what is reality (al-Haqq). Is it not enough for them that Allah is *shahid* over all things?"[174] In other words, our inherent ability to use the faculties of the five senses allows us to decipher the appearances of multiplicity and reach unity.

The whole path of divine knowledge is an uncovering of reality, an uncovering of al-Haqq. Basically there is a present moment in time, *mashhood*—which comes from the same root as *shahid*. Through the power of ash-Shahid, you can penetrate a moment and go to the center of the universe.

You arrive at the center of a circle where you are united with the source of knowledge. You look out to past, present, and future. From the center, you see that God is manifesting in every direction. That is ash-Shahid in an infinite sense. Perfecting this awe-filled witnessing with the eye of the heart is the Sufi practice of *mushaahidah*.

Understood in this grand sense, ash-Shahid would be to view everything simultaneously in the whole time and space continuum. From the standpoint of spiritual awakening, it is seeing God everywhere you look. God, the only being, plays all the parts. Several hadiths report the Prophet Muhammad said something to the effect: I literally saw God in the form of Mister so-and-so. And I saw God in the form of this and that.

Such a process of seeing, which in the hadith mentioned above is a vision described by the Prophet Muhammad, is exactly what *mushaahidah* is. The divine attribute ash-Shahid opens us to see God within every form everywhere, without exception. It is seeing the essence of God with the eye of God.

The vastness and inclusiveness of such an experience calls to mind the image in the Bhagavad-Gita where the God-realized being, Sri Krishna, in response to a request, shows the true face of his universal form to Arjuna, and that face reveals every form, both beautiful and terrible. It is all so awe-inspiring and overwhelming to Arjuna that he then says, "May I please just have back your kind and familiar face?"

In Sufism, the process of transformation into witnessing with the eye of God is described in three stages: *mukaashifah, mu'ayyinah,* and *mushaahidah,* which vary as to the characteristic duration of the state. In *mukaashifah* the discovering and uncovering are momentary. In *mu'ayyinah* they are more enduring, and in *mushaahidah* the awareness or vision of Allah becomes continual.

These levels are illustrated in three Qur'anic verses. Verse 50:22 speaks of removing the veil and overcoming heedlessness through remembrance of the divine reality in recitation of the Name. Your sight *(basaruka)* becomes keen, the eye of the heart opens, and you are able to penetrate into the deeper levels of reality, even though it is temporary. Then you fall asleep again.

The next stage is described at 57:4: "Allah is with you wherever you are, and Allah sees everything you do." This is more intimate. There is a palpable feeling of "with-ness." Now there is more sense of the eye by which you see, and there is more consistency of seeing into the inward phenomena from the outward.

Finally, illustrating the ultimate stage of *mushaahidah*, where a being reaches the center and becomes a *shahid*, there is the famous Qur'anic verse 2:115: "Whatever and whichever way you turn, there is the very face of Allah, for Allah is al-Wasi' and al-'Alim, infinitely embracing and all-knowing."

According to 'ibn 'Arabi, a truly enduring state of consciousness is seeing the world with two eyes. One eye knows the temporal and the other the eternal. Bringing these two realms into view simultaneously elicits a compassionate response. "The function of every *shahid* is to be a mercy to all the worlds."[175] Ultimately speaking, "only Allah is *shahid* in truth, in reality [*bi-l-haqq*]."[176]

Ya Khabir

(yaa ḵha-BEER)

In the previous section we saw that outward knowledge, ash-Shahid, ultimately leads the knower in stages from a place of limitation to the fullness of God's knowledge. As we look at inner knowledge, al-Khabir, we will see a similar kind of transformation taking place.

It helps to start with some physical meanings of al-Khabir. The form *khabara* means to plow the land, to furrow the land for sowing. So the very common name *khabir* means a tiller of the earth. Soft tilled soil is called *khabaar*. Metaphorically, it is easy to see that hard-packed soil is a surface phenomenon, and one breaks through this hard outward world of appearances in order to pierce the veil and go into the deeper, softer soil, *khabaar*, of the unseen worlds.

With much care, planting, and harvesting, a proper cultivator gains the fruits of inner knowledge. Another interesting physical-plane form of this root is *khubrah*, the savory food one carries on a journey. It becomes clear that inner knowledge nourishes us on the path, as the ultimate goal of all journeys is Allah.

Khabr means a field where a tree is growing. It appears in the Qur'an: "A good word is like a good tree whose roots grow deep into the earth, firmly fixed, and its branches reach up toward heaven; it brings forth its fruits at all times, or without season."[177]

Later, in Surah *Najm* (The Star) we get a description of the highest heaven, and another image of a tree. The Prophet Muhammad on his night journey or *miraj* is brought near a lote tree at the utmost boundary of the heavenly realm. The lote tree is covered in an unspeakable mystery. "His sight never swerved, nor did his heart, for truly he did see the greatest sign (*ayat-ul-kubraa*) of Allah."[178] Through the *dhikr* of the heart the complete human being journeyed deep into the unseen worlds, and brought forth the fruit of complete inner knowledge.

Some extended meanings of al-Khabir from the dictionary serve to complement all of this. The form *khabara* means to test something, to make a trial of a thing: to experiment with anything in order to know its inner reality or essence (*dhat*), and to know the nature of its connection with reality (al-Haqq).

"And we shall test you and those among you until we know who strives to their utmost and who preserves in patience, and we will test your knowledge of the unseen worlds."[179] There is a play on words in this verse. *'Akhbaara-kum,* which means *la'akhbaranna khabarak,* means, "We will assuredly know what you know." But it also means, "We will assuredly test or prove the inner reality of your state, by testing the outward manifestations of your apparent knowledge."

By a kind of divine testing of the outer information attained by the five senses, you are able to gain knowledge of the reality of the unseen inner state. What is being tested is the veracity, or correspondence, between your inner and outer state. One who is verified in this way is called *saadiq*, which is one of the highest forms of being a *waliyy*, or saint. At this stage, outward appearances never contradict the inward state.

The second extended meaning from the lexicon is the main one people have heard. It is to know the internal, inner, secret mystical essence of a thing in the light of absolute reality. *Makhbar* is the place of inner knowing. *Khabbara* and *'akhbara hu* both mean to inform someone or tell them something of the reality of their inner state of which they were previously ignorant.

Al-Khabir also deals with inward subtleties: "those who believe and have been granted degrees of mystic knowledge."[180] Mystical knowledge is deeper and deeper by degrees, and these degrees culminate with al-Khabir. In consideration of this, levels of subtlety are emphasized in the description of these degrees, rather than the contrast between outer and inner knowledge.

These subtle degrees of knowledge are emphasized and articulated by the frequent pairing of al-Latif and al-Khabir throughout the Qur'an. Reciting Ya Latif, Ya Khabir is recommended for accentuating subtle openings in the realm of inner knowledge.

Another example of the subtle mysteries of the unseen, as they are contrasted with outer appearances, is *tukhbiru 'an majhoolihi mar'aatuh*. This means that a person's outward appearance—that which is visible to the outward eye—informs one of their true inward state. A hadith says: "A believer is a mirror for a believer." That is why the outward reality of the spiritual teacher can inform students of their own inner states.

Finally, in this journey through the different forms taken by the root of this Name, we come to the particular form that appears in the list of 99 Names, al-Khabir. As the sound code tells us, it is intensive. Al-Khabir means to have a deep inner knowledge of everything, individually and totally, without exception. Such inner knowing is in the light of absolute reality and is described as an all-encompassing presence.

Past and future are aspects of the realm of al-Khabir, the unseen world. The word for historian in Arabic is *'akhbariy*. Knowledge of the future is also a dimension of al-Khabir. The word *khabr* means future harvest. It is the seed crop.

Those saints who are called the friends of God do not have fears of the future or the past. How is it, then, that the traveler on the path gets stuck in relation to the quality of al-Khabir? An underlying mistake is to divide reality (al-Haqq), which is ultimately one, into separate parts, and then to understand these separate parts as having an independent reality.

In a specific way, the mistake is to take past, present, and future as separate things, and then to get mired in one of these dimensions. In al-Khabir it is possible to get stuck in the notion of the separation of the unseen world. Spiritual practitioners easily become elitists about mysticism, and as a result, they often place physical phenomena in a lower category of reality than what they experience within.

Next we will look more deeply into this and other problems, as we explore applications of al-Khabir and ash-Shahid to conditions in the human psyche that are in need of healing.

Psychological Applications of ash-Shahid and al-Khabir

What limitations, disabilities, and disconnections in the human condition directly relate to ash-Shahid and al-Khabir? To answer this question, it helps to focus on the nature of our attachment to the world and our rejection of the world.

When you are extremely attached to the world, that attachment obscures your view and you are unable to see the world as a divine manifestation. It is very limiting to think that there is nothing more than this world, that this world is all there is. Mired in that perspective, it is not surprising that you carefully observe all the various forces of this realm, including the actions of corporations and governments, and what you mainly witness is the motive of getting whatever you can and putting your interests above everyone and everything else.

The opposite condition to being utterly attached to the world is rejection, or renunciation, of the world. You sever your relationships. Carried to an extreme, you become convinced that the world of the five senses is unreal. This can be a strong tendency in the approach of certain spiritual schools. However, if you make that claim, you get stuck with the job of describing the "reality" of what is unreal. After all, it is real enough to us. Most importantly, however, those who choose to renounce the world often are denying the world as a kind of escape or splitting off from their difficulties of being in the world.

From the psychological point of view, the extremes of attachment and renunciation present the same problem, and can be traced to the same root cause: the incomplete bonding children have with their parents. They lack a sense of belonging with their basic family members. Something fundamental is truly missing.

Those who are overly attached to the world usually suffered from not getting enough bonding in their childhood. Their relationship with their parents was unfulfilling, and they came to think that by grasping the world as hard as possible they would somehow get fulfillment. But the more they grasp at it, the greater they fix upon the surface appearances as the only thing of importance, the more they lose sight of the world as a divine manifestation.

When, however, through spiritual processes, those who are overly attached to the world begin to let go of their attitude of clinging and grasping, then they begin to feel just how much they have missed in their childhood. Now they come to recognize that all the objects in the world will not give them what they really need.

The other ones, the ones who thoroughly renounce the world, usually have experienced rejection in their families. They never became attached in a healthy way. They were not loved or honored. Consequently, their psyche pushes everything away, because anything that gets in close might lead to the anguish of experiencing the gaping hole of unfulfilled relationship.

This force of pushing away the world creates a split in the fabric of the self. They cannot see the physical manifestation as divine nor are they able to accept the unity of all spheres. If their family also was fractured, Mom against Dad, or parents were absent, that aggravates the problem further and leads to the phenomenon of splitting off, or to a continual desire for differentiation.

When the physician of the heart prescribes Ya Khabir to a student suffering from the difficulties of attachment or rejection that we have described, it will lead them to a discovery of deep splits that happened in their being. These are deep divisions that ultimately separated them from Being itself.

Al-Khabir answers this great need with the wisdom that arises from the oneness of things. Recitation of Ya Khabir first reveals your internal relationship of disconnection. It brings up your fear about entering the unified field. You are afraid to go inside. And when you do go inside, you experience deep fragmentation in your being. Your head and your body are not together. Your heart and your genitals are not together.

Looking inward, you begin to face these divisions, this splitting. When you go deeper still, you see that you have become disconnected from the unifying force. If you reach that realization, then the unified field will begin to integrate you.

Recitation of Ya Shahid, Ya Khabir together will work toward healing both of these types of affliction. Clinging to the world and aversion to the world express similarly limited relationships to the world. Bringing together the opposite poles of God's knowing, through recitation of these two Names allows each person to relate to the world the way it is, as a beautiful manifestation of the absolute God reality, differentiating itself in all forms and embodiments, within and without.

Both clinging and aversive types of people are always looking at differences instead of looking at the unity of things. They always want to split off the unpleasant and gain the pleasant. They focus on differentiation: "this is me, this is you, this is here, this is there." People who are absorbed in such a way are usually quite stuck in their lives. From the standpoint of developmental psychology, they may be stuck in the first week or two after birth.

Between birth and three weeks, babies generally are in a space of undifferentiated reality. They feel and perceive the unity of all, but they don't know what is their hand and what is their mother's hand, or what is their body and what is their mother's. They see it all floating and in a field of luminosity. How they hear can be compared to the muffled sound heard when you are deep in the ocean.

They don't even see or hear reality the way we think of it as adults, as their senses are not so much separated from Being. Adults who are stuck in this developmental stage did not achieve a healthy differentiation from the mother, which is a foundation for individuation. They are disturbed by what they feel is missing in them and continue to seek differentiation, remaining driven to split off from unity.

Repetition of Ya Shahid uncovers your external relationship with knowing. It shows the way you grasp at things. You begin to see how much you are projecting your object relation into the world. Your object relation is established by what happened to you with your parents. Such projection is a common occurrence. You look at a house and the house is not a house, because it represents Mother. You will interact with the house according to how you thought about your Mother, and thus you may reject the house or get attached to the house, and so on.

When you begin to see what it is that you are projecting in the world, what you are projecting in relation to your teachers, what you are projecting in the environment you live in, you understand that you are not seeing what is manifest as it really is. You are seeing your own inner projection. It is your mother or your father. Whatever happened to you is projected onto the object, whether the object is human or not.

Spiritual wayfarers become able to see how much they are projecting their unconscious on the here and now, and then they understand that their projection is actually not what is truly present. The veil of projection then begins to dissolve, and they begin to see what is here for what it is. At this stage, the universe is illuminated with the light of God, with the perception of God. As the veil is removed, the luminous presence of Allah's witnessing capacity comes through each person's perception.

At such a time, you see the pure wonder of what a tree is, what a human being is, what all of this manifest world of colors and dimensions is. It becomes a magical manifestation, and this leads to the perception of how the unified field of the only being is individuating itself in an infinite variety of forms. These forms are generally not seen in such a way because of the associations you give them and your reactions to these associations.

Once spiritual travelers see that they are not relating to the world in its suchness, but instead from their subjectivity, then the veil begins to thin out. That thinning of the veil opens you up to ash-Shahid. You are witnessing what is present through its realness, its thatness, and not through the lens of what you have projected upon it. Such a one can truly bear witness to the existence of God when they recite the *shahaadah: 'Ashhadu 'an laa 'ilaha 'illa allah.*

Each person's psychological lens is the veil of object relation. You are projecting the past, or projecting your mind, on the object that is here. It is your particular lens. When this limitation is removed, then you are graced to see through the real eye of awareness. 'Ibn 'Arabi says that when the transformation takes place, and the tongue and the eye become the tongue of God and the eye of God, then that is the only time that you can fully witness the oneness of Allah.

As long as your *shahid*, your witnessing of Allah, is through the lens of your separation, it may be a conceptual act of witnessing but it is not the real thing. Ultimately, Allah is the witness of Allah's own existence. It is an all-inclusive and therefore ultimately self-referential world with no "other" as a possibility.

There are several fragmentations that result in a person not having a wholesome and integrated relationship with the world. An ascetic who sees the inner world in detail, but can't handle the outer world, has an exaggerated form of this inability. They reject the world because they see it as a bad or unreal place. The problem lies in their relationship with al-Khabir.

They have become absolutists. They believe the absolute is the only truth, and the relative is not truthful. So they renounce ash-Shahid and they attach to al-Khabir. They don't want to be the *shahid.*

Whenever ash-Shahid comes, they create an inner veil, and that veil may be very powerful. It may even take the semblance of the absolute itself. But even so, it is differentiated: there is the observer and there is the absolute.

They are lost in the veil of the absolute. It's a very strange phenomenon. They think there is no veil because they are seeing the absolute, but there is a filter, a subtle filter in which they say they don't exist and only the absolute exists. Yet they are still subtly there, and that is what creates the veil of differentiation, the inner and the outer. They go all the way to the inside, to the absolute, as a way of trying to be only al-Khabir and to renounce ash-Shahid. But this is bound to fail, because ultimately there is no experience of al-Khabir without Ash-Shahid.

Most people, however, are so much on the outside, so much about witnessing this world and attached to their notion of ash-Shahid, that they strongly resist turning inward to see the source of it.

In practice, a physician of the heart has several ways to proceed.

When a student is entangled with the external, the counselor may begin to actively work with the student in that externalization. What is the student specifically doing? What are their projections? Then the student can begin to see that they are projecting on the world and are seeing through their own projections.

On the other hand, when students hide inside and declare that they don't exist, the physician of the heart should show them how they exist in all kinds of subtle ways. They are really there, but as a very subtle ego, an ego that has subtle preferences—such as that the absolute is the only thing, the only truth.

That belief creates an identity, an identity that believes it is the absolute, but it doesn't see that it is separated, really separated. When that separation, or splitting, is seen precisely and removed, then the lens of separation is dissolved.

In dealing with both of these kinds of disabilities, the physician of the heart must lead the student into the hole that exists in their relationship with the world as it truly is. Take them to the hole itself. Take them into the full extent of the feeling of being lost that is in that vacant place.

Encourage them to stop defending themselves from falling into that place, but instead to let go and feel it all. After they have that experience, there is no longer a hole to avoid. And there is no need for anyone to build bridges or perform spiritual acrobatics. When they go through the fullness of that experience, they can begin to deal with the quality that has been lost in their relationship with the world.

They fall into the hole. They find what quality has been hidden in the hole. Then they find the way to walk that walk. Such a process relies on them uncovering their own God-given resources. Success is not about a mysterious effort to have a student leap to a needed quality. They may put in a lot of spiritual effort to do such a thing, and the teacher may likewise work hard to have them make a leap, or may work to create a bridge for them, but such strategies do not lead to the integration of self that they need. There is no way that a physician of the heart can create a continuum for someone else. You can construct bridges over the hole, but ultimately the traveler will fall into the hole.

The physician of the heart can get close to root issues by approaching things in the student's childhood, and this simplifies the journey into the student's psyche. Every immense issue, or impeded quality, always goes back to something that happened in childhood. That is the hole they are trying to avoid. It may be the loss of mother, the loss of love, the loss of connection, the loss of guidance, the loss of father. All of these elements are waiting for them if they fall in the hole.

But the resolution turns out to be very simple. It is the hole itself that will provide the answer and bring what they need to them. Falling into the hole allows them access to their unconscious, and they can see how they lost their sense of intimate, loving connection with reality because of their unresolved relationships to their family.

What happened to you in childhood made you lose your connection with the innate qualities of your soul. What is needed is to get sunlight onto the event, to the dark spot, and then it can transform itself. Once it is seen, something in you begins to resolve. Nothing can fill that hole. No system—philosophical, religious, or spiritual—can fill it. The missing quality has to be born from the hole itself. The teacher might fill the hole with their grace, but ultimately each human being must give birth to the quality that can arise from there.

In conjunction with the processes described above, the physician of the heart at the same time addresses all of these complex human problems related to knowledge of the outer and inner world by drawing the spiritual travelers into prayerful recitation of the divine pair: Ya Shahid, Ya Khabir. We strongly recommend reciting them as a pair. It brings balance and leads to completeness.

How ash-Shahid and al-Khabir fit together is described in the Qur'an: "Allah, who knows the unseen and seen, visible and invisible realities."[181] This passage is also interesting because it is a reference in the Qur'an to the many beautiful Names of Allah. It starts with *hu Allah*, and then *la 'ilaha 'illalla hu*, and then goes to 'Alim, which is the first quality mentioned, the field of God's infinite knowing.

Al-'Alim is full knowledge of the outer and the inner. It is mentioned over and over again, and in a variety of forms, in the Qur'an. We will devote a full chapter to it as our journey through the Names of divine knowledge and wisdom develops. First, however, we are now at the perfect time to examine two Names that manifest the means through we come to enter the sphere of omniscience: al-Warith and al-Ba'ith.

warith

balith

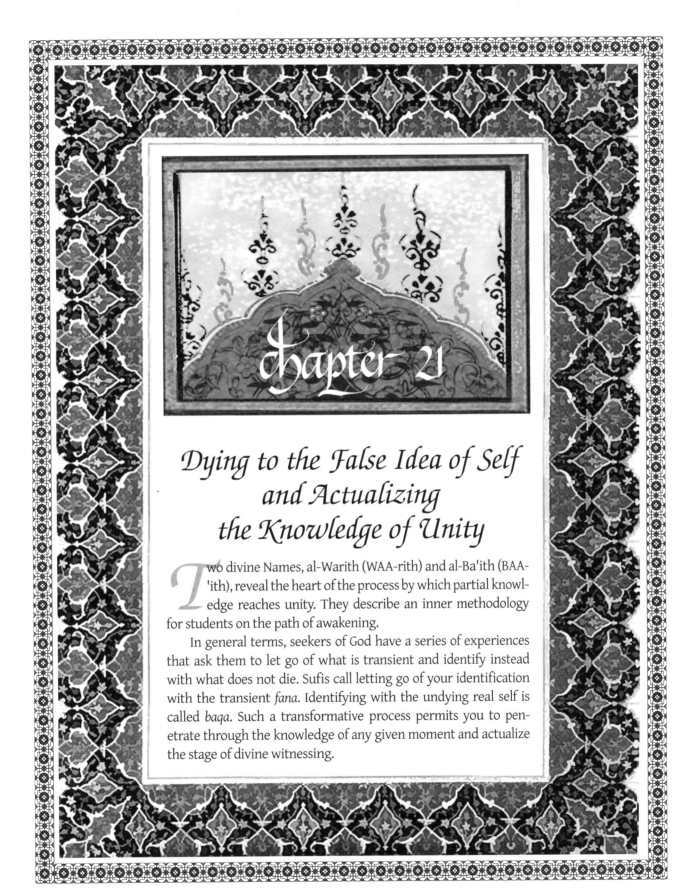

Chapter 21

Dying to the False Idea of Self and Actualizing the Knowledge of Unity

Two divine Names, al-Warith (WAA-rith) and al-Ba'ith (BAA-'ith), reveal the heart of the process by which partial knowledge reaches unity. They describe an inner methodology for students on the path of awakening.

In general terms, seekers of God have a series of experiences that ask them to let go of what is transient and identify instead with what does not die. Sufis call letting go of your identification with the transient *fana*. Identifying with the undying real self is called *baqa*. Such a transformative process permits you to penetrate through the knowledge of any given moment and actualize the stage of divine witnessing.

Continuously dying to your false idea of self and integrating afresh in what remains are required to move through all the stages on the path. There is an ultimate direction to this path of transformation. In a famous verse of the Qur'an we read that everything upon the face of the earth passes away (*fana*) except the face of Allah, who is the ever-living presence of what is real (al-Baqi).[182] The Qur'an also says: "We [Allah] give life and We give death, but We are the inheritors [*warithun*]."[183]

This is the context in which the divine Name al-Warith appears. It is the context of death and life, of *fana* and *baqa*. A traditional counsel on the Sufi path is to "die before you die" and thus realize that Allah is present as the inheritor of whatever is truly valuable in what you give up as you die. You are asked to let go of self and know that God is the ultimate return. This means to awaken to what is real. This awakening process is expressed in al-Warith's companion Name, al-Ba'ith.

The Qur'anic verse cited above describes the goal of the process and then goes on to characterize the human condition that we all face. We are told that some travelers on the path hasten forward, and others get stuck.[184] You may get stuck in the inner realms or the outer world, or in the transition between the two. The passage concludes: "Everything will return to Allah and Allah is surely Hakim and 'Alim [wisdom and omniscience].[185]

Ya Warith and Ya Ba'ith are most beneficial when recited as a pair. They can be of great benefit in overcoming the places where travelers on the spiritual path get stuck in their process of dying before death (*fana*) and awakening into what is more enduring (*baqa*).

Ya Warith

(yaa WAA-ri<u>th</u>)

Al-Warith describes the process of dying to the false self in order to awaken into what is more real. When you die you leave behind a legacy, because every moment your heart faces Allah, a reality awakens in it that transcends the material sphere. When your heart faces Allah it is transformed and becomes a legacy of light. Every other moment is essentially an experience that fades away and is gone.

In other words, what will vanish is every moment that has been absorbed in identifying with your idea of a limited self. Al-Warith expresses the divine activity of leaving your limited self behind. What transcends death, what truly remains, is called *al-baqi*. Al-Ba'ith expresses awakening to that reality. Taken together, al-Warith and al-Ba'ith point to a cosmic process that manifests the great return of all separated entities to unity.

A richer view of al-Warith will emerge as we examine some of the forms that its root takes and the context in which it appears in the Qur'an. The noun form *meeraath* appears at 3:180: "To Allah belongs the heritage [*meeraath*] of everything in the heavens and the earth, and Allah knows [*khabir*] everything you do outwardly and inwardly."

A word for fire is *wartha'tun*. The physical meaning of the verb *warratha* is to put out a fire, to stir around the ashes to kill it. The fire itself is undergoing *fana*. It is a passing phenomenon. The heat (*naar*) or the *wartha* dies away. Everything other than Allah is temporal.

Even after the ashes of the fire have been stirred to encourage its extinction, something yet endures. Light is more enduring than the smoke or heat. For example, we can see the light from a distant star long after the star has ceased to exist. The kinds of physical meanings the root takes serve as metaphors to allow us to better approach the depths of all the divine Names.

Al-Warith brings you to a condition that is more lasting (*'abqa*). This is the legacy that you offer when your lifetime is over. It is a legacy of light. Allah is the light of the heavens and the earth, the Nur. Al-Warith points to the relationship between the heat of fire and its light. *Naar* becomes *nur*. And al-Warith reveals the relationship between the temporal and the eternal, *fana* and *baqa*.

The metaphor of the fire, the *wartha'tun*, deserves further consideration. Heat is the transient aspect of fire, and light is the more lasting aspect. To heat up or to be hot emotionally is *ghadiba*, which also means to be angry, vexed, vehement, irate, wrathful, furious, enraged. There is a sacred hadith of the Prophet Muhammad in which he reports Allah to say: "My loving compassion [*rahma*] overcomes my rage [*ghabad*]."

This raging heat is directly felt in our psychological states. *Ghadbaan* means to defend or to be defensive. It is to be hot and angry and in a defensive posture. When Muslims pray *Ghayri-l-maghdoobi*, as in the opening chapter of the Qur'an, it is a prayer to not walk on the path that lacks light, where there is burning heat, or hell.

The word for "hell" in Arabic is *naar*. It has the same root as *nur*. It is experienced as hell because the burning heat totally obscures the light. When human beings don't embody *rahma* and just become full of rage, they are in a hell of their own making. As it says in the Qur'an, "In their hearts is a heat and hypocrisy, the heat of ignorance."[186]

Another way to talk about heat is *hamiyyah*, which literally means the burning sting of a scorpion. More abstractly, it means zeal, fanaticism, and fury. All Muslims, whether they know it or not, are praying every day, when they recite the *Fatiha*, to not walk the path of fanaticism and fury.[187]

Our attention is also called to how we offer our human legacy in other ways. What is the *meeraath* or legacy, of the hand? "Light will flow out [or run forward] from their hands, and they will say, 'Allah, perfect for us our light.'"[188]

To prepare for the transition from the temporal to the eternal, it helps to understand that temporal beings leave behind a legacy of light at death. It is also useful to see that some traces in the world of the unseen are more enduring than others. A simple way to understand this principle is to consider your memory. You have many long-lasting memories, which leave enduring traces on your heart even though the event remembered has passed away, yet there are more recent memories that leave no trace at all.

According to the dictionary, the usual way people understand *warith*, as *wartha*, means to inherit property. "He inherited property from his father." But according to one dictionary, *warith* is related to *baqi* in this sense: If Allah is al-Warith—the inheritor of all—that means everything else is *faa'in*, or empty. The metaphor of inheritance suggests that, just as material property passes from one generation to another, God gives life and death, and all that truly remains after physical death goes back to God, the origin of all things.

It is totally acceptable to interpret *baqi* and *faa'in* to say "everything is annihilated and *baqi* is what remains." But al-Warith puts a different emphasis on it. It is not simply a disappearance. Something that is essential returns to Allah in the end. The Qur'an says, "It is We who inherit the earth and all that is upon it, and to Us everything will return."[189]

The legacies of other things that give witness to God's presence are also mentioned in the Qur'an. Words leave a kind of light or legacy. "A good word is like a good tree; its roots are firmly fixed deep in the earth and its branches reach out toward heaven. It brings forth a fruit of all seasons."[190] "Not a word does he speak but there is a witness. It turns into light and goes back to the Throne."[191] And speaking of the Day of Judgment: "We shall set a seal upon their mouths, but their hands will speak and their feet will give witness."[192]

Finally, the heart also has a legacy. "One whose heart is opened receives the *nur* of Allah [the enlightenment of God]. Woe unto those whose hearts have been hardened to the *dhikr* [remembrance] of Allah. They are manifestly lost, walking the path of self-delusion."[193] The *dhikr* softens and opens the heart, and the light or legacy of this *dhikr* on the heart is shown through the face.

Another form of *wartha* is *tawarathahu*. It means to inherit something by degrees. The implication is that a person passes through one stage after another, going repeatedly through *fana* and returning to Allah. By stages everything returns, and it is in that sense Allah is al-Warith, and everything else is *faa'in*, is passing away.

The process of self-transformation is called *taqallub*. The very form of this word implies gradual and repetitive stages of transformation. *Taqallub* appears in the Light verse: "People whom neither trade nor commerce diverts from *dhikr*, their hearts and eyes are transformed in a wholly new way."[194] They are able to perceive in the temporal the sign of the eternal.

"It is We who give life and give death. And it is We who remain the *warithun* [the inheritors] after all else passes away."[195] God is the ultimate inheritor of all the stages and of each and every stage. God is the ultimate return of every being. When we realize this, it gives meaning to loss, death, and pain.

There's a hadith that says: *Allahuma tia'anni bisam-e'e warbasa-e waj alhu waarith.* "O Allah, let me enjoy the long-lasting benefits of my hearing and my sight and make it a *warith*." We read that "everything will be gathered." That is the activity of al-Warith. Next comes the statement that Allah is Hakim and 'Alim.[196]

The whole process we have described with al-Warith leads to the wisdom that comes from the ultimate unity of both outward and inward knowledge. Many people have a sense of sublime heavenly realms that are very much more enduring than the material realm. While this is true, in the absolute sense of things these realms are transient. They are the stages of the return described by al-Warith and al-Ba'ith.

The metaphor of incense helps us to appreciate the subtle realms. When you burn incense, nothing remains but the fragrance. It suggests movement into another dimension. The Sufi martyr, al-Hallaj, used that metaphor to answer the authorities when they were determined to burn his body, thinking that if they destroyed his body, he couldn't be resurrected on the Day of Judgment.

Hallaj's answer to that assumption was that burning his body would be "like an incense promise of a resurrection." Whether it is the metaphor of the transition of a stick of incense to fragrance, or fire to light, we are looking at a process of continuing to move into more refined realms, closer and closer to eternity.

Psychological Perspective on al-Warith

A straightforward approach to al-Warith is to address it from the perspective of letting go of everything that you cling to, in order to reach the source. It is the way of totally releasing attachment. However, there is another way that is just as important to physicians of the heart who must skillfully work through the wide variety of problems that different students present.

Let's call this other method the way of cultivating "spiritual greed." Every one of us is greedy. By increasing the greed, or as Sufis call it in a milder form, increasing yearning (*shulk*), you can ultimately achieve union. By yearning more and more it is possible to proceed on until you inherit the whole kingdom. The kingdom is your birthright by creation, but you lost it.

Cultivating "spiritual greed" is taking the attitude that you will not settle for anything less than inheriting the whole kingdom of God again. That kind of yearning is the wholesome root of greed, and it can be cultivated. When greed gets distorted, it becomes lost in materialism, trapped in the pursuit of wealth, reputation, or other goals. But when your greed is rooted in yearning for the beloved, yearning for the wholeness of who you are, then this longing becomes a quest for retrieving the totality of your inheritance.

Our eyes long to see, our ears long to hear, our heart longs to love. Every bit of us longs for its original inheritance. Unless we retrieve all the essential states that we long for, and retrieve the source from which we came, we have not gotten our inheritance.

Recitation of Ya Warith can be used as an invocation to activate the yearning and intensify the greed so that you can want more. When it comes to God, it is quite all right to want more. From the psychological point of view, the issues that come up around al-Warith are issues of entitlement.

Babies are born with a deep sense of entitlement. The baby's eyes, mouth, and hands seek the breast. The first thing that the baby is entitled to is the breast. And the breast symbolizes the totality of the blessed body of existence. The baby doesn't see just the flesh. It sees gold, honey, pearls, and jewels flowing.

With the milk, the efflux of the soul is flowing through the breast. In that experience, the baby has a vision of the totality of the universe manifesting in ecstasy. The baby feels entitled to have that breast, which means he or she feels entitled to have the totality of existence. That is where our original sense of entitlement comes from.

At the same time, babies don't have boundaries, so they are naturally merged with the infinite, with the absolute. The essential state flows into the baby and flows out of the baby. There is a natural feeling of belonging to existence, a sense that this is my home, my kingdom, my being, my mother, and my breast. It all belongs to me. The child retains this sense of entitlement until about age one and a half or two. They feel that the whole world belongs to them.

Our inner relationship with al-Warith comes from our deep sense of what we are entitled to. When we are deprived of that connection, we seek to retrieve it. Repetition of Ya Warith becomes a very effective practice at the time when this yearning has been activated.

What is needed is to validate the fundamental sense of inheritance or entitlement. It needs to be corrected in the right way and transformed so the student can journey all the way to inherit the source itself. Such a journey ultimately means dissolving in the God-reality, and requires dissolution of the personality, or idea of your self. The light remains and the crud goes away.

The personality fizzles out, and the luminous essence of each individual merges with the infinite. In that merging with the infinite, something of the individuated being remains intact. It has become an individuated part of the whole. It exists in the whole but without boundaries around it. The one and only being is your basic nature; it is what you are made of, but you are also a very specific constellation.

The real position of the complete human being is not in the absolute, nor in the relative. The human being, in essence, is like the description of the Prophet Muhammad: *sayyad-il-'aalamayn*. He is the master of the two worlds, which means one foot is in the relative and one foot in the absolute.

That is the pinnacle of the position of the human being. To simply merge with the absolute and identify with it is not yet a complete experience. It has not yet reached what al-Ba'ith has to offer. When you reach union with the beloved and become one with the beloved, there is no sense of a "me" separate from the absolute. There is just pure awareness.

Within that pure awareness there is an awakening. You realize you are a unique being with a unique frequency, a unique soul, a unique history, and a unique evolution, a being that is beautiful and delightful. You develop a consciousness that can unify and integrate the absolute and the relative. That is the great witness consciousness, the consciousness described in the previous chapter as *mushaahidah*.

Pure awareness lacks differentiation. It is aware only of unity and oneness. The moment it enters differentiation, it becomes witness consciousness. It becomes diamond-like consciousness, a consciousness that unifies the relative and the absolute. This is the middle ground where the human being resides. We weave the relative and the absolute together. We are like the spiders who are at work unifying the spiderweb.

What is desired in this process is your remembrance of the birthright of your whole soul, what is yours by right of creation. We recommend prescribing Ya Warith to students when their mind is awakening. It is especially valuable for all those seeking to make a real passage through their issues around entitlement.

Narcissism has many colors. Some people feel entitled to be special, entitled to sit in the front row. They feel angry when they don't get what they feel they are entitled to. Repeating Ya Warith, and understanding at the same time that what you are always yearning for is your true birthright, provides a doorway into your issues with entitlement.

Now you can begin to feel your entitlement in a fresh way because it is coming from a deep source. It is calling you back to inherit the whole kingdom. Everybody is entitled to have a life, to have a home, to have a decent way of living. It is an important part of the soul's purpose, though not all. If your basic issues of entitlement are not addressed, and integrated, then an important element of your life is missing. Your worldly existence, your bodily needs, your community, your manifestation on Earth as a being, are not given the precious value they deserve.

There is no human being who is not a narcissist to some degree. The fact that narcissism is such a universal condition should tell us something basic. Narcissism goes right to our attachment to our sense of self. Unfortunately, the self that we are usually holding onto is made of zirconium, and not diamond. It is an imitation of the real self.

When a person actually becomes aware that their attachment is to an unhealthy self, then they are ready to seek a self that is more authentic. Then you can direct your attention to the highest of inheritances, your soul, which is made in the divine image and likeness.

When your original nature is realized, consciousness becomes liberated. You then enter the realm of al-'Alim: knowing, learning, disengaging, integrating, and differentiating. The consciousness becomes free, even free from the effort of knowing.

You may feel you really don't know, yet now you are equipped to progress on the journey. You know there is something journeying with you. What is journeying with you is your higher consciousness: your inner Khidr, your inner guru. It is a state of awareness that gives you an ongoing connection with the activity of the Spirit of Guidance.

A necessary piece to be accomplished by the guide on the spiritual path is to liberate students, at the appropriate time, from their dependency on the outer teacher by empowering them to find their inner guide.

Al-Warith straightforwardly includes in its meaning extinguishing the flame of separateness and extinguishing the sense that the worldly kingdom will satisfy your yearning. This approach is fundamental and should be emphasized by physicians of the heart. It has received less attention only because we have chosen to describe in some detail the approach of "spiritual greed."

As we mentioned earlier, there are two methods to reach the true worth of the inheritance of the kingdom. One way is by extinguishing the fire in the personality. The other is by kindling the fire of yearning for the source. The first approach is to extinguish the heat. This heat is the unpleasant fire of attachment, and the heat of this attachment activates all the gymnastics of the false self.

The Qur'an speaks to this when the patriarch Ibrahim (Abraham) is about to be thrown into a raging fire. Allah says, "All fire, be coolness and peace. And peacefulness upon Ibrahim when he is thrown into the fire."[197] Then he gets tossed into the fire, and everyone is amazed that he dwells there and is not burned.

Taking note of all this, we affirm that al-Warith can be either cooling or heating—or both. You can be heating up the fire of your yearning while at the same time extinguishing the fire of your ego attachments. Invocation of Ya Warith can accomplish both. It shouldn't be thought of as simply a heating *wazifah*.

However, it is amazing to see, when you take somebody who is very heated and let them expand their heat and their yearning, their attachment then fizzles away. They go into *fana*. Physicians of the heart must have discriminating wisdom to know to whom to give this method of instruction, and when.

Ya Ba'ith

(yaa BAA-'ith)

Al-Ba'ith means to get unstuck from what restrains you to become free to journey through the stages of realization. It sends you forth. It is to get unblocked, to throw off death-like sleep or inertia in order to wake up!

As a practical matter, al-Ba'ith means to quicken, to awaken, to free yourself from blockages, and to go to the next stage toward Allah. It is like getting the kinks out of the hose to allow the free flow of water. Al-Ba'ith is often paired with al-Warith when it appears in the Qur'an. They naturally go together.

Our research strongly suggests that the description we have given above of the meaning of al-Ba'ith is a better and generally more complete reading than what is expressed by the term "resurrection," which is the usual translation of al-Ba'ith. Resurrection is a part of its meaning, as we shall see, but not the most inclusive.

To draw out al-Ba'ith's meanings, we will first examine some of the physical forms of expression that occur in variations of its root. The first form, *ba'atha*, means to remove that which restrains from free action. An example of its use: *a'atha-an-naqah*, which means to loosen a cord around the leg of a camel so that she may rouse herself and get up and go.

Another variation of the root means to remove the barrier from a stream of water so that the water can flow forth. The story of Jonah and the whale in the Qur'an gives a vivid example of the physical meaning of al-Ba'ith. Jonah is inside the belly of the whale. "He would certainly have remained inside the stomach of the fish until the day when he was spewed out."[198] Spewed out, vomited forth, is *yub'athun*. It comes from the same root as al-Ba'ith, and means the day or time for being sent forth.

A simple and direct physical meaning of al-Ba'ith is "to send," which is the most common use in the Qur'an for the various forms of al-Ba'ith, rather than the idea of resurrection. It is all about sending. *Ba'athuka ni'mah* means I send you blessings. The eighth form, *'ibta'atha*, means to send a letter, and implies God sends a messenger. Finally, *al-mab-'ath* means the time of sending, and that is the time when God sends messengers and sends messages to the messengers. Sending is *ba'atha*. There are many other references of the same type.

Having said all this, there is a meaning of al-Ba'ith that indeed does relate to resurrection. It is to awaken, to rouse, to excite, and to quicken. It is shaking off the drunkenness of death, and thus awakening, as is described in the Qur'an.[199] We find it also in the seventh form *'inba'atha*. This word relates to someone who is so sluggish or indolent that they will not be roused to action. There is also an ordinary meaning of awakening from sleep, and *ba'itha* is a person that is wakeful.

In the Arab society of Prophet Muhammad's time, the prevailing belief was that nothing survives death. This belief is mentioned in the Qur'an: "They swear in their strongest oaths by God that God will not raise those who die."[200] And: "Those people in the past thought as you Meccans think, that nothing will survive."[201]

Then the Qur'an says, "Don't be surprised when they ridicule you and don't pay attention when they hear about life after death and turn it into mockery and say this is nothing but charlatanism and trickery; when we die and become dust and bones who is going to raise us up again?"[202] A form of *ba'ith* is used in this verse for raised up rather than *rafi'*. The Qur'an says, "As to the dead, Allah will send forth them and then they will be returned back to Allah."[203]

God gives life and death and has power over all things, and God will raise up those who are in the graves. *Yom ba'ith* is the day of sloughing off death and being born to a new life. This could be every day, or every breath. St. Paul says in Corinthians, "I die daily in Christ Jesus." And at the physical level it is true that the body is sloughing off cells and making new ones all the time.

In the Mary chapter of the Qur'an, Jesus says, "Peace be upon me the day I was born and peace be upon me the day I die, and peace be upon me the day I shall be sent forth to the new life again."[204] The word used for being sent forth to the new life is *'ub'athu*, a form of al-Ba'ith. John the Baptist says virtually the same thing elsewhere.[205]

What all these verses refer to is the action of quickening the dead. At each stage in the processes of *fana* and *baqa* you are absorbed and spewed forth, as in the metaphor of Jonah in the whale. Stage by stage, death by death you are raised from station to station. As Mevlana Rumi puts it, "When have I ever grown less by dying?" Through the many stages and gateways of truth, you ultimately return to the divine presence.

The Qur'an says, "Reality [al-Haqq] has come and falsehood passes away, for falsehood by its nature always passes away."[206] *Ba'itha* arouses human beings when they get stuck in the process. It frees the kinks in the hose and allows for the natural flow to fully move toward the source. Al-Ba'ith clears the way, and keeps you moving forward on the path.

In the last part of the opening of the *Fatiha*, one way to understand the words *siraat-ul mustaqeem* is a prayer to flow back on the day of return, and not become lost along the way.[207] It is interesting to see that Iblis (Satan) prays to God and says "delay me until the day when everything returns and flows back to the source."[208] Referring to the ultimate return of everything to Allah, *yub'athoon* is the passive form of *ba'ith* that appears in this passage.

Abaa, "he refuses," is said to be the root of Iblis. It is the opposite of *balaa'*, "he accepts." Everyone is guided on the road of return according to his or her own character and predisposition (*shaakilah*). 'Ibn 'Arabi poetically expresses this by saying that this disposition is related to the intensity of the affirmation (*balaa'*) with which you answered the question of God in pre-eternity, *'A lastu bi-rabbikum?* "Am I not your Lord?"[209]

In delving into the forms that the roots of the divine Names take in their physical-plane meanings, there are forms that incorporate various human shortcomings. We are always interested to find these variations, as we have found they offer insight into the particular kinds of blockage that may respond to the prayerful invocation of the *wazifah*.

Ba'atha is a first-form variation that means to rush forward because of impatience, carelessness, or thoughtlessness. *Ba'atha 'ala* means to be sent against someone, like one army sent to clash against another army. Finally, the seventh form *'inba'atha* means to rush forward headlong or to hurry.

The human disability to be addressed here is that of trying to force things and not allow a natural maturation from one state to another. Zen Buddhists call it "pushing the river." It is the *nafs* that is pushing itself forward, rather than letting the power of God do the unblocking.

When Jonah is in the darkness of the whale's stomach he is moved to recite a form of the *dhikr*. Consider everything that the metaphor of being in the body of the whale might imply. It is in this dark place that you have been swallowed up where you are able to give up your clinging to the desires of the lower self. If you are Jonah, you give up your aspiration to escape to Spain, and instead remember Allah. You are ready to be sent forth anew.

In the story Jonah was just trying to escape from the inner call of God that had instructed him to go forth and deliver a message to the people of Nineveh. He was relying on a plan about how to get away by sea. But the sea rose up, and his ship was in distress. The captain got the idea that someone onboard was the karmic cause of their perilous situation. Jonah identified himself as that person and said, "Just go ahead. Cast me out."

He was willing to accept the consequences, willing to go into the ocean deep and into the belly of the whale. That too was a stage of *fana*. He lost his self and was swallowed up in a kind of darkness, a kind of unconsciousness, with no sense of how he could ever get out. There was nothing that he could do except the *dhikr*, the remembrance of God.

He did a 40-day *dhikr* in the whale: *La 'ilaha 'illah 'anta subhaana-ka 'inniy kuntu mina-dh-dhaalimeen.*[210] The use of *'anta* changes the usual *dhikr* phrase to say instead: "There is no God but you." It is intended to be more a more intimate invocation than *la 'ilaha 'illa allah.*

The verb for being spit out or spewed forth from a whale's stomach is *ba'itha.* Jonah goes from the darkness into the light, and so does the traveler on the spiritual path. The *dhikr* recited by Yunus (Jonah) in the whale is a practice in some Sufi orders.

Al-Warith can be seen in throwing yourself into the sea, in getting swallowed up by the whale, letting go of all attachments, and dwelling there in remembrance. The opening of all blockages and getting spewed out is al-Ba'ith.

More About When to Prescribe Ya Warith, Ya Ba'ith, and Ya Haqq

Human beings experience existence as a place of duality. This is natural, because creation is based on the principle of duality, not on the principle of unity. For creation to occur, something separate is conceived and made.

Invocation of Ya Warith addresses the struggle all human beings have with issues of duality. This divine Name encourages a journey into the domain of true worth, toward the inheritance of your true being. It is a means of connecting to being and uniting with the source of all being.

The physician of the heart should prescribe Ya Ba'ith when the student is dealing with the process of coming back from source to the relative. Al-Ba'ith allows each one to experience the emerging, to experience incarnation. Earlier, they were experiencing dissolution and integration into essence.

Now they are absorbed in integrating essence into life, into existence. They are coming from the source of all to the relative. Before they went from the relative to source. At the time in a student's progress when they need to learn to unify and unite all the fields, they should recite the two Names together as a pair: Ya Warith, Ya Ba'ith.

When you wish to emphasize what each quality brings in a differentiated way, you can look to each Name alone. Initially the spiritual traveler is going from the poverty of their personality into the inheritance of the richness of being. After that experience, you come from infinite richness of being into the relative poverty of existence, which you now actively enrich with being.

By invoking Ya Warith and Ya Ba'ith together you activate both principles simultaneously. The result is a powerful and potent practice. The spiritual wayfarer experiences dissolution and integration simultaneously. He or she has the ability to disintegrate the personality as well as embody the personality and in this way can accomplish integration into the fullness of being.

It is not only the qualities of al-Ba'ith and al-Warith that are realized, but you are led to reality itself, to al-Haqq. When al-Ba'ith and al-Warith are integrated, the dual principles begin to unify into one field. This field of reality can be seen either as an absolute dark nothingness or as pure radiant awareness. Allah is the union of the two. This unity gives birth to the realization of an emptiness that is luminous, numinous, and voluminous.

Al-Haqq emerges as the all-inclusive transcendental Name that contains both al-Warith and al-Ba'ith. If you recited the three together—Ya Warith, Ya Ba'ith, Ya Haqq—it would be inclusive of all possible conditions. It combines *jamal, jalal,* and *kamal.* In the Qur'an at 50:19 we read "The stupor of death comes to them and al-Haqq remains." This Name will be discussed in greater detail in subsequent chapters.

From the alchemical point of view, there is the journey of disintegration where you dismantle the structure. And there is the other journey, where you transmute the structure. For example, if you open up and attentively engage with the part of your personality that is wounded and hurt, and bring in the divine attribute that fills the hole, that isolated part begins to dissolve itself, and loving-kindness is born.

When you reach al-Warith, and go through al-Warith, you let go of your muddled inheritance from humanity, which is pain and suffering, and return to the inheritance from God, which is loving-kindness. You take the personality, the ego, and you disintegrate it through a process of *fana* until you find the source.

When the process reaches the divine quality you need, you come back to the world correcting the broken part, mending the distortion, and redeveloping the personality. In this way you build up a healthy personality. You let go of the distorted personality, the lousy inheritance, and enter the grace-filled inheritance.

You develop the structures that were missing in your personality. This is the journey activated by al-Warith and al-Ba'ith. Through stages, it leads to the dissolution of the false personality and the awakening of the body of resurrection, which is the essential personality. Even the physical body is thoroughly enlivened.

Many seekers don't want to be in the world. What they really want is to get away from the world and reach the source. For them, returning from the source is extremely challenging because they fear reentering all the limitations that obscured their vision before. At this stage, some travelers become confused by their experience. They may even be tempted to think of themselves as the next messiah, and rush out to make claims. In spite of all these kinds of hindrances, they need to take the path back to Earth.

You have inherited everything. But now you must learn how to flow forth from al-Ba'ith, to come from the real source, and transform your places of blockage. The work of the physician of the heart is to convey how a person can be in harmony with the source while at the same time flowing forth from it, actualizing individuality, and harmonizing with others. It is learning to walk afresh, as if you have just been born, or spewed forth from the belly of the whale, and need to walk step by step.

The more you dissolve the false personality, the more you emerge in an essential personality. It is made of elements of grace and beauty and other divine qualities. For a seer, it may manifest as a jeweled structure. You feel transformed, as if the absolute is awakening you from the sleep of the dead into a living body. The new self is an individuated structure that is made of elements that are truly beautiful, like the 99 Names of Allah, jelled in embodied forms. Ya Warith, Ya Ba'ith, Ya Haqq.

ya 'alim
muhsi hasib
raqib

chapter 22

God's Omniscience and the Secret of Every Heart

Ya 'Alim
(yaa 'a-LEEM)

The sacred Name al-'Alim, in all of its multiple forms, is mentioned in the Qur'an more than any other single attribute of Allah. There are hundreds of appearances of this Name in the Qur'an, and thousands of hadith that include it.

Al-'Alim is a good example of the process we saw operating in contemplating opposite divine qualities. Contemplation on any pair of divine opposites naturally leads to a Name of God whose inclusive meaning transcends and encompasses all that the opposites contain. In the case of al-'Alim, the two opposites are ash-Shahid and al-Khabir, inner and outer knowledge, which were described in a preceding chapter.

Al-'Alim is the Name of knowledge at the center of the knowledge cluster, but as all real knowledge must ultimately express wisdom, the center of the center, or heart of the heart, of this family of Names expressing God's knowing is al-Hakim, divine wisdom. Wisdom requires of knowledge that it be put into practice in everyday life, in every moment.

We first need to address a common misunderstanding. What people call "knowledge" is often restricted to the mind's understanding of outer name and form. *'Akl* is the word in Arabic for this kind of outer understanding, and *'akl* literally means "a knot." It is necessary to untie this knot. The process of untying is illustrated by the word *ma'rifah*, a name frequently given to Sufism, and it means gaining real inner knowledge.

'Ibn 'Arabi disagreed with such a degree of prominence being given to *ma'rifah*. He said that *'Ilm* or *'Alim* is a more complete Name. His point is that real knowledge is more than simply a journey from outward to inward knowing. The inward and the outward should be experienced as seamlessly interpenetrating each other. He pointed to *'ilmu-l-ladoonee*, knowledge that is drawn directly from divine presence. This is the way Khidr's knowledge when giving teachings to Moses is described in the Qur'an.

In Islam, great importance is given to the path of knowledge. Many hadith express this in different ways. Here is a sampling: "To seek knowledge is incumbent on every believer, man and woman." "Allah has made nothing more beautiful than the intellect, nothing more perfect, nothing more excellent." "Whoever leaves their home in search of knowledge walks the path of Allah." "The ink of the scholar is more sacred than the blood of the martyr." "The people of knowledge are the heirs of the prophets. They leave behind knowledge as their inheritance. One who inherits it inherits a great fortune."

Knowledge (*'ilm*) is contrasted with *jahl*, which is usually called ignorance. However, this gloss overlooks the point of how these words are used in the Qur'an and hadith. *Jahl* is not ignorance as we ordinarily understand it. One hadith shows the relationship of *jahl* to *'ilm*: "Among the many types of knowledge is that which is ignorance." This is a good indication that al-'Alim is all-inclusive.

Jahl is not just absence of knowledge. *Jahl* means to neglect the truth or the reality of a given situation. There are several types of *jahl* that are mentioned in the Qur'an. The first type is the arrogance of those who have learned something but who do not actually practice it.[211] A second type of ignorance is to pretend to know what you don't know.

The third kind of *jahl* is to be really quite sure that you know something that you don't know. You think that you know everything about it, and the more you think you know, the more ignorant and arrogant you become. The fourth type of *jahl* is to be proud that you don't know and feel superior to those who do know, and give them no respect.[212]

There is an element of self-delusion involved in all of these types of ignorance. To initiate the process of overcoming self-delusion is to begin to awaken to al-'Alim. Merely wanting to dispute, and speaking harshly and aggressively, is the mark of someone who is *jaahil*.

For example, some so-called fundamentalists have an absolute disdain for the *'ulamaa'*, the people of knowledge. When the *'ulamaa'* hear disdainful argumentative talk and receive attacks from people like this, they offer a greeting of peace and proceed in a peaceful manner.[213] Those who embody *'aleem* are called slaves of infinite mercy who walk upon the earth gently.

This teaching gives us an ostensive definition of *'ilm*, the noun form of al-'Alim: it is the reality that causes the behavior of walking on the earth gently, offering peace to all, and being the willing servant of infinite mercy. Al-'Alim is the answer to the condition of *jahl*, an answer that is so inclusive it even embraces its opposite. The all-compassionate nature does not exclude those who are lost in the darkness and filled with stubborn disdain and heat.

Root Forms of al-'Alim

We find it productive in exploration of the Names to draw out some of the meanings expressed by the various forms taken by the root of the word, including physical-plane forms. In this case, it is significant to see that the two realms of outer and inner knowledge are both included and transcended in the forms of the root A-L-M. All of its variations are divine Names that express God's omniscience in one way or another.

Let's briefly summarize some of them, using phonetic notation, as in the Pronunciation Guide. An explanation of how the structure of the Arabic language affects the meaning of a word is given in Chapter 4, The Sound Code. To make the distinctions between the variations of the root we spell these words phonetically and show stressed syllables by capitalization.

'AA-lim is the only source of knowledge; *'al-'AAM* is ever-continuing knowledge; *'a'lam* is ever-widening knowledge; and *'al-EEM* means the unlimited emanation of knowledge that reaches everything without exception. This latter form *'al-EEM* is the one that we find on the list of the 99 Names of Allah.

Al-'Alim affirms a nexus between outward and inward knowledge. From such a nexus, all things known and unknown ultimately represent deeper truth. Human beings can interpret symbols perceived in the outer world to know the secrets of the unseen. In one sense, all knowledge is symbolic or metaphorical. The word for symbols or marks is *'alaamaat*. *Ma'loom* means such secrets are known by some people, people who have been taught (*mu'allam*) by a teacher (*mu'allim*).

The Throne verse[214] speaks of God's all-encompassing knowledge. Elsewhere, Allah is called the knower of the unseen and the seen.[215] The word for such a knower is *'AA-lim*. The unique source of all knowledge intrinsically contains all possible knowledge of the inward and the outward. There is a long list of divine names in this particular verse. It begins with al-'Alim and ends with ar-Rahim, and thus suggests that knowledge ultimately blooms into love, and expresses mercy to all of creation, within and without.

In many of the physical-plane variations of the root of al-'Alim, there is an indication of an underground water source, a source that may be under a mountain. *'Ulamaa'* is an unseen source of water. *'Aylam* is an underground well. *'Alaamah* is a water source that is under a mountain.

Reading the divine signs in nature is similar to what a dowser does in locating a hidden source of water by using signs that are concealed beneath surface appearances. In a more universal sense, the whole of creation is nothing but a collection of such divine signs: *'aalam*. This is expressed in the first chapter of the Qur'an, in the phrase: *al-hamdu li-llahi rabb-il-'aalameen*.

All the possible worlds are nothing but a collection of signs and symbols to be read by those who are capable. *'Aalameen* is an animate plural of *'aleem*. It is the word for universe in the sense of a collection of all possible worlds and has the same root as the word for knowledge, *'ilm*.

The word for sign or symbol is *'alam*. If you look at the world, and all the possible universes, as a sort of theatrical presentation where the outward form is to be taken and understood as symbolic of the essence, then you may be graced to gain the eyes with which to read the universe like a book, and so derive meaning from it. In a famous Qur'anic verse[216] the world, by implication, is likened to a mirror in which the face of God is seen.

There are forms of the root of *'aleem* that also refer to receiving guidance on the path of life. *Ma'lam* means footprints on the path that give you a track to follow. It also means a river road, a road that leads to water. That same meaning is within the word *sharee'ah*: a wide track that leads to a source of water in the desert.

How al-'Alim is Used Throughout the Qur'an

It is a mammoth task to present the usage of al-'Alim in the Qur'an. Allah is described as the knower of the seen and the unseen (*'aalim-ul-ghaibi wash-shahaadah*) on 13 separate occasions. Many passages demonstrate how al-'Alim naturally moves from knowledge of the outer realms to knowledge of the inner, and from knowledge of the inner world to the outer.

Throughout the Qur'an, numerous ways are given through which human beings can come into full knowledge. Allah is further described as the knower of the secrets of the heart (*'aleem bi dhat-is-sudoor*), and there are several passages revealing the levels of what is entailed in being the knower of the secrets of the heart. These passages refer us to *taqwaa*, or divine awareness, a most important facet of God's omniscience.

Because no divine Name is mentioned in the Qur'an more often and in more contexts than al-'Alim, it is impossible, given the scope of this book on the 99 Names, to cover such a vast body of material. However, to suggest the richness that is available to the student who is inclined to dig more deeply into it, we will summarize some high points and then discuss them in some detail.

What can deepen our understanding of God's omniscience? The Qur'an broadens our initial notion by showing the relationship of al-'Alim to other Names, as these alignments suggest hidden depths of meaning in omniscience.

Al-'Alim is significantly paired with another divine Name, al-Wasi', and repeatedly linked with *kullu shayin*, which is the most inclusive possible Arabic name with which to affirm knowing every possible thing. The Qur'an also uses a unique form found in Arabic grammar, called a *kaana*, in combination with al-'Alim, to suggest the eternal present.

The Qur'an shows the inclusiveness of al-'Alim by pairing it with al-Wasi'.[217] The context is a response to those who claim exclusive possession of religious truth. It shows the quality of God's guidance cannot be limited and is truly universal, through pairing the infinite vastness of al-Wasi', a Name of God's omnipresence, with the infinitude of omniscience conveyed by al-'Alim.

The essential point is their alignment with each other, and their identification with each other. Al-'Alim is al-Wasi'. It is all-knowing and universally present. The passage ends by saying that Allah chooses love and compassion for whomever he pleases, for Allah is the innermost essence of infinite unbounded blessings (*fadl*). We are therefore invited to see that the very infinitude of al-'Alim implies divine mercy and compassion. It must necessarily be unbounded inwardly and outwardly.

Another way the Qur'an describes al-'Alim in its universal sense is to combine it with *kullu shayin*, which means "everything" in the most emphatic possible way. 'Alim thus includes knowledge of every thing and of all possible things. The phrase *kullu shayin* is repeated again and again in the Qur'an. A good example of its use is this: "He is the first and the last, the outward and the inward, and he has knowledge of all things [al-'Awwal , al-Akhir, az-Zahir, al-Batin, and *kullu shayin*]."[218] This verse is one of many universal definitions of al-'Alim.

In Arabic there is no verb "to be" such as is at the core of English grammar. However, there is a word *kaana* that you can join with a verb, and which expresses the eternal present. It is an ongoing reality, a kind of timelessness. In the classical Arabic of the Qur'an *kaana* can be past, present, and future at the same time, although in modern Arabic it usually refers to the past.

In the context of the divine Names, when you put *kaana* with any of these Names or qualities, it emphasizes in an absolute way the eternal nature of that quality, which is not restricted by past, present, or future. Albert Einstein used to refer to past and future as "persistent illusions." It is important to understand the timelessness of a divine attribute such as al-'Alim.

The Qur'an joins *kaana* with *'aleem* 22 times. That is significant. It is emphatically telling us that 'Alim is universal with respect to time. Such timeless truth is expressed by the word *kaana*. Al-'Alim is also universal with respect to space. Its universality in space is impressed on us by its frequent pairing with *kullu shayin*, everything and all possible things. Both of these pairings point to the universality of al-'Alim in its manifestation.

A famous verse says wherever you turn, there is the face of God.[219] What is interesting for us at this point in the discussion is the *daleel*, or tag, at the end of the verse, the phrase that points toward its deeper meaning. The *daleel* is *'inna allaha waasi'un 'aleem*. Al-Wasi' is the embrace of infinity. By pairing al-'Alim with Allah's infinite, all-pervading presence, our view of the infinitude of divine knowledge is magnified. It invites us to become aware that wherever we turn, the face of Allah is there.

Another way to demonstrate the infinite nature expressed by Ya 'Alim is the word *al-'allaam*. It expresses that God, in creating this world and all possible worlds (*'aalameen*), created a mirror through which God can see God's own face. Allah, who is infinite, has infinite knowledge of self, and this manifests in the unlimited possibilities of created forms.

The divine Name al-Khaliq is at the root of a three-layered process expressed by the Names of divine creation and described in Chapter 14, God the Creator. A variation of the root is *khallaaq*, which has the same form in the sound code as *al-'allaam*. The Qur'an says, "Allah is *khallaaq*, the infinite source of the infinity of continuously created forms, and *al-'allaam*, the infinite source of infinite, universal knowledge."[220]

The central point we wish to emphasize from our selections of Qur'anic teachings on al-'Alim is that God, the infinite being, is the source of the infinitude of created things. Since this is so, God may attain to unlimited knowledge of God's very self through the mirror of created being.

The Knower of the Secret of the Heart

Al-'a'lam is the elative form of *al-'aleem*. In grammar, an elative is a form that means "always more." Finite knowledge can always be increased. "Above every knower, or possessor of knowledge, there is one who knows more."[221] "Allah knows best how long the sleepers stayed in the cave, because with his knowledge are the secrets of the heavens and the earth."[222] "Allah knows best what is in the hearts of all of creation."[223] In short, God's always knows more about both outer and inner realities.

It becomes clear that Allah's purpose in knowing the innermost reality, or secret of the heart, is the purification of the heart. This human process starts with a kind of surrender that infuses the soul with calmness and serenity. God then tests the heart and purifies it to bring forth its innermost secret, which God knows.[224]

The final purpose of the process is to return the soul to Allah. "In the end unto Allah is your ultimate return and Allah will reveal to you the reality and truth of all that you have done, and Allah knows the innermost secrets of the heart."[225] God is described as the knower of the essence, or inward realms of the hearts, *'aleem bi dhat-is-sudoor*.[226]

How do we approach that secret? "God has inscribed upon God's innermost heart a word, which is *rahma*."[227] That is the starting point. God's innermost depth of heart contains a secret love. This loving compassion is at the root of everything. It is at the heart of God's knowing.

There is a hadith, "I seek refuge in Allah from a knowledge which is useless." Useless knowledge is that which creates in you a sense of separation from divine compassion, and useful knowledge is that which causes you to have intimacy with divine love.

Taqwaa

Throughout the many different avenues of investigation of the wonderful Names of Allah in the course of this book, we have again and again been led to the subject of how God's infinite nature is hidden within the human heart. God knowing the innermost secret of every heart is an act of self-knowing. Consequently, human beings can become fully aware of the presence of God in their hearts.

In his last sermon, the Prophet Muhammad spoke about the secret in the human heart. He pointed to the Qur'anic verse that says, "O people, we created the whole human race from a single pair, male and female, and then we made you into different races and tribes, so that you might become well acquainted with one another, not so that you might despise each other; and the best of you are the ones who are most aware [*taqwaa*]."228

The verse brings up the common heart of all humanity in a beautiful way. In this talk, the Prophet Muhammad spoke about males and females, blacks and whites, rich and poor, as all being essentially the same. He was himself a person who reached beyond cultural, racial, and religious delineations. For example, he married Mariya, an Egyptian Christian.

The Prophet went on to say that if you wish to think of some people as being better than others, it could only be those who are most aware, who are most conscious of Allah. He then tapped his chest three times and said, "*Taqwaa fi-l-qalb, taqwaa fi-l-qalb, taqwaa fi-l-qalb.*" *Taqwaa* is in the heart. God consciousness is in the heart.

Every human being has the capacity to become aware of God in his or her heart. The main function in all our consideration of al-'Alim is to unveil *taqwaa*. It is impossible to properly treat divine knowledge without including divine awareness.

Taqwaa is frequently mentioned in the Qur'an. We will offer a few examples.229 At the outset, a passage says that you should turn away from ignorance by turning toward knowledge in the form of saying '*astaghfiru-llaah*. By praying in this way, you yearn for and turn toward the divine, whose nature it is to forgive. It is a turning from *jahl* to '*aleem*.

The passage ends by saying that when those who have intense awareness of the omnipresence of the divine (*taqwaa*) are even touched by a negative thought, that very occurrence brings Allah to remembrance. At such a time they will be able to perceive with God's seeing, and if they are confused or angry, God will open their eyes.

Taqwaa qualifies as a kind of knowledge. It is a heightened consciousness of both the immediate and transcendental omnipresence. And it includes both the outward and inward. We read that you should not put yourself forward, but instead have *taqwaa* of Allah, for Allah hears and knows all things.230

Taqwaa is at the higher end of the scale of knowledge. One station of knowledge is reading the inward in the outward. *Taqwaa* has the awareness that inward and outward are absolutely one. They aren't different dimensions; they really are one thing. *Taqwaa* takes us into the door of wisdom itself and directs us to al-Haqq, the ground of all knowing.

Allah uses the Qur'an as a way of seeking to make things clear, or to interpret inward reality from outward signs. The Qur'an should be read in order to enter the deeper reality. However, in addition to receiving the book, you need the wisdom or knowledge to read it. Only those who have *taqwaa* can read it in its depth. They know that Allah has universal knowledge of all things, and it is by operating in accord with this fullness of knowledge that they are enabled to more properly approach and read the book.231

If you are imbued with this state of super awareness, *taqwaa*, it is Allah who teaches you, and Allah has knowledge of all things.[232] This kind of universal knowledge is gained through the process of self-effacement, or *fana*. It is a device through which God guides students onward from spiritual station to spiritual station in their evolution, through their dissolving of a mistaken identification with an isolated and deficient idea of an ego-self. This process is described in Chapter 21, Actualizing the Knowledge of Unity.

A chapter of the Qur'an starts with ar-Rahman and links this quality of compassionate love with the activity of teaching the Qur'an.[233] It can be translated, "It is endless love who teaches the Qur'an and who has brought humanity into being, and has taught meaning." It then refers to the next stage of the teaching and learning process, which is God's creation of the complete human being, *al-'insaan kaamil*, and then instructing *al-'insaan kaamil* to read the signs of God in his or her own self and in the world. In Arabic, "teaching" has the same root as "learning," *'aleem*.

The divine Names themselves are not entities but instead are ever-changing relationships within the heart of the God reality, which are revealed through a particular vibration. They are pathways, *subbul*. A famous story in the Qur'an illustrates this.[234] In pre-eternity, the time before there was time, so to speak, God taught Adam the Names of all things. Adam in this sense is *al-'insaan kaamil*, the complete human being.

In the story, when God asks the angels to speak about the Names, the angels respond by saying they don't know such things because they only know what they have been shown by God. So God tells Adam to teach the angels the real Names of all that is, which Adam does. God then says, "Did I not tell you that I know the secrets of the heavens and the earth? I know what you reveal and conceal."[235]

Considerations for the Student on the Path

There is a progression that a spiritual wayfarer makes as he or she experiences various states of blessing. What becomes awakened is a heightened aspect of knowing, an enduring capacity of witnessing, integrating, and differentiating all the dimensions of being. This place is so strong and solid it can endure the onslaught of life's confusing issues.

For students to develop such an enduring capacity of witnessing in all domains, they need to go through an empowerment that allows them to move from ordinary consciousness to objective consciousness.

Ya Muhsi, Ya Hasib, Ya Raqib
(yaa MUḤ-ṣee, yaa ḥa-SEEB, yaa ra-ḴEEB)

Three Names directly relate to ordinary mundane consciousness and provide a window for seeing what must be learned for us to progress to a clear state of witnessing. These qualities also bring up an important psychological dimension that should be addressed for the seeker's process to be successful.

We will begin with brief summaries of al-Muhsi, al-Hasib, and ar-Raqib, and then look at their relationship with one another and to spiritual practice. Finally, we will examine their intimate connection with an aspect of the formation of the superego, an aspect that can be disabling on the journey.

Al-Muhsi is omniscience in the sense of the full knowledge of each and every quantifiable thing. The root *ahsa'* means to take everything into account without losing track of anything. A physical form that the root takes means to count sheep with little black stones. For example, God knows the number of hairs on your head, and all such things.

Al-Muhsi is the one who enumerates and quantifies. Nothing is ever lost in the knowledge of God. Theologically, this capacity of God is often used to show that human knowledge of things is limited, and God knows best. When we feel the things we are lacking and identify with this deficiency it brings up personal fears, and questions like "How much wealth do I actually have?" become very worrisome.

Al-Hasib is God's action of accounting for the full meaning of everything. Nothing goes unrecorded, and nothing is ever lost. From the standpoint of how human beings can realize this quality, it is to become completely accountable. To become honestly accountable allows for a fresh beginning. It means taking full responsibility for one's actions, words, and even one's thoughts.

A root meaning of al-Hasib is to record a business transaction in an account book with exactitude and honesty. The account book, with its red column and its black column, was a natural metaphor for a mercantile society to use to understand accountability. Taking stock of yourself is compared to balancing a checkbook. Balancing your checkbook doesn't mean you don't have debt any more, but now you know where you stand.

An advanced Sufi technique called *muhaasibah* is an honest taking account of oneself while never forgetting you are within the ocean of divine mercy. A Sufi Shaykh, Muhasabi, of the 3rd century after the Prophet Muhammad wrote about sincerely practicing this method every day.

He took stock of all his actions, and whenever he felt he had made a mistake, he repeated *'astaghfiru-llaah* and turned to Allah for forgiveness. When he thought he had done well, he remembered God as the real cause of his action, and the cause of all causes, and he gratefully repeated Alhamdulillah. When he didn't know how to assess an action, he recited Subhanallah and emptied himself in acceptance of the divine reality.

Whatever the accounting of al-Hasib means to you personally, it needs to be rooted in the relationship of your soul to God. Muhasabi did his honest self-accounting while always maintaining his central relationship with the ocean of God's love. That is what allowed him to be successful! It is essential to get beyond the religion of a merchant who sees his relationship with God defined in only the most literal terms of the balance sheet.

If you sit judging yourself every night, asking "What did I do right or wrong, and how can I correct the wrong?" you soon become exhausted and confused. It leads to a huge superego that can drive you crazy. This is the negative way the ego forms a relationship with the attribute al-Hasib. It even impacts one's physical health in a negative way.

A superego ordinarily forms around the basic things that caretakers determine a child needs, such as: it's dangerous if you cross the road without looking and a car is coming. The superego can work as a reminder of these dangers, expressing an attitude of "if you do this, it's wrong, and if you do that, it's right." In this way, the superego serves a healthy function as a protective guide. It involves learning about the dangers of navigation in the world, and how to be cautious about what you do.

The important difference between the healthy and unhealthy state of the superego is the difference between learning about conditions and feeling shame about the state of affairs. Al-Hasib is a form of conscience. The question becomes "How can conscientiousness be aroused and at the same time freed from the shadow of the superego's assertion of dominance?" We will return to this question shortly.

Ar-Raqib combines the qualities of protection and watchfulness. Its meaning of "watching over" integrates two concepts: to watch the stars until the dawn comes, and to watch a baby while it is sleeping. Ar-Raqib means to fully give loving attention, and at the same time to possess the inner quietude that makes real concentration possible. As in the case of how you protectively observe a sleeping baby, concentration can best be held and grow out of a caring for what you love.

From Ar-Raqib comes *muraaqabah*, an advanced Sufi technique of concentration that begins with *hush dar dam*, merging with the rising and falling of the breath. The one-pointedness attained by patient, loving attention to the present moment results in a liberating unity of consciousness. *Muraaqabah* is pure, passive, loving observation, without any clinging (*ta'alluq*). Such loving attention allows you to be interested in whatever is arising. You are interested, but you are nonreactive.

Briefly speaking, al-Muhsi allows you to see what is there. It emphasizes knowledge. Al-Hasib gives rise to conscientious action based on observing what is there. It is the reckoner that knows what to do with the information. Ar-Raqib gives your full focus of heart attention and awareness to whatever is present.

Invocation of Ya Muhsi is an antidote for those who think that what they know really doesn't count and who consequently feel that their lives don't count. Repetition of Ya Hasib can be an antidote for those who get lost in minutiae and is recommended for those who are fearful or who have the habit of scheming and blaming themselves and others. Repetition of Ya Raqib is helpful in attaining proper focus in concentration.

The Obstacle of the Superego

It is necessary to address issues that are connected with the superego, as these issues are a formidable obstacle standing in the way of the student's development of a diamond-like clarity of consciousness, which would give them enduring access to wisdom's guidance. Al-Muhsi, al-Hasib, and ar-Raqib are easily associated with a big piece of psychological trouble that people have with the superego.

It is important for the traveler on the path to be aware of this from the beginning. The superego is always present: watching, calculating, and judging. The superego assumes the part of God and plays the judge. It believes that it is the Muhsi, the Hasib, and the Raqib. Students confuse this voice with the voice of knowledge, of conscience, and of guidance. Really it is the voice of the false controller, the commanding self, and the blaming self.

In general, repetition of Ya Muhsi, Ya Hasib, Ya Raqib may help address such confusion. Without skillfully dealing with this problem, students lack the capacity to be steadfast in their journey. When the superego is playing God, the student is caught in a realm of the unconscious that is particularly difficult to disengage from in order to witness objectively.

The superego is like an octopus. It has tentacles in every domain. You can find it in the domains of the heart, the body, the mind, and even the divine. In each of these domains there is a voice that diminishes you. Whether it is a gross or subtle voice, it is saying the same thing: you are no good and you have it all wrong. The student mistakenly associates this voice even with the emanations of the divine reality.

Earlier in this book (in Chapter 8, Divine Forgiveness, and in the section of Chapter 7, Allah's Opposite Qualities, that deals with al-Muntaqim and al-A'fuw) we addressed the dominating voice of the superego in relation to issues of self-worth and revenge. Now we are addressing it within a different family of Names. We could have taken a different pedagogical route and organized our whole text around psychological constellations such as the superego—an approach similar to that taken in Chapter 17, The Seven Levels of the *Nafs*—but we chose to organize around the families of divine Names.

The point is that there are many ways to approach the obstacle of the superego, but deal with it we must, and in more than one realm. Now we meet the superego in the midst of the family of knowledge, where it stands in the way of our evolution toward a more objective view of the self and the world.

The blaming self can often manifest as the superego playing God, in the form of al-Hasib. A person in the grip of this force becomes so belittled that they are incapable of doing anything. What also may occur in this confused state is utter grandiosity, where you blame yourself for everything that happens in the universe. Both of these conditions are paralyzing to the self.

The spiritual counselor should assist in an excavating project of all this terrain. A way is needed to deconstruct the inner configuration that enables this diminishing voice to have its way. People need to be led to go right into the superego, to go into that place where this kind of might is expressed.

They can then be shown how the superego is the oppressor and the dominator. It causes them to regress, and it prevents them from opening up and having the courage to walk their walk, in just the way a child becomes inhibited. The superego stymies the wisdom to examine and truly cultivate the higher octaves of self-awareness.

Because we can be disabled by the activity of the superego in any particular sphere, and because the shadow side of any particular quality appears when our ego claims the quality as its own possession, physicians of the heart need to be skillful in their approach. To have a seeker honestly face *an-nafs ul-'ammaarah*, for example, is painful. It is at the heart of boring, sober Sufism.

The physician of the heart should be careful not to negate what is inside the seeker. What is happening is the building of an inner structure. For example, if you tell them that what they are seeing is delusional, it may break them down. Tell them that the process of real seeing can evolve until they see the truth unmixed with shadows, but don't directly negate their experience. Instead, suggest a process. For example, they may go from seeing images, to seeing lights and colors, to seeing essential states, to seeing luminous beings.

The attributes of God all have a palpable presence, a living presence. They have depth, texture, color, and sound. And the presence of the divine quality changes how you are experiencing yourself and reality. On the other hand, the fakery of the superego is dead, deadening, and distorted. It brings mental and emotional disturbance rather than pristine presence.

The physician of the heart works to cultivate in seekers the discernment between what is real and what is artificial. The unreal might generate some emotion, or some energy, but it does not have the refined vibration of what is really in al-Hasib or any other divine quality.

So they cultivate these inner senses, these capacities, and they begin to differentiate. This process stabilizes them. The discipline required for practice of *muraaqabah*—to steadily hold an object of concentration for an extended period of time—likewise builds a structure. It helps to develop some very necessary skills.

At times, the physician of the heart will encounter individuals who have weak ego structure and sometimes extreme difficulty maintaining healthy interpersonal boundaries. The physician of the heart needs to help them build an ego structure. And there are many layers of being and inner players which need the imposition of such a structure. Murshid Samuel Lewis used to say, "My secret is controlled schizophrenia." That's really a good name for what needs to be achieved in bringing a masterful structure to any realm.

Those who have developed on the path have more capacities to look at the inner realm, thoroughly examine it, and control its various elements. A more complete description of the work of the physician of the heart in the process of dissolving and building up the ego-structure, along with some parting advice for physicians of the heart, is provided in Chapter 25.

Having led the seeker directly into the realm of their superego, the physician of the heart needs to point to the full presence of God's compassion, the love behind all the Names. They need to demonstrate God's love manifesting even within the particular qualities that have been distorted by the student's superego. The student may then be inspired to move past self-criticism and do a simple accounting of what is happening in their life. Then the time is ripe for the counselor to recommend the invocation of an appropriate Name or Names that are particularly connected with their condition.

Some Applications to Spiritual Practice

When you have the diamond-like jewel of your consciousness developed, through realization of al-'Alim, you can witness the visible universe, and make sense of what is. A state of consciousness emerges that is a doorway to inner truth and ultimate essence.

All knowing stems from one source, but the usual course of human consciousness is to drift in one domain of being or another and to become lost in a particular domain. Students become trapped in these limitations by identifying whatever is occurring in a given realm with their sense of self.

However, once consciousness takes root in the source, you can see the thoughts, feel the emotions, and sense the sensations without identifying with them. All these become like passing clouds. You witness them passing. You begin to perceive the patterns of what they are. And you remain present.

Since you still remain connected to the inner flow of those energies, you can now ask, "What are those concepts? What are those emotions? What is the deeper pattern underneath it?" You begin to see the undercurrent of your personality, and also to see, below that, just how unconscious your personality is to the source of knowledge.

All people can become trapped in their preferences. There is some prejudice inside each of us for something we desire. Every seeker who comes to the path wants something, but they are hiding it, even from themselves. So as the diamond-like body of witnessing arises, it begins to excavate your hidden agenda.

This knowing faculty does not invalidate your hidden agenda, but it gives it space to be present, and such spaciousness allows you to be guided to see why you so desire what is in your hidden agenda. Viewing it from this perspective reveals a crucial piece that is missing in your soul's awareness. It then guides you through that particular treasure to more and more fulfillment, all the way to the source of all.

Such a process is one way in which the diamond-like capacity present in al-'Alim is retrieved. A consciousness dawns that is very concrete and powerful. It has the quality of supreme witnessing consciousness. The merely ecstatic realms are not to be confused with this realization. There are influences of emotion in the ecstatic realms, and there is a sweet kind of drunkenness.

An inspired saying of the Sufi Pir Hazrat Inayat Khan expresses the fullness of the process well: "I am the Wine of the Holy Sacrament; my very being is intoxication; those who drink of my cup and yet keep sober will certainly be illuminated; but those who do not assimilate it, will be beside themselves and exposed to the ridicule of the world."[236]

Awakening to the level of knowledge being described here can be equated with the kind of knowing expressed by Khidr or Elijah. In the description of how Khidr receives directly from the source, the Qur'an says *'alama hu'ilmu-l-ladoonee*.[237] *'Ilmu-l-ladoonee* is to know the essence in the *'alam*, to see Allah in the infinite collection of all the possible manifestations of all the possible universes. *'Alama hu'ilmu-l-ladoonee* is a play on words in Arabic that reveals the purpose of the relative in the absolute and of the absolute in the relative.

An enduring and clear embodiment of guidance begins with the realization of al-'Alim. This state is different from the state of merging with the absolute. In the absolute, you let go of the witness consciousness and you unite with pure awareness. Pure awareness lacks differentiation. Pure awareness sees only unity and oneness. Actually, it is not a final stage but a birthing stage, and it is necessary for the dissolution of the personality.

The moment pure awareness enters afresh into differentiation, it becomes witnessing consciousness. It becomes the embodiment of the Spirit of Guidance, the inner guide. What emerges is a medium of witnessing that unifies the relative and the absolute.

Human beings reside in the middle ground between the relative and the absolute. We have the innate potential to weave them together into a kingdom. As our journey through the Names of knowledge, wisdom, and guidance continues, we will have occasion to revisit in a variety of ways this place of inner guidance.

The danger, not only among scholars, but among mystics as well, is that because they have access to knowledge of unexplored and unseen realms, they have a tendency to become arrogant. When that happens, they lose the love element. Arrogance is a form of ignorance, and it stains the mirror of your knowing faculty. The diamond body of guidance is made of pure *rahma*, pure love. The inner guide is a manifestation of Allah's perfect love—ar-Rahman, ar-Rahim.

Our discussion of omniscience leads us to the divine Names of wisdom and guidance that will complete this relational cluster. To do this properly, we first need to direct our attention to al-Haqq, and in the next chapter we will investigate the ground of all knowledge, the ground of reality itself. Consideration of al-Haqq will enhance our understanding of divine wisdom and the nexus of spiritual guidance.

ya·ḥazz

ḥakim

ḥakam

Chapter 23

The Ground of All Knowing and the Dawning of Wisdom

Ya Haqq

(yaa ḤAKK)

Throughout his famous book *Fusus al-Hikam*, 'ibn 'Arabi consistently uses the word *haqq* instead of "Allah," and it has driven scholars crazy. Why doesn't he say Allah instead? In this, his most famous book, he hardly mentions Allah. It is all about Haqq. Haqq does this; Haqq does that. Why he chose to write in this fashion is a fascinating question.

We think he is using al-Haqq to point to a quality of God's knowledge that is virtually impossible to describe. The key to this may be hidden in the introduction to *Fusus al-Hikam*. When 'ibn 'Arabi is drawing the reader's attention to all the big philosophical questions, he says there are two ways of knowing: how a being knows itself directly and how it knows itself through a mirror.

Out of this thick book, he spends half a page on the all-important subject of a thing knowing itself directly, and the rest of the book is about the other way of knowing. That secondary way of knowing is how a thing knows itself through another thing. What 'ibn 'Arabi then describes is how the ineffable reality of Allah knows itself through the mirror of the complete human being, *al-'insaan kaamil*. How God knows God's own self without the mirror is expressed by the pure awareness of al-Haqq.

The divine Name al-Haqq directs our attention to the nature of reality. It is the very ground of being, a field that is both active and potential, known and unknown. We have seen that al-'Alim is a mode of knowing that includes both visible and invisible, and how its knowing is an embrace of infinite love. And we have seen that it knows itself in everything. Still, al-'Alim can be said to know itself through another thing.

The beloved looks at its face in the mirror of what appears to be other than itself. But how does the beloved appear to itself without the mirror? Al-Haqq orients us toward the answer to that question, the supreme reality of God's self-knowledge. But before we try to go further into such sublime aspects of meaning, we think it will be useful to look at al-Haqq in terms of physical-plane forms the root takes, especially with regard to action. We hope such an approach will restrain us from viewing this great Name in only an abstract sense.

As a verb, the root of al-Haqq becomes *haqhaqa*. *Haqhaqa* means to journey into the heart of the night, and, at the same time, to exert oneself to the utmost degree. A first-form variation of the root means "I am vehemently desirous for a thing." What we can garner here for human beings is a sense of yearning, of exerting oneself, and journeying into the darkest part of night.

Another part of al-Haqq's meaning is found in the phrase *'ihtaqqat bihi at-ta'nah*, which means to pierce directly inside. It is to take an instrument and pierce the belly directly in its deepest part. This stage of meaning in al-Haqq is the journey from the outside to the inside. You go from the outside of the animal into the inside, and you go right into the heart of the night. Al-Haqq brings not only a driving desire, but also a sense of direction.

A second stage of meaning is being outside in the dark when the sun begins to rise and its light makes everything visible to someone. That is called *haqqat-nee ash shams*. The sun goes from being invisible (or inside) to being visible (or outside). It moves from the hidden to the fully manifest, from al-Batin to az-Zahir.

A third meaning of al-Haqq is to become necessary, incumbent, or obligatory. It is associated with *taqdeer*, which expresses the whole realm of al-Qadir, the inexorable power of divine purpose moving through all of manifestation. A fourth meaning of al-Haqq is for a thing to become suitable and in accord with the requisites of wisdom.

It is important to notice the activity that is associated with al-Haqq throughout all of the examples cited. This divine Name clearly connotes more than just the abstract reality of all that is. One Qur'anic verse particularly demonstrates what we are emphasizing, and spells out all the meanings we have alluded to: *Fata'ala-llahu-l-maliku-l-haqq laa 'ilaaha 'illa hoo. Rabb-ul-'arsh il-kareem.*[238]

Ta'ala is the transcendental aspect; you can think of this as the ascent. Al-Malik is the *malakut*, the descent into manifestation, the immanent. Al-Haqq is both. There is nothing else but al-Haqq. To underline this point, the verse goes on to say there is nothing else but *hu*. In the last sentence of the verse *rabb-ul-'arsh* is the center point of a circle, also called the Throne of God or the Heart Throne. It is paired in the passage with al-Karim, which is the boundless generosity that reaches everything without exception.

We would therefore render the translation as: "Allah is both absolutely transcendent and absolutely immanent. This reality, this truth, is al-Haqq. There is no other reality but the reality, the *hu*. It is the cherisher of the essence of the universe that is everywhere all at the same time."

We also read that Allah is *qadir* over all things.[239] This aspect conveys the feeling of a necessary being, a power that is unavoidable. It is as if there is a line, *taqdeer—haqq*, passing infinitely in all directions, and there is a sense of inevitability about that truth line proceeding in such a way.

The Qur'an also addresses how our ability to discern becomes marred.[240] It is the anxiety that is created in the lower self, or *nafs*, and the resultant feelings of doubt and confusion that serve to make humanity unaware of al-Haqq. The condition is described like this: "They have no knowledge and they are attached only to their pure conjecture, but conjecture is not related in any way to al-Haqq."[241]

There is a dynamic described in the Qur'an that is set up to distinguish between *haqq* and *baatil*, between reality and unreality.[242] This ability to discern is based on knowing there is a sense of permanence to al-Haqq. You are able to verify the *haqq* by experiencing the permanence of its undying reality. At the same time, you are noticing the *baatil*, which shows itself to be unreliable and impermanent by fading away. The ability to discern is rooted in the sense of inevitability of al-Haqq enduring through time without end.

Al-Haqq Considered in Relation to the Names of Knowledge and Wisdom

Is al-Haqq a Name of knowledge or of something more than knowledge? How should it be viewed in relation to the divine Names we are exploring in this large family?

In the big picture, al-Haqq is the basic field of reality, and that places it beyond any particular family of Names. One very suggestive form that the root of al-Haqq takes is *hulkh*, which means the spiderweb. Al-Haqq is the unified field of reality, a field in which all possibilities and potentialities can emerge and actualize, or remain hidden. It has the potential of being all-knowing and all-loving, it has the potential for all-action, and it has the potential to be fully unmanifest and unseen. It is the field from which any manifestation or activation can be generated.

One of the potencies within this basic field of reality is the realm of knowledge. The realm of knowledge can be divided into two domains. One domain differentiates into ideas and concepts; the other domain is undifferentiated.

On the path of the mystic, it is possible to gain knowledge of a dimension of reality through a kind of union with al-Haqq. After the merging experience, you might attempt to articulate it, differentiate it, and communicate it. Perhaps you have an experience of merging with al-Haqq, and it opens up and activates the field of love. You might then differentiate that field of love into 33 gradations, as some Sufis have written.

On the other hand, you can simply enter the field of al-Haqq and become a state of being. This state is neither knowing nor loving. It is just being. There is no concept, no idea, and no direction. There is no differentiated content to your knowing.

There is nothing like "I know this or that." Instead, you are all the elements of knowing, itself. After such an overwhelming event your knowledge might become differentiated into all aspects and gradations of what "being" means: on the personal level, the cosmic level, and the social level.

The important thing to see is that the field of al-Haqq can express itself in the conceptual and non-conceptual domains. In the nonconceptual domain you can be merged in al-Haqq and feel the whole universe as music. You can celebrate the field without needing to articulate or differentiate it. But then the moment comes where you will begin to articulate it and differentiate it, which can lead to further and further intricacies.

For al-Haqq to be differentiated to the level of knowing, a certain lens has to be applied. For example, when white light comes, you must put it through a prism to see the rainbow. To differentiate the cosmic field into love, a certain prism must open it into love. If you want to differentiate it into knowledge, a different prism has to be set in place to do so. In the hidden realm there are many of these generative archetypes, *'a'yaan thaabitah*, ideas in the mind of God, lenses. This is a good way to look at the divine Names.

When al-Haqq goes through such a lens it begins to differentiate, and what you perceive is seen as love, as joy or knowledge, and so on. The absolute in its basic nature comes through lenses, such as the divine Names, differentiating it through different realms. Human beings assimilate these realms and realities according to their development. Those who are evolving in the dimension of love can experience love, but if they are blocked in that area, they have no notion of it.

These lenses are essential vehicles, essential archetypes made of light. It is as if they are prisms of condensed light. They are like crystals. They are described in different ways by the Sufis, the Buddhists, the Kabbalists, and others. In the Jewish tradition this reality is called *merkabah*, which is also an Arabic word that means "vehicle." In an earlier chapter, we talked about experiencing all the divine Names in the abundance family as a chandelier.

We are speaking here of a vehicle that takes the absolute and differentiates it into various domains—joy, love, ecstasy, knowledge, omnipotence, and so on. There is a dimension a seer might call the diamond dimension, for it is luminous and shining. It takes the absolute and differentiates it into the domain of knowledge. It is made of light, yet it is alive, full of consciousness, and full of capacities to differentiate the abstract.

The absolute is not consciousness, as we are describing it here. The absolute is pure awareness, which differentiates into consciousness. The differentiation into consciousness is the level at which you begin to notice particular things and conceptualize about them. When you come into a room and simply see it as such, directly and without interpretation, that is awareness. Differentiation occurs when you begin to notice that the room is designed in a certain way or has certain characteristics. There is a fireplace, there are books, it looks like a living room. Consciousness has begun to differentiate awareness into many interrelated details.

The pure capacity of differentiation is what we are calling the diamond dimension. In this dimension, the spiritual wayfarer discovers an entity that acts as a guide. It may be the collective wisdom of all the illuminated souls. Some have called it the angel of revelation Gabriel, or the cosmic bodhisattva Avalokitesvara. It has been called Khidr or Elijah. No matter what name it may be given, this guidance is usually experienced in a personal form as an individual entity.

This cosmic entity filters the absolute into all the differentiated domains. It gives you the capacity to know not only what there is to be known, but also to know what needs to be known. Its way of knowing moves consciousness into different centers and different depths, and according to such movement, it reveals.

The diamond body of guidance is the facilitator of knowing. If it goes into the heart, it reveals what is in the heart. If it goes into the liver, it reveals what is in the liver. If there is fear in the liver, or anger, or ecstatic, passionate love, that conscious entity goes there, opens the area, and reveals its content. The same is true of all the contents of our psyche and of our relationships.

By finding this crystal-like body of guidance, you are connecting to an entity that is all-knowing. This entity is not exactly al-Haqq. It arises from the pure potentiality of al-Haqq. Stored in al-Haqq is all that there is to know, but it is purely undifferentiated. When al-Haqq becomes the domain of the all-knowing, it manifests as a particular guide, or deity, or entity, in order for human beings to perceive.

When a human being connects with guidance in such a way, they wisely use the boundless reservoir of all knowledge to meet the needs of humanity and the world. Such a one represents the divine reality in manifestation. Sufis look at the Prophet Muhammad, peace be upon him, not simply as an Arab of the sixth century but as a representative who has fully entered the niche of lights in just this way. It doesn't matter what individual lamp lights up this globe, its essence will have the same universal function.

There is only one guide, the guiding spirit of all souls. The wisdom that is expressed through the Spirit of Guidance is the main function of knowledge in the human realm. The spiritual nexus that we are describing can be seen also in the *logos* doctrine in Christian theology.

For the Names of Knowledge, al-'Alim is the umbrella. Through the experience of ash-Shahid and al-Khabir, we arrive at a knowledge that includes what is visible and what is invisible. The unity of outer and inner knowledge is al-'Alim. At this stage the diamond body becomes al-'Alim. The body of guidance, with all the wisdom it brings, is the nexus between the visible and the invisible.

When you are able to allow knowing and not knowing equally into the ground of your awareness, the diamond body moves to an absolute dimension. True wisdom, al-Hakim, is the heart center of the diamond body in the absolute dimension. When knowing becomes centered in the heart with a wisdom that is discerning and healing, then the Names of guidance, such as ar-Rashid and al-Hadi, enter the picture.

Al-Haqq is the matrix of all. It is how Allah knows Allah, and thus it is almost a synonym for Allah. Yet Allah is beyond even al-Haqq, as Allah must be totally complete in all domains as well as the potential of all the domains. The combination of potential and completeness as one field, interactive, manifesting, generating, is Allah.

No matter how we might try to approach understanding al-Haqq, it should be evident that we won't get very far by just conjecturing and projecting our various ideas and concepts about it. Perhaps a visual metaphor will be more suggestive. We can describe al-Haqq as a spiderweb matrix of light and dark, of form and emptiness. The human being then could be seen as the "spider" uniquely positioned to weave together the strands of the absolute and the relative into oneness.

A nexus is emerging which combines knowing (al-'Alim) and not knowing. When this occurs, the diamond body manifests as pure wisdom, al-Hakim. When you stand at this nexus of knowing and unknowing, it is not that you are absent. You are aware, and at the same time there is a potential to know. It is a field of utmost potentiality and utmost knowing. Awakening of this pure wisdom is the very heart of what we are investigating in the large cluster of Names related to knowledge.

What is needed at this point in our discussion is to understand divine wisdom and its manifestations better and to direct our attention to the different Names of divine wisdom.

Healing Wisdom and Discerning Wisdom

The Prophet Luqman is described in the Qur'an.[243] He is affectionately given the nickname Hakim, meaning the wise, and it may prove helpful to ask why Luqman is called wise. God's omniscience (al-'Alim) is an all-inclusive umbrella for what can be known about the visible and invisible worlds. For human beings, however, higher wisdom is discovered when we become able to know what we don't know. This kind of wisdom is embodied in the person of Luqman.

Scholars have argued that Luqman could be a number of historical figures, including Socrates, who we think a likely choice. In a famous story, the Oracle at Delphi pronounced: "There is none wiser than Socrates." Socrates said that he couldn't believe such a statement because he was certain that he didn't really know anything. So he investigated those who made claims to knowledge. When he probed in this way, he found that these people thought they had knowledge when they really didn't. Socrates came to see that the oracle was right because in this one small area Socrates was actually wiser.

Luqman gives some sound advice to his sons based on his accumulated wisdom. Somewhat later the Qur'an says, "We have given to Luqman wisdom [*al-hikmah*], for he expressed gratitude to Allah and gratitude for his own self [or *nafs*]. Allah is *ghaniyy* and *hamid*."[244]

Yusuf Ali comments upon this passage in his translation of the Qur'an: "This kind of wisdom perfects one's relationship with Allah and at the same time perfects the imperfections of the self. Luqman is the prototype of the sage who passes up worldly benefits and strives for inner perfection. He is the best example of wisdom and spiritual maturity and an example for how one ought to practice the wisdom within."

At the end of Surah *Luqman* there is a treatise on what can never be known. It is suggested that true wisdom (*hikmah*) comes from knowing what you don't know. Overcoming the arrogance that arises from thinking you know something when you really don't is the crucial step to take to be able to receive guidance from God and to act with wisdom in the world.

What you know and don't know is like a latticework of form and emptiness. Higher wisdom arises when you are aware of the whole fabric. Then you don't have to decide if what you are perceiving is a positive or a void, outer or inner.

You are at the nexus of knowing and not knowing. The Spirit of Guidance is attracted into that in-between space. This witnessing place at the heart center of the known and the unknown is the beginning of wisdom. Awareness of God, or *taqwaa*, can originate in the space where you are not clinging to knowing.

There are two components of wisdom: knowledge and practice. *'Imaan* is the highest kind of knowing. It is a certainty that is both inward and outward. *'Amal* is ability and skillful practice. *'Amal* is also described as *sulh*, which is the nexus between knowledge and practice.

To be a wise healer, to be what we call in this book a physician of the heart, you must know how to heal, have the ability to heal, and engage in the actual practice of healing. Being truly wise involves joining what you know with what you practice.

Ya Hakim, Ya Hakam

(yaa ḥa-KEEM, yaa ḤA-kam)

Two principal Names for divine wisdom, al-Hakim and al-Hakam, appear on all the lists of the 99 Names. They will be the next focus of our discussion. However, there are other forms that the root H-K-M takes that also should be emphasized, and we will begin with the most important such Name.

A very common form of H-K-M is HAA-kim, with the accent on the first syllable and the long "aa." Al-HAA-kim is an accepted Name of Allah that doesn't appear on any of the lists of 99 Names. It means the source of all wisdom. *Haakim* shows up in the Qur'an as a superlative and in the plural form *'ahkam-ul-haakimeen*. God is the most wise of all instances of healing wisdom.

Knowledge that is healing in some way is the only kind of knowledge that qualifies to be called wisdom. The Name al-HAA-kim means that Allah is the source of all healing wisdom. This healing wisdom is expressed in time and space through al-Hakim (ḥa-KEEM), which is the infinite manifestation of such wisdom, and through al-Hakam (HA-kam), which is the true discernment that brings clarity as to wisdom's purpose.

Al-Hakim manifests into everything without exception. It is so universal that it includes al-Hakam as part of its meaning. The theme of al-Hakim is expressed in two distinct parts. It has the intellectual aspect (al-'Alim) and the practical aspect (al-'Aziz) united in it.

In the Sufi tradition, when al-'Alim is fully reflected in your awareness you are in the state of knowing that is called *yaqin*. When al-'Aziz is fully reflected in your awareness, you realize the appropriate manner of expression in all your relationships in life, and this results in behavior that is described as having *adab*.

What we find most interesting is that in the 80 or so occurrences of al-Hakim in the Qur'an, it is almost always paired with either al-'Alim or al-'Aziz. The pairings are about equally divided between the two. Given the teaching that the mystery of the sacred Names is encoded in the Qur'an, these pairings are a very straightforward way to make the point that both aspects of wisdom are contained in al-Hakim.

The nominative form of H-K-M is al-Hikmah. It means both wisely reflecting on the secrets of divine essence (the silent or still wisdom), and living actively in harmony with that reflection. Al-hikmah has several levels of meaning. The first one is *al-hikmat ul-maskutu 'ana*, the wisdom of the secrets of divine essence. This knowledge is connected with al-'Alim.

The second level is *al-hikmat ul-mantuq biha*, the wisdom of the secrets of articulating and practicing the knowledge that is drawn from the essence. Skillful practice of the healing arts is associated with the name al-'Aziz.

Let's look at some basic meanings that the root H-K-M takes at the physical level. *Hakama* means to attach a bridle made of untanned leather or hemp straws around the head of a horse, to guide the horse's movements and not let him run wild—unbridled—and injure himself. It is to rein in.

The ability to control unbridled passions such as anger requires a wisdom that is practical and that expresses itself in skillful action, putting into practice all that you know. It requires patient perseverance (*sabr*) to see the process through to completion. The Sufi analogy between controlling the horse and controlling the *nafs* comes directly from the Arabic.

Hakama, we have seen, means to prevent from acting in a harmful or injurious manner. *Hakam-tu 'alayi bi-kadhaa*: I prevented him from suffering or doing injury to himself or others. Along those lines, the noun form is *hukm*, which means prevention or restraint. *Hikmah* in ordinary speech is what prevents or restrains you from acting in an ignorant manner. A second form of the root, *hakama*, means to control events rather than have events control you. You ride the appetite rather than having the appetite ride you.

There is a fourth form, *'ahkama*, that means to manufacture a sword in a firm, stable, strong, well constituted, established, and skillful way. *'Uhkima*, a passive fourth form, means "it was secured from corruption and made free from defects by acting in a well constituted, firm, and determined manner."

We recommend recitation of Ya Hakim and Ya Halim for this taming process of the *nafs*. This invocation combines the gentle healing love of al-Halim with al-Hakim, the emanation of healing wisdom. Ya Sabur and Ya Rahim are also an excellent combination of qualities to repeat as a pair toward the accomplishment of controlling the ego. You tame a horse in a gentle, loving, and persistent manner.

In the same way, you manage your own lower self, and control the excitement of unbridled passions, particularly anger. Such skillfulness is based on the excellence of the knowledge that opens our hearts to the secrets of divine essence. Those who realize al-Hakim perform skillfully the arts and sciences of mystical knowledge.

The word *hakama* means a bridle, but by extension it also means the head, face, and spiritual rank or station. An example of this usage is *rafa'allahu hakamatah*: Allah has raised his spiritual state or station. So it is by gaining the ability to control the *nafs* that Allah accordingly raises one's state or station.

In modern Arabic, a *hakim* is a skilled physician. A *hakim* is one skilled in the healing arts who is using their well grounded education and abilities to perform their profession. They are competent in knowledge and practice and reliable as healers. It is easy to see how this contemporary meaning grew from its classical roots, which we have glossed as a physician of the heart. Another dictionary meaning for *hakim* is a wise old man or woman.

Let's turn our attention now to al-Hakam, discerning wisdom. Al-Hakam is described by such words as sapient, sagacious, wise, and judicious. It is to be clear-eyed, percipient, penetrating, knowing, aware, and perspicacious. It is a seeing from the eye of the heart, by means of the light of God. A hadith says that we should be aware of the penetrating insight [*firaasah*] of the believer, because such a one sees by the light of God.

The dictionary also describes *hakam* as mindful, clearheaded, thoughtful, watchful, intelligent, smart, and bright. Another group of synonyms for this discerning quality is subtle, discrete and sensitive. A last group of dictionary meanings expresses skill in discerning, practice of discernment, and the finding of skillful means. All of these things describe the divine name al-Hakam.

Discerning wisdom is called the goal of all knowledge, inner and outer. Through this wisdom you become able to discern between what is real and what is transient (*al-haqq* and *al-baatil*). The ability to discern erases all doubt so that a seeker of wisdom can focus on the truth amidst the most confusing of conditions.[245]

Here's an example from the Qur'an of how such discernment manifests in human beings: *'inna-allaha kaana 'aleeman khabeeraa*.[246] Those truly wise ones who are working for peaceful resolution in family matters are called arbiters. Taken as a whole, all the qualities we named as being connected with discerning wisdom offer everything you could ever desire to have in a proper arbiter of affairs.

Returning to the more inclusive Name al-Hakim, on 56 occasions it is paired with al-'Aziz in the Qur'an. On almost as many occasions it is paired with al-'Alim. In other words, practice without knowledge is not wisdom, and knowledge without practice, or the skillful ability to be able to practice, is not wisdom either. Balance is essential. You need to have the wisdom and ability to put into practice what you know to be true.

Its pairings illustrate the universality of al-Hakim. Here are a few examples from the Qur'an of some of al-Hakim's pairings. At 4:140, al-Hakim is combined with al-Wasi'. When it is used with al-Wasi' what is emphasized is its unlimited manifestation. When it is paired with al-'Aziz it emphasizes the capacity to practically achieve wisdom's ends. The end result is *'inna-ka 'anta al-azeez al-hakeem.*[247]

A typical Qur'anic verse reads, "Allah will set forth clearly the signs and symbols, for Allah is 'Alim and Hakim."[248] This is repeated in over two dozen verses. The divine Name al-Mubin expresses this kind of wise discrimination, as used to interpret the signs and symbols of unity found in the sacred book of nature. "After these clear symbols have come to you, then know that Allah is both 'Aziz and Hakim."[249]

God's explaining signs and symbols to Abraham and his descendants is both Hakim and 'Alim.[250] "From the messengers on the straight path, God reveals this wise message. God is 'Aziz and Rahim."[251] Clearly, both divine knowledge and the capacity to accomplish are necessary for wisdom.

The next passage brings us back to the gateway of all the Names. We have come full circle to the outpouring of divine love. "It is ar-Rahman who has taught the Qur'an and every other message in the book of nature, and has created humanity."[252] Wisdom must be rooted in infinite love, compassion, and kindness. Wisdom, to be wisdom, must come from love.

Many times the Qur'an is described as full of wisdom, as a wise book. The attributes of al-'Alim and al-Hakim are applied to it.[253] The important thing to know, however, is that the word *kitab*, which is usually translated as "book," doesn't mean a collection of printed pages. When the Qur'an was first recited there was no physical book. *Kitab* does mean the writing. It is a verbal noun that comes from "to write."

What is being written is called *ayat*, a word that means signs or symbols of God. *Ayat* is the name for all chapters in the Qur'an. The chapters (*ayat*) of the Qur'an are completely filled with the signs of God (*ayat*). These signs are seen in heaven, earth, trees, shadows, rivers, mountains. Thousands of verses support this view. Qur'an means divine song or recitation. Wisdom is *written* in the sacred book of nature. That is the *kitab* being referred to here. It flows through all of nature, and what is collected in the Book is a microcosm of it.

From the psychological perspective, there will be some people who have personal conflicts and resistance in relation to the qualities expressed by al-Hakim. They might manifest as "wise guys" or "know-it-alls." Grandiosity is their defensive strategy. Grandiosity is a cover over an extreme vulnerability. The more the physician of the heart excavates this terrain, the more this vulnerability will come into view.

People in this condition are generally afraid to enter the space of not knowing. They are unwilling to venture there because it is threatening to them. For example, if they should happen to imagine the forest is full of mischievous djinns and evil forces, their grandiosity will say in defense, "Who needs forests?" The counselor needs to expose the grandiosity, and to show the student that it is a defense over their vulnerability. This will expose the terror that is inside them as well as the depth of what is unknown to them.

When the physician of the heart begins to reach that person and gets through the grandiose cover the student begins to feel safer in the condition of not knowing. They recognize their own habitual strategy of defending their vulnerable place, so they don't have to go right into grandiosity. Healing wisdom begins to dawn.

The depth of not knowing is usually a very dark place. But it has potential! Consciousness can enter the dark matter of the universe, and instead of feeling it as a terrible thing you can experience the pure potentiality of knowing that it is there. In this way, wisdom is born. Getting acquainted with the unknown is in fact becoming acquainted with a gentleness and depth that is numinous.

Spiritual travelers usually want to transcend the abyss rather than descend into it, but that means ignoring an important aspect of wisdom. Dark, deep, gentle wisdom is the feminine aspect of wisdom, called *sophia* in the Greek. It can be contrasted with radiance, which is the masculine aspect of the absolute.

Al-Haqq, as a field, can be divided into luminosity and darkness. According to a hadith, there are 70,000 veils of light and 70,000 veils of darkness. The field is divided into form and emptiness. Yet all these opposites are inseparable. What is forming, that is emptying; what is emptying, that is forming.

Discerning wisdom and healing wisdom manifest in the world through the emanations of the Names of divine guidance. The particular ways that divine guidance operates, and how such wisdom informs the work of the physician of the heart, is the direction to be explored in the concluding chapters of this book.

hadi
rashid
muthim

chapter 24

The Names
of Guidance

The pathways through which divine wisdom is communicated to humanity are the emanations of the Names of guidance. Al-Hadi, the most general and inclusive of these emanations, means the source of all guidance. Al-Hadi's guidance is for the whole of humanity or a whole community of people.

Ar-Rashid has a more specific focus and can be particularly seen in the relationship of the spiritual guide or Murshid (*mu-ra-sha-da*) to a student. Al-Mulhim points to the inner guide, the guidance of the heart; it is a guidance that is received directly and not in response to anything exterior.

In societal terms, al-Hadi manifests in canonical guidance from a holy book and a structured religion. A traditional treatment of the Names of guidance would begin with al-Hadi, and this would be the perfect place to begin if we lived in a settled society where people were thoroughly reared in a religious context and then developed from those roots into a deeper inner relationship with the God-reality.

However, that is not the world we presently live in, certainly not in America, and the seekers of the way of mystical union almost always come toward the path as the result of inner experiences. Something happens that touches their soul. Inspirational experiences arouse them in specific ways and give them access to a new realm. They are being touched by the emanation of al-Mulhim. The new realm that is experienced may be ecstatic and heart opening, but it is also shattering to their settled sense of self and very confusing for their egos. Nevertheless, it activates their process.

The traditional cultural model says to begin the subject of divine guidance with al-Hadi, but our overwhelming experience in Western culture strongly suggests to us to begin with a discussion focused on al-Mulhim. So before we do a more detailed analysis of these Names as we have done throughout this book, laying out the roots and the usage in the Qur'an and so forth, we think it important to have a more general discussion in the context of psychological growth and the spiritual path.

We will consider how the different qualities of guidance are manifested in life experiences and how their presence leads seekers to go forward on a spiritual path and to progress through the stages of the path. We will discuss how we think a teacher, functioning in our time, can best connect with students by meeting them where they are in their process at the time when they are drawn to the teachings, and moving forward from there.

The stages of the spiritual journey are demonstrated by our evolving relationship with the divine qualities of guidance. This is not solely a modern phenomenon. Events in the life of the Prophet Moses, as described in the Bible and the Qur'an, illustrate the kind of developmental relationship with divine guidance that we are focusing on in this chapter. It begins with a primary experience—the encounter with God, the fire of divine presence, called the burning bush.

At another stage in his development, Moses is seen as being in training as a student of the great spiritual guide, Khwaja Khidr. (We discuss important details of this relationship in Chapter 17, The Seven Levels of the *Nafs*, and in particular *an-nafs ul-mulhimah*.) Finally, at the end of his maturation process, Moses brings the scripture and offers the law, the divine covenant, and guidance for the whole community. The principles and teachings brought forth at this stage of the path apply equally to all levels of society and all people.

Today we can see the echo of this cosmic pattern acted out again and again. A typical scenario might be of a man or woman who in their youth, perhaps on psychedelics or other drugs, has a primary experience of the infinite. It is an experience that offers light and also unsettles their view of the world. Becoming inspired to learn more, they are eventually led to accept a spiritual guide and to receive some specific guidance.

In time they become a member of a community of people that has a standard of ethical and harmonious behavior and a stability of practice. The outer forms of the scenario vary, and certainly drugs are not necessarily a part of it, but the pattern of discovery, beginning with some direct inner experience, tends to be the same. There is no established outer standard that all people in our society accept, and at the outset of their journey a typical seeker might not even imagine that their awakening experience has anything to do with religion.

As a spiritual guide, you could be dealing with a second generation American Muslim, who is a transvestite right out of the jail cell, with a heroin habit, and who came to you because they read a book of Rumi's poetry. We think it is wise for a teacher to find something positive to build on from the inner experience that led them to you, and after making a connection and gaining their trust you can gradually deal with issues such as the heroin addiction, rather than telling them everything about themselves is wrong, and initially trying to make them fit into an outer religious norm.

We think that there has been a kind of paradigm shift. In the past, people were first trained how to behave in society, and then they were taught what constituted the roots of such behavior. Finally, they were encouraged to find the inner experience of unity with humankind from which it is all derived. Now we are in a world where we can't effectively teach that way. So our method of teaching is to look for the inner experience that will inform a person's understanding of how to behave in the world.

For example, an experience of seeing everyone as part of yourself would naturally lead you to exercise fairness in all your relationships. It can be argued that we are recommending the path of mysticism, not the path of religion, but it is also true that this approach often leads people back into areas they have discounted and enables them to see a new spiritual depth and wisdom in religion. Then they are able to interpret religion in a living way.

Fundamentalism is an extremely closed system. In the end it is incapable of sustaining growth, and as a consequence, things fall apart. What tends to happen with people in such closed systems is that rather than nurturing, affirming, and in some way cultivating inner heart experiences, they choose to ignore them. The Sufi teacher Murshid Samuel Lewis used to describe the attitude of most church establishments: "If you say you believe in angels you're in, but if you say you have experienced angels, you're out."

When an inner experience activates the seeker, then their soul begins to ask love to awaken it and to send it deeper insights and further experiences. Such an activating inner experience, whether it comes with clarity or not, begins to dismantle some of the psyche's grip on things, and the psychological structure loosens. In Western society, LSD and other psychedelics rocked the psychological landscape, and the aftermath entered the overall conceptual structure and became part of the mainstream of society and its evolution.

An extreme example of the phenomenon of dismantling the psychological structure can be seen in the *madzub* who have no grip on this world at all. They are completely taken up by inner inspirations and are constantly pulled by the divine. However, generally a teacher today deals with students in varying degrees of dissociation and not those who are thoroughly *majnun* (God-crazy).

Most human beings are thoroughly encased and insulated. We experience ourselves as an island separated from the whole. We are individualized rather than individuated. We wanted to individuate, but instead we ended up isolated. Because of this isolation, the ego or personality structure lacks resilience and becomes quite narcissistic.

Such an ego is a solid structure, and you need a bulldozer as well as laser beams to make a dent in it. Each one of us is trying to survive as an ego! Consequently, initiating our relationship with a flow of inner inspiration can only happen as a kind of miracle, something massive and powerful. This is the stage of *ilham*—the noun form of al-Mulhim.

The activation of al-Mulhim is full of opportunities and pitfalls. Great inspiration comes from it, and sometimes an encounter with the absolute occurs. There are enthusiasms and realizations all mixed up with a person's prejudices, concepts, and distorted image of self. One in this condition needs integration. A relationship with a real spiritual guide becomes important.

At this stage of the journey, the teacher might recommend repetition of Ya Mulhim. Calling on the reality of the One who truly inspires from within can help the student begin to clarify their inner experiences. What they ultimately need to develop, and what is later seen in the quality of ar-Rashid, is the clarity of the diamond body of awareness discussed in Chapter 23, The Ground of All Knowing and the Dawning of Wisdom. This luminous accommodation of wisdom is the individuated being. It can integrate, unify, and explain the relative and the absolute.

At this time in their journey, this realization is not readily available to them, and indeed any kind of objectification seems quite foreign. What is needed is that they begin to find a way to relate to divine wisdom as a stabilizing and grounding force. Recognizing the need for guidance in the confusing terrain they have entered is important.

The ego needs some encouragement and nurturing to gain the confidence to move through its various experiences. And that is a large part of what the spiritual guide does. At this point the quality of ar-Rashid fully enters the picture. It is a guidance that is particularly focused on what they need in their development, which stabilizes and balances them.

Then, as the student's experiences get more embodied and actualized, the natural maturation of their process is to become engaged with the way of life of a spiritual community, or *sangha*. You naturally feel that you want to walk a walk that is grounded in your deep experiences, and you seek the community with which that can resonate.

Finding the strength to follow through in this way activates an essence, another dimension, which is a kind of citadel. It gives perseverance, patience, and support. It is the capacity to walk that walk of your soul's intention regardless of the influences that come up. Your soul has been touched by the flames of the burning bush, and its fire has aroused the yearning to live the truth behind the experience.

The function of the spiritual guide, or Murshid, is to represent a clear and balanced capacity of knowledge and wisdom. They take the student and say, "What you saw is only part of you, and part of the great being, and it has a meaning." Their quality of guidance decodes the hidden realm all the way to the absolute and shows how the absolute differentiates itself in myriads of forms in the inner and outer worlds. The guide also serves to balance the emphasis on form given by al-Hadi and the lack of structure of al-Mulhim.

Repetition of Ya Rashid is of benefit when the student is ripe for developing their inner capacity for accessing and accommodating divine wisdom into all aspects of life. And it is appropriate when they are ready to find their inner guide.

The stage in which the student is encouraged to find the inner guide can be a real challenge for the teacher. At this point, the student has integrated inner guidance more and more. Their relationship with the teacher no longer has so much transference involved in it, and it has become more vivid. They begin to see the teacher as another human being. Now, when the student looks at the teacher without so much projection, there is continuing love, honoring, and respect.

However, in the undercurrent of the unconscious what comes is the breakage of their idealization. And when that ideal is broken, what is aroused is a layer of rage and disappointment. First of all, the teacher needs to show the student it is appropriate that they see the teacher more objectively, that in fact they are now honoring the teacher properly.

At the same time, the guide should be prepared to be under attack. The student will now unleash their rage at having no guidance in their life, and their projections on the teacher will take a new shape. Their anger at their father or mother, and the relation to guidance that was taught in their childhood, spills over in their relationship to the teacher. "Where were you when I needed you?" In this phase, the student has to be held accountable and responsible.

The teacher should find the capacity to tolerate it, knowing that the part of the student that is devaluing them is just a child throwing a tantrum. Still, the teacher should hold them accountable and clearly reflect it back to them so they can see it for what it is. The breaking down of the idealization with which they have held the teacher needs to be navigated with utmost care and utmost cautiousness to stabilize the companionship and to heal.

The approach we are suggesting will bring up in the student's awareness the deep wound of their separation from God, a wound which no teacher can heal for someone else. Even so, the student may be outraged that the teacher has failed to heal this wound, and after the anger come the tears. The student needs to gently but firmly be turned to face this pain of separation from God directly, to wait at the door of the beloved, and to be open to grace.

In time the student reaches the stage of the spiritual community or *sangha*. In its fullest sense, this stage has to do with a certain quality of guidance. We could call it the Holy City, the Jerusalem of Being, the Shambala. Within this essential state there is a quality that encompasses all the essential states and integrates all of the essential domains.

In general terms, these domains can be called the boundless ever-potent reality of the transcendental absolute, all the possible accommodations of the heavens or different planes of existence, and the mystery of the constant transformations of all material things. In Buddhist terms, these domains are called *dharmakaya*, *samboghakaya*, and *nirmanakaya*.

The stage of al-Hadi is the stage of actualization. Gradually a time comes in your spiritual process when you begin to feel a kind of citadel settling into your consciousness. You feel rooted in your process no matter what happens. You continue steadily like a camel crossing the desert, even in the face of a sandstorm. The blessings of the divine are manifest in daily life. This is the realm where the daily bread of heaven comes into the daily bread of breakfast. It is the landing of the essential domain in daily life.

Ego consciousness can't accomplish this stage. When the essential domain we have called the Holy City comes, there is a great relief and ease in knowing that the kingdom of heaven is with you, that you can enter by meditation, by relaxing, by feeling, by sensing, by invoking. At this point the *ilham* has become fully integrated into the rhythm of everyday life, and it is no longer just an isolated experience. The experience has been tamed.

"The kingdom is at hand," as Jesus says. So what are the stumbling blocks that prevent us from becoming rooted in guidance and experiencing these further stages of the path? After all, each of us wants to live our truth, to fully develop what our soul came here to embody.

One significant element of our situation is referred to in psychological terms as "merged support." It is the support that an individual gains from merging. The negative aspect of merging can be explained by starting with the common experience each of us has of seeking individuality, of seeking to identify who we are. This longing for identity drives humanity crazy. "Who am I? What I am? Where am I? You don't see me. You don't love me." People don't have a real sense of self, so they seek for it and long for it. It's all about "I" "me" "my."

It turns everyone into a narcissist. In the Greek myth, Narcissus didn't have a sense of self so he looked into the pool to see who he was, and he fell in love with the image. The image we are talking about here is the image of the ego. We hold on to the ego because the ego is the image of the beloved.

All humanity is seeking for the real self, but they don't know how to find it, so they hold on to the ID card, the image of it in the ego. It goes along with a story. I am from this tribe, this religion, this society, or this family. And there is the unconscious feeling of these values, which we use as a crutch to sustain our ego identity. There is power in it. A whole nation or religion can become inflamed by it.

This identification with a society, even a spiritual community, builds a kind of superego. I am a Buddhist. I am a Sufi. What does that concept have to do with your flesh and bones, which are the living manifestation of the divine being? Such ego identification can transform what is taken from a religion or spiritual community into the worst enemy of that religion or community's real goals.

Since the approach to seeking spiritual identity by identifying with a community or society is subtler, people believe they are free, but they have fallen into the trap of using the group to support the ego and to fill in the missing sense of self. When they give up the sense of self that comes from being "an American," "a church member," and so on, it feels like the ground they were standing on has been removed.

They plummet into a giant hole and experience no direction and no sense of self. Ya Hadi is the *wazifah* that is most appropriate when the student is approaching this stage: to actualize insights, to walk the walk, and to move from states to stations, from *hal* to *maqaam*.

The mind structure needs to be continually opened and to be regrouped each day according to what comes. Sometimes you have to build an ego before you can let it go. Incorporation and embodiment are necessary stages in the process. The kind of disintegration of the personality structure we have described is only encouraged in the very late stages of the journey.

We have been shaped and limited by our family constellations. Here is Mom and here is Dad, and their unhappiness and misery, which we have internalized. Ultimately, we let go of all these structures we have used to provide our identity. When the spiritual traveler lets go of it all, they fall into a vast emptiness. There is no ground and no identity.

Not shrinking from this, you begin to feel you are landing somewhere. Where you are landing is in the absolute, and you experience the essential state. You become established in the light of freedom, and what emerges from within you is the being of light that you are.

It is as if a holy city has landed in you, a domain filled with realized beings and with great beauty. It is pervaded by the luminosity of the absolute coming through jeweled structures and illuminated beings, praying and praising in temples upon temples of light. The feeling of this kind of manifestation is very sacred.

With the landing of the holy city in you, you experience the everyday kingdom in which you live as precious and holy. It is equally beautiful and magical and filled with all virtues as the inner world. That is what *taqwaa* means. It is to live in this awareness of the presence of Allah in your own heart. In the words of the Prophet Muhammad, "There are those who act in the world as if they see God." Mevlana Rumi quotes another famous hadith: "The reason why we are in this world is to find the hidden treasure in everything."

The holy city protects itself from those who just seek bliss but are unwilling to forego their ego attachments. If a person loses the frequency of being that is in harmony with the holy city, then they are in self-imposed exile. The temple of God, which is the human body, should be treated with great respect. If the soul is not purified of its identification with its limited notion of ego-self it cannot sustain being at home in this accommodation.

When you are freed from the trap created by narcissism, your Sufism, for example, becomes your heart's desire to walk the authentic walk of your soul's manifestation. Now the way of the *sharee'ah* or of any outer form is illuminated from within. You embrace your particular path but you also embrace the Buddhist who is sitting next to you.

'Ibn 'Arabi calls *al-'insaan kaamil*, or complete human being, the *wahdah*. It is the middle ground between the absolute and the relative. The complete human being unifies knowledge, weaving together the absolute and the relative. This nexus is expressed in the spiritual guide through the quality of ar-Rashid. Having access to this divine quality allows the spiritual guide to accept the inspirations of al-Mulhim given by students and to show their deeper meanings.

The whole process of ripening in the Names of guidance grows from the original response of the teacher to keep alive the primary experience of inspiration that activated the student's journey, al-Mulhim. By keeping this connection alive, the teacher avoids turning the process into some sort of personality cult—the creation of a new substitute Daddy or Mommy.

There are warning signs that should be mentioned. At a certain point in the life of a cult mentality, the individuals in the group isolate themselves from the world more and more, and they become more and more dependent on one person. This is quite different from the balanced approach to the world offered by *al-'insaan kaamil*.

When the spiritual process becomes stale, a seeker may begin to sleepwalk through the teachings because they have lost their connection with inspiration. Repetition of Ya Mulhim may be of great value at this point. It is also helpful for the student to repeat Ya Mulhim in the early stages of enthusiasm and inspiration that characterize their initial approach to the teacher.

On the other hand, sometimes students have been drawn by some small experience or have heard about beautiful things that are happening in a group or with a teacher. Hearing of such things awakens a kind of longing, but they have had no primary experiences of inspiration. They don't even have an inspiration to call for something beautiful. Recitation of Ya Mulhim may awaken them somewhat and allow them to connect to inner experiences beyond everyday life, which will help activate their journey.

In dream work, a counselor may work with someone for years, and then hear about a dream from their childhood where an angel of light came to them and gave them guidance. They had repressed the dream because their mother had told them it wasn't important. That is pure gold for the physician of the heart because you can affirm it and kindle the flame of al-Mulhim.

The issue you must deal with in this case is the loss of the basic trust that was connected with their initial experience of inspiration. They have lost a basic trust that they can be nurtured by Being itself. Because they got very disappointed so early, they have never been able to trust that there is some goodness or love that will come to them.

In the long run, the teacher wants to help the student be drawn into the experience of the inner world but also to value everyday life. They need to move from being tossed about from experience to experience to becoming established in a station of realization that is not so dependent on circumstances.

This middle ground is brought through the quality of *rushd*, the Name ar-Rashid. It brings an established and clear consciousness that balances inner experience and worldly life. A person who has this doesn't get overinflated or underinflated. So when the student is going through amorphousness, through inflation/deflation, you take them to ar-Rashid to see exactly what is the experience they are having.

The invocation of Ya Rashid encourages balance, steadiness, and objectivity. It could be combined in repetition with Ya Matin. It stabilizes both the *ilham* and the experience of the world. If a person is really stuck then Ya Mulhim can be prescribed, but for someone who is stuck and needs guidance badly, you could combine Ya Rashid and Ya Mulhim in repetition. Ya Hadi will become most effective toward the end of their overall process toward actualization.

The stage of *ilham* can knock people off their rocker. A primary experience in *ilham* is unpredictable and varied like the flickering light of a fire. It destabilizes your relationship with the world. The daily news is full of extreme cases, and we can learn something by looking at them. Recently we heard about the man who said he built a box inside himself to listen to God, and what he heard was to kidnap and rape an 11-year-old girl and hold her hostage for 19 years.

One of the writers of this book was called in as a chaplain to speak with a woman in prison who had thrown her three children in the Bay and drowned them. She sincerely believed that God had told her to do it. She had had an experience of some kind. She wasn't making the story up.

The stage of al-Mulhim is dangerous terrain because people are beginning to hear an inner prompting but they cannot sort out the voice of the *nafs*, or the ego-self, from the voice of Allah. There is no ability to distinguish between what is genuine guidance and what is the product of fear, inner confusion, and ego-blindness. The result can be a kind of fanaticism, replete with absurdities like suicide bombers blowing up children while quoting from the holy Qur'an.

The stage of *ilham* is discussed in the context of the third stage of the *nafs*, an-nafs ul-mulhimah, in Chapter 17, The Seven Levels of the *Nafs*. There we see its positive manifestation in the quintessential spiritual guide Khwaja Khidr. The activity of al-Mulhim is an intense state, or *hal*. It is a powerful experience, but it is a transient one, even if it takes you to the eternal.

Inspiration passes through the globe of the heart, which according to a hadith is covered with 70,000 veils of darkness and 70,000 veils of light. You think you are serving God, and your intention may be to serve God, but who is the God you are listening to and what are you really serving? Understanding is obscured because of the coverings over your heart.

As we mentioned earlier, most people today approach the different *tareeqahs*, or spiritual orders, having being aroused by al-Mulhim in some way and needing guidance in relation to inner experiences of different kinds. If you can meet them in their particular state, and help them to ground it and overcome confusion, they will be able to make progress on the path of their life.

Repetition of Ya Mulhim paired with Ya Nur may be a helpful practice for the student at this early stage. Ya Mu'min and Ya Muhaimin is another pair of Names that may be useful at this stage to give grounding and divine protection. Also, for the person who is totally deadened to the realm of *ilham*, repetition of Ya Mulhim, Ya Nur would be effective.

However, the activity of *al-Mulhim* for some people inflates their ego to such a point that they reject any outer help. Compare this condition with that of Moses at the burning bush. Moses' response to his powerful experience was not that of an egomaniac who would grasp at the chance to appropriate all that intensity into his ego-self. He spoke of his inadequacy to convey it to Pharaoh. He said he couldn't speak well, that he stammered, and someone else would be a better spokesperson.

For a moment let's consider the *ilham* from the ego's point of view: "God talks to me, so I am a special, chosen one." The experience of *ilham* brings great inspiration and the enthusiasm to connect to God and to be in union with God, but there is something beyond even this. For the core of every ego, there is one highest aspiration, and that is to be God. It is not to reach God, not to connect with God. It is to be God.

Every ego wants it. Every ego narcissistically aspires to be God and is plagued by this longing. Why does this condition exist, and does it have to be a narcissistic disease? It helps to understand that the very seed of the ego was planted by Allah. You were made in the divine image, and because of a kind of memory of that, the ego wants to find Allah at the individual level. There are hadiths of the Prophet Muhammad where he describes an experience of seeing Allah in the form of a beautiful human being on the throne.

There is a divine spark within each one of us. If you magnify it, you will see the Lord. Each one of us has our own Lord sitting on its own throne in the image of the Great Lord. From this perspective, every ego aspires to reach the domain of individuated Godhood.

Gradually, children, whose very nature is to be born as the light of the soul in its glory, lose the spark within and the sense of their essence. At some point, generally from seven to nine years old, the child fully separates from that identity and forms an ego identity. I am such and such. Then, when push comes to shove, you hear them saying, "This is me and this is how I am, and I know myself, and you don't know me and you don't love me," and so on in this vein.

In the core of the ego there is a crystallized sense of an identity, and this identity is godly. We all believe that we are gods, and that nobody sees us. Even for those who go into the deepest despair, in that despair there is grandiosity about the hopelessness of it all. "I will never reach the optimum." And the optimum here is not about being a fully functioning human being; it is about wanting to be God on Earth.

The motivation of the ego that brings each person to the spiritual journey is a narcissistic pride, a narcissistic need to be seen as the ultimate special one. This deserves deep reflection; it shouldn't be passed over lightly. Everyone wants to be seen as the most beloved daughter or son. They want to hear, "You are the one. You are the most special of all."

This aspiration is a built-in desire in the human being, and that desire, if it is not turned into a pathological condition, becomes the flame that leads the ego to reach the goal. The deepest *ilham*, the deepest inspiration is to become al-Mulhim, the one who inspires. This is the *ilham* that can consume the ego and lead it to be absorbed by the divine reality and become the individuated God. When the student reaches the core of the personality structure and uncovers this deepest aspiration to be God, then repetition of Ya Mulhim as a sacred phrase is most appropriate.

The other aspiration is to reach al-Haqq, the undifferentiated ground of all reality, and not just to reach the individuated soul within, or God within. The ego seeks the personal God reality, and the soul seeks the cosmic God reality.

What is the difference between the story where Moses swooned on the mountain when he experienced *tajalliyyat* and saw God and the one where he did not swoon on Mount Sinai when he saw God? In the first instance he tried to see God with his ego but couldn't contain the experience. In the second instance he received the Torah and communicated it to the community because he received the experience through the purified heart that is an infinite container.

Once there was a 12-year-old boy sitting on a throne that ruled the whole civilized world. It is conceivable that he might even have been the Pharaoh of Moses' time. And while that Pharaoh was probably much older, there is a psychological truth here.

When Moses came to the Pharaoh, the King was quite surprised by what Moses said. He conveyed this amazement by saying essentially, "You tell me you worship God, but I am God. Everyone says so." What a natural reaction, since each one of us has a 12-year-old boy or girl sitting on a throne ruling the whole world and saying, "I am God!" Imagine what would happen if that condition were inflated all the time by everyone telling you that you were God.

It is interesting to consider the possibility that both Moses and Pharaoh were having *ilham* experiences when they had their historic encounters, and that the condition of the veils or covers over the heart determined the radically different conclusions of each: God-realization and egomania. The stream of guidance is constant, but it can be received in a useful or damaging way.

When in its manifestation the ego lost awareness of the one who is truly sitting on the throne, it pretended to be the one enthroned there. If there is no one else there to take the job, the ego is glad to take it. Some egos become inflated and some deflated by this, but there is the same grandiosity in both reactions. If you look into the core of it, you will see a child sitting on the throne pretending to be God, helpless, deficient, and grandiose. It is a little pharaoh having tantrums and screaming orders such as, "Kill all the first born males."

The physician of the heart must find a way expose the student to this inner structure at a point when they are ripe to face it. Then the light of awareness will reveal the ego's game of a little demigod pretending to be Allah. It is a mistake to judge or condemn this inner child. See and honor that it holding the position of the loved one, the higher self. It's not a bad guy. It is the part that God put into the world to struggle and develop, and through divine love and mercy to return home and merge with the light.

This is described in a Sufi story. There was a prince who was living in a palace. Telling a servant he was going on a pilgrimage, he asked him to stay by the door to protect the palace. So the servant waited and waited. After a few months, he began to feel cold. He said, "I'll just go behind the front door and stay there." Then he waited some more but the prince didn't show up. He said, "I'll just go to the living room suite." Finally he said, "The prince is not coming. It's my house anyway. Maybe I am the prince, but I forgot." This is the story of the ego.

What is needed is to say kindly to the enthroned ego, "You are not the prince. You are playing the role of the prince, but you are not the prince. Thank you for holding the position of the prince. But now merge with the prince, become one with the entity that is God-like within you."

At this time your soul is speaking directly to the most wounded part, the shamed part, the core of the narcissistic structure. This core part is like the hub of the wheel. All the spokes are connected to its desire to be the center of the universe. When it is faced in this way the center becomes transparent.

When you acknowledge and honor the ego and see what it has been doing—a little child playing God, overwhelmed by it all, ashamed and vulnerable—you see it needs to be hugged instead of demolished. When a compassionate attitude is directed toward the 12-year-old child, the child is willing to let go of that post. Healing comes for the grandiose part; it releases its woundedness and there is active remembrance of Allah. Grandiosity is replaced with grandness. In the image of God, every one of us is grand, and exists within a grand luminous field.

The psychological state of the student at the time when they become ripe to deal with this core issue should be considered. For a long time they have idealized the teacher, placing the teacher in the position of God for them. Now they have reached the stage where they want to claim it for themselves. The teacher must be dethroned and nobody can sit in the throne except their own self. That place belongs to their own inner God/Goddess.

A challenge often arises here for the teacher because they may also want to occupy that position in the student's heart and not want to be dislodged. Some gurus really want to be worshipped. It is important that the teacher look into his or her own state. When they are clear about their own desire to be God, and resolve it, then they can remain balanced and compassionate during the student's narcissistic rage.

The physician of the heart already understands that the wound of not being seen as God is now opening up in the soul of the seeker, and they can be moderate with the student and respond with joy. The teacher should cherish that at last the student is getting to the core of their mandala. It is beautiful when you journey into that aspiration of every ego—to be God in the most special way.

After all, every soul is special. Every soul has its own station, and that station is the particular emanation that comes from it. If the physician of the heart is able to properly engage in their own process and respond to the student in the ways we have described, the student will journey with the teacher as their friend to receive the divine guidance from a unique frequency.

At this stage, the physician of the heart should encourage the student to reveal their hidden ambition to be the most special, and that is to be God. It helps for the teacher to become playful at this time. "Which God would you like to be today?" Such playfulness takes away the superego, the judgment, and the pathology, and then the child—the 12-year-old—begins to show up. Take the opportunity to embrace it. "Hallelujah! You have the throne, but understand that it is all imitation."

Then you invite that child to join with the reality of its higher self. It is a mistake if you condemn their ego and say, "You are playing God. I know you are sneaking about. Stop trying to pretend." Then the ego feels intimidated, and it really hides. It goes far underground; it can even hide in the absolute where it could never be found.

If there is no competition with the teacher and the teacher embraces the student's passage, then the teacher can give some guidelines to the student—telling them that their rage comes because everybody wants to occupy their own throne, and that what is happening is a process of returning to one's throne in a real way. Then the student may gain insight into their passage, and the interaction at this stage does not become devastating.

Not only can you explain that returning to the individuated godhood is a very beautiful, complex process, but you can show that they want to be a very special kind of God, and not just God. Each soul has its own flavor, and the ego longs for that particular flavor of godhood. It is what is missing. They want to color the universe that way.

So you have people saying, "God is all loving" or saying, "God is all wisdom," and each one is saying it through their own emanation, through their own lens of seeing. Al-Haqq is beyond all of that, of course, but each one thinks that God is their flavor, their own little lens of perceiving the universe, and the ego thinks that that flavor is the ultimate.

A final gloss to this overall discussion: Al-Hadi expresses *sharee'ah*, the large road that everybody travels, the source of guidance for all. Ar-Rashid expresses *tareeqah*, the manifestation of divine guidance in a particularized form in order to discover the infinite treasures within. It is the intimate, exact path of an individual soul, and the way of the Sufi orders. Al-Mulhim expresses *haqqiqah*, enlightenment directly from the essence of God. It expresses the cause and effect of the state of being divinely guided. Al-Mulhim reveals this grand reality of *haqqiqah* because it is direct from the essence. It is called *'ilmu-l-ladoonee* in the Qur'an and ascribed to Khwaja Khidr in the Moses story.[254]

Our central theme in this introductory treatment of the emanations of divine guidance is to give proper respect and continuing attention to the quality of direct inner inspiration in spiritual development, and to see how it leads to realization of the other aspects of guidance.

Now we can turn our attention to an individual analysis of these divine Names, which will add substance and detail to the picture we have painted above. We will begin with the most general and inclusive Name of divine guidance.

Ya Hadi

(yaa haa-DEE)

Hudaa, or guidance, is remembrance of God (*dhikr*), and its opposite, *dalaalah*, is forgetfulness, which is also known as *ghaflah*. To understand guidance more fully we will contrast it with its opposite. Being disconnected from divine guidance is described in the Qur'an as a veil of the heart, "a veil from remembrance of me."[255] Human beings who suffer from this malady are directly confronted and prodded many times in the scripture. "They do not understand, their eyes are closed up they see not, their ears are closed up, and they are further away from receiving guidance than cattle. They are heedless and forgetful."[256]

When the Qur'an says that Allah does not guide the *kaafir*,[257] what is meant by this word is not "infidel" as it came to be translated. The word *kaafir* is derived from the verb *kafara*, which means to cover over. *Kaafir* comes from *kufraan*, which is a cover over the heart made by the *nafs*, or lower self.[258]

The main function of the *kufr* is to obstruct.[259] The people of *kufr* obstruct themselves and others on the path of Allah while imagining they are on the path. One of the features of this cover over the heart is self-delusion. It can be said that God does not guide them because they are in denial about the guidance that exists. This relationship between guidance and its loss is described time and again in the Qur'an.[260]

If you are engaged in the practice of self-effacement (*fana*), then the *kufraan* can become as thin as a silk handkerchief, but if the *nafs* is attached to its vain desire the *kufraan* becomes thick and dominant and obscures the light. When the *kufraan* is thin and the accommodation made by the *ruh*, or highest aspect of soul, is dominant, then there can be confidence that you are acting with guidance.

It is interesting that when Moses is sent by Allah to confront Pharaoh, the Prophet is accused of being a *kaafir*.[261] Pharaoh is speaking of the fact that Moses killed an overseer of the slaves and fled Egypt. Moses responds to this accusation by agreeing. He says my heart was covered, but now I have *hukm*, discerning wisdom, and this is an ecstatic gift. He explains that at that time he was frightened and he panicked. He found the cure for his condition—the light of certainty, *nur-ul-'imaan*.

We can think of the covering over the heart as a disease of the heart. In 22:53 the Qur'an actually uses the term "disease of the heart." The heart is tested to see how open it is. But if the heart is diseased it becomes hardened. The calcified state of the heart is an important cause of forgetfulness. The very first chapter of the Qur'an contains the prayer not to be led astray, *Ghayri-l-maghdoobi*. *Maghdoobi* is the path of panic and raging anger rising from forgetfulness. Its opposite is guidance, which comes from remembrance and is a path of patience and trust.

There is a verse on guidance in the famous Surah of Light in the Qur'an, chapter 24. It starts with Allah and Nur. "Allah is the light of heavens and earth… Allah guides to this light whomever he wills."[262] Earlier, there is the description of reality as "light upon light,"[263] and contrasted with this is the state of "darkness over darkness."[264] The depths of darkness are a vast, deep ocean, clouds over clouds, darkness over darkness, where you can't see your hand before your face. From this place we can observe the path of light, or guidance, and the path of darkness, where there is no guidance to be found.

Nevertheless, self-delusion (*dallah*) makes us mistake the darkness for light but feel sure that we are rightly following guidance. "They obstruct the path but they imagine they are guided on the path."[265] "They are lost, confused, bewildered, and befuddled, and after receiving guidance from Allah they still call on their little gods"[266] and they sneer at others, all because of lack of the ability to be receptive to guidance.

Takdheeb is the essence of denial, the sense of being in denial about meeting the face of the beloved. "Surely those who are lost, and who deny or refuse the meeting with Allah, they refuse to receive true guidance."[267] The opening chapter of the Qur'an, the *Fatiha*, is the most repeated prayer of all Muslims. One part of the prayer is to be guided on the straight path, the path that is life-giving water. *Hady(un)* is the name of such a path. The prayer is also to avoid the way of self-delusion and anger (*maghdoobi*).

Discerning wisdom (*hakama*) allows us to distinguish between guidance and its opposite, between remembrance and forgetfulness, between reality (*haqq*) and illusion (*baatil*). It is not evil to be off the path, for you can realize your condition and pray for guidance. The problem is willful denial. It is the ego's insistence that it is right that is the problem. Similarly, it is not anger that is bad but the unwillingness to change and the insistence that your anger is a virtue.

Moses apparently had a hot temper, as recorded several times in the scriptures. When he returned from Mount Sinai with the 10 commandments he was angry and grieved that his people, whom he had left with his brother Aaron, had made an idol to worship.[268] He threw down the tablets and pulled his brother Aaron by the hair. But then he prayed to God to forgive him and Aaron: "Admit us into your loving mercy because you are *'arham-ur-raahimeen*."[269] This last phrase can be translated "the most supremely, ultimately loving, kind, and merciful of all possibilities of being." This prayer is traditionally made during family difficulties.

Finally, the anger that is said to characterize those who are strongly attached with their egos to the outward form of things is like a malignant serpent. Several forms of this word for anger in Arabic mean: eating too much, stuffing oneself, swollen belly, unable to void, getting angry, raging, and self-deception.

The dictionary gives its opposite as *radiyyah*, which is synonymous with *hudaa*. "O soul in complete peace [*radiyyah*] return to me, completely contented, cool, calm, peaceful. Enter you my paradise among the slaves of love."[270] This stage is treated in Chapter 17, The Seven Levels of the *Nafs*.

For those who receive guidance, Allah increases the light of guidance and gives them *taqwaa*, universal awareness of the divine presence. Guidance is described as light perfected.[271] Your relationship with the light of guidance matures. We can see the light of guidance is ever being perfected.[272] There is a famous hadith: "Speak to each person according to his or her degree of understanding." It is important to realize that the degree to which the inner light of the soul is covered or transparent determines the appropriateness of the specific guidance given to different types of human beings.

The level of guidance seen in al-Hadi is the most universal and cosmic. "Allah gave everything its existence, and then guided it."[273] "Everything" in the text (*kulli shayin*) includes all possible realms, the seen and unseen worlds. And it includes all human beings and all communities of beings, such as the communities of the Jews and Christians and others who were filled with the very same light of guidance.

"And we sent to every community [*'ummah*] a messenger."[274] Lists of specific messengers are mentioned in the Qur'an. They include Abraham, Isaac, David, Noah, Jacob, Job, Solomon, Zachariah, John, Jesus, Ishmael, Elijah, Noah, Lot, Dhul Kifl, Dhul Nun (Jonah), John the Baptist, and finally Mariam (Mary) at the end of one passage.[275] In the hadiths of the Prophet Muhammad the number of 124,000 such messengers is given.

There are many references unmistakably stating that there is a continuity of guidance, and the Qur'an is confirming the guidance that came to the Jews and the Christians and other communities.

In several places in the Qur'an we read how everything that exists circles in devotion around Allah.[276] This includes all creation, from the spheres of the angels and all the inner worlds, to the galaxies of the physical universe, to the circle of prayer beads circling in remembrance of the Name of Allah. The whole universe is involved in this devotion to the highest and most exalted reality, the One who makes everything in existence, informs it to perfect proportions, determines its path of return, and guides it.

Again and again we are invited to follow the guidance of Allah. Al-Hadi is the guide, and the grammatical form of the word itself emphasizes that Allah is the only guide. Every messenger of Allah is called *haad(in)*.[277] So Allah is the guide and the messenger is also the guide. What manifests through the messenger is the message of guidance, the *Hudaa-an-noor*. It is a faculty of the complete human being, *al-'insaan kaamil*. God is the guide, the guided, and the goal of guidance.

Most of us have lost our trust in guidance. Guidance may knock on your door, but you are heedless of it unless you perceive it is useful for the accomplishment of specific desires. If it doesn't move you toward what you want, you push it away and negate it. Most of us don't have the capacity to decide what is guidance. Often this is because of a prejudice based on an early wound of being misguided as a child.

Sometimes a teacher tells students to trust in God, trust in being, but such an admonition doesn't work because there is a fundamental distrust of life. Travelers on the path may become devotional, and try their best to trust, but they won't really have it. When a spiritual counselor hears them say, "I trust," you can be sure they don't mean it, because at a deep level they have learned not to trust. Instead of demanding a devotional blind trust, the physician of the heart should make it a friendly challenge: "You are not capable of trusting!"

A person who has lost the clear sense of witnessing and who is identifying with an isolated sense of self will project their father or mother and their notion of God onto the teacher. If teachers haven't become empty of their own ideas of self, they will buy in to the projected identity at the ego level and will enable it in a different form.

The teacher might as well be saying, "Well, yes, as a matter of fact I am God, thank you very much for seeing it." This misses the point of the process, which is to facilitate the student's deep inner connection with the wisdom of divine guidance. Our experience is that most students don't enter the path from the place of seeking the kind of universal guidance, or *hudaa*, that we have been describing. Most real students come because of being stirred up and activated by experiences of *ilham*.

Hazrat Inayat Khan, who in 1910 was the first teacher to bring the Sufi message to the Western world, advised those who would be teachers that most people will not come to you seeking God. They will come with a problem, and if you can help them with their problem they will trust your guidance on the path to God-realization.

We will turn our attention to al-Mulhim next, and conclude our discussion of the family of guidance with the divine quality ar-Rashid, which balances al-Hadi and al-Mulhim in people's lives.

Ya Mulhim

(yaa MOOL-him)

We introduced this divine quality in some depth at the beginning of this chapter. What we aim to do now is to put some meat on the bones of what we previously said. Al-Mulhim is the illumination or guidance of the inner heart that is the beginning of the mystical quest. It comes directly, without any intermediation, from the infinite source of all, *nur-ul-'anwaar*, the light of all lights.

As explained in Chapter 4, The Sound Code, al-Mulhim is a fourth-form participle. It is a causative. It expresses both the cause and effect of the state of being divinely inspired. Its root meanings include to devour, to consume like fire, to swallow, and to be swallowed.

If the seeker is consumed by fire they are *mulham*. But the tension comes in that they are also *mulhim*. That is to say, they desire and swallow and consume the spiritual experience and they are also consumed by it. Seeing both sides of the experience of this quality is important, and also recognizing how all these experiences are filtered through the state of our ego or *nafs*.

How this quality of *ilham* is used depends exactly on the state of the *nafs*. Karen Armstrong in her book *The Case for God* gives an illustrative example of Richard Rolle, who described his inner experience in this way: "For the first time I was surprised and felt my heart beginning to warm. It felt as if it was actually on fire. It surged up surprisingly and brought unexpected comfort. It came entirely from within and no material or sinful cause, but was the gift of my maker. I was then delighted and wanted my love to be greater."[278]

However, she writes, after this experience Rolle said that he continuously called others who hadn't had such an experience fools, would explode at anyone who disagreed with him, and refused to have a spiritual director who could have instructed him in techniques and attitudes. This account is typical of an initial encounter with al-Mulhim. It is a study in contrasts—you are swallowed but you are also swallowing.

The root of al-Mulhim occurs once in the Qur'an in the Sun chapter. The chapter is itself a study in contrasts. Its teaching is that divine inspiration is eternally itself, but it is observed by us through a healthy or unhealthy *nafs*. The key verse is: "And she [the *nafs* (*alhama ha*)] is enlightened in that way whether she is fractured and broken or integrated and self-aware of God."[279] *Alhama ha* is the name the *nafs* is called at this stage of its awakening.

To be fractured is *fujoora*, and to be integrated and self-aware of Allah is *taqwaa*. This is the lens through which we must view al-Mulhim's manifestation in our life. Just the experience of inspiration is not sufficient for awakening. When Allah, al-Mulhim, inspires the *nafs*, it inspires only to the degree the *nafs* is whole or healthy.

When there is a filter or covering (*kufraan*) over the heart, this diseased condition radically mediates the inspiration that is coming. The first half of the Sun chapter deals with the healthy, balanced condition (*taqwaa*) and the second half with the unhealthy condition (*fujoor*).

We will take a few meanings of *fujoor* and *fajara* to more fully understand its meaning. *Fajara*, the first form of the word, means to cut open, to split, to explode. The earth meaning is to dig up the ground when plowing. This gives a good picture of the fractured ego. What is interesting is that the *nafs* is enlightened by this emanation, *alhama ha*, and yet is fractured and cut off.

The last half of the chapter describes the bad things that happen to such people. These people are arrogant and cruel and oppress the poor. The chiefs of the tribe of the Thamud are portrayed as cutting the hamstring of a prize camel not only to disable her but also with the purpose of causing maximum pain.

This image works to show the emotional landscape of the fractured *nafs*. *Fujoor* means *'aqara*, to cut, and also *'aqeer*, the one who experiences being cut, terror-stricken and frozen with fear. *'Aaqar* means to cling to and to be addicted to something. This is the diseased condition of the ego or *nafs*. A second meaning of *fujoor* is to overflow and trespass the bounds of self and others with utter disregard for proper limits of behavior.

An-nafs ul-fujoorah is the most unhappy, most wretched, most wounded, and most distressed. And that very person is the exact one who is the most vicious, cruel, severe, ruthless, inflexible, vengeful, heartless, unforgiving, pitiless, and compassionless. This fractured *nafs* is contrasted with the state of the divine messenger, *rasulu-llah*, mentioned in the chapter's last verse: "For him there is no fear."[280]

The one who is the most wounded wounds the most. These are the ones the chief of the tribe of Thamud chose to carry out the vicious and cruel act mentioned earlier against the counsel of the Prophet Salih, whose name means the peacemaker, the one with a peace-loving nature.

All these negative qualities certainly have a bad effect on others, but the point the Qur'an emphasizes over and over is the bad effect it has in poisoning your own self and distorting what you receive from Allah. Self-delusion and falseness are harmful to the soul who carries out the act. Every time a lie is perpetuated it makes the covering over the heart thicker and more rigid.[281]

One last contrast between *fajara* and *taqwaa*, between the fractured and diseased *nafs* and the integrated and wholesome *nafs*, is that *fajara* means to become weak of eyesight, while *taqwaa* means to be fully aware. Allah is all around us: To perceive this is *taqwaa* and not to perceive it is *fujoor*.

In Surah 7 (*al-Araf*) we have the same story of Salih and the Thamud retold.[282] In this account, the quality of arrogance is emphasized. It is one sign of Iblis, who is also called Shaitan (Satan). Arrogance acts as a veil over the heart. It is that very arrogance that made Iblis refuse to bow down before the perfect essence in Allah's creation of Adam. Early verses in the chapter talk about that act of refusing to bow down.[283]

Shaitan suggestively whispers to Adam and Eve, inflating them and seducing them into eating the forbidden fruit. Consider this in the context of dealing with the quality of *ilham*. After the enthusiasm and inspiration there's the whisper that says, "you are the greatest," which the fractured *nafs* takes to justify itself.

Shaitan should not be taken as some kind of independent power. The Qur'an reminds us of this:

"But Satan has no power over them."[284] And at 2:102-103 we read of the misuse of the spiritual power that is given to you in the state of inspiration, such as casting the evil eye on people. The source of all these kinds of problems does not lie with some exterior force. It lies in the enthused but fractured heart.

On the spiritual path the fractured heart is offered a step-by-step healing or integration. This process, called *darajaat*, appears in a passage about Abraham: "And so we raise whomever we will, step by step, and Allah is Hakim and 'Alim."[285] Earlier, Abraham worshipped God in the moon, the sun, the stars, but renounced that worship when the natural object set. Finally he reached the station of seeing the one God everywhere. At this stage, his vision is not limited, because his heart is integrated and whole.

Ya Rashid

(yaa ra-<u>SHEED</u>)

There is no compulsion in religion.[286] Divine guidance must be brought into a particular clarity of focus to communicate a healing wisdom that addresses the particular needs of particular souls. *Rushd* (the noun form of ar-Rashid) is guidance that brings that emanation. It brings hope to human beings. Its opposite, *ghayy*, leads to despair. Some of the practical meanings of *rushd* in human affairs can be seen by contrasting it with *ghayy*.

The following actions of *ghayy* are all things the real spiritual guide, the one who is the vehicle of ar-Rashid, does not do. The first form of *ghayy*, *ghawaa*, means to mislead, seduce, disappoint, covet, and use deceit. It is to give way to passions such as anger, lust, and greed, all of which lead to despair.

An example of following your passion in such a way is the word *ghawi*. It means locusts, whose voracious appetites destroy crops and destroy hope. Another meaning of *ghawaa* is to lead you into a trap, a pitfall, a place of calamity, misfortune, or death. The ones who deceitfully dig a pit for others to fall into have already fallen into the pit. All of these meanings of *ghayy* are offered as opposites to *rushd*, the light of guidance.

A final meaning of *ghayy* makes the connection between it and *rushd* quite clear. It is to obscure the light with clouds or shadows, to be inert, or to obstruct movement on the path toward unity by blocking the activity of discerning wisdom. The state of the real Murshid, the one who embodies *rushd*, is empty. It is *al-fanaa'u fi-llaah*, ego effacement in Allah, and this allows all the light of guidance to pass through without being obscured.

Al-Mubin is a name of Allah; it has the same root as *al-Bayan*. "He taught humanity al-Bayan."[287] Al-Bayan is the particularization of this guidance, ar-Rashid. The manifestation of ar-Rashid brings integration and balance. In the next verse the Qur'an describes how the sun and moon follow their courses in nature. The sun is outward knowledge and the moon is inward knowledge. The outward manifestation, which is *qur'an* and *hudaa*, is combined together with the inward realization, which is *ilham*, by the activity of al-Bayan.

The manifestation of everything, all put together into a grand whole, is called *tawfeeq*. Both God and ar-Rashid, as the manifestation of God, are called *muwaffiq*, the balancer. The guidance of *rushd* is sent to balance the outward and the inward. "The skies are set on a delicate balance [*al-miyzaan*]."[288]

A meaning of *qur'an* is to put together. *Qara'a* is a variant form of the root of *qur'an*, and it means to recite and gather together. *Bayana* is to take apart. All of this is seen in the activity of the teachers who are a focus of ar-Rashid. They accept the inner experience of *ilham* and take it apart piece by piece. Then they put it together in a fresh way.

When the outward and inward are balanced, it may be called *siraat-ul mustaqeem*. It is the clear path of balance between too much outward form and too much inwardness or *ilham*. Too much attachment to outward form makes you angry (*maghdoobi*), and too much inwardness leads to *dalaalah*, which is the condition of wandering without direction. It is instability, as opposed to anger.

What is truly in the middle, *ni'mah*, balances these extremes. *Ni'mah* means blessing. It is the happiness and joy of being in balance and in harmony. It is described in the Qur'an: "that I may complete [or perfect] my joyful balance for you, and you may be guided."[289]

In the classical Sufi teachings of al-Qushayri, *taqleed* is the name for blind imitation of form. It is too much attachment to the outer. In this blindness there is a conception of *hudaa* (al-Hadi) that excludes *ilham*, inner illumination. It is described in the Qur'an as a loss to one's own soul.[290] It is an imbalance caused by too much outward form. *Talween* is too much *ilham* without sufficient outward form. It means to be inconsistent and unsteady. The balance between the two is *tamkeen*, which is the stability and consistency that are a result of this balance.

We all want balance and guidance and protection so that we can grow on every level. The human being who is the vehicle of ar-Rashid is the nexus for all those levels. It is vital for wayfarers on the spiritual path to have such a link. The value of such a person is described in the Qur'an where it talks about *imam* and *mubeen*.[291] This verse really personalizes the Murshid. It tells us that ar-Rashid is clearly manifesting through the heart of a human being.

Such a person has *firaasah*. *Firaasah* means to be thoroughly perspicacious, to have both penetrating sight and deep insight. It is to be transparent as crystal and to be bright and luminous. A man or woman who has this guidance can actually read the writing in the heart by the light of God.

Ultimately, to have this awareness is to see the inner reality in the outer signs. *Firaasah* decodes the outer meaning and consequences of inner experiences. That is the activity of *imam mubeen*, one who stands forth to offer guidance with integrated clarity of awareness. It is all part of what was taught humanity, described as al-Bayan.

The Qur'an further illustrates how a human being can be the nexus of divine guidance. "With him are the keys of the unseen, the treasures that no one knows but Allah. He knows whatever is in the dry land or in the sea; no leaf falls except with his knowledge, not a grain in the darkness of the earth or any fresh or dry seed but it is written in a clear record [*al-kitab ul-mubeen*]."[292]

The dry land and the sea and so on are all symbols for the nexus or balancing of outer and inner experiences. It is all reflected in clear hearts that are the shiny mirrors in which can be read the treasures of the unseen that are the essence of everything. These are treasures of *rahma*, loving compassion.

It is that quality in a human being that allows the Qur'an to say, "If you follow him [Muhammad] you shall be guided, for the messenger's duty is only to be a clear guide [*balaa' mubeen*]."[293] In other words, if you are guided by the messenger, you will be guided by God.

A last function to identify in human beings who are the nexus of guidance is that they act with the divine authority. The word *sultan* simply means authority. It does not mean to be a king. Moses is described like this in the Qur'an: "And Moses we sent to pharaoh with a clear authority [*sultan mubeen*]."[294]

From all this we can conclude that the essence of the Murshid is the functioning of *muwaffiq*, the balancer of outward and inward. What makes ar-Rashid and the state of the one who embodies it so important is that it keeps balance between inner and outer guidance, between *ilham* and *hudaa*.

It balances these two realms while at the same time continually balancing in the inner and outer worlds every single spiritual station the student goes through on their path. The sound code of the Arabic language informs us that the doubled "f" in *muwaffiq* means this activity of balance and integration is continuous.

The Murshid (*muwaffiq*) keeps the opposites in balance. Without a balancing guide at this stage of your journey you can easily become out of balance in either direction. Too much form without inner experience makes you angry, and too much inner experience without balance leads to idle wandering about.

Let's examine some of the balancing acts of *rushd* as the embodiment of the *bayaan* or guidance that is given to humanity. It finds a balance in the experience of being wounded. *Balaa'* is the wound or affliction. In 44:33 *balaa'* and *mubeen* are treated together. *Mubeen* is able to clearly define each one's inner wounding.

Another way balancing this affliction is discussed elsewhere.[295] The context is inner wounding (*balaa'*) and the manifest fulfillment of all desires (*fawz*), the greatest bliss. "It is due to God's mercy [*rahma*] that this [*balaa'*] is the obvious fulfillment of all desire."

Our interpretation of this is that happiness or affliction comes from the power of God, not from the illusions of life. By finding the courage to face your wounded condition and allow it to open up so that real healing can occur, you discover the loving mercy of God, and that allows you to fulfill your deepest desires. The role of the Murshid is to hold a focus for balancing the inner wounding and the fulfillment of desire.

In general, when a person slips off the path of balance in one direction you get sanctimoniousness, hypocrisy, and excessive formalism. "Have you not meditated upon those who claim sanctity for themselves; they are the furthest from purity."[296] It is a kind of hypocrisy when you imitate the form but there is no reality behind it.

Those who are sanctimonious look at others and condemn them for not being as holy as they are. It is a rat hole. "If anyone slips and then blames someone else who is innocent, he carries that falsehood."[297] And they start to harass or molest people whom they perceive to be less holy than they are. They annoy and harass believing men and women undeservedly.[298]

So the *rushd* is a kind of balancer between *taqleeb* and *talween*, between being overly attached to form and being unstable. Emotionally, it is between the extremes of anger and confusedly wandering about. The manifestation of ar-Rashid is activity of the *meezaan* or *muwaffiq*. The physician of the heart needs to know where the imbalance is at each stage, and then proceed to take it apart and put it together anew. The role is to interpret or decode the symbols of the inner world for the purpose of integrating and actualizing it in everyday life.

Al-Furqaan is this method of teaching, of taking apart and putting back together. "Ramadan is the month in which is sent down the Qur'an, the *hudaa* or guidance to humanity. Next is *bayyinaatin min al-hudaa wa-l-furqaan*."[299] It is a particularization of guidance. Guidance has to be passed through another level of particularization. *Faraqa* means anything that can discern between reality and unreality. *Farooq* and *mufriq* mean anyone recovering from a disease.

The one who has this kind of awareness, this *taqwaa*, is like a physician who heals the hearts of anyone suffering from a disease. They offer this particularization of focus, a diagnosis of a particular diseased condition. *Farooq* is doctor and *mufriq* is patient. "And we gave *al-furqaan* to Moses and Aaron, and a spreading light [*diyaa'* (zia)], and a *dhikr*."[300]

Furqaan is all of that. It is a particularization, a light whereby you can read the manuscript of the heart. The opposite is inner confusion and darkness. *Furqaan* is like the time just before daybreak when the morning brightness appears. It is enlightening every part of the soul and seeing how everything works together. The spreading quality of the light of dawn helps separate the darkness of night and the lightness of morning.

David is described hearing the mountains giving *dhikr* every morning and evening; birds gather around him in this awareness. The pre-eternal light was strengthened in him and he could perceive it through this universal *dhikr*, and he got wisdom and discrimination.[301]

Furqaan captures all the best parts of *rushd* and the Murshid process. How the Murshid takes the *ilham* apart is portrayed in the Moses and Khidr story. It is *ta'wil*, the interpretation of each and every sign.[302] Moses learned his lesson; we read elsewhere: "And we gave to Moses *al-kitab* and *al-furqaan* so that perhaps you may be guided."[303] This is not only the guidance in *rushd* but the realization and actualization in *hudaa*.

This particular function of the prophet is opened up to all humanity. Any human being can become filled with this guidance, and be a Murshid. "Anyone who believes and has this *taqwaa*, Allah will grant you *furqaan* and unveil the veil that covers you, and forgive you and bestow maximum blessing [*fadl 'adheem*]."[304] This teaching is repeated elsewhere.[305]

"In that blessed night is made distinct every instance of wisdom."[306] This ties *furqaan* to knowledge, wisdom, and finally guidance. *Furqaan* is made distinct and particular here. Because of this, every *tafsir* (commentary) says that *imam mubeen* is *al-kitab ul-mubeen*.

In his commentary, Yusuf Ali paraphrases these Qur'anic verses: "In the heart of the being of this *imam mubeen* We sent this light of clarity into the darkness of the night, which made it *mubaarakah*, extremely blessed, in order that we can make the guidance explicit, and in that night is made distinct every letter of wisdom by the will of the sacred and divine presence that we cause to be sent down as a mercy, a *rahma* from Allah, and he hears and knows all things." This passage is talking about the process of realization from every level, *hudaa*, *rushd*, and *ilham*.

The inner wound (*balaa'*) is the opposite of *fadl*, which means intensive *barakah* and healing.[307] Being tested is one way to understand the experience of affliction. It allows you to see truly what state your heart is in, whether it is covered or clear. "The difference between the two was seen by you in a clear light [*yatabayyana*]."[308]

So at first a distinction is made, but ultimately all the pairs come together. That is *mubeen*; it particularizes and then brings together. The action of *mubeen* is described: "His heart did not falsify what he saw."[309] The inner state does not differ from the outer appearance. If it does, then it is *takdheeb*, denial.

The Prophet Solomon said, "Soon we shall see whether you have lied or told the truth."[310] *Sadaqa* here means telling the truth; it is clarity and pure vision in the heart. Solomon's affirmation did not come from his personal desire. It was not *nafs* desire; it was only divine guidance. What he taught was intensely powerful, imbued with wisdom.

The diamond body is very concrete. It is not amorphous, so when a student is going through ambiguity the physician of the heart takes them to ar-Rashid again and again. Sometimes they may feel sensation that goes into their emotional body and they become hysterical. The teacher objectifies it and asks, "What did you experience?" "I felt some burning in my heart." By taking them to an exact experience the teacher can help them see they are jumping from this simple impression to heaven and hell and doomsday, for example.

Take them to that impression exactly. By applying the clarity of the diamond body of awareness to that experience they know the suchness of that experience. It brings them to basics. It is that *tamkeen*, that consistency, that the physician of the heart provides. A hadith says that to be *mubeen*, to be perfectly clear, you must know the subtle distinctions, every single letter on the manuscript of the heart.

The Qur'an talks about the Torah, an actual physical object (*suhuf*) of Abraham and Moses, and it talks about the Qur'an itself, which is a recitation.[311] The Qur'an is not an external form. There is no book unless its depth of meaning can be found. It requires the awareness of a human being who has the clarity and light to read it, truly to know it by heart. This writing in the heart is a mystical reality, an *imam mubeen*.

hakim
rashid
atim l'aziz
nur

chapter 25

Some Parting Words for Physicians of the Heart

Our underlying purpose in writing this book on the Names of Allah is to offer a useful resource for individual growth and to create a guidebook for those who are drawn to become physicians of the heart. If you are called to help others in the ways we have described, you must be willing to continue to work on your own spiritual growth and awakening. Your own process of awakening must be alive, especially if you are in a position of guiding others as a spiritual teacher or counselor.

Throughout the book, within the context of each chapter, we have made practical suggestions about how best to proceed as a student and as a physician of the heart. Most of the chapters focus on the Names of Allah grouped together within common families of meaning, such as the Names of divine forgiveness. Within each cluster of Names we explain how the qualities the Names embody relate specifically to each person's fundamental experience of feeling disconnected from humanity, from God, and from awareness of their own soul.

Fortunately, your experience of disconnection actually connects you intimately to that very attribute of being you feel is missing in yourself: You first discover your relationship with a divine quality by experiencing its lack. It is like a hole or a blocked door. The necessary response to your discovery of deficiency is to focus your active attention on awakening that missing divine attribute as an essential aspect of your real self.

We recommend consistent prayerful and contemplative invocation of the 99 Names of Allah, combined with devoted attention to using the Names as agents for bringing healing wisdom into your life and, if you are working as a physician of the heart, as active agents in the lives of those you are counseling.

A physician of the heart should pass on some simple guidance about the way to use the 99 Names of Allah, such as the following: They are best recited aloud with a devotional feeling of calling out to the source of all perfection while also knowing that God is in the very vibration of the sound. The quality of God that is evoked moves in and through you. By listening to the sound you make when you recite the Names, you begin to gradually bring the tone of your voice into harmony with their essence.

Often you will be asked to let down your defenses around a wounded place so that a particular quality of God can reach you. It is important to feel the sound in your body. That will give you a vehicle to sense your own resistance to a particular quality and your own profound resonance with it.

Among the Sufi orders there are traditional numbers of repetitions for the recitation of the *wazaif*, such as 33, 101, and 1001. Whether a fixed number of repetitions is used or not, a fixed period of daily recitation should generally be undertaken and prescribed for others.

At this concluding point in the book we want to focus on the role of the physician of the heart as a spiritual guide. We need to look into the nature of the guide's relationship with their students. How can a physician of the heart best serve the process of each student's self-realization? How should they handle themselves in the midst of the difficult issues that come up when working with students, and what are the pitfalls that often arise?

In general, the question we want to explore here is "What background of knowledge and practice is most helpful for the physician of the heart to have?" To answer this question, we first should frame what is behind the whole discussion. We think it is always important to keep the big picture in view.

We begin with reality—being, itself—the essence of all essences, the pure nature of all things, which becomes differentiated. These differentiations—human beings call them love, joy, happiness, and so on—are embodied and magnified to the maximum of what is possible through the 99 Names of God. Each Name is a glorious emanation of being, an archetype that both represents and manifests a quality. Its presence makes clear the nature of the particular quality and its connection with each person's body, mind, and sense of self.

The divine qualities are inherent in the human soul, which is an activity of God. Like a ray of the infinite sun, the soul is individuated and yet not separate from the source. It is this immortal essence in human beings that is "created in the divine image and likeness." Every human being is born with many of these divine qualities intact, and everyone has the potential to develop the qualities that have not been realized. It is our God-given birthright of perfection.

What happens then, in our childhood, is that we encounter difficulties in our environment, and in particular with our parents or parental figures. As a result of the conflicts that arise, we lose connection to the inherent qualities, one after another. These conflicts are mostly due to human ignorance. In our ignorance we don't even know there is an all-pervading being. We don't know that the one and Only Being is differentiated, or that its individuated attributes are part of the human nature, and not just of the divine nature.

These divine qualities are an integral part of human nature, and their presence provides the basis for real psychological work. In our ignorance, our personal self develops with no awareness of connection to the source of our being. As a result, we live continually in a hole of disconnection, and we pass it on from one generation to another. There is no child born who is immune to becoming disconnected in this way. The "fall," the trauma of disconnecting, appears to be part of incarnating in this reality.

From another perspective, we can say that the soul is bound up with certain karmic consequences, positive and negative. Our causal conditioning brings with it the loss of certain qualities but also the empowerment of other qualities. The path of realization partakes of both grace and karma. The grace reflects what the soul has already evolved into. The karma is connected with what the soul has not learned yet, and what it came to Earth to learn.

The divine qualities manifest sequentially during the child's development. In the first weeks there may be one attribute or essence that is more dominant; later, as the child further interacts with their parents, another quality enters the picture. This continues in stages. In each stage there may be a dominant quality or a few principal qualities.

In the midst of conflict around a particular quality—let's say, generosity—the child struggles with, and often loses, that quality. In a given case, the environment might be supportive, and the child might be able to retain that quality, but they will definitely lose another. Children manage to save some qualities, or partial qualities, but lose most of them.

Years later, as adults, when they start the process of retrieving what has been lost to the soul and reconnecting to the source of being, they run into the obstacles that made them lose connection with the source in the first place. Each time you activate one of the attributes of essence—one of the 99 Names of Allah—a psychological complex (a cluster of emotionally toned valences and associations) is activated with it.

If you can respond to guidance, you can make excellent use of this whole cluster of impressions that is being aroused. As you begin to understand and sort it out, the particular Name of Allah you have engaged to work with will become active and manifest in your system. By gradually overcoming the obstacles you have to connecting with the source in relation to, let's say, the quality of generosity, you become able to naturally merge with generosity's ceaseless flowing.

Having a precise understanding of the divine qualities and the psychological issues associated with them is a very powerful tool for the practitioner and for the physician of the heart. It speeds up the process of each soul's retrieval of the essential states, which are called the 99 Names of Allah.

There is also a great deal of modern research into the developmental stages of children that is relevant to this process. In general, psychologists say a child's development begins in a merged condition: the baby clings to and is not inwardly distinct from the mother. Later the child begins to individuate and separate. But it sometimes happens that the baby is already individuated from day one. They are looking, they are precise, and they do what they do. They begin to cuddle and merge perhaps at the age of three or four years old.

Such things happen because the soul's development is not generic; each soul is unique. Modern psychology doesn't have the scope to acknowledge that sometimes the soul does not exactly conform to established developmental stages. Nevertheless, what psychologists know about the developmental stages of the child does help shed light on the picture, even though babies and children sometimes go through the stages in a sequence that varies from the norm.

Operating at another level, a master teacher can know the stations of the soul by insight. Such a teacher has the capacity to design a path for each student that best takes into account the student's particular purpose at their present stage of realization. In this book, however, rather than basing the approach of the physician of the heart on such a degree of comprehensive mastery, we approach the goal in a more sequential way.

We focus, particularly in the beginning of the student's process, on their *hal*, or transient state, rather than on their *maqaam*, or spiritual station. The active and transient state becomes the focus of our attention in the counseling relationship. The physician of the heart needs to know what a student is currently struggling with. Is it issues of strength? Will? Intimacy? Abundance? Joy? What?

Generally, the physician of the heart will find one quality that will strongly present itself to focus on as a vehicle for the student's growth. This quality, in association with a cluster of related qualities, directly and intimately connects with the underlying issues that are affecting their life.

In this book, we briefly summarize each of the qualities individually in Chapter 5, The 99 Names in Summary Form. However, they are discussed at greater length in chapters that are based on clusters or families of the Names of God. By dealing with the family of forgiveness, for example, or the family of divine omnipotence, you have a whole realm to work with, and not just the one vibration of a single Name.

The physician of the heart needs to identify the general area that has been activated in the student and hold it in their heart as a field of qualities that exists in and of itself. If the guide becomes sensitive to the general field a student needs to work with, the guide and student can work effectively together with the combined richness of a whole cluster of Names.

We have gone to some lengths in this book to articulate our psychological view and to show its practical application in different realms of experience. There are so many different stages that a physician of the heart must be able to face with the student.

However, some of those who are drawn to counsel in this way lack the experience of being professional therapists. Such people may see their role as simply that of a spiritual guide, but they cannot afford to ignore the psychological realm. Even as spiritual guides, they frequently have people come to them with issues that call for resolution on the psychological level. We encourage spiritual teachers to seek more skillfulness in dealing with this realm and to consider the various approaches we outline in the course of this book.

It is very important for the physician of the heart to be at ease and to hold the bigger picture at all times. The practices that we have given in this book offer powerful tools of dissolution and creation. Critical situations arise that you must be prepared to face. For example, you must know what to do when the practices you have recommended bring up the very nightmare that students have been defending themselves against for many years.

What follows now is some general and fundamental advice for those who would be physicians of the heart.

One key requirement is that you must be capable of actually experiencing the states of the different Names of Allah—and not just know about them. You might be quite masterful in relation to some, but not all, of these divine emanations, and there is always scope for further development and deepening. The counseling relationship gives the physician of the heart a chance to increase their experience of the divine qualities that are being evoked and to develop a variety of skillful means of working with others.

Teachers should not hold themselves back from the process of growth. It is not just the student who learns and grows. The teacher's role is to facilitate the student's ability to go through real inner and outer change and growth. But if the teacher does not become involved in the student's process, and if they are not involved in their own inner process, their disengagement will impair the student's development.

If the teacher has not experienced a particular state, or is holding back because of lack of knowledge, their condition will hold the student back. The student learns through merging with the teacher. By connecting in a deep way, the teacher naturally shares his or her realization, and this is empowering to the student. Any absence or disconnection on the teacher's part is subtly and critically felt.

It is crucial that a physician of the heart have the humility to remember that they are not fully actualized in every divine quality. You might have only a glimpse of a certain quality. But regardless of how much of it you have realized, you also need to continually evolve and cultivate the quality. As a physician of the heart you need the humility to know that students are often more advanced than you are in certain qualities. When you gain this insight, you can teach them and learn from them at the same time.

In honoring the soul of each student and its evolution, the soul of the teacher evolves as well. The difference between the teacher and the student is mostly that the teacher has more experience and more knowledge, and they are a few steps ahead in certain domains; they can hold an integrated field before the student to help them go through their growth process. But teachers are not above and beyond the process. They are within the process, and they need to be able to simultaneously process for the student and for themselves.

The physician of the heart has to keep practicing this skill, this art, because it never ends. It is like a jewel mine, so that every session you go into you are learning something, excavating something, and evolving. Then the journey becomes very rich. You are not just a teacher. You are teacher, student, and companion. The result is a vibrant, living field that enhances and empowers the companionship.

Two souls genuinely journeying together bring forth more treasure than does a single soul who works hard to achieve. The difficulty of the individual soul working alone may be fed by a sense of self-deficiency. Also, this difficulty may be fed by a relationship with a teacher who persists in maintaining an appearance of perfection, but who cannot actually connect with the student, and therefore basically leaves them on their own. Genuine humility on the part of the physician of the heart is the greatest quality to cultivate to avoid this debilitating pitfall.

Teachers need the objectivity to see where they themselves are weak and where they are strong, and at the same time they need to keep evolving and holding the field for the student. Skillful means are important. Breathing exercises, *dhikr* practice, working with the body as the temple of God, knowing its centers of light and magnetism, are all important. All the various disciplines of the spiritual path are helpful. In general, a genuine personal connection with the path and a commitment to awakening the heart of the complete human being are most essential.

There are some other things to know. We think a very basic review of child development will help all those who wish to work deeply with the practices in this book. What happens in childhood? It doesn't have to be a complex Freudian or Jungian analysis. It can be quite simple. What generally happens between two and three years of age? What happens in the individuation phase? What happens in the separation phase? If the physician of the heart knows some of this it helps them to locate what stage a student is going through as an adult.

It is also important to acknowledge the power of the unconscious. Much of the time the unconscious rules human beings. You think you are operating consciously; you think you are making decisions based on thoughtful reflection, but most of the time you are under the influence of your unconscious. The more the physician of the heart is able to help the student become aware of their unconscious, and how the unconscious manifests in their tendencies and mechanisms, the more the student can feel at ease with facing their life situation, and the more they can wholesomely integrate newly conscious material.

To simplify, unconscious influences repeat themselves again and again in different scenarios. They are mainly personified in the threesome of mother, father, and child, or the figures who represent Mom or Dad in a particular case. Our unconscious relationship with mother, father, and child keeps coming into play in every realm of our life and in our experience of the Names of Allah as an absence or a presence in our life.

The moment you activate a particular divine quality, some kind of complex around father or mother, or with the levels of the ego-self in its formation, also gets activated. It is important for the physician of the heart to keep a keen eye on this and to constantly direct the student to check in with their childhood situation. How old are you when you are going through a particular feeling or process? Who in this manifestation do you think God is associated with? Is it Dad? Is it Mom? Is it Grandpa?

Through delving into this association behind your conscious awareness, the physician of the heart is able to help you see that at any one moment your "I" is actually the complex connected with your relationship with your mother, or your father, or yourself at a certain stage of development. It simplifies the task of the counselor to work from this point of view. One sees a pattern repeating itself time and again through different scenarios. There is the scenario of love, there is the scenario of hurt, and maybe, afterwards, the scenario of anger.

In the course of bringing awareness to this aspect of their experience, the student becomes familiar with the fact that their unconscious is linked with certain situations and asserts itself in certain ideas and images. And they come to see that this unconscious element responds directly to the different qualities evoked by the 99 Names of Allah. When this starts to happen, the associations and images begin to break down, and the student can begin to let go, for example, of their projections onto their mother.

When trying to focus on what the student is struggling with, you can ask, "Is it father issues? Mother issues? Issues the child faced as their sense of self was forming? Is it a combination of these, and which combination? This simple and repetitive approach is useful. The student begins to feel they have a handle on the journey because there is something they can easily see. They become more conscious of which of these forces is driving them on a given day. It makes the process simpler, and they don't need to face symbolism and analysis and other complexities which may be difficult for them to grasp as a vehicle of self-understanding.

A physician of the heart ought to be comfortable with the psychological realm, at least in this kind of simple and clear way. If they are, it will help them in speeding up the student's awakening of the essential states of the 99 Names of Allah in themselves. Just as it is important for the physician of the heart to develop some of this kind of psychological knowledge, it is equally important for them to develop resiliency in engaging with their own evolution.

You need to be conscious of the projections that are placed on you by the student. Transference is constantly happening. Who are you to the student in this moment? Part of the responsibility of the spiritual counselor is to hold the space for such a process to occur. The student projects onto you, and if you can bring that into your mutual conscious awareness, you can explore that projection or transference together.

Similarly, teachers must investigate their own counter-transference. Counter-transference could take the form of getting angry with a student, or soliciting love from a student, or acting out some other projection. It is imperative to watch your own need and how it comes up in the counseling relationship. If the one you are counseling intensely dislikes you, and you get angry or afraid, you should watch and see who you have unconsciously become and who the student has become. At that moment, he or she may have become your mother or father.

You must own up to your own process. You are working with a person in a mutually committed relationship. The opportunities in this kind of friendship on the path are great. In working with a student, the overall goal of wholeness may be approached in different ways.

Some approaches focus on what is missing in the person, their deficiency. A physician of the heart would then amplify and intensify awareness of that deficient condition for the sake of healing. A connection to the source, such as a *wazifah* that embodies the missing quality, would then be offered to the student so that they can draw on the divine being as a resource for what they really need to awaken and embody.

Parenthetically speaking, if you are someone who is simply trying to benefit from the teachings in this book on your own, it is important to continually strive for clarity so that you can learn to recognize the indications of what *wazifah* practice you yourself need.

The other main kind of approach in working with a student is to enhance whatever he or she has that is the most developed in their nature. Some people are very intelligent, and so you use their intelligence. Some people are very full of heart, and so you use their heart. Some people are very willful, and you use their will. These are qualities that they are already connected with, but as yet they remain only doorways for them and not pathways.

The teacher brings these more developed qualities forward in the consciousness of the student so that, for example, they begin to know their innate strength. Then you encourage that strength and confidence to circulate through their system more and more. As it circulates more in them it builds their ability in other areas as well. The student then has a progressively greater foundation of strength and courage, wisdom and guidance to go into all the areas where they are broken, to face and bring healing to their deficiencies.

For the greatest success, it is necessary for a physician of the heart to keep a keen eye toward balancing these two approaches, the one that focuses first on brokenness and the one that first accentuates abundance.

There is danger in being extreme. Suppose a teacher hammers on the personality and on the ego of the student and succeeds in breaking it. Then they continue to focus on the deficiency until the student crumbles, falls apart, goes through psychosis, and *maybe* comes to the absolute. Meanwhile their life falls apart and they become nonfunctional. Or perhaps their ego structure is already very weak, and what they needed first was to be nurtured and built up. In general, a balanced approach will always serve best.

There is a field of blessing that comes when an authentic relationship between teacher and student is created. When using practices of personal dissolution and deconstruction, the existence of such a relationship allows the grace of God, and the grace of the teacher, to support the student in their process. At the same time, the teacher does not strive to protect the student from the breakage or dissolution of long-held personality structures. There are jewels waiting in the breakage.

Harmonizing the two approaches we have been describing will prove most effective. We want unfoldment to take its natural course, and we also want to support the unfoldment. "Don't push the river" is a famous Zen saying. Yet everybody pushes the river one way or another: Sufis, psychologists, Buddhists, everyone. We all push the river! So pushing the river becomes a part of the journey. But we must learn to make it moderate.

Perhaps a person you are working with is stuck in one stage of transition for years. You love them and want them to move out of it and evolve, but the breakage in that domain is severe and profound. The truth is that even if it takes ten years to go through the terrain, it will be worth it. That breakage is the foundation of their personality dysfunction. It occupies them completely. It happened in the womb, perhaps, during the first, early stages of life, and during all their life.

This "stuck" situation can be difficult for you because you want to see progress, but the quality of this particular kind of breakage in the human structure of personality is very enduring. As the student keeps coming back and revisiting that place, you may feel it is boring and redundant, but as a counselor you must not lose focus. In that breakage, if the student goes through it wisely and is guided patiently, they will be able to retrieve the 99 Names of Allah in time and heal the schism in their personality.

They will find flavors of their missing qualities in the breakage. It was in that primal experience of breakage that they lost the totality, not just one piece or another. Understand it is a primal domain for them. They can't easily reach it, and they can't deal with it. It takes time. If the counselor can retain focus, one day the student can make light-years of progress.

When the breakage heals from within, it is as if the soul has mended its connection to the source, to Being itself, and all of a sudden it knows how to access essence. Then the process speeds up, even though particular qualities that have been missing still require time and patience to be realized. The student, along with the physician of the heart, can now begin to attend to the rebuilding of the personality structure itself, in order to allow a natural unfoldment to take its course.

Throughout this whole process, when the student falls into a crack or deep hole in their personality structure—and we can't emphasis this too much—the counselor should not feel deflated. On the contrary, they may have just hit the jackpot! Perhaps together you have journeyed into the domain that reveals what their deepest breakage is all about.

They need to be nurtured in that domain. In that arena of their life they have not developed any qualities, and they have lost so much. The physician of the heart should hold a field of protection in which the student can work. Deep nurturing is called for. It takes many years to grow from childhood to adulthood, and it might take an equivalent number of years in the psychological and the spiritual domain to develop the quality that is needed.

Some people didn't have love, and it is in this realm that their breakage occurred. When you deal with the attributes in the divine cluster of love, you want them to experience love, but they cannot. They might take ten years to experience love. You must be patient with their process. Eventually they may come to experience one kind of love and then another one, and then reach fountains of love, and rivers of love, and the heavens of love.

If they gradually mature with this specific quality over time, they will also mature more generally in the other families of the divine Names as well—knowledge, ecstasy, protection, abundance, forgiveness, strength, and so on, because the most broken place will have healed and become strengthened from the source. Now they can catch up in the other domains.

When you come across a student who falls into the abyss, and you are able to see that this is their primal issue, that it is where they are really broken, it is crucial that your attitude embody healing. A deep acceptance of the timing of inner processes enables you to refrain from becoming impatient. And if their primal difficulty in some way triggers some of your own issues, then you too need to go to school on what is coming up in your own being.

In your mirroring process as a physician of the heart and your merging with the student, the student may touch you, the counselor, at your own breakage point. You need to keep with you, to respect and nurture, your own breakage point as a place of continual healing for the rest of your life. Give yourself time and space to engage in the inner process. Protect yourself from your superego's demand that you be a perfect teacher, an enlightened master.

Take all of this projection out of the picture, and acknowledge your humanness. Acknowledge your limitation and your own potential to evolve and grow. By doing this for yourself, you invite yourself to relax and simply look at the issue. When there is no interference on the part of the superego, it is much easier for the teacher to go through their process, and for the student as well.

One pain that the physician of the heart sees again and again is the pain that comes because each of us is born into a family that was missing a major quality, missing one aspect of the 99 Names of Allah. Mom didn't have that quality at the time. Dad didn't have it. Brothers and sisters didn't have it. There was a big hole where this quality was missing in the family.

A great many struggles of the human soul occur on this most basic plane. The baby is born into this family hole and struggles with issues connected with the missing quality. The importance of it comes and goes, depending on their merging with their environment. In time, their personality begins to develop, focused around this quality. This quality and its absence become centrally important to them.

Love could be the missing factor, or intelligence, or abundance, or any one of the 99 Names or families of Names could be the answer. The personality begins to try to generate this particular quality, to connect to this quality. The child tries to be always loving, or always fair, or always intelligent. But no matter how much the child tries to heal the family hole, to heal Mom and Dad, and all of it, usually the parties involved refuse to be healed. Mom doesn't want to understand Dad, Dad doesn't want to understand Mom, and so on.

The child feels that no matter how much they try to develop understanding, for example, they fail. Such failure generates a deep hurt in the psyche. It is a major wound. The ego feels "no matter what I do, I keep failing." This wound is extremely tender, and as a child grows up and becomes an adult, they continue to try to heal the hole, to find ways to compensate for the pain, and most of all to protect that wounded place from being stirred up.

When a student is going through such a process and is open to going into their wounded place, it resonates in the teacher. And the teacher, feeling tenderness for them, might try to expand their own abundance, or bring out more love from their own store of love, but doing that doesn't solve the problem. What you should do is mirror, simply and lovingly, the field of the family of this divine quality.

Keep in mind that what is getting triggered in your counter-transference to want to fix things and make them better may be the same pain as the student's, but in a different domain of your own. Still, you both are feeling the hurt and the frustration. The teacher needs to keep aware, because when this great pain emerges in the student it will trigger your own pain.

Some teachers react to feeling this pain by rejecting the student, and becoming harsh with them. Their own narcissistic issues are now emerging, and it leads them to entanglement with their student. It often happens, and is not really escapable, but it does become fertile ground for growth.

The student you are having so much trouble with in the way we just described is a teacher for you in disguise. The student is giving you an opportunity to revisit in a deeper way the domain of the missing quality you have struggled with in your own life. Through this outer means, and your inner attentiveness to what it is directing you toward, the major quality your personality is focused around can now be renewed from the source. Then the divine quality is restored as part of your essence, and you become more engaged in its continuing embodiment and development.

Each quality can be a grand awakening for a student. Experiencing a state is a wonderful condition that allows you to become beautifully aware of the presence of the God reality. But it is part of a greater process. Let's look at an example of how that larger process might play out.

A student is working for years with different aspects of divine abundance. They take one aspect of abundance and then another and another. To them, this realm appears to be infinite and rich, even though you may remind them it is only one domain. A stage then comes when they become able to experience this domain as a totality, holding the whole field of it in their heart at the same time.

Now, having experienced abundance as a totality, the student can now expand beyond it and enter another domain. And in this new domain, let's say divine strength, they may need to start from the zero point. They don't know much about strength, but their confidence has grown and they progress in a similar way in this realm.

In addition to the particular family of qualities involved, each time the student enters a new realm, they are learning to move on from individuality through a linear expansion, and then suddenly to achieve totality. The physician of the heart should be especially attentive to the student as they move toward such a quantum leap.

In the inner realm there are what can be called vehicles of consciousness, which empower the student to cultivate greater capacities than is possible when they simply dwell in any one state. These vehicles bring personal power so the individual can integrate a whole dimension, diversify it, and see it in all its richness and all its totality of possibilities. Some of these vehicles are immense.

Earlier in the book we spoke, for example, of holding all the qualities of divine abundance with the image of a chandelier. Such a structure powerfully unites and holds a whole field of individual lights as one. Another vehicle might take the totality of the body for the function of the whole field, while another might take the totality of the psyche. In Judaism, the mystery of the *merkabah* points to a vast and powerful vehicle.

The form of the chandelier is a visualization of a functional dimension of abundance. The vision of such a vehicle arises spontaneously from within the field, and when it does, you become confident that you can address the divine quality in its totality. The form is like a gestalt for the student, and it brings with it the active function of the vehicle, which is empowering.

The essence of a realm manifests in relationship to the spiritual practitioner's senses. If you are a visual person, it manifests through seeing forms. For a musician, it might come as music. Some people are "feelers"—it doesn't come to them as seeing or as hearing, but they feel the texture: this feels dense, this feels cold, this feels liquid. Some are smellers. They can smell the essence states. This is amber, this is rose, this is jasmine. They blend those! Some are tasters. It tastes like gold; it tastes like silver.

Encourage the student to find their own strength and their own bliss. Essence will present itself to each soul's deepest desire in the way the soul can best perceive it. When you are ripening in a domain, it will bring itself to you in just the way and form you need. So when we speak in visual terms about the inner world, such a description is simply one of many ways of saying what is present at the time.

This stage of working with the student in embodying great structures that preserve and generate families of qualities is often reserved until after the student passes through *fana*, or dissolution of their false idea of self. After becoming empty of self, the real self arises from its intrinsic connection with the God-reality. Then the qualities of essence spontaneously shine forth. You don't need to do much further homework. The homework was to undo the personality. Then grace effortlessly brings forth essence.

A good illustration of the emergence of a vast vehicle of empowerment was given when we spoke about the diamond body of awareness in Chapter 23, The Ground of All Knowing and The Dawning of Wisdom. Let's briefly revisit the diamond body here. Knowledge is a capacity of human consciousness, and mind can differentiate the vast field of knowing into infinite areas of kinds of knowledge.

But, if knowledge is not connected, if it is not integrated, it misses its purpose. Knowledge has little value if your mind is not connected to your heart. In that case, the mind becomes merely an intelligent mechanism that is used in a way that is not intelligent and not useful. You can diversify millions of ideas and concepts, but what does that have to do with being wise? How does that heal the soul? How does it touch the human realm?

When the diamond consciousness is activated and has landed in the heart, then the heart is the bigger mind that takes the little mind of intelligence and abstract knowledge and gives it meaning, wisdom, and warmth. Even though it might originate in the head, the diamond-like body of consciousness ultimately must land in the heart.

When it lands, it becomes the vehicle through which you can reach your inner guide in the form the guide presents itself to you. Through a living connection with the Spirit of Guidance, the student gains wisdom and warmth of heart and begin to generate qualities that heal the human psyche and liberate the human soul.

A luminous inner structure of knowing heals the imbalance and blindness of mind as it is frequently experienced. What such a structure offers is perception and knowledge of Allah on the differentiated level. The absolute is Allah on the undifferentiated level. People often get confused at the level of differentiation because they are conditioned to only think of Allah as the undifferentiated. But in restricting your idea of God to that, you are actually imagining a God that is split off from part of reality.

The 99 Names of Allah come forth as the grandest of vehicles, a structure covered with a great array of jewels. It feels like a thousand-winged angel, a most glorious being. This is the palace of God, where God resides as an entity, and also as a cosmic presence.

This vehicle takes the Godhead from the undifferentiated cosmic presence to individuality. The individuality of Godhood is a universal archetype. It is this embodiment we aspire to reach in our very humanity, as Jesus Christ, for example, has shown is possible for a human being.

The 99 Names of Allah are the vehicle of Allah. In a sense, the vehicle of the Names is the body of Allah. Allah, however, includes the vehicle of the Names and the infinite field as well. We aspire to God-realization because our soul is created in God's image and we want to recover our true nature. When our true nature reveals itself, individuality is intact and integrated. Grace, humanness, love, and divinity come together.

If you only take the undifferentiated aspect of God as real, you feel something is missing. You have a sense of loss because the absolutist view lacks individuation. The individual human being is born to be able to integrate three realms: the realm of the absolute, the 99 Names of Allah as the differentiated state of the absolute, and the worldly domain.

You are a body, a soul, and reality itself. If you are not fully awake, if you experience disconnection in any of these realms, this absence is felt as a missing part of yourself. Longing for wholeness inspires you to continue the journey. Physicians of the heart are wise to cultivate their hearts for this ever-continuing process.

Notes

Chapter 1

¹ Rather than citing each
  reference to individual
  traditions quoted in this book,
  we refer our readers to the
  References chapter, which
  lists several fine collections of
  hadith.

² 2:136 (Notes in this format
  refer to chapter and verse in
  the Qur'an.)

Chapter 4

³ 6:12

Chapter 5

⁴ 6:12
⁵ 5:52
⁶ 1:2
⁷ 7:100
⁸ 22:46
⁹ 2:152

¹⁰ Abu Talib al-Makki, *Qut al-qulub*
¹¹ 40:60
¹² 2:115
¹³ 50:1
¹⁴ 37:144
¹⁵ 38:19
¹⁶ 93:8
¹⁷ 24:35
¹⁸ 15:23
¹⁹ 18:66–82

Chapter 6

²⁰ 3:18
²¹ 1:6
²² 1:2
²³ 48:4, 48:18
²⁴ 11:75
²⁵ 9:114
²⁶ 21:103
²⁷ 19:96
²⁸ 11:90
²⁹ 85:14

30 60:7
31 2:114, 9:117, 9:128, 16:7, 16:47, 22:65, 24:20, 57:9, 59:10
33 57:9
34 9:117
35 3:30
36 6:12
37 9:128
38 Surah 18, *Kahf* (the Cave)
39 33:34

Chapter 7

40 5:95–98
41 3:4, 5:95, 14:47, 39:37
42 39:37
43 55:5–6

Chapter 9

44 17:70

Chapter 10

45 3:174
46 2:225
47 9:129, 23:86, 27:26
48 9:72
49 24:37
50 2:115
51 3:64
52 50:16
53 53:9

Chapter 11

54 az-Zujjaji, *Ishtiqaq asma' Allah*, pp. 395-410
55 Abu Talib al-Makki, *Qut al-qulub*
56 8:63
57 65:3, 5:23

58 63:7
59 2:152
60 5:52
61 2:255
62 2:62

Chapter 12

63 2:62
64 93:8

Chapter 13

65 112:3
66 30:11

Chapter 14

67 27:40
68 55:29
69 2:222
70 2:261
71 26:137, 37:36

Chapter 15

72 4:57, 5:122
73 55:26–27
74 40:68 "It is He who gives life and death; and when He decides upon an affair, He says to it, 'Be,' and it is." Also cited in 2:117, 16:40, 36:82.
75 Surah *Ikhlas*:112

Chapter 16

76 41:53
77 9:128
78 21:19–22
79 2:30
80 17:44

81 2:30, 15:97, 20:130, 32:15
82 2:26
83 2:255
84 9:72
85 20:50
86 108:1
87 17:20
88 92:1–5

117 35:15
118 35:15
119 20:23
120 79:18
121 79:20
122 53:18
123 53:14
124 53:17–53:18

Chapter 17

89 12:53
90 12:23
91 12:23
92 12:24
93 12:53
94 12:23
95 75:2
96 14:22
97 91:7–91:10
98 32:9
99 32:9
100 32:19
101 18:60–82
102 89:27
103 16:112–114
104 16:114
105 89:27
106 13:28
107 48:18
108 88:8
109 3:162
110 3:163
111 3:164
112 9:40
113 2:207
114 3:163
115 91:9
116 35:18

Chapter 18

125 8:4, 22:50, 24:26, 34:4, 33:31
126 33:31 "But any of you that is devout in the service of Allah and His Messenger, and works righteousness, to her shall We grant her reward twice: and We have prepared for her a generous Sustenance." (Yusuf Ali trans.)
127 27:40
128 36:58
129 80:13
130 56:74–80
131 17:70
132 69:40
133 81:15–20
134 17:70
135 23:116
136 Marvin Meyer, *The Unknown Sayings of Jesus*, p. 40
137 7:143
138 41:53
139 12:18
140 12:83
141 5:13
142 13:22
143 11:61
144 56:9–11
145 50:16

146 2:186
147 Yusuf Ali commentary on Qur'an 2:186
148 53:9
149 40:60
150 11:71–73
151 50:1–2
152 85:15
153 85:21
154 85:22

Chapter 19

155 39:36
156 93:8
157 11:85
158 55:7
159 42:17
160 6:153
161 10:47
162 5:45

Chapter 20

163 85:9
164 3:17
165 24:34
166 22:46
167 50:15
168 50:16
169 50:21
170 48:8
171 85:9
172 16:84
173 16:89
174 41:53
175 43:86
176 21:107
177 14:24–25
178 53:13–18
179 47:31

180 58:11
181 59:22–24

Chapter 21

182 55:26–27
183 15:23
184 15:24
185 15:25
186 48:26
187 66:8
188 66:8
189 19:40
190 14:24
191 50:18–21
192 36:65
193 39:22
194 24:37
195 15:23
196 15:25
197 21:69
198 37:144
199 50:19
200 16:38
201 72:7
202 17:49
203 6:36
204 19:33
205 19:15
206 17:18
207 1:6–7
208 38:79
209 7:172
210 21:87

Chapter 22

211 61:2
212 25:63
213 28:55

214 2:255

215 59:22

216 2:115

217 3:73–74

218 57:3

219 2:115

220 15:86

221 12:76

222 18:26

223 29:10

224 3:154

225 39:7

226 57:6

227 6:12

228 49:13

229 7:199–201

230 49:1

231 37:117

232 2:82

233 Surah *Rahman*, 55:1–2

234 Surah *Baqara*, 2:33

235 2:33

236 Hazrat Inayat Khan, *Dance of the Soul*, p. 246

237 18:65–66

Chapter 23

238 23:116

239 22:6

240 3:154

241 53:28

242 42:22–24

243 Surah *Luqman*:31

244 31:12

245 6:114

246 4:35

247 2:129

248 24:18

249 2:209

250 6:83

251 36:1–5

252 55:1–3

253 31:2, 36:2, and elsewhere

Chapter 24

254 18:60–82

255 18:101

256 7:179–180

257 9:37

258 21:94

259 4:167

260 39:3

261 26:19–22

262 24:35

263 24:35

264 24:40

265 43:37

266 6:71

267 10:45

268 7:150–155

269 7:151

270 89:27–29

271 9:32–33

272 17:84

273 20:50

274 16:36

275 6:83–86, 21:51–93

276 87:1–3, 57:1–3

277 13:7

278 Karen Armstrong, *The Case for God*, p. 163

279 91:8

280 91:15

281 6:23–25

282 7:73–79

283 7:11–13

Chapter 24 continued

[284] 34:20–21

[285] 6:83

[286] 2:256

[287] 55:4

[288] 55:7

[289] 2:150

[290] 39:15

[291] 36:12

[292] 6:59

[293] 24:54

[294] 51:38

[295] 6:16

[296] 4:49–4:50

[297] 4:112

[298] 33:57

[299] 2:185

[300] 21:48

[301] 21:79

[302] 18:78

[303] 2:53

[304] 8:29

[305] 36:21–25

[306] 44:1–4

[307] 27:40

[308] 9:43

[309] 53:11

[310] 27:27

[311] 87:19

References

Dictionaries, Grammars, Glossaries

Fischer, Wolfdietrich. *A Grammar of Classical Arabic.* Translated by Jonathan Rodgers. New Haven, CT: Yale University Press, 2002.

Lane, Edward William. *An Arabic-English Lexicon: Derived from the Best and Most Copious Eastern Sources.* Cambridge, UK: Islamic Texts Society, 1984. First published 1863. Available online: www.laneslexicon.co.uk

Penrice, John. *A Dictionary and Glossary of the Qur'an with Copious Grammatical References and Explanations of the Text.* Des Plaines, IL: Library of Islam, 1988. First published 1873.

al-Qashani, 'Abd al-Razzaq, comp. *A Glossary of Sufi Technical Terms.* Edited by David Pendlebury. Translated by Nabil Safwat. London: Octagon Press, 1984.

Wright, William. *A Grammar of the Arabic Language,* 3rd ed. Cambridge, UK: Cambridge University Press, 1967. First published 1859.

In Arabic

al-Makki, Abu Talib. *Qut al-qulub fi mu'amalat al-mahbub wa wasf tariq al-murid ila maqam al-tawhid* [The Nourishment of Hearts in Dealing With the Beloved and the Description of the Seeker's Way to the Station of Declaring Oneness]. 2 vols. Edited by Basil 'Ayun al-Sud. Beirut: Dar al-kutub al-'ilmiyah, 1997.

'ibn Mandhur, Jamal al-Din. *Lisan al-Arab.* 15 vols. Edited by Amir Ahmad Haydar and Abdul Munim Ibrahim. Beirut: Dar al-Kutub al-Ilmiyah, 1956.

al-Zubaidi, Muhammad al-Murtadza Husaini. *Taj al-'Arus min Jawaher al-Qamus.* 20 vols. Beirut: Dar al-Kutub al-Ilmiyah, n.d.

az-Zujjaji, 'Abd al-Rahman. *Ishtiqaq asma' Allah.* Al-Najaf al-Ashraf: Matba' at al-Nu'man, 1974.

The Holy Qur'an in Translation

While we recommend no specific translation of the Qur'an, we offer the following suggestions.

Ali, Yusuf Abdullah. *The Holy Qur'an: Text, Translation and Commentary.* Lahore: Sh. Muhammad Ashraf Publishers, 1938. As recent editions have been censored, the older versions are preferred.

Arberry, Arthur J. *The Koran Interpreted: A Translation.* New York: MacMillan, 1955.

Bakhtiar, Laleh. *The Sublime Quran.* Chicago: Kazi Publications, 2007.

Durkee, Abdullah Noorudeen. *The Transliterated Tajwidi Qur'an: With Meanings Rendered in Early 21st Century American English.* Charlottesville, VA: An-Noor Educational Foundation, 2004.

Collections of Hadith

'ibn 'Arabi, Muhyiddin. *Divine Sayings: 101 Hadith Qudsi: The Mishkat al-Anwar of Ibn 'Arabi.* Translated by Stephen Hirtenstein and Martin Notcutt. Oxford, UK: Anqa Publishing, 2008.

ul-Karim, Maulana Fazl, comp. and trans. *Al-Hadith: An English Translation and Commentary of Mishkat-ul-Musabih.* 4 vols. New Delhi: Islamic Book Service, 2001.

Syed, M. Hafiz, comp. *Thus Spake Prophet Muhammad.* Madras, India: Sri Ramakrishna Math, 1963.

at-Tirmidhi, Muhammad 'ibn 'Eesa. *Jami' at-Tirmidhi.* Translated by Abu Khaliyl. Edited by Hafiz Abu Tahir Zubair 'Ali Za'I. Dar-us-Salam Publications, 2007. Available online at http://www.scribd.com/doc/16768046/Jami-a-Tirmidhi-Sunan-alTirmidhi

Other References

Almaas, A.H. *Essence with the Elixir of Enlightenment: The Diamond Approach to Inner Realization.* York Beach, ME: Weiser Books, 1998.

———. *The Pearl Beyond Price: Integration of Personality into Being, an Object Relations Approach (Diamond Mind).* Boston: Shambhala Publications, 2000.

Armstrong, Karen. *The Case for God.* New York: Alfred Knopf, 2009.

Chittick, William C. *The Self-Disclosure of God: Principles of Ibn Al-'Arabi's Cosmology.* Albany: State University of New York Press, 1997.

———. *The Sufi Path of Knowledge: Ibn Al-'Arabi's Metaphysics of Imagination.* Albany: State University of New York Press, 1989.

Corbin, Henry. *Alone with the Alone: Creative Imagination in the Sufism of Ibn 'Arabi.* Translated by Ralph Manheim. Princeton, NJ: Princeton University Press, 1998.

———. *The Man of Light in Iranian Sufism.* New Lebanon, NY: Omega Publications, 1994.

Dalai Lama. *The Buddha Nature: Death and Eternal Soul in Buddhism.* Woodside, CA: Bluestar Communications, 1997.

Greenberg, Mitchell. *Object Relations in Psychoanalytic Theory.* Cambridge, MA: Harvard University Press, 1983.

Guntrip, Harry. *Schizoid Phenomena, Object Relations, and the Self.* Madison, CT: International Universities Press, 2001.

Horner, Althea. *Object Relations and the Developing Ego in Therapy.* Lanham, MD: Jason Aronson Publishers, 1995.

'ibn 'Ata'llah 'Iskandari. *The Book of Wisdom* [Kitab-al-Hikam]. Translated by Victor Danner. New York: Paulist Press, 1978.

Khan, Hazrat Inayat. *The Sufi Message.* 14 vols. Delhi: Motilal Banarsidass, 1995. Available online at wahiduddin.net/mv2/index.htm

———. *The Dance of the Soul: Gayan Vadan Nirtan.* Delhi: Motilal Banarsidass, 1993.

Kohut, Heinz. *The Analysis of the Self: A Systematic Approach to the Psychoanalytic Treatment of Narcissistic Personality Disorders.* Chicago: University of Chicago Press, 2009.

———. *The Restoration of the Self.* Chicago: University of Chicago Press, 2009.

Lewis, Samuel L. The Jerusalem Trilogy: Song of the Prophets. Novato, CA: Prophecy Pressworks, 1975.

Lowen, Alexander. *Bioenergetics: The Revolutionary Therapy That Uses the Language of the Body to Heal the Problems of the Mind.* New York: Penguin Arkana, 1994.

———. *The Betrayal of the Body.* Alachua, FL: Bioenergetics Press, 2005.

Mahler, Margaret. *The Psychological Birth of the Human Infant: Symbiosis and Individuation.* New York: Basic Books, 2000.

Meyer, Marvin. *The Unknown Sayings of Jesus.* San Francisco: HarperCollins, 1998.

Miller, Alice. *The Drama of the Gifted Child: The Search for the True Self.* New York: Basic Books, 2008.

Qushayri, Abd Al-Karim 'Ibn Hawazin, Abu'L-Qasim Al-Qushayri, and Laleh Bakhtiar. *Sufi Book of Spiritual Ascent (Al-Risala Al-Qushayriya).* Translated by Rabia T. Harris. Chicago: Kazi Publications, 1997.

az-Zujjaji. *The Etymology of the Beautiful Names of Allah.* Najaf, Iraq: an-Ni'man, 1974.

Websites

Murshid Samuel Lewis's Living Stream: www.murshidsam.org
Physicians of the Heart: www.PhysiciansOfTheHeart.com
Pir-o-Murshid Hazrat Inayat Khan's Complete Works: www.nekbakhtfoundation.org
Sufi Ruhaniat International: www.ruhaniat.org
The Diamond Logos Teachings: www.diamondlogos.com

Index

Appendix A:
Hadith Regarding
the Recitation of the Names

❖ ❖ ❖

From *Jami' at-Tirmidhi*, also known as *Sunan at-Tirmidhi*:

Allah's Messenger (peace be upon him) said, "Allah most high has ninety-nine names. The one who enumerates them will enter paradise. He is Allah who is none but He [*La 'ilaha 'illa huwa*], ar-Rahman, ar-Rahim, al-Malik, al-Quddus, as-Salam, al-Mu'min, al-Muhaimin, al-'Aziz, al-Jabbar, al-Mutakabbir, al-Khaliq, al-Bari', al-Musawwir, al-Ghaffar, al-Qahhar, al-Wahhab, ar-Razzaq, al-Fattah, al-'Alim, al-Qabid, al-Basit, al-Khafid, ar-Rafi', al-Mu'izz, al-Mudhill, as-Sami', al-Basir, al-Hakam, al-'Adl, al-Latif, al-Khabir, al-Halim, al-'Azim, al-Ghafur, ash-Shakur, al-'Aliyy, al-Kabir, al-Hafiz, al-Muqit, al-Hasib, al-Jalil, al-Karim, ar-Raqib, al-Mujib, al-Wasi', al-Hakim, al-Wadud, al-Majid, al-Ba'ith, ash-Shahid, al-Haqq, al-Wakil, al-Qawiyy, al-Matin, al-Waliyy, al-Hamid, al-Muhsi, al-Mubdi', al-Mu'id, al-Muhyi, al-Mumit, al-Hayy, al-Qayyum, al-Wajid, al-Majid, al-Wahid, al-Ahad, as-Samad, al-Qadir, al-Muqtadir, al-Muqaddim, al-Mu'akhkhir, al-'Awwal, al-Akhir, az-Zahir, al-Batin, al-Wali, al-Muta'ali, al-Barr, at-Tawwab, al-Muntaqim, al-'Afuw, ar-Ra'uf, Malikal-Mulk, Dhul Jalali wal 'Ikram, al-Muqsit, al-Jami', al-Ghaniyy, al-Mughni, al-Mani', ad-Darr, an-Nafi', an-Nur, al-Hadi, al-Badi', al-Baqi, al-Warith, ar-Rashid, as-Sabur." (5/530, Hadith no. 3507)

Appendix B
Alphabetized
List of Names

For introductory information and chapter references to any Name, see its numbered entry in Chapter 5, 99 Names of Allah Discussed in Brief Summaries.

Number	Name	Pronunciation	Sound Code Form	Summary Page
29	'Adl	'ADL	I-5	49
81	'Afuw	'A-fooww		68
66	Ahad	A-ḥad	I-6	63
73	Akhir	AA-k̲h̲ir	I-1	66
19	'Alim	'a-LEEM	I-2	45
36	'Aliyy	'A-leeyy		52
72	'Awwal	OW-wal	I-6	65
33	'Azim	'a-ḎHEEM	I-2	51
8	'Aziz	'a-ZEEZ	I-2	41
95	Badi'	ba-DEE'	I-2	74
49	Ba'ith	BAA-'ith	I-1	57
96	Baqi	baa-ḴEE		74
12	Bari'	BAA-ri'	I-1	42
78	Barr	BARR	I-5	67
27	Basir	ba-ṢEER	I-2	48
21	Basit	BAA-siṭ	I-1	46

Number	Name	Pronunciation	Sound Code Form	Summary Page
75	Batin	BAA-ṭin	I-1	66
91	Darr	DAARR var. ḍarr		72
84	Dhal Jalali wal 'Ikram	DHAL ja-LAA-li WAL 'ik-RAAM		69
18	Fattah	fat-TAAḤ	I-4	45
14	Ghaffar	ghaf-FAAR	I-4	43
34	Ghafur	gha-FOOR	I-3	51
87	Ghaniyy	GHA-neeyy		71
94	Hadi	haa-DEE		73
38	Hafiz	ḥa-FEEDH	I-2	52
28	Hakam	ḤA-kam	I-6	49
46	Hakim	ḥa-KEEM	I-2	56
32	Halim	ḥa-LEEM	I-2	50
56	Hamid	ḥa-MEED	I-2	59
51	Haqq	ḤAḲḲ	I-5	58
40	Hasib	ḥa-SEEB	I-2	53
62	Hayy	ḤAIYY	I-5	62
9	Jabbar	jab-BAAR	I-4	41
41	Jalil	ja-LEEL		54
86	Jami'	JAA-mi'	I-1	70
37	Kabir	ka-BEER	I-2	52
42	Karim	ka-REEM	I-2	54
31	Khabir	kha-BEER	I-2	50
22	Khafid	KHAA-fiḍ	I-1	46
11	Khaliq	KHAA-liḳ	I-1	42
30	Latif	la-ṬEEF	I-2	49
48	Majid	ma-JEED	I-2	56
3	Malik	MA-lik		39
83	Malikal-Mulk	MAA-li-kal-MULK		69
89	Mani'	MAA-ni'	I-1	72
54	Matin	ma-TEEN	I-2	59
71	Mu'akhkhir	mu-'AKH-khir	II	65
58	Mubdi'	mub-dee'		60
25	Mudhill	mu-DHILL	IV	48
88	Mughni	mugh-NEE	IV	71
7	Muhaimin	mu-HAI-min		40

Number	Name	Pronunciation	Sound Code Form	Summary Page
57	Muhsi	MUḤ-ṣee	IV	60
60	Muhyi	MUḤ-yee	IV	61
59	Mu'id	mu-'EED	IV	61
24	Mu'izz	mu-'IZZ	IV	47
44	Mujib	mu-JEEB	IV	55
6	Mu'min	MU'-min	IV	40
61	Mumit	mu-MEET	IV	61
80	Muntaqim	mun-TA-ḳim	VIII	68
70	Muqaddim	mu-ḲAD-dim	II	65
39	Muqit	mu-ḲEET	IV	53
85	Muqsit	MUḲ-siṭ	IV	70
69	Muqtadir	muk-TA-dir	VIII	64
13	Musawwir	mu-ṢOW-wir	II	43
77	Muta'ali	mu-ta-'AA-lee		67
10	Mutakabbir	mu-ta-KAB-bir	V	41
90	Mu'ti	mu'-ṬEE	IV	72
92	Nafi'	NAA-fi'	I-1	73
93	Nur	NOOR		73
20	Qabid	ḲAA-biḍ	I-1	46
68	Qadir	ḲAA-dir	I-1	64
15	Qahhar	ḳah-HAAR	I-4	43
53	Qawiyy	ḲO-weeyy		58
63	Qayyum	ḳaiy-YOOM	I-4A	62
4	Quddus	ḳud-DOOS	I-4A	39
23	Rafi'	RAA-fi'	I-1	47
2	Rahim	ra-ḤEEM	I-2	38
1	Rahman	raḥ-MAAN	I-7	38
43	Raqib	ra-ḲEEB	I-2	54
98	Rashid	ra-SHEED	I-2	75
82	Ra'uf	ra-'OOF	I-3	69
17	Razzaq	raz-ZAAḲ	I-4	44
99	Sabur	ṣa-BOOR	I-3	76
5	Salam	sa-LAAM		39
67	Samad	ṢA-mad	I-6	64
26	Sami'	sa-MEE'	I-2	48